THE GREAT NAVAL RACE

By the same author

The Battleship Era

THE GREAT NAVAL RACE

The Anglo-German Naval Rivalry,

1900-1914

Peter Padfield

David McKay Company, Inc., New York

First American Edition, 1974

Library of Congress Catalog Card Number: 74 78662
ISBN: 0 679 50472 9
Printed in Great Britain

Viscount Esher to Lord Fisher, 1918:

'Memories of old days crowd upon me, and I have thought much of you these last few hours. It all seems so far away and yet so near. Where should we all be today, were it not for your foresight, your bold determination? ... Really, the prophets were not in it with you. And what a story the whole thing would make ...'

Contents

List of Illustrations

Acknowledgements

In the first place I should like to thank Drs Paul Kennedy and Volker Berghahn of the University of East Anglia for their help and unstinting generosity in guiding me to the most recent research on Wilhelmine Germany and the incredible 'Tirpitz Plan', and in particular for making available the hard-won fruits of their own copious researches into this period and this Navy; also for many enjoyable arguments about the aims and calibre of Wilhelm II and Tirpitz and the practicability of their grandiose schemes. I should also like to thank Dr Berghahn for loaning me the typescript of his latest work before publication, and for reading the first draft of this book and putting me right on many points of fact and interpretation; any errors that remain are, of course, my responsibility.

I am grateful for permission to quote from Dr Berghahn's *Der Tirpitz Plan*, Droste, Düsseldorf, 1971, and *Germany and the Approach of War, 1914*, Macmillan, 1973, and from his other works, particularly *Zu den Zielen des deutschen Flottenbaus* ... from *Historische Zeitschrift*, 1970, *Der Tirpitz Plan und die Krisis* ... from *Marine und Marinepolitik*, Droste 1972 and the startling *Neue Dokumente* ... on the *Kaiserlichen Marine*, which he edited with W. Deist for *Militärgeschichtliche Mitteilungen*, 1970; these last contain the evidence for the frantic preparations for war of the German Navy in early July 1914.

I should like to thank Dr Kennedy for permission to quote extracts from his penetrating researches into the strategy of the 'Tirpitz Plan', notably *Maritime Strategieprobleme der deutsche-englischen Flottenrivalität* for *Marine und Marinepolitik*, Droste 1972, *Tirpitz, England and the Second Navy Law of 1900* for *Militärgeschichtliche Mitteilungen*, 1970, *Second Navy Law of 1900* for *Militärgeschichtliche Mitteilungen*, 1970, 2, *German World Policy and the Alliance Negotiations with England, 1897-*

1900, for *The Journal of Modern History*, Dec., 1973, and *The Development of German Naval Operations Plans against England, 1896-1914,* for *English Historical Review*, Oct., 1973. My debt to other authorities on this period is great; those familiar with the Fisher era in the Royal Navy will realise that it is impossible to explore these waters without reference to the detailed charts of the area contained in Professor Arthur Marder's classic works: *From Dreadnought to Scapa Flow*, O.U.P. 1961-1970 (but particularly volume 1); *British Naval Policy 1880-1905*, Putnam 1941; *Fear God and Dread Nought; the correspondence of Admiral of the Fleet Lord Fisher of Kilverstone*, Cape, 1952-9; I am extremely grateful to Professor Marder for permission to quote extracts from memoranda cited in these splendid volumes, and from very many letters from the correspondence in *'Fear God'*. And I am most grateful to the present Lord Fisher of Kilverstone for his prior permission to quote what I needed from his grandfather's letters, surely some of the most uninhibited masterpieces of the Edwardian era. And I am grateful to Lt Cdr Peter Kemp and the Navy Records Society for permission to quote other 'Fisherisms' from *The Fisher Papers*, another fascinating source essential for an understanding of the British naval reforms of the early twentieth century.

Returning to the German side of the story, I should like to acknowledge my great debt to Dr Jonathan Steinberg of Cambridge University for his work on the genesis of the 'Tirpitz Era', published as *Yesterday's Deterrent*, Macdonald, 1965, and for his many other colourful articles on aspects of the Anglo-German naval rivalry, particularly *The Copenhagen Complex* from *The Journal of Contemporary History*, and *Germany and the Russo-Japanese War* from the *American Historical Review*; I am most grateful to Dr Steinberg for permission to quote extracts from these works. I am indebted also to Drs P. J. Kelly and J. E. Sutton, whose researches into the Imperial German Navy as detailed in their impressive doctoral dissertations (cited in references and bibliography) were of vital help; I am grateful for permission to quote extracts from Dr Kelly's work. I am extremely grateful to Dr J. C. G. Röhl of the University of Sussex for permission to quote from his fascinating *1914: Delusion or Design?* (Elek 1973), and his other works on the naval rivalry, particularly *Vice Admiral von Müller and the Approach of War*, from *The Historical Journal*. And I should like to thank Professor Michael Balfour of the University of

East Anglia for permission to quote extracts from *The Kaiser and his Times* (Cresset Press 1964), which provides fascinating background information on Wilhelmine Germany.

I should like to acknowledge my debt to the late Sir Llewellyn Woodward, whose *Great Britain and the German Navy* (O.U.P. 1935) blazed the trail I have followed; it was published at a most timely moment—but how many heeded the message then? That Sir Llewellyn's conclusions were correct is only too evident now that the German archives have been opened to public view.

I should like to thank Her Majesty the Queen for her gracious permission to quote extracts from letters in the Royal Archives, and Viscount Esher for permission to quote numerous extracts from his grandfather's letters and journals, published as *Journals and Letters of Reginald, Viscount Esher* (edited M. V. Brett) by Nicholson & Watson in 1934.

Rear Admiral P. N. Buckley and the staff of the Naval Historical Branch, Ministry of Defence were, as always, unfailingly helpful; I should like to mention in particular Mr J. D. Lawson of the Foreign Documents Section. And I should like, once again, to express my gratitude to the Library Interlending Service which makes an author's lot so much more travel-free than it would otherwise be. I should also like to thank Mr Christopher Legge, librarian, U.S.A.F., Bentwaters for his help, particularly with many problems of German translation.

I am indebted to the following publishers for granting permission to quote from their books, and, naturally, to the authors: Heinemann Ltd for R. Churchill, *Winston Churchill, 1901-1914*; The Hamlyn Group for W. Churchill, *The World Crisis, 1911-1923*; Butterworth Ltd for Crown Prince of Germany, *Memoirs*; The Bodley Head for B. v. Bülow, *Memoirs*; The Observer Ltd, for A. M. Gollin, *The Observer and J. L. Garvin*; The Clarendon Press, Oxford, for A. J. Marder, *From the Dreadnought to Scapa Flow*, and E. L. Woodward, *Great Britain and the German Navy*, and L. Albertini (transl. I. M. Massey), *The Origins of the War of 1914*; Eyre & Spottiswoode and Collins & Sons Ltd for V. Bonham-Carter, *Winston Churchill as I knew him*; Yale University Press for A. Dorpalen, *Heinrich von Treitschke*; Princeton University Press for L. Cecil, *Albert Ballin* ...; Hutchinson Publishing Group Ltd for A. Tirpitz, *My Memoirs*; Hodder & Stoughton Ltd for R. H. Bacon, *The Life of Lord Fisher of Kilverstone*, and Viscount Grey, *Twenty*

Five Years, and A. Hurd, *The German Fleet*; Macmillan Ltd for S. Lee, *King Edward VII*; John Murray for C. V. Usborne, *Blast and Counterblast*. And I should like to thank the editors of *The Times*, *The Daily Mail* and *The Daily Telegraph* for permission to quote from their newspapers, also all those contributors to the journals devoted to contemporary historical research, particularly perhaps C. Andrew, R. Cosgrove, R. J. Crampton, R. Hyam and R. Langhorne, whose work added so many dimensions to the story. If I have overlooked anyone I apologise.

I

Imperial Germany

While the sea powers of western Europe carved the world between them and England, the greatest sea power of them all, took the lion's share, the Germans lingered in the realm of dreams. Divided in petty princedoms jealous of their sovereignty and mostly far from the sea, the high road for commerce and world influence, they made their contribution to European life in analytical thought, writing, immortal music. And when they awoke in the last quarter of the nineteenth century all the good places of the earth had been taken. This was how Germans looked at the world—and with some reason.

Going deeper, they saw two distinct branches of the German race: on the one hand the southern and western states, generally favoured by nature, whose princes had patronised great men of science and art and raised the magnificent edifice of German intellectual life, on the other hand Prussia, kingdom of the eagle, whose stiffer character had been formed on the sandy soil of the northern marches east of the Elbe and Oder. Lacking natural barriers, forced to maintain itself in battle, Prussia had become a nation of warriors united under the soldier kings of the house of Hohenzollern, with a Spartan code of self-sacrifice and individual subservience to the good of the State. This code had received philosophical justification in the teachings of Hegel. The State was 'the Divine idea as it exists on earth'; individuals possessed spiritual reality only through the State. Therefore the State was its own highest law and relations with other States were not governed by normal codes of morality, only by the will of the State. Armed might was a right, indeed the instrument of this will, and in the wars which, in the natural order of things, had to occur the only justification and the only judgement was success.

The doctrine was given political reality by Bismarck in the second

15

half of the nineteenth century. In a series of sudden, calculated, skilfully localised wars directed against one opponent at a time— 'those terrible but splendid years'[1]—he extended Prussian State power over all the German peoples except Austria, creating a great central European Empire under Wilhelm I of Hohenzollern, the new Caesar—the Kaiser. Afterwards it became apparent that this had been Prussia's historic mission. Through the long German sleep, she had been preparing herself by privation and discipline to become the political teacher and taskmaster of the Germans so that their high civilisation whose manifold facets were brought together in one emotional word, *Kultur*, might have an appropriate power base. For civilisation without power was an empty shell. Throughout history higher civilisations had been spread by armed conquest. This was a 'law of history'; it was the way mankind had progressed, and without this constant clash between higher and lower civilisations there would be no hope of development for mankind. If the Germany of Goethe and Schiller meant anything, it needed the strength and purpose of the Germany of Bismarck, von Roon and von Moltke. This was the trend of German historical thought.

Its most influential exponent was Heinrich von Treitschke from the chair of history at the University of Berlin, the Prussian capital —now the Imperial City. This deaf, passionate high priest of State power, born into the nobility but unable to follow the customary military career, had built his model of history upon Hegel's framework and, having made history fit doctrine had argued the doctrine upwards from the 'history' into a mystical concept of Prussian destiny through the sword. In this closed, circuitous system, war was both the instrument and the realisation of the 'Divine idea'.

> Only in war a nation will truly become a Nation. Only common great deeds for the idea of the Fatherland will hold a nation together. Social selfishness must yield ... The individual must forget himself and feel part of the whole; he must realise how insignificant his life is compared with the whole ...'[2]

Such an idealised concept of war was not unique to Prussian thought. But it took the Prussian genius to raise a world-wide fascination with the ancient qualities of heroism and self-sacrifice —as purgative for gross 'materialism'—into a dynamic philosophy. Treitschke was first among the prophets. He told Prussians what they wished to hear; they were the chosen people; their mission was to extend the borders of Prussian State power as in the past regardless of means or moral scruples and finally, because it was inevitable, with the sword. Year after year he preached this doctrine in University lecture halls filled to overflowing not only with students but with a cross-section of Berlin official, professional and Service life, Generals and Admirals among them. Year by year his language grew more violent, his aphorisms more predictable, the ritual and atmosphere of his courses more characteristic of a revivalist meeting than an academic institution. His entry, followed by acolytes who took up appointed places either side of him on the dais was a solemn procession; his address, begun immediately he ascended the rostrum, was delivered in a continuous, howling roar which rose and fell as rhythmically as a liturgical chant without regard to meaning or punctuation, broken only by the responses of his audience who stamped and clapped ecstatically on cue—or by his own visible emotions momentarily choking the breathless torrent of words.

His language was as unrestricted as his delivery, ranging from paeans to the German *Volk* to elemental shafts of hatred for peoples outside the mystic circle. In such a charged atmosphere as he created neither analysis nor argument found any place. His audience was there to dedicate itself to the truth, not question it; Treitschke, pouring out his soul before it with such prodigal vehemence that by the end of each performance he was spent and his handkerchief soaked with tears of emotion, seemed the embodiment of Prussian truth. His message intoxicated. Generations of students and men who came to wield immense power in Germany found their inspiration at his feet.

'It is impossible to describe the impression which Treitschke made on my cousin and me,'[3] wrote one director of the Pan-German League; 'it was as if everything noble, great and strong had taken form in this man.' Innumerable similar recollections testify to his remarkable impact. Not all were favourable. Critics recognised that his lectures, while based on the denial of self before an all-mighty State and couched in mystical, lyrical language, ultimately appealed to the basest instincts of his audience. But criticism was swamped in the rising tide of young Germany feeling the growing material strength of the Empire and dazzled by the bizarre mixture of idealism and power he held before them.

Everything came down to power. Power was the supreme force in the world; to nurture power was the highest duty of the State. 'The State,' went one of his best-known, most thunderously applauded phrases, 'is not an academy of art. It is power!'⁴ Power, in the final resort, was armed force. Therefore the State was armed power; therefore the concept of the State implied war; this was because relationships between States were never static but altered constantly as some nations and empires grew, others decayed. Darwin's theory of the evolution of species applied to the evolution of races and civilisations; the fittest became dominant; the fittest class—in Germany the Prussian nobility—imposed its will on the lower orders within the State; the fittest State imposed its will on less fit, that is less powerful States and spread a higher culture in the cause of human progress. The mechanism of change and progress was war. 'Unceasingly history builds and destroys; it never tires of salvaging the divine goods of mankind from the ruins of old worlds into a new one. Who believes in this infinite growth ... must acknowledge the unalterable necessity of war.'⁵

By mixing up the State and power and war and human destiny until they seemed but different faces of one dynamic whole, which was nothing less than the spirit of creation moving on earth, therefore its own highest sanction, Treitschke elevated war from a simple extension of political action into a high moral necessity. That was the message which came through. 'The diplomat is the *servant*, not the master of the soldier.' And by according to the State and the acquisition of State power—which was the same thing—the sanctity of the highest moral law, he placed statesmen outside all other systems of ethics. 'The statesman does not have the right, like the ordinary citizen, to hold sacred the spotless purity of his life and reputation as the supreme of all moral goods ... the statesman must, for the victory of his idea, resort to tactics of deception which the individual may not use to further his own small objectives.'⁶

The effect of Treitschke's teaching was to extract the evils, imperfections, ambitions and race hatreds of current European politics and raise them into the highest forms of political virtue. Taken to its logical conclusion—and new Germany prided itself on logic—it was a system which glorified any internal tyranny, any external aggression for the good of the State.

Deplorable as this philosophy appeared to liberals, it was easy to justify as a simple exercise in realism. Look where they would the policies of the Powers spelled it out. To the east, the vast Empire of the Tsars sprawled across the top half of Asia, its divers peoples held in check by secret police whose odious methods shrank from the light of any conceivable system of ethics or law, whose external policy was cynically expansionist. 'We shall proceed southwards along the road of history', one of her leading statesmen wrote in a memorandum for Tsar Nicholas II. 'The more inert countries in Asia will fall prey to the powerful invaders and will be divided up between them ... the problem of each country is to obtain as large a share as possible of the inheritance of the outlived Oriental States ... Russia, both geographically and historically has the undisputed right to the lion's share.'[7] Other advisers believed that it was Russia's destiny to rule the entire Yellow Race. To the west was France with similar large ambitions for a Mediterranean Empire, and England whose lust for power, unassuaged by possession of India and the great English-speaking dominions, was manifest in her bullying attacks on the Boers and her grand design for an African Empire to stretch uninterruptedly from the Cape of Good Hope to Egypt and the Mediterranean. This lust was the more despicable since it was hidden behind a humanitarian mask. 'Take up the White Man's burden, send forth the best ye breed; go bind your sons to exile to serve your captives' need.'[8] Kipling's naïvety was easily penetrable by German intellect. And the English Music Hall sang a different, more elemental tune: 'Back to back the world around, answer with a will—England for her own, boys! It's Rule Britannia still!'

Further west across the Atlantic lay the other great 'Anglo-Saxon' nation, the United States of America, which had driven its civilisation right across the Continent with scant regard for the native peoples; now finding itself unable to spread further, it was looking towards South America, the Pacific, even Africa, justifying vital expansionary urges with ideas from the same source as Treitschke's or Kipling's. Further west still was the island Empire of Japan, which had absorbed the techniques of European material civilisation in remarkably short time since emerging from feudalism in mid-century, and had shown herself an equally willing pupil in its political expression.

Everywhere it was the same: 'advanced' nations spread their influence by force of arms and rationalised their conquests by reference to a 'civilising' mission or glorification of the State through the divine ruler. The only check to one nation's ambition was the superior armed power of other nations; there was no law except might. The Germans prided themselves on seeing the world as it was, and having this clear vision and virile ambitions of their own, they drank from Treitschke's tainted well, worshipped at his shrines to the *Herrenvolk*, pledged themselves to the one Commandment of *Realpolitik* and looked to the coming of the greater Germany.

Deutschland! Deutschland über alles, über alles in der Welt!

In contemporary terms 'greater Germany' meant an extension of the Empire overseas through colonies and trade, spreading 'Germanism' and German influence and power throughout the world. Here it was evident they must come up against Great Britain with her existing world Empire and her mighty navy whose battle squadrons were supreme in every ocean. Britain would never give up her supremacy voluntarily. Here, then, was the great struggle of the future and although Treitschke professed to see it as a struggle for a power *balance* at sea, therefore a moral struggle for the freedom of all States against Great Britain's arrogant assumptions as mistress of the seas, this scarcely fitted his general theories of power and aggrandisement, evolution and decay; to his followers at least, it was evident that the balance would need to be in Germany's favour. Treitschke *felt* this; as he grew older his passions became more violent, expressions of hatred for England assumed greater prominence in his lectures and the inevitability of the struggle with England became even clearer to him. Seeing on the one hand the young German Empire with its intellect and scientific vigour harnessed under the Prussian leadership in iron discipline and with the all-important will to greatness, on the other hand the impressive but ramshackle system that British tradesmen and 'pepper jobbers' had strung together haphazardly across the globe in fits of enthusiasm, he looked forward amidst frenzied stamping and cheering to the day when a German army marched on London.

This was the fare which nourished German imagination towards the end of the nineteenth century. It was a powerful vision and a driving force that began to mould the real world closer to its own image.

The foreign policies of nations, so far as they are not the mere expressions of the individual ambitions of rulers or the jog-trot opportunism of diplomats, are anticipation of and provision for struggle for existence between the incipient species. Arsenals of war, navies and armies, are the protective and aggressive weapons of the species-corporate, as the antlers of the stag or the teeth and claws of the tiger are the weapons of the individual. War itself is the most striking expression of the actual struggle ...[9]

This biological view of power politics came not from Berlin, its spiritual home, but from the *Saturday Review* published in London in 1896, the year that all the vague anti-British feelings of Treitschke and his school burst out into the open over British colonial action against the Boers in southern Africa—particularly over German impotence to intervene while the British navy commanded all seas. The article was not representative of British thought which was too unspeculative and, as Treitschke noted contemptuously, 'utilitarian' to lend itself to such gross abstractions; it was only significant as one of the earliest signs of British alarm at the new spirit stirring in Germany, and—because of its violent, pseudo-scientific and peculiarly un-English approach—as the most widely-quoted article in subsequent German nationalist and 'navalist' propaganda; it was proof of Britain's compulsive enmity. It went on :

Feeble races are being wiped off the earth and the few, great incipient species arm themselves against each other. England as the greatest of these—greatest in geographical distribution, greatest in expansive force, greatest in race pride—has avoided for centuries the only dangerous kind of war. Now, with the whole earth occupied and movements of expansion continuing she will have to fight to the death against successive rivals. With which first? With which second? With which third?[10]

Here the western world, with its glittering veneer of a civilisation at once courtly and animated by the prospect of unending scientific advance, had reverted to a jungle where great beasts lay in wait with nothing but their strength and primaeval instincts to guide them. Pressing the analogy to its limits, the anonymous biologist went on to assert that the most deadly conflicts in the animal kingdom occurred between those species which were most similar.

Of European nations, Germany is most alike to England. In racial

21

characteristics, in religious and scientific thought, in sentiments
and aptitudes the Germans, by their resemblance to the English
are marked out as our national rivals. In all parts of the earth, in
every pursuit, in commerce, in manufacturing, in exploiting the
other races, the English and Germans jostle each other. Germany is
a growing nation expanding beyond her territorial limits, she is
bound to secure new footholds or perish in the attempt ... Were
every German to be wiped out tomorrow there is no English trade,
no English pursuit that would not immediately expand. Were every
Englishman wiped out tomorrow, the Germans would gain in
proportion. Here is the first great racial struggle of the future; here
are two growing nations pressing against each other, man to man all
over the world. One or the other will go.[11]

This pitiless view of European rivalry with its mixed and unrelated
arguments from the jungle and modern commerce may have struck
some chords in English businessmen and shipping magnates who
believed themselves to be suffering from the efficiency of German
competition, but it was chiefly significant as a small surface indication of the world-wide undercurrents sucking reason into the
maelstrom of images emanating from the schools of history and
philosophy at the University of Berlin. The conclusion of the
article revealed the depth of the vortex.

Be ready to fight Germany as *Germania est delenda*; be ready to
fight America when the time comes. Lastly, engage in no wasting
wars against people from whom we have nothing to fear.[12]

This was the phantasm conjured from the once simple and manly
code of the Prussians by a self-indulgent and degenerate intellectual-
isation. 'Be ready to fight...' not a limited war for limited objectives,
but a struggle to the death between two similar races for the
overlordship of the world.

'It needs no custom house to tell you that you have come to
Germany,' wrote an English visitor in 1896. 'You are in a new
atmosphere—an atmosphere of order, or discipline, of system rigidly
applied to the smallest detail. The officials carry themselves stiffly
and seem to live with their heels together at attention.'[13]

This was the hallmark of the warrior race. The discipline of the
Prussian troops had always been the quality most marked by

observers. Frederick the Great himself had attributed to this 'wonderful regularity' a large measure of his success. 'The discipline of the troops, now evolved into habit, has such effect that in the greatest confusion of action and the most evident perils their disorder is still more orderly than the good order of their opponents.'[14]

Such habits of obedience carried into everyday life struck strangely on the English visitor whose self-reliance, sharpened in the subtle blend of muddle and convention at home, had nothing to bite on. Everything had been thought out. It was almost as if the country had been turned into a giant army camp. The stations were functional transit points of lofty but naked brick and glass, all alike, carrying no posters displaying commercial products, simply holding out directions in imperatives: 'Go Right!' 'Have Ticket Ready!' There was a multitude of other rules which needed careful study; when travelling with baggage it was necessary to book it in at least fifteen minutes before departure—otherwise it meant a wait for the next train. When the carriages drew up at the platform it was not in order to alight until the Guard had commanded it; those waiting on the platform received a similar order to board. Inside each carriage was a blue-covered booklet containing several pages of further directions to meet any eventuality; it might be necessary, for instance, to lower the window—the circumstances in which such an operation might be carried out were clearly listed.

The Teutonic style was quite as marked in social life. Standards were set by the Kaiser's entourage drawn mostly from the oldest noble families of Prussia, an aristocracy bred to arms, which provided nearly all the officers, not only for the Guards but for most cavalry and some infantry regiments as well, allowing a mere sprinkling of recruits from the new industrial and professional classes to infiltrate its proud preserve. Their arrogant bearing and harsh, rattling, nasal speech with its highhanded violation of grammar and pronunciation and deliberate crudities of expression emphasising contempt for any effeminate refinement had spread down through the aspiring industrial, commercial and professional classes, even to petty officials and civil servants who oiled the clockwork of State. The outward show of aggressive manhood was not sufficient, however; it was necessary to prove hardihood and loyalty to the State by bearing arms. For a professional man this meant gaining a commission as an officer in the Reserve; without this badge of conformity, self-respect, even career and social life could be blighted. A mere civilian was scarcely a man.

The same Junker class which provided the social and military élite filled the positions of power in the State. This was partly a result of the voting system in Prussia which gave those who paid most taxes most votes and gave agricultural areas in the pockets of the great landowners greater proportional weight than the new industrial conglomerations, partly a result of the peculiar constitution of the Empire. At the head, naturally in the Prussian ethic, was the King of Prussia whose deliberately vague position was President of the Union of Federated States, with the title of Kaiser, or Emperor. The States themselves, which retained their own Royal Houses and many autonomous rights sent representatives to an assembly known as the *Bundesrat*, in which the sovereignty of the Empire was vested. However, Bismarck had seen to it that Prussia, the largest State, dominated the *Bundesrat*; nothing could be done against the will of Prussia. There was also a lower House, the *Reichstag*, whose members were elected by the people on a Party basis irrespective of State boundaries. But the *Reichstag's* functions were confined to debating and passing or amending legislation which came in theory from the *Bundesrat*, but was actually put through by State Secretaries chosen by and responsible to the *Reich* Chancellor. The Chancellor, in theory the sole *Imperial* Minister, was also Prime Minister of Prussia, who was appointed by and responsible to the Kaiser.

This complex system gave the representatives of the Princes of the Empire who sat in the *Bundesrat* and the representatives of the people who sat in the *Reichstag* the appearance of power to throw out measures which they disliked and to control the Imperial Budget, and on occasions they did place the Chancellor in an impossible position without authority for his policies. But in practice there were so many parties with narrow interests within the Empire that a skilful Chancellor, playing on their fears and ambitions could usually construct a majority. So the responsibility of the government to the people was more apparent than real, and effective power, maintained by the most ancient policy of 'divide and rule' was vested in the Chancellor, thus in the King of Prussia, who in his Imperial mantle appointed him. Meanwhile the armed Services, the ultimate sanction, lay outside the civil constitution in all matters except budgetary control, the senior officers appointed by and responsible to the Commander-in-Chief—who was the Kaiser. The Kaiser was also empowered to conduct the foreign affairs of the Empire—although there was a State Secretary for Foreign Affairs responsible to the Chancellor—and the ultimate decision of war or peace was his sole prerogative.

Wilhelm II discharged all these supreme responsibilities, which have been recognised in a recent study as endowing him with an 'almost absolutist position',[15] through three personal Secretariats, or Cabinets, one Civil, one for the army, one for the Navy. These were filled from the Prussian élite which surrounded him. As the chiefs of these Cabinets were natural enemies of democracy— the antithesis of their class ideal of popular subjection to the will of the State as expressed through its Divine Ruler—so absolutism was nourished. Kaiser Wilhelm II, who needed no encouragement to believe himself an autocrat, scarcely made a speech in which the theme of absolute Monarchy was not hammered home in his peculiar, high-flown, emotional idiom: 'Sovereignty by the Grace of God, sovereignty with its never-ending, ever-ending toils and anxieties, with its awful responsibilities to the Creator alone, from which no Minister, no people, no Parliament can absolve the Prince,'[16] or more directly, 'My course is the right one and that course shall be steered ... There is only one law and that is my law.'

Treitschke's myth was, it seemed, close to reality. The Empire was knit under the will and by the standards of the warrior race in fealty to its heaven-sent Commander. And yet ...

Stretching west from the heart of the Imperial City, the suburbs of the new rich suggested another Germany.[17] Mansions and apartment blocks aping styles from every great age and corner of the world rose in tasteless opulence, their miscegenated architecture and excessive ornamental detail attesting 'materialism' run riot. And were these the *Volk*, so many with gross flesh from beer and gargantuan meals swelling their sober suiting![18] And their loud wives, so many wide ankles and baggy shapes under extravagant couture, was this *Kultur* for exploit—were these the Spartans to spread the new Athenian age?

A Prussian officer might have greeted the suggestion with an oath. '*Wirklich!* The effete display of a decaying Empire—a typical manifestation of the new Germany, with its huckstering, obtrusive manners, more a snobbism than a symbol of true German ability!'[19]

In the heart of Berlin the lesson was evident. Extending westward from the Kaiser's Castle was the beautiful avenue, *Unter den Linden*, culminating at the Brandenburger Gate, whose restrained columns and simple yet majestic outline crowned by a chariot of victory had been designed at the end of the eighteenth century. Other public architecture of the same or earlier periods was similarly dignified with clean, often stark lines traced in simple stone. Later periods became successively more pretentious. The *Reichstag* building, completed in 1894, epitomised the most recent style; it was ablaze with gilt, encircled by statuary representing knights, goddesses and all the heavenly hosts, the four corners emphasised by massive edifices structured with diverse columns and arches. Over the entrance façade the words DEM DEUTSCHEN VOLK were graven in letters of gold. Opposite in the great square, the Königplatz, a column of victory erected to celebrate the triumph over France and crowned with a gilt angel so enormous that it threatened to snap its base, was similarly tortured with a profusion of sinuous allegorical episodes. Everything of the Imperial epoch, it seemed, was double life-size, ornate, gilded, ostentatious.

Warriors were in the saddle. But while they faced backwards the new Germany galloped away beneath them in the press of industrial nations pursuing material progress and profit; they held the reigns, but it was the industrialists, entrepreneurs and speculators who provided momentum and the real power behind Germany's position in the world. Not so much Prussian discipline as Krupp steel cannon outranging French field pieces which had cut down Napoleon III's soldiers at Sedan, Krupp steel siege pieces which had pulverised the French garrison in the fortress of Metz. And it had been the network of German railways based on Krupp steel tyres and track, whose construction had been the catalyst for her rapid industrial growth, which provided the key to the rapid, and in the Prussian style exact deployment of her troops and cannon.

The Junker aristocracy enjoyed the prestige of these great victories, and the great industrialists who had provided the means were content, for the moment, to affect their manner and, hopefully, marry their sons and daughters into the nobility of the sword, often poor by comparison. At the same time business had given them a different outlook on the world, and most of their real interests were in conflict with those of the landed class they aped. The Junkers, for their part, were naturally resentful of this highly successful industrial element which threatened their established way of life with new ideas, different standards, particularly resentful of the parvenu wealth which must eventually threaten their tight hold on power. So they retreated further into the glorious past and closed ranks, exaggerating their distinguishing features as a natural consequence. Meanwhile the new Germany thundered on beneath them. It had come up too fast from too far behind to be halted by any reaction above, and could already see the winning posts in view. German steel production was double that of England; German science and science-based industries led the world; German exports and sea trade were growing rapidly.

The furious pace and iron grip caused serious strains. In the tenements stretching in rows about the industrial quarters of Berlin, beneath the smoke overcast from the chimneys of the rich coal and mineral areas centred on Essen, in the warehouses of Hamburg and Bremen, the antithesis of Treitschke's power State had taken form as the Social Democratic Party. The Party was opposed to everything that Imperial Germany seemed to stand for. Nationalism, especially with military or Monarchical overtones was anathema; the workers recognised no national borders nor hereditary rulers. In the calendar that the Socialist journal *Vorwärts*, published every year, the schoolbook heroes of Germany, Bismarck, Moltke, Blücher, Scharnhorst, were not so much as mentioned, nor the famous battles; instead Nihilists and Anarchists were listed with their desperate attempts against authority. The prophets of the Party were Marx and Engels, the elimination of differences in wealth by the abolition of private property, and the nationalisation of the means of production and distribution formed its dogma; to achieve these ends revolution was held to be inevitable. And while other western European parties tempered their Marxism with pragmatic attempts to wrest better conditions from the system as it was, the German Party confronted by the most inflexible system, campaigned for absolutes in the bitter language of class hatred. For it was a German creation—the reverse image of the power State it sought to destroy. It was as arrogant in its belief that German workers were the most useful, competent and admirable members of society as the Junkers in their stiff assumptions; it had the same strength in abstract justification of its purposes, and its members had the same

27

gift for detail and individual subordination to the good of the whole.

The authorities recognised these qualities and saw the Party, which grew in strength every year, as the most serious danger to the State. 'It is so dangerous because it is typically German. No other nation has such a gift for organisation, no nation submits so willingly to discipline.'[20]

Other strains caused by Prussian domination were apparent in arguments over individual State's rights, in the small political parties representing minority groups within the Empire against their will, and in the religious differences between the predominantly Catholic southern and western States and the colder Protestant north. While Prussian politicians ruled by exploiting these flaws they knew that in the long term all the tendencies towards class and State separatism could destroy the Empire as they knew and willed it. To prevent such a relapse into the tribalism from which Prussia had rescued them the German peoples needed a great unifying vision—so went the ruling orthodoxy; their gaze needed to be lifted from petty internal squabbles and directed outwards. 'Kaiser Wilhelm's government,' Baron Holstein wrote in 1897, 'needs some tangible success abroad which will then have a beneficial effect at home.'[21]

Analysed 'beneficial effect' can be seen as preservation of the peculiar system by which the Junkers, 'a pre-industrial élite' whose 'social and economic base was the German countryside', sought to preserve their privileged power position against the threats posed by an industrial society—specifically against the wealth of big business, the political ambition of the middle classes and the Red spectre conjured from the growing urban proletariat. Granting greater participation to any of these forces would necessarily weaken the closed political system whereby the Junkers and the House of Hohenzollern mutually supported each other and, it was feared, would eventually lead to 'democratic government' on Westminster lines. Junkers despised this on ideological grounds as much as they feared it as the end of their supremely privileged position. In this respect, 'lifting the gaze' of the German people and 'directing it outwards' were euphemisms for 'distracting' attention from the Junker stranglehold on power.

One of the most brilliant of the coming men in Germany, Bernhard von Bülow, put it clearly when he advised a 'wide-minded foreign policy' for the purpose of 'restraining the majority of the nation from pursuing the revolutionary aims of the Social Democrats', meanwhile strengthening the middle classes, 'the vast majority of whom steadily uphold the Monarchy and the State.'[22]

This strategy—which was in another sense, perhaps, only German rationalisation of the drive for overseas adventure that swept all Europe and America too—came naturally to Kaiser Wilhelm II. He delighted in beating the national drum and did so without prompting at home or on his frequent travels abroad. Each performance was given in full martial costume with a wealth of heroic symbolism. He seemed the embodiment of Treitschke's vision. Visitors to his capital, who might have been deceived by the hustling commercial and shopping quarters, the profusion of telephones, electrical novelties and signs and pfennig-in-the-slot automation that they were in a European version of Broadway or Chicago, were brought back to the different ethic of Prussia by a glimpse of the Kaiser. In company with officers whose chests glinted with as many crosses and orders as their splendid tunics could bear, he stepped with the stiff stride of the Prussian soldier, or rode bolt upright on a white charger, his public features set in a mask appropriate to his position as the earthly representative and focus of the Creator's will for Imperial Germany.

A dead yellow skin, hard pencilled brows, straight masterful nose, lips jammed close together under a moustache pointing straight upwards to the whites of his eyes. A face at once repulsive and pathetic, so harsh and stony was it, so grimly solemn. A face in which no individual feature was very dark, but which altogether was black as thunder. He raised his gloved hand in a stiff, mechanical salute and turned his head impressively to left and right. But there was no courtesy in the salute, no light in the eye, no smile in the tight mouth for his loyal subjects. He looked like a man without joy, without love, without pity, without hope. A man might wear such a face who felt himself turning slowly into ice.[23]

Wilhelm's private face was very different. Behind the vertical waxed moustaches, the sensitive features of his youth, when he had been described by his tutor as almost girlishly good-looking, were little changed. And when he relaxed his heroic mask his eyes lit with animation, interest or gaiety as they had in boyhood. 'Willy is a dear, interesting, charming boy ...' his fond mother had written when he was seven. 'He is growing up so handsome and his large eyes have now and then a pensive, dreamy expression and then again they sparkle with fun and delight.'[24] He had shown great promise in those days.

His mother was Queen Victoria's daughter, 'Vicky', the Princess Royal of England, an attractive, clever, eager girl who had been very close to her father, the Prince Consort, and had imbibed all his earnestly progressive liberal views. She married Crown Prince Friedrich of Prussia also of liberal persuasions, and gave birth to Wilhelm in 1859, some years before Bismarck carved out the greater Empire for his dynasty. Bismarck's repressive internal policies which pushed Prussia and then the *Reich* violently away from English constitutional ideas towards the despotism of Russia, were bitterly opposed by Friedrich and his 'English Princess'—she more than he as she was intellectually the dominant partner. Bismarck had responded with a characteristically unprincipled campaign which had isolated the liberal couple. His greatest triumph had been to take Wilhelm from them. This was the beginning of high tragedy. 'Vicky' had tried earnestly to instil 'all that is most Christian, therefore most liberal'[25] into 'Willy', and bring him up 'without that terrible Prussian pride which grieved papa so much';[26] he turned out more conceited, more arrogant, more illiberal and a more breath-taking liar than if she had given him over to Bismarck from his cradle; it was the stuff of nightmare.

'Willy's' birth had been violent. In their efforts for his mother, the doctors had injured the nerves on the left side of his neck and extending down his arm, leaving him with a permanently crippled hand and arm, uncertain balance and a rightward tilt to his neck and head. The sight of the poor mite with his left arm withered and dangling uselessly and his head to one side had torn his mother's heart as he grew to boyhood and it had been a constant source of anxiety to find some treatment which would at least disguise the infirmities and enable him to lead a more normal life, for he could neither run so fast as others of his age, nor climb, nor with his lack of balance ride, nor even cut his own food. One of the first remedies was an iron and leather machine designed to screw his head around and stretch the muscles on the right side of his neck. To see him in this cruel apparatus was an additional torment for his mother. Later she had to endure watching him suffer a far more painful electrical treatment for his arm. She wondered if, in consequence of his afflictions, she spoiled him; whenever he didn't wish to do anything he flew into such a violent passion.[27]

At the age of seven 'Willy' was given over to a tutor, a stern Calvinist who sought as earnestly as his mother to overcome his physical disabilities while instilling a classical education and the virtues of hard work, self-denial and duty. It was a pitiless régime, unrelieved by humour or praise, which began at six or seven in the morning and lasted until the evening. During the course of it Wilhelm was obliged to master his imbalance in the saddle; the simple method his tutor employed was to deny him stirrups and, each time he fell off, to remount him. After weeks of torture which his mother watched like a Stoic, the treatment worked. Wilhelm had *wanted* to ride; later he taught himself to swim with only one arm and play tennis and shoot with equal success. But his tutor found it impossible to force him against his inclination; his 'inner self' resisted all pressures designed to guide it in an unwanted direction.

As he grew older a natural shyness and timidity which his tutor ascribed to his physical backwardness in all normal, boyish pursuits, were obscured by less pleasant traits which his mother had noted much earlier as inclinations to be 'selfish, domineering and proud.'[28] She had blamed the peculiar circumstances of his upbringing for encouraging rather than checking these tendencies. Now his tutor, alarmed by his charge's increasing vanity and autocracy suggested that he be sent to a State school where he would have to compete with boys of his own age, and thus gain a more balanced idea of his own abilities. Wilhelm was already painfully aware that other boys were better at most things; to make up for it he played on his position as future Monarch, and if that were not sufficient invented stories to display himself in the most favourable light. He was clever and amusing at it. It was only a surface cleverness; in his studies, despite all the earnest zeal and long hours his tutor had lavished, he proved incapable of concentrating on any topic for long; he became bored and anxious to move on to something new and more exciting. One of the only exceptions was an interest in ships acquired on summer holidays which he loved at Queen Victoria's Palace at Osborne overlooking the Solent and Spithead, or on tours around the British dockyards with his uncles.

From the school, whose pupils had quite failed to knock the

conceit out of him, he was sent to Bonn University, where deferential treatment enhanced it and his other disagreeable traits, and from thence to the traditional initiation for Prussian Monarchs, the First Regiment of Guards at Potsdam. By the time he emerged from this swaggering, masculine stronghold of Monarchical and nationalist values his mother had given up hope for him. His towering arrogance and grotesque sense of his own importance, rudeness and obvious contempt for all the ideals her beloved father had passed on to her were almost past bearing. In place of the cultured and intellectual eldest son she had hoped for, she found a melodramatic braggart without depth of mind or interest living in a fantasy of Teutonic Knighthood and cheap nationalist sentiment.

This was just the tool Bismarck needed against her and the Crown Prince Friedrich and he cultivated Wilhelm, inspired him with his own attitude to statecraft in the jungle of European politics and Marxist subversionaries, and used him for his own ends both at home and abroad. All the cards seemed to fall into his hands. Before Prince Friedrich could inherit the Crown of Prussia a fatal illness overtook him, and he reigned, literally speechless after a throat operation, for only three months after the old Kaiser, Wilhelm I, died. During this time in which he was too weak and ill to attempt any reforms of Bismarck's noxious system, Wilhelm made no secret of his impatience to ascend, and made a typically bombastic, unfilial speech in which he urged Germans, in view of the new Kaiser's incapacity, to rally about 'the great Chancellor'.[29] While his father was dying he had the Palace surrounded by a regiment of Hussars with orders to let no one in or out without signed authority, and afterwards he had the palace ransacked for his father's papers. But his mother, suspecting something of the sort, had already had them smuggled to safety in England.

Having ascended, Wilhelm lost little time in dismissing his former idol and teacher, Bismarck; there was no room for two autocrats at the head of the Empire. 'I perfectly understood the terrible task which heaven had shaped for me; the task of rescuing the Crown from the overwhelming shadow of its Minister, to set the Monarch in the first row at 'his' place, to save the honour and future of our House from the corrupting influence of the great stealer of our People's hearts ... and I felled him, stretching him in the sand for the sake of my Crown and our House.'[30] Bismarck should not have been surprised; he had encouraged this imperious adolescent in his dreams of Imperial grandeur, in his belief in the Divine Right of the Hohenzollerns; he had recognised his wilfullness and nervous changeability, marked his capacity for self-delusion, his natural bent for intrigue, his genius for lies, his inability to grasp essentials about men or problems or to apply himself to any consistent idea for any length of time, above all his over-riding ego. He had used all these traits for his own purposes; he should not have been surprised that in his old age they should be turned against him. Although apparently he was.

Such was the man of straw at the head of the most dynamic industrial power in Europe. He took to himself the title 'All-Highest', surrounded himself with courtiers who would play up to his own images and threw himself into the role of warrior Lord, clothed in 'shining armour', raising his 'mailed fist' as a warning to his enemies that he would smite them to the ground, making up for inability to concentrate on more mundane affairs of State by compulsive travelling and rhetoric in which mediaeval allegory and nationalist sentiment were mixed with visions of overseas dominions and the 'Sea Power' necessary to realise them. He loved to dwell on the glories of the old Germanic Hansa League which had raised fleets 'such as the broad back of the sea had never borne up to that time'.[31]

Older Germans looked back nostalgically to the first Kaiser, whose lack of ostentation had reflected a simpler, truly Prussian style. But to the young he seemed the very embodiment of the new Germany. 'He is German through and through. He means to make Germany the only nation on earth.'

'Our Kaiser,' one young German told an English correspondent in 1897, 'is one of the greatest men in history. He has the clear eye and the strong will. He sees the time for a Continental policy is gone by; first of the Germans he pursues a world policy. Up to now England has pursued world policy while all other nations pursued Continental policy. England has had no rival. From now on we Germans pursue a world policy also. To do this is the greatness of our Kaiser. But, alas, nowhere is this greatness less appreciated than in Germany. The strong Navy is the essential condition of world policy, but the people as a whole are dead against spending the money. They say they spend quite enough on the Army for one nation. But I am thinking that one day we shall have the Dutch colonies also—not by force, but because we must naturally absorb

33

Holland. And then—what rich colonies! It will be well worth the fleet. And though we can never be a naval power like England, yet, together with France and Russia, and two Corps—only two Corps landed in England—we would take London, my friend!'[32]

Tirpitz

Early in June 1897, a comparatively junior Rear-Admiral named Alfred von Tirpitz arrived in Berlin from the Far East to take over as State Secretary of the Imperial Naval Office. He was charged with the task of creating the fleet without which the grand design for *Weltpolitik* would be impossible.

Tirpitz had risen rapidly in the Service. He had made his mark early in charge of the 'Whitehead' torpedo section when first formed, applying himself with devotion and personal application even to the blacksmith's tasks about the machines, and succeeding in making a high proportion run straight. Later he had been given responsibility for developing and codifying fleet tactics, and had brought Service doctrine out of a slough of out-of-date theories with precision, earning himself the nickname 'Master'. Now forty-eight years old with an unbroken record of successes behind him, he was an impressive figure. Physically he was massive. His presence could never escape notice. But while heavy, a fondness for exercise had prevented him running to fat. His head was large and wide, bald at the top, the lower features obscured by a great, tawny beard parted curiously into a fork which was a gift to later cartoonists. What could be seen of his mouth had a hard, downward tilt at the corners and his enemies spread the story that if he ever shaved his beard the ugliness of expression revealed would cause men to recoil in horror. But he never did. More immediately striking was the 'calm, steadfast look in his expressive eyes' beneath heavy, arching brows. Surprisingly for such a commanding frame, his voice was thin and low—it was said because of an asthmatic complaint— but this took little from the air of dominating calm and competence which he radiated.

In manner he had nothing of the taciturn brusqueness of so many of the 'unnatural, stiff and affected people'[1] in Imperial Germany.

He was a Prussian, but from a middle class home in the western region, and his speech and conscious charm reflected an earlier, liberal Germany which had looked towards England for many of its ideals. He dressed elegantly, affected the style and habits of a man-of-the-world, even sent his daughters to Cheltenham Ladies' College and kept an English governess as an integral part of his home circle. His style was so agreeable and determinedly genial when he wished to persuade that he impressed some as a poseur; to rigid Prussians his preference for conciliation in argument, even retreat on some points to achieve his main objectives was remarkable, not to say pusillanimous!

Such was the smooth or bluff outer shell of the man. Beneath it volatile elements demanded outlet. As a young officer he had shown obsessive concern for his health, frequently complained of sleeplessness and loss of appetite, and dosed himself with a variety of remedies for his imagined ailments. After marrying, much of this emotional charge had been transferred to his wife and family, to whom he was deeply devoted, but the positive aspects of the nervous self-consciousness remained as the driving force behind his professional successes. Personal pride demanded that everything he touch reflect his mastery; any set-back was felt as a personal failure. This tendency had been exaggerated by the mediocre intellectual level of the Service as a whole; in a nation which glorified the Army, the Navy had not attracted the best ability and Tirpitz, who had seldom been under officers of his own intellectual calibre, had acquired a supreme confidence in his own abilities—a confidence he never troubled to hide.

He had been spotted some years back by the chief of the Kaiser's Naval Cabinet, Admiral von Senden Bibran. Senden was in most outward respects the opposite of Tirpitz, a gruff-mannered Silesian aristocrat with no interests outside the Navy, 'neither wife nor child, and only a very few friends',[2] whose consuming passion for the Service found its most violent expression in hatred of everything English. His sole ambition for Germany was to build a 'monster' fleet, and when it was ready—'then we will talk seriously to England!'[3] His lack of tact was remarkable even in high Court circles where tactlessness was equated with manliness, and his wild talk about German fleet plans even in the hallowed atmosphere of London's Clubs when he did errands for his Imperial master caused numerous incidents. Not surprisingly he had no use for Tirpitz

as a man; his suavity smacked too much of a salon, a London salon
at that. But he recognised Tirpitz, the administrator, as the one
ranking officer with the intellect, energy and force of character to
give reality to his dreams of naval power, and burying his dislike he
had kept Tirpitz's name constantly before Wilhelm, and schemed
to have him replace the State Secretary of the Naval Office, Admiral
Hollmann.

Hollmann was a failure. Throughout his tenure of office the
Reichstag and the German people had preserved their land-locked
view. He had given them no vision of the power that could flow
from a great fleet and consequently no reason to revise their
objections to paying more taxes to finance one. His construction
policy appeared to be dictated more by the amount of money
hopefully available than by defined purpose; his Estimates modest
in themselves for a nation with such expanding industry and overseas trade, had been trimmed downwards continually by the Budget
Committee of the *Reichstag* at a time when all other Powers had
been expanding their navies.

Hollmann was too reasonable a person. Looking at the British
Navy, substantially stronger than a combination of its two nearest
rivals and probably more than equal to any three Powers allied
against it, guided by Boards of Admiralty patently determined to
preserve this measure of strength, it had seemed ridiculous to
challenge it, particularly for a nation keeping the most powerful
army in Europe to preserve her borders against France and Russia.
The most that could be hoped for was a strong coast defence force
of torpedo boats and small-displacement battleships to keep open
the Baltic and prevent a junction of the French northern squadron
and the Russian Baltic Fleet and make it costly for any power
attempting a naval blockade, meanwhile keeping a force of ocean-
going cruisers to protect German trade and deter other Powers by
their own potential for commerce-raiding. Besides this Hollmann
was astute enough to recognise that naval technology, which
appeared to have settled down after a bewildering flux of experiment and innovation in the 1870's and '80's was still changing
rapidly, and that any cut-and-dried construction policy would
probably be overtaken by events.

Tirpitz lacked Hollmann's brand of realism. His compulsion was
to make reality conform to his own images; as revealed to Senden
and Wilhelm in the years leading to his high appointment, these

were conceived on a grand scale; his goal was the same as Senden's, his analysis, made with painstaking attention to the smallest details, was rigorously logical; his ability to see beyond the details, and thus construct an integrated system upon them had been marked in his many independent posts of responsibility; so had his ability and energy in realising his schemes.

What had also been clear—although not to Tirpitz—was a certain narrowness of vision. His great force and intellectual clarity was achieved—like Treitschke's—by assuming mental blinkers to cut out all distractions, particularly those concerned with the feelings or reactions of those outside his system. One contemporary report on his career noted:

> His otherwise successful performance in responsible posts has shown a tendency to look at matters one-sidedly, and devote his whole energies to the achievement of some particular end without paying enough attention to the general requirements of the Service, with the result that his success has been achieved at the expense of other objectives.[4]

The upper levels of the Imperial government and the Navy itself might have been designed to allow such single-minded zeal the utmost scope. For the great departments of State and the Army and Navy all worked in separate, closed compartments pursuing their own ends. In theory the Chancellor co-ordinated policy and gave direction under Wilhelm's guidance; in practice, because Wilhelm was temperamentally incapable of rational leadership and because the chiefs of his personal Cabinets had closer contact and greater influence than his Chancellor, he ruled by whim and interference and momentary enthusiasms caught from the latest audience granted or the most extravagant flattery from one of his unblushing advisers. The administration of the Navy was conducted in the same Byzantine fashion. Instead of one professional chief, as in London, presiding over one Board of Admiralty responsible to one Civil member of the government, there were three separate departments, each responsible for their own aspects of the Service, each with chiefs of equal status. These were the *Oberkommando* (High Command), responsible for strategic and tactical planning, the *Reichsmarineamt* (Imperial Naval Office) responsible for construction policy and the Estimates which had to pass the *Reichstag*, and the *Marine Kabinett*, responsible for officer appointments. In addition to this triumvirate, assumed to be co-ordinated by the Commander-in-Chief, the Kaiser, but in practice bickering with extraordinary bitterness as they attempted to enlarge their own responsibilities at the expense of their rivals, all the important fleet and area commanders had equal rights of audience with the Kaiser to put forward their own ideas or dissatisfactions, as had all naval attachés from abroad. Under a strong man devoting his whole attention to the Service and guiding the departments along a common policy, the system might have worked more efficiently than the British counterpart. Under Wilhelm II, with all his other responsibilities and capacity for infinite distraction, it was a formula for intrigue and muddle.

Tirpitz already had a considerable reputation for intrigue. He had contributed enthusiastically to Senden's campaign against Hollmann. As Chief of Staff to the chief of the *Oberkommando*—now his rival department—he had conducted a sustained attack on the *Reichsmarineamt*—now his own responsibility. He had first disputed their right to interfere in fleet tactics, or with military matters which were the 'direct expression of the supreme authority of the Kaiser'[5]—and here was a key theme of flattery—later lifting the argument into personal abuse of Hollmann's competence. Meanwhile he had been pressing his own policy on Wilhelm personally or through Senden. Senden had noted, 'Tirpitz is a very energetic character. He has too big a head of steam not to be a leader. He is ambitious, not choosy about his means ...'[6]

The views on policy which Tirpitz pressed during these years of intrigue were developed from the three main sources of intellectual stimulus which he had received during his career. First had been von Stosch, who as chief of the Admiralty, had given him his head with the torpedo section in the early days. Stosch had been the one superior who ever matched his own ability; Tirpitz always revered him, and three of Stosch's premises for the German Navy of the early '80's formed the core of his plans. First was the necessity of removing the financial Estimates from the control of the *Reichstag* and placing them on a permanent basis so that a construction policy, once decided, could be followed through without being subject to cuts at the whim of the people's representatives—as Stosch put it, 'a creation such as the German Navy cannot live from hand to mouth.'[7] Second had been Stosch's conviction that a Navy could exert real influence only by seeking decisive battle; consequently his aim had been to build a fleet of powerful battleships rather than rely on cruisers or torpedo boats. And from this conviction Stosch had drawn the conclusion : 'If in a major war against a power with superior naval strength the German flag cannot maintain itself on its own, Germany can have no value for maritime allies.'[8]

The second influence on Tirpitz, as on naval men throughout the world, was the American naval historian, Alfred Thayer Mahan. When his works on 'Sea Power' appeared in the 1890's they provided what had been most lacking during the frenetic decades of experiment and change ushered in by the industrial revolution; that was a theory of naval strategy and tactic based on universal 'laws' largely independent of technological change. They returned thought to the old certainties. To Mahan, a battleship, whether she sailed under canvas and pointed 32-pounder cannon from hull gun-ports, or steamed 100-ton turret-mounted breechloaders into action, was the 'capital' unit, the unit on which command rested, and around which the rest of the fleet had to be planned. Cruiser warfare against trade, which enjoyed great theoretical popularity, he rejected as annoying but always indecisive on its own, never 'commanding', and similarly torpedo boat warfare. The prime units of command on which all ultimately depended were the great gunned ships strong enough to lie in the line of battle, massed in battle fleets whose aim was to destroy enemy battle fleets or blockade them in their own harbours and so retain command of the oceans outside.

Mahan had a great deal to say on wider aspects of naval strategy and economic and political power, enthusing particularly about the undeviating building policy of Colbert which had given France a great fleet of ships-of-the-line and could have given her a commanding position in the world had Louis XIV not changed direction and dissipated the effort in land campaigns. To Tirpitz, with his intensely systematic approach to any problem, Mahan's principles came as a revelation. They said little that had not been implied in Stosch's programme, but they gave the ideas solid intellectual backing; they seemed to have the authority of scientific 'laws'. More, they offered a unified vision of the indissoluble links between naval and world power.

For the other great influence on Tirpitz was von Treitschke—'that splendid man whose lectures I had attended at the University after 1876, and who had given me advice as I sat at his side at Josty's scribbling my questions on a slip of paper.'[9] Treitschke's view of the world which had been pointed up for Tirpitz during his foreign service by the chain of British naval fortresses and squadrons encircling the globe as the very visible manifestations of her world power, informed his whole approach to the German fleet question.

All these elements can be seen in his correspondence during 1895-6 with his one-time chief and mentor, von Stosch. Referring to the need to concentrate all the naval and maritime interests of the nation in one department, the *Reichsmarineamt*, he went on:

> Regarded from the historical view it is the standpoint adopted by Colbert and Richelieu in their day, when they engaged in extending the power and economic sphere of France in this direction ... In my view Germany will swiftly sink from her position as a great power in the coming century if these maritime interests are not brought to the forefront energetically, systematically, and without loss of time; in no small degree also because there lies in this new great national task, and the economic gain bound up with it, a strong palliative against educated and uneducated Social Democrats. We cannot allow these interests to develop with a free hand ('Manchester' fashion) because there is no time left for such methods.[10]

Von Stosch replied that German maritime expansion had to reckon with the opposition of England whose policy was dictated solely by commercial considerations, and he asked Tirpitz to answer the question, 'how could we conduct a naval war with England with any success?'[11] A naval war with the greatest sea power was not Tirpitz's aim—not in the short term. His immediate goal was to build up a battle fleet so that, in the spirit of von Stosch's own policy of giving 'value for maritime allies', it would represent a *political* power factor which England could not ignore.

> England puts up with a slight from America because the latter is a source of some anxiety to her, and more than anything else because she is an unpleasant opponent, and Germany pays the bill because at the moment she has no sea power of any weight. At the present our policy is building on the army alone as a material basis; but the army is only effective on our land frontiers ... Our policy does not understand that Germany's alliance value, even from the point of view of European States, does not lie altogether in our Army, but to a great extent in our fleet ...
>
> If we intend to go out into the world and strengthen ourselves commercially by means of the sea, then if we do not provide our-

41

selves simultaneously with a certain measure of sea power, we shall be erecting a perfectly hollow structure. When we go out into the world we shall run against interests everywhere that are either already established or to be developed in the future. How then does the most skilful policy think to attain anything without a real world power which corresponds to the many-sidedness of world policy ...[12]

Tirpitz never revealed his hand fully. While his immediate aim was for 'a certain measure of sea power', obviously heavy enough to weigh in the European balance to exploit the enmity between Britain and her historic enemies, France and Russia, this was only the first step in a larger design. Senden boasted publicly of that design; so did Wilhelm who was incapable of restraining his tongue; his one aim, according to his mother was to have a fleet as large as England's.[13] Tirpitz was a subtler character. His methods were described by one subordinate as the deliberate creation of an atmosphere of fog out of which he could operate in any direction. 'People can never tell what his next move will be.'[14] For his fleet plans the fog had to extend to England. It would be fatal to alert the British to the full extent of German naval ambitions lest he provoke them into an arms race which would both strain his limited financial resources and endanger the internal *rationale* of his scheme which aimed at wresting financial control of the Navy from the *Reichstag*. Alternatively the British, once alerted under a latter-day Pitt, might create a pretext for striking and destroying the infant rival before it could grow strong enough to defend itself. This was the 'Danger Zone'; references to crossing the 'Danger Zone' in safety recurred again and again in Tirpitz's memoranda and in discussions with Wilhelm and his Ministers;[15] it is this constant preoccupation with the English threat and his constant, usually ineffectual attempts to restrain Wilhelm and Senden from publicly revealing the total design in all its daring colours which provide the clue to Tirpitz's goal from the very beginning.

On the face of it the fear was irrational. All Powers were increasing their battle fleets, Japan, America, France, Russia, Italy; why should Britain single out the young German fleet for destruction? It was not worth destroying; in any case Germany's natural enemies, France and Russia, were also England's, so the wisest course would have been to foster a certain amount of German sea power. Then why look back as far as Pitt when all recent experience in the long duel between British and French naval policy since 1815 showed that Britain now preferred to *outbuild* her rivals; many opportunities for a reckoning by arms had been let slip and she had contented herself with ensuring a crushing *numerical* superiority based largely on greater industrial strength and a single-minded devotion to the sea affair while France oscillated between a naval and a Continental policy.

Fear of Britain and consequent absorption with the 'Danger Zone' were only explicable in terms of 'guilt' about future intentions. Tirpitz was a disciple of Treitschke; it would be intolerable for the German Navy to remain simply an 'alliance value' fleet, forever having to rely on the squadrons of her decadent Continental rivals whenever it came to a clash of interests with England. In the new division of the globe which he and Senden and Wilhelm, Treitschke and the new Pan-German and Colonial Leagues all confidently anticipated,[16] Germany would need a force at sea at least equal to that of the greatest sea power to ensure a fairer distribution of the good places. They did not regard this as impossible; the dramatic rise in German industry and trade and the flattening of Britain's graph suggested that England had passed her peak, and in the coming century Germany must overtake her. As the fleet was essentially an industrial creation a Navy as strong as England's, given good management of resources, was only a matter of time. Then—why be content with parity?

All this was clearly perceived inside Germany. The Press and the *Reichstag* were alive with rumours of 'limitless' fleet plans—not surprisingly as Senden, wherever he went, continued to bluster about a great naval expansion and the three hundred million marks which would be necessary to finance it. And if the *Reichstag* would not grant the money they would be dissolved—again and again until it was passed. It was intolerable that the Kaiser's wishes should be flouted; 'There must be an absolute Monarchy—His Majesty to command how large the Navy is to be.'[17] Baron von Holstein, a Prussian of the old school who had received his political grounding among the web of Bismarck's continental alliances, wrote to the German Ambassador in London, 'With the Kaiser the Navy question now takes precedence over everything. Senden is said to dominate him completely ... The Kaiser wants a fleet like that of England—with twenty-eight first class battleships—and wants to direct his entire policy to that end, i.e. to a fight.'[18] In

43

the alarms caused by the wild talk and rumours, Tirpitz's name was cited, even before Hollmann was retired, as the captain for the new course. In April 1897 Holstein noted, 'Our doom embodied in Admiral Tirpitz is closing in upon us.'[19]

In these circumstances Tirpitz's first task as he strode into the Naval Office at 13 Leipzigerstrasse with the balancing gait of a seaman bred in sail was to dispense oil on the seething waters, in particular to convince moderate opinion in the *Reichstag* that he was not the 'Militarist' he was being painted in the Socialist Press, and that his fleet plans were not 'boundless'. It was not too difficult. In the first place his immediate plans *were* limited, both by fear of England's reaction, and by Germany's relatively small ship-building and naval armament capacity. As for 'militarism' it was easy to produce figures showing Germany's expanding sea trade and her consequent need for a Navy to *protect* that trade—not to take the offensive on others' trade or colonies.

At the same time he had to start on the construction of a battle fleet and persuade the *Reichstag* that it was both the essence of his *defensive* policy, and would cost no more than Hollmann's ever-changing schemes, and—this was the bed-rock of his plan—could only be completed economically and systematically by adopting a fixed programme over a specified number of years in place of the present system of annual appropriations.

The scheme had been maturing in his mind for some time; within a very few days of reaching Berlin he had the outline drafted in a memorandum which he showed Wilhelm in audience on June 15. It was a momentous paper with implications reaching far beyond Tirpitz's new office, for it portended both the assault on the *Reichstag's* control over the Navy's budget, and a complete reorientation of German foreign policy; in place of the 'two-front' Continental enemies, France and Russia, against whom all former fleet plans had been directed, Tirpitz put England.[20]

Very Secret   June 1897
General considerations on the construction of our fleet according to ship classes and designs:
1. In the distinction between one class and another, and in the choice among ship designs within the various classes, the most difficult situation in war into which our fleet can come must be used as a basis ...
2. For Germany the most dangerous enemy at the present time is

England. She is also the enemy against whom we must have a certain measure of Fleet Power as a political power factor.

3. Commerce raiding and transatlantic war against England is so hopeless because of the shortage of fleet bases on our side and the excess on England's that we must ignore this type of warfare against England ...

4. Our fleet is to be so constructed that it can unfold its highest battle function between Heligoland and the Thames ...

5. The military situation against England demands battleships in as great a number as possible ...

The memorandum went on to establish the basic principles that even vessels for overseas service should be designed according to the specification for the home fleet. For:

16. Only the main theatre of war will be decisive. In this sense the selection of a ship design in peacetime is applied naval strategy.

The total force Tirpitz envisaged for his first programme was one fleet flagship, two squadrons of eight battleships and one material reserve each—making nineteen battleships in all—eight coast defence ships—already built—six large and eighteen small cruisers, and twelve divisions of torpedo boats for the home fleet; for overseas service and as material reserve for the home fleet, six large and twelve small cruisers. These ships were to be completed by 1905 at a cost of approximately 408 million marks or some 58 millions per year—no more than Hollmann had asked for.

It was a brilliant document. It knitted grand strategy, construction policy and tactics as never before in one supremely economical design. Typical of its creator it achieved maximum force by complete disregard for all the distractions which had plagued his predecessor; gone were all ideas of trade warfare, protection of Germany's overseas trade and colonies, or even coastal defence in its passive form; gone too any doubts about the ability of the battleship itself to maintain supremacy in the face of changing technology, instead one concentrated power force operating at the decisive point of the world balance—as Tirpitz expressed it, *'Der Hebel unserer Weltpolitik war die Nordsee.'*[21] For here was England's weak point. With her main battle strength in the Mediter-

---

* 'The lever of our world policy was the North Sea.'

ranean against the Dual Alliance of France and Russia, and her other squadrons scattered around the globe to protect her vast trade and possessions she would not be able to meet the new threat pointed at her heart without leaving other parts open to others. The plan revealed all Tirpitz's great power in intellectual synthesis —and his inability to see things from any angle but his own.

In the years to come the glaring faults in each apparently logical proposition were revealed one by one, but at the time the ideas scintillated in their new boldness and simplicity. To Wilhelm, who had been preaching, demanding, working himself into paroxysms of nervous frustration for a fleet worthy of his own status in the world, it was almost too much to bear with composure—especially when Tirpitz revealed that it was only the first step in a larger design. Truly Tirpitz was the 'Master'!

Returning to the Leipzigerstrasse after attempting to calm his Imperial Commander-in-Chief and prevent him transmitting the substance of the very secret memorandum to the four corners of the world, Tirpitz set about knocking the details into shape with an energy and flair for management that transformed the bureaucratic style of the Naval Office into the image of an aggressive American business Corporation. His method was to set up study groups and permanent committees for each area of the total design, meanwhile keeping an open mind himself and chairing their final discussions, not as the 'Master' but as *primus inter pares*.

> There is nothing I consider more irrational than for the superior officer to emphasise his position in discussion. There always comes a point when one person must decide; but I may say that it rarely came to a command at the *Reichsmarineamt*; we almost always came to a mutual decision, in the course of which I ... spared my colleagues the feeling of being overruled, and left them with the pleasure of achievement, while I, myself, did better and more than if I had wanted to see myself in everything ...[22]

There is no doubt that he did inspire his teams with the 'Band of Brothers' feeling he wished to create, and at his own desk by 7 o'clock each morning, set an example of energy and dedication which resulted in a phenomenal and enthusiastic output. Within ten days of his audience all the figures for the Naval Estimates 1898-9 had been revised for his new plan, and the vital committees for drafting the text of the proposals to go before the *Reichstag*, and for News and Publicity to enlighten the general public to the need for a fleet, had begun their work under gifted subordinates.

In London, tennis was played on the Admiralty lawn. Inside the building with its eighteenth-century rooms scarcely changed from the heady days when Nelson and St Vincent, Howe, Collingwood, Lord Barham had breathed their spirited defiance of a continental tyrant, the reigns of a great naval empire were held with leisured assurance.

> If one had not chosen to work there was little incentive to do so. This was largely due to so many of the higher posts being filled by men who had entered by patronage and the vicious system of promotion by seniority without regard to merit. The Second in my branch was quite incompetent, in fact even seniority could not get him promoted.[23]

The routine business began at some time between eleven and half past in the morning and ended without urgency at about half past five in a style hallowed by tradition. Typewriters were few and telephones non-existent save for members of the Board; shorthand writers were unknown. Letters were written out in draft in cursive longhand and despatched by messengers in frock coats to the copying branch where clerks made fair copies in a special ink which allowed duplicates to be taken by pressing damped paper on the original. Files of memoranda gathered dust as they waited weeks, even months before being read, initialled and passed on to the next desk in their slow round. Only the occasional arrival of a coded telegram could jolt one or other of the Secretariats into a show of unseemly haste.

On the first floor the Lords of the Admiralty met in the Board Room between dark oak-panelled walls and fluted corinthian pilasters as historic as any in England. Above the fireplace with its exquisite festoons of nautical motifs carved in pearwood was the wind dial whose face had been the subject of so much anxious study in former years; filling one end of the room was the long table with its unique recessed end containing nests of drawers for the Naval Secretary, around which so many Boards had debated portentous decisions for the island Empire and the world.

The present First Sea Lord, Admiral Sir Frederick Richards, matched the setting. A taciturn man with 'an astounding disregard

for all arguments',[24] his single-minded determination was to preserve for the British Navy a crushing superiority over any probable
combination of enemies. The most probable combination was still
France and Russia; 'there can be little doubt that the navies of
these two countries whose interests clash with ours *must* be
regarded as one in the determination of the naval policy of England ...'[25] His memoranda abounded with battle fleet comparisons,
interrogatives—'Have they gained on us?'—and blunt assertions
—'What this country wants is clear and undoubted superiority.'[26]
To ensure this the Estimates had been swelling each year; for the
current year they were up again to nearly £22 millions. Their size
was defended in parliament by Richards' civil chief, the First Lord
of the Admiralty, as 'not the Estimates of provocation', but 'Estimates of self-defence. If foreign countries look at these Estimates
they must not compare them with what they spend on their navies.
They must consider comparatively what they spend on their
armies, because the squadrons which we send to sea are the *corps
d'armée* that we place on our frontiers as they place *corps d'armée*
upon theirs. And an increase of these, even a large increase in our
Estimates, ought not to any degree to excite the jealousy or emula-
tion of any foreign nation. We are doing no more than we consider
absolutely necessary for our self-defence.' He ended, 'The British
people are unanimous that our fleets should represent the self-
reliance of a great nation.'[27]

That June—in the same week as Tirpitz's office completed their
new Naval Estimates—the British people were treated to a sight of
their unparalleled fleet in a display which seemed to *The Times*
correspondent 'memorable beyond all others in the spectacular
annals of the British Navy'.[28] The occasion was the Spithead
Review, the culmination of a week of Imperial pageant to celebrate
Queen Victoria's Diamond Jubilee. In the wide sleeve of water
between Portsmouth Harbour and the Isle of Wight 21 battleships,
53 cruisers, 30 destroyers, 24 torpedo boats and other small craft
had been assembled in five parallel lines each some five miles long
and so straight they might have been ruled. All the ships had been
drawn from home commands; neither the Mediterranean nor more
distant squadrons had been weakened. Outside the British vessels
was another line composed of foreign men-of-war, and close in to
Ryde pier a line of passenger ships serving as floating hotels for
the privileged.

The morning of the Review broke dull and misty, enhancing the impression of a vast concourse of vessels for the spectators aboard the yachts and launches that were plying from first light, for the ends of the lines could not be seen; the dark hulls, white upperworks, glistening yellow funnels and masts dressed overall with flags appeared to melt away into the distant haze. In Portsmouth shorebound sightseers, denied any view of the ships, gathered around the station to watch the de-training of troops who had come from every part of the Empire for the celebrations, then lined the route as detachments of every race and colour and magnificent variety of uniform marched to the Town Hall behind the band of the Shropshire Light Infantry playing 'The Soldiers of the Queen'. From thence they marched through more cheering crowds to Clarence Pier to board the steamer *Koh-i-noor* for the Review. Later two special trains carrying the Princes, Chiefs and representatives of the Dominions and Colonies, and the Royal guests arrived at the Dockyard station where six Admirals of the Fleet, glittering gold against dark blue waited to receive the Prince of Wales, representing the Queen. With the Prince, also in the uniform of an Admiral of the Fleet, was his sister, the Empress Friedrich of Prussia, mother of Wilhelm II. As they boarded the Royal yacht, *Victoria and Albert*, both British and German Royal standards were hoisted at the main where they fluttered side by side in the light breeze.

Precisely at two, guns on shore fired the Royal salute, and the paddles of the yacht started to turn. By this time the sun had dispersed the mist and the whole of Spithead lay revealed. Warships stretched in every direction, their white and yellow paintwork, brightwork and brasswork throwing off darts of light, their black hulls above red waterlines rippled with reflections from the waves, their sides, barbettes, turrets, bridges lined with men; above, coloured bunting between the masts, line upon line, blew out in the breeze. Set against an ever-changing pattern of white-flecked blue and sea-green shades pointed up with the white and coloured wings of countless sailing craft, it was a sight to catch the breath and make every British heart beat faster.

'Truly a marvellous pageant and one which Britons may take pride in knowing to be such as could be exhibited by no other nation, nor indeed by all of them put together.'[29]

The *Victoria and Albert* steamed out to become a part of it, past Haslar Creek where the masts and yards of Nelson's flagship,

Victory, stood up above the land, past enthusiastic crowds massed deep along the Southsea shore, to the head of the centre lines. Here she received a Royal salute from the guns of the 1st division ships. She turned and steamed down the lines and as she passed each ship the band played and the men roared 'Hurrahs' and swung their caps high in unison; following her came the P & O liner, *Carthage*, carrying the Indian Princes and other Royal guests, then the smaller Royal Yacht, *Alberta*, the Admiralty yacht, *Enchantress* with the Lords of Admiralty and their guests, the liner *Danube* carrying the members of the House of Lords, the *Wildfire* with colonial premiers, the Cunarder, *Carpathia*, whose great bulk dwarfed all the war-ships there, carrying the members of the House of Commons, and last the liner *Eldorado* carrying foreign Ambassadors. When the procession reached the end of the lines it turned and steamed back between the outer lines composed of the most modern battleships on the one hand and foreign warships on the other. The difference was striking. Whereas the British 'Majestics' and 'Royal Sovereigns' presented a handsome, uniform and assured appearance, the foreign ships were generally smaller 'polyglot and uncouth'; few had emerged from the hideous era of transition to the new style of steam-powered armourclad. The Royal yacht dropped anchor abreast the British flagship *Renown* for the Prince of Wales to receive all Flag Officers present; when the ceremony was concluded she weighed and steamed back for Portsmouth to the accompaniment of three simultaneous cheers from every ship in the fleet.

> As the echo of these hearty cheers rolled along the lines in a tumult of acclaim, every one who heard it must have felt that no Throne was ever more securely guarded by the loyalty and might of a world-wide Empire, and no Sovereign ever more sincerely loved and revered by subjects of every class and clime.[30]

As if to mark the solemnity of the occasion, the heavens opened while she was steaming back, and a tropical downpour blotted out sight of any ships save the nearest and thunder and lightning provided a Royal salute dwarfing all the guns that had sounded that day.

The storm was short-lived; when the final act was staged, the evening was clear. At 9.15 precisely every ship in the fleet switched on strings of fairy lights which traced the outlines of their hulls, bridges, funnels and masts, and even the colours and shapes of the Admirals' flags. The effect was startling in its suddenness and beauty; continuous aisles of scintillating light filled the length and breadth of the anchorage. Rockets and other firework displays and individual ships' displays of alternating coloured lights tracing loyal motifs continued to delight the spectators until midnight, when the Royal salute was fired from all ships for the last time and, as suddenly as it had been lit, the anchorage went dark.

Weary but glad at heart at the brilliant success which from first to last had crowned the proceedings, the few spectators who remained to witness their solemn and impressive closing retired at last to rest, full of inspiring thoughts about the Empire and the bond of sea power, and of loyal respect and sympathy for the beloved Sovereign in whose person, even more than in her office, its unity is so nobly embodied.[31]

3

The Fleet Bill

While the Royal Navy staged its triumph in Spithead, Wilhelm was attending Kiel Week. Here, amidst the sailing Regattas and Yacht Club functions with which he had tried, over the years, to evoke the excitement and internationalism of Cowes Week in the beautiful Baltic harbour, Wilhelm liked to reach large decisions on policies and persons; here, on the very day of the Spithead Review, he received the second key figure in the design for *Weltpolitik*, Bernhard von Bülow, to become his new Foreign Minister.

Bülow was an elegant and accomplished figure. He came from Frankfurt, a meeting place of the north with the south German States, and had mixed in the highest political circles from his earliest days and travelled and read widely. Fortunate both in an astonishing memory for facts and apposite quotations in several tongues, and a sharp wit for repartee or anecdote to turn away wrath, he was a glittering example of the European diplomat at his most cultivated and cynical. He also admired Treitschke; underlying the urbanity and international sophistication, he carried an essentially Treitschkian view of Germany and Germany's place in the world.

Wilhelm was alone, pacing the upper deck of the Imperial Yacht, *Hohenzollern*, when Bülow was summoned to him. 'My dear Bernhard,' he started as Bülow clicked heels and kissed his outstretched hand, 'I'm sorry for you, but you must go to the front', and he launched into a breathless diatribe against the man Bülow was to replace, accusing him of intrigues behind his back, and betrayal by attempting to diminish the prerogatives of the Crown and establish a parliamentary system!

Bülow was hardly surprised by the greeting. On the way to Kiel he had been warned of the difficulties of the task that lay ahead. Count Philip Eulenburg, most intimate of Wilhelm's advisers, had come to meet him to impress on him the dangers of Wilhelm's impetuous attempts at directing policy and inflammatory public outbursts. He had begged Bülow to accept the post if offered; he was the last hope for Wilhelm and the Empire. As the two parted he had handed Bülow a note to guide him in his dealings with his master.

> Wilhelm II takes everything personally. Only personal arguments make an impression on him. He wills to teach others, but he is unwilling to be taught himself. He endures nothing that is boring. Slow, stiff or too serious people get on his nerves and have no success with him. Wilhelm II wants to shine and to do and decide everything for himself. But what he wants to do often goes wrong. He loves glory; he is ambitious and jealous. In order to get him to accept an idea you must act as though the idea were his. You must make everything easy for him.[1]

The note went on to stress Wilhelm's need for praise; he was 'as grateful for praise as a good and clever child', and ended, 'We two will always keep to the border line between praise and flattery; we will keep exactly on the line.' Bülow had thought the note revealed almost as much of Eulenburg as of Wilhelm.

When at length Wilhelm had exhausted his diabolical tale of intrigue against the Crown, he told Bülow that he must accompany him to St Petersburg in August. 'The English are behaving so disgracefully towards me that we must cultivate relations with Russia still more assiduously.' The talk moved in logical progression to the fleet question, never far from Wilhelm's mind. Here Bülow had no need to disguise his opinions with flattery; he was quite as convinced as Tirpitz that a powerful fleet was essential for Germany's world destiny, essential also to promote the patriotic feelings and growth in prosperity with which he hoped the 'workers' could be enticed from the 'ensnarements' of Social Democracy and, with the middle classes, united enthusiastically under the Hohenzollern. He told Wilhelm that the basic problem in foreign affairs would arise from Germany's need to build a fleet, yet not become involved in a war with England in the process.

The talk was resumed in greater detail in August when Bülow joined the *Hohenzollern* for the Russian trip. 'Now,' Wilhelm said, 'what about my ships?' Bülow replied that it would take an hour or two to deal with that matter and Wilhelm, who had not lost the habits of exercise instilled in boyhood, decided to take the discussion on a country walk. They went ashore and cut across the Holstein sandhills at a brisk pace, Wilhelm at thirty-eight the picture of vigour and restless curiosity with all about him.

'What about my ships?' he asked again.

Bülow replied that German industrialisation was proceeding at a pace which had no parallels outside America and was entrusting an ever-increasing share of its products to the high seas; this wealth on which the welfare of so many Germans depended, must be better protected than hitherto, and Germany must have a power factor in overseas affairs commensurate with her growing strength. Then again he posed the question uppermost in the minds of all privy to the fleet plans: could a sufficiently powerful Navy be created without coming to blows with England?

'Now that's *your* job,' Wilhelm cut in.

Bülow begged him not to doubt his good intentions, but they would not be sufficient; he must have His Majesty's support. Wilhelm clapped him on the shoulder with a typically hearty gesture and assured him of his absolute confidence. Bülow stressed that he also needed 'negative support'; he explained this as never doing or saying anything which might endanger peace, and he touched on the delicate issue of Wilhelm's recent public utterances. There had been, for instance, that most unfortunate phrase—so far as England was concerned—in the speech at Hamburg two days after Tirpitz had presented his revolutionary memorandum, 'The trident belongs in our fist!' Wilhelm looked put out. Bülow hastened to pour oil: as things were in Germany at present it would not be possible to build the fleet without arousing national feeling first; the parties in the *Reichstag* would only consent if a strong wave of sentiment for the fleet could be aroused throughout the country. It would be necessary to beat the national drum.

'Agreed! Agreed!' Wilhelm exclaimed, delighted once more with his new Minister.

'We two will always keep to the borderline between praise and flattery; we will keep exactly on the line.'

After discussing the practicalities of manoeuvring Tirpitz's proposals for the fleet through the *Reichstag* and concluding that it would be possible provided sufficient interest in the Navy could be worked up in the country as a whole, Bülow eased the talk into more entrancing regions—the Pacific, the Far East, Asia Minor, these were ripe and fruitful areas for German enterprise, where colonies must be acquired. As they arrived back aboard the *Hohenzollern* for lunch Wilhelm was in excellent spirits. Bernhard was a splendid fellow!

'I adore him. My God, what a difference to the South German traitor! What a pleasure to have to deal with someone who is devoted to you body and soul, and can understand and wants to understand.'[2]

While Wilhelm and Bülow discussed the prospects for the fleet law in general terms, Tirpitz in retreat at his home at St Blasien in the pine-forested mountains and ravines of Baden near the Swiss border, devoted himself to the practical details. Relieved from the pressures of office, he and a few of his closest subordinates pondered tactics and went through each phrase, every sum of marks in the draft Bill and accompanying explanation, to foresee and meet all probable counter-arguments. The task was a delicate one, for the explanation which had to convince the critical Budget Committee which had savaged Hollmann's best efforts also had to conceal the true purpose of the Bill and the true meaning of the fleet programme. The purpose of the Bill was to establish a battle fleet whose size was fixed by law, therefore outside the control of the *Reichstag* deputies who were being asked to vote for it! The purpose of the fleet was to alter the power balance with England. Neither of these dangerous ideas could be allowed to surface without fateful consequences.

> Every word of the draft Bill was altered quite a dozen times in our discussions at St Blasien. I used to 'revolve' the matter, an expression about which I was often teased.[3]

The easiest aim to conceal was the positive policy against England. It was simple to argue that the German Navy had not kept pace with the great increases in German overseas trade because it was true. To support it Tirpitz had a statistical section compiling details of the expansion in industry, commerce, population, merchant shipping, fishing fleet, exports and imports since the birth of the *Reich* in 1871. It was not so easy to relate the protection of these interests to the creation of a battle fleet as trade defence was linked in most minds with cruisers and coast and harbour defence with

55

torpedo boats. However, Tirpitz was able to state quite sincerely his conviction that the rate of technical change had slowed sufficiently for various distinct and unalterable types of warship to emerge; of these battleships were the prime units, and cruisers or torpedo boats without the support of a battle fleet carried no weight. It was only in battle with an enemy's major units that a navy could exert decisive effects. The programmes of all other naval powers bore this out. The battleships once established as the decisive factor, it was easy to argue, as Tirpitz did again quite sincerely, that tactical exercises had demonstrated the need for the battle fleet to be organised in homogeneous squadrons of eight ships each. A fleet of two such squadrons with a fleet flagship would give Germany an effective force to protect her coastal waters and, under certain circumstances, 'to seize the offensive', although he hastened to add that this would simply be a tactic in the defensive strategy.

Given the numbers and types of ships necessary, it was essential to reach this goal with a systematic programme which would ensure continuity of work for the shipbuilding and armament industries; it would be uneconomic for yards to expand their plant and workforce to meet the expected orders one year only to find them idle the next because the programme had been cut or altered. Similarly with personnel intake and training for the Service itself. So, he argued, it was necessary to establish the building and replacement of ships by law—the fleet to be completed at a fixed rate over a fixed number of years, in this case seven, battleships to be replaced automatically after twenty-five years life span, cruisers after twenty years. Here was the nub of the matter. It could not be disguised that such a law must take control of the fleet out of the hands of the *Reichstag*—it could only be denied. And in the hope that the modesty of the annual financial demands and the sound arguments for system and regularity would conceal the probability of future increases in the size and armament, therefore the cost of individual ships, it was denied.

> There is no infringement of the rights of the *Reichstag* because of the establishment by law of the size of the Navy and of the annual proportion of the battle fleet on active service because the constitutional co-operation of the *Reichstag* in the legal resolution of these questions is preserved in full.[4]

Few of those whom Tirpitz consulted expected the deputies to swallow this. The head of the Reich Treasury was particularly sceptical and naturally hostile to the open-ended financial commitment implied. Tirpitz played him ruthlessly, first demonstrating sweet reasonableness in the formation of a joint Treasury/Naval Office Committee to thrash the matter out, then gaining a month's postponement of the first sitting by spinning a tale that his own representative was away—he was away from the office at St Blasien with Tirpitz—and finally using the respite to get his draft Bill agreed by Wilhelm and his Chancellor over the head of the Treasury Minister.

Meanwhile the effects of the News and Propaganda Department Tirpitz had set up earlier began to show in a flood of inspired news paragraphs and articles demonstrating the benefits of sea power. The refrain was taken up enthusiastically by the publicists of the Pan-German and Colonial Leagues, who had long supported Wilhelm's campaign for 'more ships'. 'Wide circles of our people do not yet know what the naval question means',[5] the Pan-German *Blätter* had complained the previous year. 'To enlighten them, to spread understanding for and interest in the meaning and present position of our Navy ... is during the next few years a task of the greatest importance for the League.' Tirpitz's News Bureau gave them the professional arguments and all the statistics they needed.

With such a satisfying Press response behind him the likeable young head of the *Marineamt* News Department, von Heeringen, set off on a tour of University cities to charm support from the academic world. His task was not difficult. There was a long tradition of intellectual support for a united Germany, a long absorption with power; Treitschke had been the angry crest of a great Hegelian surge. And the Navy, besides expressing German power in the wide world where the academics quite as much as commercial and industrial interests willed it, was a product, hence a symbol of unity. Unlike the land forces of the Empire which were still organised on a State basis with a Prussian, Bavarian, Saxon and lesser Armies wearing different uniforms and remembering different battle honours, the Navy was the *Reich* Navy, recruited from all States, directed by an Imperial office, solely an instrument of Imperial will. Academics needed little prompting to recognise its potential for strengthening national feeling and unifying the separatist tendencies within the Empire. Besides this, the officers of the Navy were very largely drawn from the same upper middle class as the Professors, who consequently had more sympathy for their aspirations than for the outlook of the nobility who dominated the Army and government—and vice versa. Able and personable as Heeringen was, the enormous success he soon achieved in the Universities was due to the fact that he was simply giving their *own* dogma a practical focus.

Tirpitz, meanwhile, was tackling the men of decisive political influence, the Princes of the different States, the heads of the political parties, even the redoubtable Bismarck himself, whose good opinion was still worth any number of technical arguments in some quarters.

Wilhelm exulted over the dynamism of the 'Master'.

Tirpitz has just organised a huge office which both directly and through intermediaries will look after *maritima* in some thousand to fifteen hundred newspapers and magazines. In the great University towns all over the country the Professor class has met us willingly and is going to co-operate by speaking, writing and teaching Germany's need to possess a strong fleet. Furthermore Tirpitz took advantage of his stay in St Blasien to get in touch with Uncle Fritz of Baden and tell him all about it. The result has been that the Grand Duke, who, like the majority of our Princes and people, was completely without knowledge or understanding on the matter, was quite surprised at the modesty of the demands, at the dangerous aspects of our present position, and at the revelation of the national necessity that the Bill should go through. He has thus become an enthusiastic defender of my ideas which have been carried out by Tirpitz. The Admiral brought me this message from Uncle, that he was quite convinced of the rightness of my policy and with all his energy would support and help in the 'battle for the fleet'. He would manage the Baden Press, but even more and at once would he explain to all the Princes of the Empire that it was 'their duty and obligation' to support the Kaiser in this matter ... So much for Tirpitz and the German Princes. You can understand that with such an advocate in prospect I naturally keep my mouth shut and use it only for eating, drinking and smoking. What a noble harvest is beginning to grow and what a reward God is giving me for all the care and anxiety that I have experienced over this business![6]

Despite Wilhelm's enthusiasm, despite a pounding of articles and lectures from Heeringen's sea-green *Flottenprofessoren*, arguing the need of a strong Navy for economic, world-cultural, historic viewpoints, despite envy of Britain and malice whipped up by the emotional organs of the Pan-Germans, there was still a majority in the government which doubted the wisdom of introducing the Navy Bill, and could not imagine the deputies passing a law which would reduce their own control so much.

However, Tirpitz had negotiated with the leaders of the Right wing parties whose traditional agricultural and continental outlook made them suspicious of the 'new course', and was assured of their support in return for a government commitment to higher tarifs on imported grains; the National Liberals, who represented the industrial, commercial and professional classes were behind naval expansion in any case, and it was evident that the balance of votes against the Social Democrats and other Radical opponents of unrestrained nationalism would lie with the Centre Party, the political wing of the Roman Catholic Church. Preliminary approaches to the Centre leader, Dr Ernst Lieber, had revealed that he was sceptical about the long-term planning at the core of Tirpitz's proposed Bill because of the constant changes in naval technology. However, it was as evident to him as to Tirpitz that his Party might hold the balance of power in the *Reichstag*, and that it would be in his interests to see what concessions he might wring from the government in return for his support. He agreed to a meeting, and as it had to be in secret lest his opponents within the Party accused him of collision with the Navy, Tirpitz paid his expenses for a discreet stay in the capital.

After three sessions in which the draft Bill and Explanation were discussed in detail Lieber still retained doubts about a fixed programme, but appreciated Tirpitz's strong technical arguments for imposing system and regularity, and expressed himself as 'perhaps' able to support the Bill—especially if the annual expenditure could be limited to, say, fifty millions, or if the term of the construction programme could be more flexible, or if the idea of a fixed programme could be applied to the home battle fleet only, leaving the numbers of ships for overseas to be determined annually. Evidently Tirpitz had been successful in obscuring his larger designs behind overwhelming technical arguments. But as the two last suggestions would have allowed the *Reichstag* to retain some control over naval affairs he kept only the first proposal in play.

Before he left Berlin Lieber was given four hundred marks for his expenses 'in the interests of the Navy, now and in the future.'[7]

After Tirpitz, Lieber had an interview with the Reich Chancellor, the ancient Prince Hohenlohe, to make clear his conditions for supporting the Bill. The frail old Prince, who usually preserved 'the calm and detached air of one who has seen it all before',[8] allowed his dislike of the whole policy to show clearly. If the first Kaiser were still alive no one would be thinking of the naval question. But now—the Navy found reasons to support its convictions everywhere. In the end the taxpayers would have 'to spit out hundreds of millions and have their purses permanently open.'[9] This was not Lieber's concern; he left the Chancellor with the idea that Centre Party support could be had in return for the repeal of Bismarck's anti-Jesuit laws.

To Hohenlohe the Navy programme was a personal aberration of Wilhelm's similar to so many others he had experienced, but more than usually serious for being so passionately held. He had often wondered whether Wilhelm was quite sound in mind, and twice already had asked Bülow's opinion, begging him not to dilute the wine, but tell the absolute truth. Bülow had replied that in his opinion Wilhelm was quite sane. But he was neurosthenic, always oscillating between excessive optimism and excessive pessimism. His boastful and exaggerated talk which was so politically dangerous arose simply from a desire to conceal feelings of insecurity and anxiety, for underneath it he was fundamentally timorous. 'I may hope I may be believed,' he had concluded, 'when I say on my honour that, to the best of my knowledge Wilhelm II is not insane. Wilhelm II, so far as human experience can judge, never will be insane.'[10]

Hohenlohe had replied, 'Insane or not, there's many a subtle distinction. In any case the young gentleman needs abler and cleverer advisers at his side than any other Sovereign.'

Bülow could only agree. On the Russian voyage he had experienced the whims and violent changes of mood which served Wilhelm for policy. There had been his fantastic scheme to send a warship to the Bear Islands north of Spitzbergen, seize them in the name of Germany and offer them to Russia as compensation for a Far Eastern port; Senden had been keeping a warship at short notice for the adventure. When Bülow had pointed out the international hornet's nest this would raise Wilhelm had flown into a rage. He had never expected this from Bülow—he had thought they understood one another in *everything*—now he was being as difficult and dogmatic as his predecessor, the south German traitor. It was only after Bülow had offered his resignation that Wilhelm calmed down, asked him not to take it amiss and promised to forget the Bear Islands.

Even more difficult was the attempt to prevent Wilhelm's excitement about Tirpitz's fleet plans from overflowing into his public speeches. In frequent talks with Wilhelm and Tirpitz together and separately Bülow stressed that the critical point in the whole fleet programme was not so much the *Reichstag* support—that could be managed—but 'whether England would give us the chance and the time to carry out these extensive and far-reaching plans';[11] he continually emphasised the extreme delicacy of their future relations with that country.

> If we allied ourselves to England by Treaty that would, more or less mean that we would renounce the execution of our naval plans for they would scarcely be reconcilable with a really definite Anglo-German alliance based on mutual confidence. But even if we retained complete freedom of action, we must avoid everything that might become an occasion of unnecessary mistrust between us and the greatest naval power. Our concept of the 'risk' must exclusively guide us in German naval construction and must remain well in the foreground. We must never fail to insist that our naval construction has no offensive purpose behind it but is intended only to create a steady increase in the risk which any power threatening our peace must take to attack us.[12]

This was the line Wilhelm followed with admirable restraint when he opened the critical session of the *Reichstag* on November 30 that year. Singling out the fleet Bill as the most important matter before the House, he described the German battle fleet as insufficient for the tasks before it; it could not secure home waters from blockade or other offensive operations and it had not kept up with the growth of overseas interests. To emphasize the defensive point, he denied any intention of competing with 'sea powers of the first rank'.

Hohenlohe, who was still against the programme being given the sanction of law, and had only recently been persuaded to keep the government firm behind the Bill by a threat of resignation from

Tirpitz, followed the same line at the first reading a few days later, after which Tirpitz, in his maiden speech, repeated the fictions: 'a protective fleet', 'compel even a sea power of the first rank to think twice before attacking our coasts', and the ultimate absurdity 'to give a chance against a superior naval enemy'.[13] Hastening from these sporting allusions, so alien to his real thinking, he plunged into the financial and technical arguments which had proved his strength in private talks with the Party leaders. His voice was low, his manner utterly reasonable—he was the new company chairman explaining to the shareholders why it was necessary to put their business on a more rational footing. It was surely plain to everyone that the constant changes of direction in construction policy, the annual scenes of dissension about the aims and financing of the fleet, the rumours of 'limitless' plans which did so much harm both at home and abroad were the opposite of good business sense. It must be obvious that a programme bound by law would put an end to all that. And he emphasised the modesty of the financial demands with the same mixture of sincerity and cynicism which had marked his explanation of the modest aims of the battle-fleet; the pace of technical change had slowed, leaving fixed classes of warships: no changes in type were contemplated; thus the *Reichstag* could be certain that the programme would cost no more than outlined in the Bill. It was a masterly performance. The muted and matter-of-fact delivery, the close dovetailing of constructional, financial, strategical requirements gave the impression that he considered the law itself a mere technical detail, part and parcel of the overall argument which his listeners, as rational men, could not dispute.

The Social Democrats and Radicals were not taken in. There were sarcastic references to the extraordinary wave of artificial propaganda and academic apologia for the fleet throughout the country, and Tirpitz and the government came under bitter attack; above all, the proposed law was another clear indication that the government did not *trust* the people or their representatives.[14]

This was to be expected. Tirpitz waited for Lieber to reveal the mood of the Centre. He was not disappointed. The Party had not reached a decision, Lieber implied, but how could it be expected to do so in view of its position of ultimate decision in the House, and he reminded the government that little had been done about the anti-Jesuit laws. This was clear political trading. But when he spoke of the fleet Bill itself Lieber came out in favour, remarking that he had been first to suggest a legal basis for the fleet; the only point that seemed to concern him was the cost, and he repeated the suggestion made in his private talk with Tirpitz that a maximum limit be placed on expenditure.

Tirpitz rose, expressing surprise; such an idea had never occurred to him. He had done his best with the sums but—moderate that he was—he would consider the proposal sympathetically so long as the main purpose could be achieved. His courtesy and evident willingness to meet Lieber's anxiety were disarming; each day that passed he looked less like the extreme militarist he had been painted in the Socialist Press.

Dr Lucanus, chief of the Civil Cabinet, listening to the debates from the gallery, sent a telegram to Wilhelm to say that passage of the law could be assumed certain; 'The Centre has made the difference.'[15]

Early in the New Year, 1898, the Bill went before the Budget Committee for detailed scrutiny. The Parties were represented in much the same proportion as in the full House, with the Centre holding the balance, and Tirpitz's tactics, positively aided by Dr Lieber, who was the official Reporter for the Committee, hardly varied from those he had used in the earlier debates. When explaining the strategic basis of the programme in the opening session he asked for the hearing to be off the record, no doubt to avoid creating alarm in England, yet his explanation followed the same 'defensive' pattern as before: naval experts were agreed that any attacking power would need a fleet at least twice the size of Germany's proposed fleet to invade her waters successfully—for England this would mean some twenty-eight battleships, for France her whole Mediterranean fleet, hence the size of the battle fleet the government considered necessary. Lieber found the explanation satisfactory and—over the objections of the Left—the discussion passed from strategy to the legal framework of the Bill. Again Lieber allied himself to Tirpitz, insisting that an organism such as the fleet needed the assurance of its programme beyond the span of any one *Reichstag*, only asking as before for a fixed upper limit to expenditure. Again Tirpitz had his answer ready, neither agreeing, nor dismissing the proposal, but sidestepping with the utmost geniality: 'In my opinion the Navy Law would be unacceptable to the Associated Governments if it were not to provide legal certainty that the fleet will be completed within the time specified, and within the proportions which these governments regard as necessary.'[16]

The only serious moments for the Bill came in discussion of the *Reich* tax proposed to finance it. Under the constitution the Federal States each had the right to tax income and property and the *Reich* government only levied indirect taxes—making up any deficit with 'matricular contributions' from the States. Now some members of Lieber's party argued that a *Reich* tax for the Navy would undermine the financial independence of the States, while others from the same party argued in favour of a graduated income tax to place the cost of the Navy on the shoulders of those best able to bear it. This, however, was opposed by the 'patriotic' parties who supported the Bill—for theirs were the shoulders. The deadlock was only broken when Tirpitz agreed to a clause being inserted providing that if the Navy proved more expensive than forecast, the additional costs would *not* be covered by raising the level of indirect taxation, or the number of indirect taxes. This compromise which appeared to protect both the lower paid and States' rights was to prove a serious handicap to Tirpitz in later years. But at the time it was necessary to keep the Centre Party behind the Bill, which was then passed by 19 votes to 8.

After this it was clear that Tirpitz was home. The Socialist Press continued to denounce the 'deal between the government and the Centre',[17] and at the final reading of the Bill in the *Reichstag* the Socialist and Radical speakers tried their utmost to bring home the real implications of the legislation: 'If Neptune's trident belongs in our fist, then for the great *Reich* with its great fist a little fleet is not enough ...'[18] and even more explicitly, 'There is, especially on the Right side of the House, a large group of fanatical Anglophobes made up of men who want to pick a fight with England and who would rather fight today than tomorrow. But to believe that with our fleet, yes, even if it is finished to the very last ship demanded in this law, we could take up the cudgels with England is to approach the realms of insanity.'[19]

The Centre remained deaf. These larger questions posed by the Bill, the possibility of an English response and a consequent arms race, of tension with England and a demand for more ships to be added by law, the possibility of the ships themselves becoming larger or more costly, all paled beside the immediate gains in home politics; Lieber held the balance in the *Reichstag* and the Centre was the 'government Party'; its reward would follow.

On March 26, Tirpitz was able to wire Wilhelm 'All paragraphs of the Navy Law in the version approved by the Budget Committee have been passed in full house in second reading.'[20] His triumph was complete. Against all the doubters in government and in the Navy itself his own assessment of the 'possible' had been correct. A modest proposal which came nowhere near his final goal had established the vital principle of a programme sanctified by law; the thin end of the wedge had been skilfully inserted through the cracks in the Party system of the *Reich*. Moreover the programme had been justified without any reference to the theme of competition with England which had dominated the discussions and internal memos of the Navy Office. The English were not seriously alarmed.

There were some signs of awakening though: in the autumn of the previous year the first of a genre of stories about invasion of the British Isles by German forces—in collaboration with the traditional enemies, France and Russia—was serialised in the *Naval and Military Record*. Just prior to this British military and naval Intelligence departments had been alerted to an article by Baron von Lüttwitz of the Great General Staff, which let many of Tirpitz's cats out of the bag:[21] a powerful German fleet would enable Germany to follow *Weltpolitik* and gain her a 'place in the sun'. This must lead to a collision with England or a deal. But if the German fleet were only strong enough to deal with the English Home Fleet the issue could be decided by a sudden strike before the English had time to recall their overseas squadrons. This was a crude version of Tirpitz's theory of the fleet as a political lever, but it relied on the same premise, that the hostility between England and France/Russia was fixed and unalterable. Von Lüttwitz could not be blamed for such a simple view; it was held by everyone of power in Germany, even such a sophisticated diplomat as Bülow.

But Lüttwitz's article and Tirpitz's Law were both remarkable for the assumption that Great Britain would allow Germany to mass a fleet so powerful so close to her own shores without matching it by increased construction or recalling overseas squadrons, or both. After all, what was the Mediterranean or China compared with London and the English Channel? If history, military theory or common sense were any guides England would both outbuild and concentrate her forces to meet the vital threat. Or—in Tirpitz's and Bülow's nightmares—stage a preventive war and cut out the canker before it grew too large.

The ingrained British response was to build more ships. That autumn, in discussions about the following year's programme, Sir Frederick Richards argued for more battleships than the 'Two-Power' standard of equality with France and Russia; otherwise Britain would 'have to trust to the forbearance of Germany, perhaps the greediest and most determined of our commercial rivals, not to take us at a disadvantage when so circumstanced. This is not a satisfactory position for the Power which lives by the sea, and claims to be supreme upon it. The only true policy lies in unquestioned superiority.'[22]

4

The Turn of the Screw

Wilhelm's and Tirpitz's most willing allies in 'the battle for the fleet' had been the great industrialists. They stood to gain in every way—not simply in home orders and the boost that increased capacity and experience would give for overseas orders, not simply for the national prestige and very visible proof of advanced industrial technology which battleships conferred, but for those in armaments and ship construction at least, because of the effect the German programme must have on the worldwide competition in fleet building. It would be another twist in the upward spiral which must, sooner or later, react back on the home programme. While some of the speakers in the *Reichstag* debates had pointed out the danger of 'yet another turn of the screw' for international armaments, the full implications had not been grasped. To the decisive figure, Dr Lieber, a naval programme established by law was a programme *limited* by law; the nature of the man he was dealing with and the elemental strength of the tides of navalism and nationalism were beyond his view.

The men in heavy industry were not so naïve; they may not fully have understood Tirpitz—few did—but they understood the leap-frogging nature of technological progress very well, and they were experienced in exploiting the trail of obsolescing weapons to stimulate the cycle of national suspicion and ambition, response and counter-response that fed the growth in armaments. Of all the industrialists the one with the most at stake was Krupp, inheritor of the gigantic family steel complex centred on Essen. His empire was organised vertically from the coal and ores in the ground, through furnace, forge and workshop to the finished products and horizontally through international trusts to embrace the world. Arms formed a major part of his production, especially heavy guns and mountings, shells and armour plate, the teeth and skin of battleships. The firm's latest triumph was a complicated hardening process for armour so much more effective than earlier processes that it was being used wherever battleships were built—in America, Great Britain, France—with a royalty of $45 a ton coming back to Krupp. It was not surprising that Krupp's newspaper, *Berliner Neueste Nachrichten*, had been among the loudest advocates of naval expansion in the frantic months of debate over the Bill, nor that Krupp himself should be prominent in a heavy industrial lobby which not only contributed to Tirpitz's funds 'for Press purposes' mark for mark with the government,[1] but was engaged in forming a new and independent organ of propaganda for the Navy. This was the *Deutscher Flottenverein*, or German Navy League as it came to be called in Britain. On April 30, 1898, a few weeks after Wilhelm had signed his assent to the Navy Law, the League was officially formed by Viktor Schweinburg, Krupp's business manager for the *Neueste Nachrichten*. Its avowed aims were to arouse and strengthen in the German people an understanding and interest in the meaning and purpose of the fleet, which it held essential for 'securing the coasts of Germany against the dangers of war', 'maintaining Germany's position among the world Powers', protecting her 'commercial relations' and 'the honour and security of her citizens engaged in business abroad.' The chief aim of the League which could not be published was the encouragement of 'a long period of warship building in the fastest possible tempo'[2] so that the manifold branches of industry affected would gain contracts.

The *Flottenverein* was another institution taken directly from a British model and exaggerated. Like the fleet programme itself with its emphasis on squadrons of homogeneous battleships, like the desire to play *Weltpolitik*, it was a symptom of Germany's peculiar emotional relationship with the older Empire, again revealing the two faces of envy—on the one side contempt for English institutions because Germans could do better, on the other, frank imitation.

The British Navy League had been founded three years earlier in the very different circumstances of a clearly supreme fleet on the 'Two-Power' standard. Its avowed aims had been to keep things that way by urging on the government and electorate 'the paramount importance of an adequate Navy as the best guarantee of Peace'. It had begun its campaign by preparing or reprinting and distributing a great mass of books and leaflets with titles like 'Command of the Sea', 'Brain of the Navy', 'England Expects', 'Our Next War', many of them aimed specifically at the working man, whose Clubs according to the first copy of the *Navy League Journal* 'echoed with Socialistic denunciations and detractions of an Imperial policy.'[3]

> He (the working man) is only half convinced of the value of our Empire, and but a lukewarm supporter of large Naval Budgets. We must be at him and teach him. It is the duty of the better-educated amongst us to go down into the market place and refute the sophistries of the blind leaders of the blind. The lower classes can be led, but they want leaders ... men with devotion to the great ideals at which this nation should aim. For our end is to strengthen that England which has made us what we are; to retain the inheritance of greatness which our fathers bequeathed to us; to confirm that proud national position without which many of us feel that life in this smoky island would be intolerable; and to do this by making the Navy strong. For by the Navy we stand or fall; if that is weak there is the unspeakable trial of war before us, war in which we must be worsted and trampled upon by our conquerors; if that be strong there is peace and prosperity ...

The *Flottenverein* contrived a similar argument by reversing the actual relationship between Germany and Great Britain; Germany was the honest trader, Britain the nervous rival jealous of Germany's success in winning new markets and only waiting a favourable moment to strike her down. The favourite pieces of evidence for Britain's hostile intentions were drawn from anti-German diatribes in the London *Saturday Review*, particularly the startling conclusions of articles in 1896 and 1897, '*Germania esse delandam*'. The last and most inflammatory of these declared that 'if Germany were extinguished tomorrow, the day after tomorrow there is not an Englishman who would not be the richer. Nations have fought for years over a city or a right of succession; must they not fight for 250 million pounds of yearly commerce ...'[4] These arguments gained vastly greater circulation in Germany than in England as a picture was drawn of the pure, hard-working German building up his business overseas under the ever green and greedy eyes of the English. Other nations were jealous too; the world was literally 'filled with enemies' for the poor German.[5] But the chief target of the propaganda was Great Britain; only thus could the necessity for a great fleet be argued. But it was more than that; emotion played as strong a part as reason, and emotionally the British Empire was the only target.

The other groups with similar goals, the Pan-Germans and Colonial Societies joined in blocks as corporate members, swelling the numbers rapidly, but it was to the unconverted working man and the young that the League directed its programme, organising dances, social evenings, lectures and seaport outings to introduce those middle and southern Germans who scarcely knew what a warship looked like to real ships and sailors. The money for these activities and for printing the League Journal and scores of books and pamphlets ranging from Mahan on Sea Power to the effusions of the more popular *Flottenprofessoren* on the urgent need for German sea power, came partly from membership subscription, rather more from interested industrialists.[6]

That same year, 1898, there were two practical examples of the importance of sea power which the League was able to exploit. First was the Spanish-American war fought over Spanish possessions in the Caribbean and Pacific which could only be reached by sea. Two American naval victories at Manila and Santiago which wiped out the Spanish squadrons decided the issue in short time. Later in the year there was a trial of strength between the two foremost naval and colonial Powers, when rival parties of British and French Empire builders met at Fashoda on the upper reaches of the Nile. Neither would retreat and there was a period of extreme tension, and on the French part nervousness; their fleet was in poor shape and they feared that Britain might force a war so that she could use her great naval superiority to sever France from her overseas possessions and settle the colonial disputes between them once and for all. These fears seemed to receive confirmation from outspoken sections of the British Press urging a 'preventive war', and when their ally, Russia, refused to help, they backed down leaving the British in possession of the Sudan. No one doubted that the British Navy, in particular the first class battleships of the Mediterranean and Channel Fleets had been the real instrument of the bloodless triumph in the heart of Africa.

At the British Admiralty Fashoda became the classic example of how a predominant British fleet was the best guarantee of peace! For the Germans it was a demonstration of the vulnerability of their own world position without any counter to the British Navy. The message was hammered home, not only by the *Flottenverein* and Tirpitz's publicity department at the Marine Office, but by the central 'Literary Bureau' which Bülow and the *Reich* Chancellor used to disseminate official news and views. The Bureau controlled political aspects of the editorial policy of a number of influential German papers, known as the 'informed', or by British journalists as the 'semi-official' Press, by reserving scoops and other highlights of news and interpretation for those correspondents whose papers could be trusted to follow the official line. In this case the official line was for the fleet; Bülow's directive to the Press ran:

> i) How necessary the increase of the fleet has been. No successful overseas policy without a strong fleet. The role of the fleet in the Spanish-American war and during the Fashoda quarrel. Why does Spain lie on the floor? Why does France retreat before England?
>
> ii) So long as we possess insufficient naval forces, their deficiency must be made up by unanimous consolidation of the Parties, the *Reichstag* and the nation in all great matters of foreign policy. Never would there be more cause to direct the gaze from petty Party disputes and subordinate internal affairs to the world-shaking and decisive problems of foreign policy.[7]

For Wilhelm, who had been following the foreign conflicts as avidly as a theatre-goer at a stimulating play—according to Bülow he could hardly wait for the curtain to go up when any foreign war threatened—the excitement of all the naval strategy and the frustration of his own and Germany's position induced further demands for more ships and tirades against 'that fool *Reichstag*' which had 'continually refused'[8] all his earlier explanations and requests. Tirpitz was also affected by the Press coverage and especially by the increased public understanding of the lessons to be drawn from these events by inferior naval Powers such as Germany, and he wondered whether the time might soon be ripe for an extension of the Navy Law. Some decision about the future of the Law had to be taken in any case because increases in the size and cost of ships were making it impossible to keep within the financial limits set. He discussed it with Wilhelm at the end of November. If he went to the *Reichstag* for more money it would scarcely be possible to avoid inquiries about future plans; it might be better therefore to establish a positive objective by including the increased costs in a Supplementary Law or *Novelle* to increase the size of the fleet. But the question had to be decided now because if a *Novelle* were to be presented at some time before the present term of the Law ended, it would be necessary in the meantime to hold expenditure within the set limits so as not to annoy the *Reichstag* and prejudice the *Novelle's* chances. Wilhelm wanted more ships, and as soon as possible, and a decision was taken to introduce a *Novelle* some time before 1904.[9]

Tirpitz still faced the problem of how to convince the *Reichstag* of the necessity for adding to the fleet without at the same time alerting England to its real purpose. As he had said to the Chancellor the previous month while discussing a hare-brained naval staff plan for war against England which involved a sudden descent on parts of the Belgian coast as a springboard for invasion across the Channel, 'All policy hostile to England must wait until we have a fleet as strong as the English.'[10] Adding to the German battle fleet programme was obviously a hostile policy and in his discussion with Wilhelm he suggested cloaking it behind a request for more cruisers for foreign service and a third squadron of battleships to accompany the cruisers as a 'Flying Squadron'. England had assembled a Flying Squadron during the Fashoda crisis.

Despite his caution and care in not exceeding the financial limits of the law, rumours of an impending *Novelle* were circulating before the end of the year, and in the Budget Committee debate the following January Dr Lieber asked him to deny them. 'The administration,' Tirpitz replied, 'intends to stay strictly within the given limits.'[11]

Meanwhile a colonial dispute was brewing up in the Samoan group in the Pacific, which threatened—at any rate in Tirpitz's fervid imagination—to realise his worst fears. The Powers involved in the dispute were Germany, Great Britain and America, who jointly administered the islands, and when in March some German colonists were imprisoned and British and American cruisers bombarded Apia, he thought the moment had arrived. Sitting next to Bülow in the *Reichstag* debates over the crisis, he said in a low voice, 'You can do no good by speaking. It is clear that the action of the British and Americans points to their determination to go to war with us in order to destroy us before our fleet has been hatched out of its shell. Otherwise one would have to assume that both John Bull and Jonathan had gone mad.'[12]

Bülow reflected on the extraordinary one-sidedness of the military mentality, and replied that neither the British nor the Americans meant to take the first chance of going to war with Germany, nor had they gone off their heads. All that had happened was that some consuls and naval officers had got excited and kicked over the traces

In the event Bülow negotiated with some skill and acquired the two principal islands in the group for Germany, a feat which was hailed by the delighted Wilhelm as miraculous and which was trumpeted by the German Press as though 'a Continent had been divided'.[13] Such favourable colouring of all news affecting German foreign policy was a feature of the 'Literary Bureau' system which was building up within the country quite a false sense of optimism about Germany's relationship with the outside world. In this instance self-congratulation was tempered by the knowledge that if it had come to a real showdown with Britain and America, Germany would have been impotent, and so well had the naval publicists done their work that there was an outcry, not simply from navalist and industrial organs, for a supplementary programme to increase the fleet immediately.

Meanwhile there was an *entr'acte* for idealists. Appalled at the pace at which armaments were growing and alarmed by the increasing cost and terrifying powers of modern weapons, groups in all countries sought a way of solving international disputes without the threat of force or the cruelties of war. The financial arguments of these groups were particularly appealing to Russia, economically the most backward of the great Powers, but faced with the need to spend huge sums, particularly in new ordnance, if she were to keep pace with her European rivals; the Russian Finance Minister therefore suggested to the young Tsar, Nicholas II, that they might avoid, or at least postpone this heavy investment by supporting the pacifist movement. And in August 1898 telegrams had issued from St Petersburg to the Chancelleries of the Powers, suggesting that a Conference be held:

i) to find some means at once of diverting progressive increase of military and naval armaments. ii) to prepare ground for possibility of averting armed conflicts by pacific diplomatic means ...[14]

It was a surprising proposal; coming from Russia, it simply invited cynicism and charges of impracticability and it duly received them.

Wilhelm was the first to react; horrified by the 'immature Tsar's sudden and stupid step', he had immediately and without consulting either his Chancellor or his Foreign Minister vented his annoyance in a wire to Nicholas reminding him of historic Russian feats of arms and asking whether he intended to hang up 'the glorious standards of his Regiments in a temple of Peace'.[15] It was a cry from the heart; after all his years preaching the need of a great German fleet and his countrymen only just beginning to come around to his view—now international limitation! His wife told Bülow that Wilhelm had not for a long time been so annoyed over anything. Count Eulenburg remarked, 'Our dear Kaiser simply cannot stand anyone else coming to the front of the stage.'[16]

In England Liberals were excited by the proposals, but the predominantly Conservative Press ascribed them to Russia's need for peace and economy to assimilate her recent sensational gains in Manchuria and deal with a famine which was afflicting her own peoples. At the Admiralty the Director of Naval Intelligence listed the practical difficulties of the proposal—which came down to disarmament:

> It is believed that—
> a) disarmament is impossible without the assurance of a durable peace
> b) a durable peace cannot be assured without adjustment of all differences such as Alsace, China, Egypt, etc., etc.
> c) the adjustment of differences is impossible without a force to enforce the decrees of Congress
> d) No such force exists.
> The fact is that after a long peace each Power is prepared to fight for what it considers its legitimate aspirations. It will only yield when exhausted by war ...[17]

The Admiralty submission to the Cabinet observed that any restriction in modern weapons would 'favour the interests of savage nations, and be against those of the more highly civilised. It would be a retrograde step ...'[18] and on a more immediately practical level it pointed out that 'any agreement to limit naval budgets would necessarily have to be accompanied by such safeguards as to inspection of accounts that, in the opinion of their Lordships, the scheme could not fail to break down ...' While completely sceptical of Russian motives and the workability of limitation or international arbitration, their Lordships were bound to acknowledge that a freeze on the present naval situation, in which Great Britain was so clearly predominant, would not be to their disadvantage. And when the First Lord introduced the Estimates, which allowed £15½ millions for construction and repairs against the French and Russian £6 millions each, the Germans £3 millions, he made an offer that if Powers which had adopted programmes of naval construction would abandon or reduce their schemes, 'Great Britain would be only too happy to follow suit.'[19]

It was part of the international condition that such a proposal should be greeted with as much merriment as the Tsar's—especially in the year after Fashoda. Naturally Great Britain would prefer to preserve her supremacy by agreement rather than costly construction programmes! The breath-taking cynicism was most evident to Tirpitz and Wilhelm; to them the important implication was not so much the perpetuation of Britain's long lead as of Germany's position trailing behind the field. The offer evoked no public response in any capital.

In such an atmosphere the first Peace Conference met at The Hague in May. All Powers, acting in the spirit of Bülow's mot, 'Above all undertake as seldom as possible the odious role', had sent delegations. The German delegation had instructions from Wilhelm—difficult to reconcile with Bülow's—to bring some 'healthy realism to bear on the mass of Russian hypocrisy, bunk and lies,'[20] but in the event the British naval delegate, Admiral Sir John Fisher, stole their show. Cutting through the ambiguities of diplomatic language, he startled the Conference with a mixture of forthrightness and exaggeration which naval officers were wont to get their points across to ships' companies or wardrobe guests.

> My sole object is peace. What you call my truculence is all for peace. If you rub it in, both at home and abroad that you are ready for instant war with every unit of your strength in the first line, and intend to be first in, and hit your enemy in the belly, and kick him when he is down, and boil your prisoners in oil (if you take any) and torture his women and children, then people will keep clear of you.[21]

Fisher had 'such a terrific face and jaw, rather like a tiger'.[22] With his uninhibited expression of the deterrent philosophy and its corollary that 'the supremacy of the British Navy is the best guarantee for peace in the world', with a jaunty assurance and boyish love of swagger and effect, he seemed the very embodiment of British naval power and ruthlessness.

For the moment his role was confined to demonstrating British common sense fully equal to German realism. Discussing with a friend at the Hague some of the motions for limiting belligerent rights and bringing civilisation to bear on warfare he wondered if the delegates imagined they would be recognised in war. 'Suppose war breaks out; I am appointed to command the Mediterranean fleet and expect to fight a new Trafalgar on the morrow. Some neutral colliers try to steam past us into the enemy's waters. If the enemy gets the coal in his bunkers it may make all the difference in the coming fight. You tell me I must not seize these colliers. I tell you that nothing you or any power on earth can say will stop me from seizing them or sending them to the bottom, for tomorrow I am to fight the battle which will save or wreck the Empire. If I win it I shall be far too big a man to be affected by protests about the neutral colliers; if I lose it I shall go down with my ship into the deep and then protests will affect me still less.'[23]

While the delegates argued over similar details of neutrality and 'humanity' in the conduct of war, the two big questions affecting the likelihood of war were shelved. The establishment of a permanent Court to settle disputes by arbitration instead of force offered the illusion of progress, but recourse to it was optional, and it was plain that nations would make use of its facilities only if it suited them—and otherwise employ more traditional methods. As for arms limitation, the practical problems of mutual inspection, of agreeing what were '*effectifs actuels*', and of quantifying armed strength in terms of national necessity and aspirations were baffling. As many of the delegates were opposed in principle the difficulties looked insuperable. In the naval field, Russia and France, while apparently anxious to meet British mutual limitation proposals, could not do so while Germany and Japan insisted on completing their programmes—as they did. Both these emerging naval Powers were quite explicit that they intended to catch up with the leaders before they would listen to talk of limitation. One analyst put it:

> The difficulties in the way of naval disarmament are not at the top of the graduated scale of naval powers, but at the bottom ...

and the crux of the problem is that no Power will call a halt while the one next below him on the scale continues to arm, and the latter will not cease to arm until he has reached equality with the rival above him.[24]

When the delegates dispersed from the Hague it was in the knowledge that no artificial barriers had been or were likely to be erected in the way of the natural forces and balances which had operated over many years to preserve peace between the great Powers. Of these the greatest was fear of the consequences of war.

In such a spirit, entirely in accord with his own nature, Fisher went to take command of the Mediterranean Fleet. This was the Queen on the chessboard of British Imperial strategy; it marked the main French fleet at Toulon and the Russian Black Sea Fleet to prevent them either joining forces or breaking out via Suez or the Straits of Gibraltar. With the main enemy fleets contained or smashed, lesser British squadrons stationed around the globe could deal with enemy cruiser squadrons of single commerce raiders and keep open the vital sea lines of communication. As Fisher summarised it:

> The Mediterranean is of necessity the vital point of a naval war, and you can no more change this than you can change the position of Mount Vesuvius, because geographical conditions, Sebastopol and Toulon and the Eastern question will compel the Battle of Armageddon to be fought in the Mediterranean.[25]

The point had always been quite clear to Tirpitz; it was against just this strategy that his own fleet plan was directed. How could the British bring their battleships home from the Mediterranean to mark the new German battle fleet without leaving their eastern Empire wide open to Russian and French main fleets? In the same month that Fisher hoisted his flag in the *Renown* at Malta, Tirpitz defending his strategy against internal criticism minuted that England, because of her 'overseas interest routes':

> can only employ a small portion (of her ships) in the North Sea. Thence is the weak point of England the North Sea, then here can *we* concentrate all our ships.[26]

The simplicity and the emphasis were childlike; all children are born with such an egocentric view. That his own machinations might cause some changes in the pattern did not, apparently, occur to Tirpitz. The only flaw that he could see was the possibility that England might discern his intention and force a preventive war before the German fleet was ready. *But*—if his programme, and German foreign policy and Wilhelm's tongue could be conducted with sufficient skill to lull the British and give them no opportunity for sudden attack until the 'Danger Zone' had been crossed, then they would simply have to accept the new power balance. As he told Wilhelm that September, once that position had been reached, 'General political grounds and the absolutely prudent standpoint of the businessman' would cause them to lose all inclination to attack 'and as a result concede to Your Majesty such a measure of naval prestige (*See-geltung*.) and enable Your Majesty to lead a great overseas policy.'[27] Whether this was necessary flattery to carry his point with Wilhelm, or self-delusion, it was a remarkable argument. By treating the political groupings as immutable and British mentality as either Treitschkian or business-like as it suited, he ignored the most likely responses. An open-minded examination of the question must have suggested that by pointing the heavy guns of his battleships at London Tirpitz was inviting, indeed forcing the British to come down from their splendid isolation and take sides in the European struggle. If this was too much to expect, at least they must regroup their squadrons to face the main threat to the homeland. Tirpitz couldn't quite see it, or didn't want to; in any case he was not in the habit of putting himself in anyone else's position.

Fisher, meanwhile, concentrating his thoughts on the main theatre for the Battle of Armageddon—which he expected off Port Mahon on Minorca—was already aware of the latent threat in the German programme. In the lectures with which he inspired the Mediterranean fleet with purpose and readiness for instant war, there were many echoes of the uncompromising views of Sir Frederick Richards, with whom he had sat as Third Sea Lord.

Nelson said 'Only numbers can annihilate'; Napoleon afterwards said 'God is on the side of the big battalions'. No use the British Empire having two or three more battleships than the French and Russians, etc., etc. as so stupidly argued by those who ought to know better. You want a sufficiency of battleships left over, intact, after settling with the first hostile combination, as to be ready to

deal with, say, our German cousin, who has kept neutral ready
to bag the booty.[28]

Fisher was not yet aware of the full extent of Tirpitz's ambition.

Towards the end of September each year Wilhelm retired to the
Imperial lodge at Rominten; there, dressed in green hunting uniform
with boots and feathered hat and confronted with a single, specific
and undemanding task of shooting beasts, his restless nature found
brief peace. It was there that Tirpitz liked to approach him for big
decisions.

> He was calmer and more collected there ... always ready to hear me
> and weigh reasons; there were no sudden outbreaks of nervous
> excitement such as occurred elsewhere, announcing themselves by
> a certain restlessness in his eyes. On the appearance of such symp-
> toms I used to put all important decisions silently under the table.
> This was not always practicable with questions which required
> haste. I came to the conclusion that the Emperor's constitution was
> not equal to the pressures of responsibility.[29]

It was at Rominten at the end of September 1899 that Tirpitz laid
before Wilhelm details of the *Novelle* which had been agreed in
outline earlier that year. The principal technical reasons advanced
was the desirability of giving the expanding shipyard and armament
capacity of the country a steady volume of work, or as Tirpitz
always phrased it a steady building-tempo (*Bautempo*). He thought
that three capital ships a year was the correct or 'normal' rate for
the German Service at its present level, and as the Navy Law only
provided for such a 'three-tempo' for 1899, after which it fell to
$1 : 2 : 2 : 1$ in succeeding years, he wanted the *Novelle* in 1901 or
1902 at the latest. The other technical reason was that he hoped to
minimise the effect of revealing that it would not be possible to
keep within the financial limits of the original Law by linking this
discussion with an increase in the scope of the Law itself. Underlying these reasons was a simple estimate of what the *Reichstag*
would swallow.

Like the original Law, the *Novelle* was not an end in itself, but
a 'step directed towards a distant goal', which Tirpitz defined as an
'Iron Budget' or '*Marineaeternat*'.[30] This would be reached when
the size of the battle fleet and the statutory life span of each ship

in it combined to produce a permanent building tempo of three ships a year; he had in mind a battle line of 60 ships each with a life span of 20 years. Once this was embodied in Law the *Reichstag*, which could neither propose, nor alter legislation, would be powerless to object to its financing and the fleet would be a permanent, self-perpetuating organism under the unfettered control of the Kaiser. While the pace of approach to this distant goal was not absolutely clear, the method of reaching it was. 'I had in mind the idea of proceeding in "spurts", nursing the *Reichstag* as much as possible meanwhile.'[31]

The considerable 'spurts' Tirpitz confided to Wilhelm on September 28th were, first the creation of a third battle squadron, together with five battleships and four large cruisers for service abroad, subsequently the creation of a *fourth* battle squadron by replacing the small coast-defence *Siegfried* class boats at the end of their life with modern battleships. This would give Wilhelm a total of forty-five battleships and fifteen armoured cruisers—sixty ships to lie in the line of battle; he scarcely needed to remind Wilhelm that only England would have more.

> But we have an undoubtedly good chance against England also through geographical position, weapons system, mobilisation, torpedo boats, tactical training, systematic organisation and development, and unified leadership through the Monarch.[32]

Again, it is difficult to know how much of this was necessary flattery, how much self-delusion, blind self-justification for what Tirpitz wanted to do, although, from the optimistic tone which prevailed in high government circles at this time and which Tirpitz shared fully, it is probable that he had convinced himself of most of it. Many marginal comments on internal documents suggest it: referring to the impossibility of keeping the sea lanes open in a war against England unless Germany was first victorious in *fleet* battle, he noted 'Victorious is the decisive word. Hence let us concentrate our resources on this victory.'[33]

Yet practically all the points he mentioned to Wilhelm were false.

Germany's geographical position was well nigh hopeless for a naval war with England which stood like a giant break-water off her exits to the sea; even the incorporation of Holland, desired by

Pan-Germans and others, could scarcely improve the position. As for weapons, the shallow and tortuous entrances to the German North Sea harbours either limited the size of the ships Tirpitz could build, hence the size and power of their armament, or enormously increased their cost by reason of dredging and other non-fighting works. England, on the other hand, had splendid deep water bases. Both factors had worked decisively for England in the Anglo-Dutch wars of the seventeenth century; Tirpitz, who prided himself on his study of naval history, must have known it.

Mobilisation was another point about which he was too optimistic; earlier he had told a colleague that the British dislike of conscription would prevent her maintaining her naval lead, for whereas the German Service would be able to man as many ships as the British from the Reserve created by the three-year conscript system she employed, the British with their long-service volunteer system had no Reserve worth speaking of. This was another failure to put himself into his enemy's position: would the British carry their dislike of conscription so far as to endanger not only their Empire, but their very existence, entirely dependent on sea trade?

His point about torpedo boats rested on the assumption that in the event of war the British would close in and attempt to blockade the short German coastline; then, in his view, their fleet would be reduced gradually by German flotilla action until it had been whittled away to equality, when the German fleet would sally forth and destroy it. This was egocentric to a degree, according the British such sluggish intelligence and arthritic reactions as to defy belief. Certainly British strategy rested on close blockade, but would it always do so, and would they stubbornly persist in it while their great fleet was thinned out before their eyes!

By 'tactical training' Tirpitz meant that the British Service, with a century of undisputed superiority behind it, had not adapted itself to the potential of the modern weapons and ship classes, whereas the young German Service, by concentrating on the single task before it, and bringing scientific spirit and German thoroughness to bear on tactics and training, would prove superior. Yet again he underestimated his opponent. The British Service, while carrying some deadwood at the top and devoting too much time to the outward show and obsolete evolutions which deceived Tirpitz was bursting in the middle ranks with a new breed of scientific officer as enthusiastic and able as any in the Royal Navy's long history, who only needed the right man at the top to bring them on. Besides this, the British Service had more experience than any other in fleet tactics and evolutions and was far ahead of all other navies in the study and practice of battle tactics; some of her Admirals notably Sir Arthur Wilson, could not have been matched by any in the German Service.

As for 'systematic organisation and development, and unified leadership under the Monarch', this was just what the split command structure of the German Navy denied them. It is scarcely credible that Tirpitz, whose intrigues had helped to sustain the friction between the various high departments of the Navy, and who was even then manoeuvring on behalf of his own office against the *Oberkommando*, could suggest that system or unity were on the German side.

Many of these points were apparent to the more thoughtful of Tirpitz's colleagues and subordinates, but the 'Master's' strength of personality and the prestige he had gained by his consummate skill in passing the Navy Law through the *Reichstag* ensured that his own arguments were decisive. In any event the alternatives to a battle fleet policy were not promising; they were either cruiser warfare against trade—which Mahan had characterised as indecisive without a supporting battle fleet, and which demanded more overseas bases and protected coaling stations than Germany possessed— or abandonment of the struggle for world power. This was simply out of the question in the mood of the new Germany. As Tirpitz expressed it in his notes for the audience at Rominten :

> The creation of a battle fleet is for Germany an absolute necessity without which Germany will meet her ruin. Four world powers : Russia, England, America and Germany. Because two of these world powers can only be reached over sea, so State power at sea (must be) in the foreground ... As Germany has fallen behind in payment for seapower, so making up this neglect is a life question for Germany as a world power and great *Kultur* State. The evolution of Germany through industry and commerce and the growth of industrial developments (are) the contact- and conflict-points with other nations, therefore power, sea power (is) indispensable if Germany does not wish to decline.[34]

Having inflamed Wilhelm with such arguments and the vision of a sixty-ship battle-line comparable to England's, and having received his assent to press on with the *Novelle*, Tirpitz stressed the need to keep it all secret while he negotiated with the Party leaders, and weighed the chances in the Reichstag. And after he had left Rominten he wrote to Bülow asking him to use his influence to calm the Kaiser and prevent him blurting out the great plan—all to no avail. On October 18 Wilhelm travelled to Hamburg for the launching of the battleship *Karl der Grosse,* and at the sight and smells of the great sea port and the leviathan on the ways the threads of his discretion snapped; in a widely-reported speech he proclaimed to the world, '*Bitter not ist uns eine starke deutsche Flotte !*'*[35]

At once all the rumours of an impending naval law were blown into fresh flames by the Press, and now they were given added meaning by a wave of Anglophobia which swept the country on the news of the outbreak of the second Boer War. The Boers were blood-brothers of the German *Volk,* a small community, brave and Godly, only desiring independence from the 'mammonism' of the great bully England. Bülow attempted to calm the frenzy:

> With regard to the British defeat at Ladysmith our Press should assume a calm and quiet tone. Public acclaim and too clearly manifested *Schadenfreude* would only direct English resentment against us, when we are not equal to her on the sea; and at the same time it will strengthen the hopes of the French and Russians that we were ready to allow ourselves to be pushed alone into conflict with England ...[36]

The semi-official Press followed the Bülow line; the rest, not content with slanting all news against the British, vied to outdo each other in the manufacture of atrocity stories: British soldiers were killing and robbing the wounded, violating field hospitals, shooting doctors, raping, encouraging the native Kaffirs to burn and loot the homes of their former masters.[37]

The turgid public outcry was echoed by Wilhelm in private and served to increase his nervous frustration. Here was another international situation in which he should be involved but, because of weakness at sea, could play no part; he must have the ships Tirpitz had promised him, but sooner—the *Novelle* must be brought in immediately. The Pan-German, Navalist and industrial organs were arguing the same theme, and Tirpitz found himself being pressed

---

* '*Bitter need* we have for a strong German fleet !'

to move faster than he wished by the very machine he had done so much to create. On October 23 he saw Wilhelm again and persuaded him to wait for one year for his *Novelle*, which was not yet fully prepared for the *Reichstag*. It was only a temporary respite. The Press vilification of Britain and demand for sea power, now recognised everywhere as the passport to *Weltpolitik*, which also had become recognised quite suddenly as the goal towards which Germany was steering, rose in volume—'We want to be a world power and pursue colonial policy in the grand manner. That is certain ...'[38] The strength of feeling impressed even the old Chancellor, Hohenlohe; as Bülow thought it a favourable moment to present a *Novelle* while England's attention was engaged in South Africa and the Civil Cabinet wanted some large measure to divert Social Democratic attention from a forthcoming 'Willing Workers' Bill, Wilhelm soon forgot Tirpitz's arguments; on November 2 he wrote to the German Princes to tell them he intended to bring in a *Novelle* that winter. Tirpitz led his team in a furious drive to polish the rough draft and accompanying explanation in time to do so.

The most teasing question was whether to bring England into the explanation. It seemed madness to alert her publicly:

> But such an usual demand as was presented here, namely the doubling of our small force, made it scarcely possible to avoid hinting at the real reason for it.[39]

On November 16 Tirpitz wrote to the German Naval Attaché in London:

> We must know if the English government plans to introduce to parliament any naval proposals as a result of the German *Novelle* and if the English government considers us an opponent at sea, or whether it has made reference to the German fleet.[40]

It was an interesting paradox; his naval ambitions were being floated on a wave of Anglophobia, yet this same wave might easily produce sufficient hostility in Britain to sink them.

Bülow was worried by this and by a heated personal relationship which had developed between Wilhelm and the English Royal family and Prime Minister; if allowed to harden this would restrict Germany's freedom of action in foreign policy, especially at a time 'when, in view of our naval inferiority, we must operate so carefully, like the caterpillar before it has grown into the butterfly'.[41] In the hope that relations might be 'normalised' again he advised Wilhelm to accept an invitation to visit Queen Victoria at Windsor towards the end of November, and he made arrangements to accompany him.

Before they went Wilhelm was handed an *aide memoire* prepared by the Foreign Office to guide him down the middle line between his present bitter relationship with England and too violent a swing the other way—which was always a possibility when Wilhelm visited his 'English grandmama', and particularly so now that a section of the British people led by their Colonial Secretary, Chamberlain, was seeking to ease the dangers of 'isolation' by an understanding with 'our natural ally, the great German Empire'. The *aide memoire* began:

> Beyond any question Your Majesty is more gifted than any of your relations, male or female. Your relations, however, do not extend to you a respect commensurate with the brilliance of your qualities— quite apart from the powerful position held by the German Kaiser. The reason is that Your Majesty has always met your relatives openly and honourably, has initiated them into your plans and hopes, and has thus provided them with the opportunity of putting obstacles in your way. For the most adroit of thrusts, if announced in advance, can be parried by a weaker fencer. This English journey offers Your Majesty at a stroke the authority which is properly due to Your Majesty's high qualities and great power. All that Your Majesty need do to secure this is to avoid all political conversations ...[42]

Above all, Wilhelm was advised against conversation with the Prime Minister, Lord Salisbury, well known as the spokesman for all English forces hostile to German ambitions. Lord Salisbury was to be treated with 'immaculate politeness, but with everyday small talk and no more, asking how his wife is and so on.' The same went for Chamberlain 'though for quite a different reason. Mr Chamberlain will try to rush matters and, while ready himself to offer substantial concessions, will try to push Your Majesty there and then into definite promises with their point aimed against Russia ...' With his own relatives Wilhelm was to keep an equally tight mouth, permitting 'no glimpses of Your Majesty's own plan'; if forced to speak of politics he was to insist on the fact of German neutrality. Bülow and the Foreign Office officials, like Tirpitz, saw the enmity between England and the Dual Alliance of France and Russia as a fixture in international relations; Germany, steering a course between them, would hold the balance of power and influence. As Bülow put it before the English journey:

> I see the future task of the German government as being, in possession of a strong fleet and under preservation of good relations with both Russia and England, to await calmly and collectedly the future development of elemental events ...[43]

Wilhelm was accorded a splendid reception at Windsor, and as always immediate impressions banished previous thoughts from his mind; the grandeur of the Castle and the beauty of its English setting, the exotic flavour lent by the Hindu servants of the Queen flashing with rich silk and jewels as they bore her on a priceless litter, the colourful uniform of her Guardsmen 'enormous, magnificent officers on splendid horses such as are only to be seen in England',[44] all turned his head. Impulsively he confided to Bülow, 'This is the finest reception of my life. Here, where as a child I went along holding my mother's hand and marvelling modestly and timidly at the splendour, I am now staying as Emperor-King.'[45] Every morning he boasted to his military aides, 'From this tower the world is ruled.'[46]

Bülow was soon being sounded by the English politicians, particularly Chamberlain who gave him a frank outline of his views for an Anglo-German-American grouping that would control the world, relegate the barbaric Russians to their proper bounds and compel France to keep the peace. Bülow parried his advances; friendship and the closest collaboration with England were eagerly desired by the German government, but not collaboration aimed *against* Russia—in any case they must tread warily while German public opinion was so roused by the Boer War. Chamberlain remarked that there was no such thing as German public opinion; the German people simply registered the emotions their government required them to have. Bülow replied that, while Germany had a less well-informed public opinion than Britain, and while its people were more gifted in philosophy, art and science than politics, yet public opinion, even in Germany, had to be reckoned with by every government—and by the Kaiser.

Before he left England Bülow recorded his impressions in letters to Hohenlohe and Holstein:

The British politicians know little of the Continent. Many of them do not know much more of Continental circumstances than we do of the conditions in Peru or Siam. They are also, according to our ideas, rather naive in their artless egoism, as well as in a certain blind confidence. They find difficulty in believing in really evil intentions in others, they are very calm, very phlegmatic, very optimistic ... The country exhales wealth, comfort, content, and confidence in its own power and future. It is clear that the people have never seen an enemy in their country and simply cannot believe that things could ever go really wrong, either at home or abroad. With the exception of a few leading men, they work very little and leave themselves time for everything. It is physically and morally a very sound country. In general there is no question that the feeling in Britain is much less anti-German than the feeling in Germany is anti-British. For that reason those Englishmen who, like Chirol and Saunders (*The Times* correspondents in Berlin) know from personal observation the acuteness and depth of Germany's unfortunate dislike of Britain are the most dangerous to us. If the British public clearly realised the anti-British feeling which dominates Germany just now, a great revulsion would occur in its conception of the relations between Britain and Germany.[47]

Bülow did his best to have Saunders removed from Berlin in the interests of Anglo-German relations but he was not successful. *The Times* continued to be the chief serious paper warning the British of the spirit of the new Germany.

Shortly after Wilhelm had left Germany Chamberlain made a speech at Leicester putting forward the ideas for an Anglo-German alliance which he had skirted with Bülow. It could scarcely have been worse timed. Pro-Boer feeling in Germany was higher than ever, and the offer simply aggravated the fury and impotence felt throughout the nation. Bülow made use of these feelings in December when he spoke in the *Reichstag* debate on Tirpitz's new Naval law which Hohenlohe had announced for the New Year. In a pointed reference to Chamberlain's proffered hand he reminded the deputies that Germany's centre of gravity was the Continent of Europe, where their position rested on the Triple Alliance, and on friendship with Russia. Popular as Bülow knew this sentiment to be, it was not justification for a large fleet, and he moved on to the equally popular theme of envy; Germany's good fortune and growing prosperity had brought a good deal of envy in its wake.

> There is a great deal of envy of us in the world ... there are groups of interests, and there are perhaps even nations, who feel that the German was a more comfortable and pleasanter neighbour to live with in those past days when, in spite of our education and in spite of our culture, foreigners looked down on us in political and economic respects as stuck-up aristocrats look down on a modest tutor. Those times of political impotence and economic and political insignificance must not return ... The one condition, however, on which we shall maintain our position is that we realise that without power, without a strong Army and a strong Navy, there can be no welfare for us. The means of fighting the battle for existence in this world without strong armaments on land and water, for a nation soon to count sixty millions, living in the centre of Europe and at the same time stretching out its economic feelers in all directions, have not yet been found. In the coming century the German nation will be either the hammer or the anvil.[48]

After him Tirpitz rose to explain the technical considerations which had led the government to seek a larger naval programme. Technicalities were his long suit, but it was impossible to get around the fact that according to his own arguments during the debate on the first Navy Law two squadrons of battleships were sufficient to protect Germany's interests; now, less than a year later, *four* squadrons were necessary. Not only that but during the earlier debates he had promised to keep to the six-year programme and within its financial limits. The Socialists and Radicals wanted to know what value could be put on his word or the government's. The debate generated great heat, but the Parties split on the same predictable lines as before leaving the balance of power with the Centre. As before Dr Lieber kept his cards close to his chest during the public speeches and the issue was still in doubt when the *Reichstag* adjourned for the Christmas recess. Tirpitz was cautiously optimistic; the old Chancellor feared that Lieber would demand too much for his support.

Shortly after Christmas the position was transformed. The British Navy blockading Delagoa Bay against contraband supplies for the Boers, seized the German East African Liner *Bundesrath* and took her into Durban for examination; shortly afterwards they seized two more ships of the same company, which they suspected of running arms. The German Press rose immediately and, representing the detentions as arbitrary and arrogant displays of British naval might, surpassed all previous standards in abuse. Heeringen's *Flottenprofessoren* who could not have hoped for a more convincing case to bring their points home added their well-rehearsed arguments to the hue and cry, and Wilhelm joined in by releasing the text of a telegram which he had sent to the King of Württemburg: 'I hope that events of the last few days will have convinced ever-widening circles that not only German interests but also German honour must be protected in distant oceans, and that to this end Germany must be strong and powerful on the seas.'[49]

Bülow, trying to preserve the delicate balance of hostility necessary to rouse his own people but not the British, wired the Director of the Literary Bureau, 'His Majesty desires that the seizure of the *Bundesrath* should be utilised (without impolitic bitterness or heat against England, but factually) with vigour and persistence for the fleet measure ...'[50]

The necessary arguments were disseminated by Heeringen's department at the Marine Office; they were the same as those which another of Tirpitz's departments was polishing and repolishing for the Explanation to accompany the Navy Law in the *Reichstag*, and rested chiefly on the vital necessity of providing an 'Alliance value' fleet to protect Germany's growing trade and vital interests. Battleships were necessary both for maximum 'alliance value' and its corollary that 'even the most powerful fleet' would not be able to attack the German fleet without getting so mauled as to leave itself wide open to others. These were compelling arguments. Here is Albert Ballin, the shrewd and sensible Managing Director of the Hamburg-Amerika line, echoing them without a hint of a question in the *Hamburger Nachrichten*:

> Without a strong fleet Germany will be very much reduced as a power for friend and foe alike in a future war; with a strong fleet the German Empire will hold the balance in its hand for a long time perhaps. But in time of peace as well, Germany needs a powerful war fleet. If England, France, Russia and the United States of America make great efforts from year to year to strengthen and increase their navies so the German Empire, as a competitor in world markets, dares not content itself with a modest instrument and should put an end to the miserable, makeshift fleet of the last

fifteen years. In the brutal struggle of nations for light and air, strength alone counts in the final analysis ...[51]

And for the 'iron core' of the fleet Ballin considered that only battleships would do. All the arguments for fast torpedo boats putting paid to blockading fleets or for submarine or cruiser warfare against trade which had animated previous discussion had been stilled.

Power was not the only consideration. A strong moral factor was introduced into the campaign. The Socialist claim that the government was bent simply on a policy of prestige and adventure, was denied by Ballin and all navalists, and the fleet itself was represented as an instrument of national prestige, 'the bearer of another, higher mission' to those less favoured with *Kultur*, 'as it were the embodiment of the national purpose'.[52] This was how Tirpitz saw it.

At the height of the agitation in the middle of January, the *Bundesrath* was released; no arms had been found aboard and the British Prime Minister, Lord Salisbury, offered his apologies to the German government and compensation for her owners. It was all that Heeringen and Tirpitz needed; after so many weeks the apology merely aggravated the anger and frustration within the country; 'Now,' Tirpitz remarked, 'we have the wind we need to blow our ship into port; the Navy Law will pass.'[53] And, suddenly anxious about the triumph in prospect he instructed his naval attaché in London to find out whether it would be possible for the English similarly to double their fleet by 1916. The reply came at the end of the month; it would not be possible.

Early in February Tirpitz presented his new Law to the *Reichstag*. He had dropped the battleships for the 'Flying Squadron' which had featured in his original scheme but the idea of a four squadron battle fleet to be reached in two stages remained the same; the first stage provided for the three-tempo construction until 1906—by which time events, perhaps the British response which Tirpitz expected, might allow another 'spurt'! The second stage provided for replacement of the old coast defence vessels by battleships. This would give Germany thirty-eight battleships by 1916—two fleet flagships, four squadrons of eight and four reserves. Tirpitz took great care to detail the programme in terms of squadrons as an additional safeguard against cuts being demanded. With the organisational and tactical unit the squadron, the implication was that anything less than a squadron was unsound; thus it was not possible to drop one or two ships without destroying a tactical unit, while to drop a whole squadron would affect the purpose of the fleet itself. This was tied in neatly with all the financial and rationalised planning arguments for a *legal* establishment of the programme which had marked his first law so that the *Reichstag*, once it passed the legislation would be bound by the whole plan and nothing less; as Tirpitz phrased it the passage of the Law would mean recognition of the 'will to create a fleet'.

He was attacked again by Radicals and Socialists for breaking his pledges and wantonly increasing the vicious spiral of European armaments and challenged to explain what changes had taken place to make it necessary to *double* the original fleet establishment so soon. This was impossible to explain; as he had remarked in private to the Saxon Military representative, 'One could not say directly that the fleet increase is in the first line against England, with whom we must doubtless come into conflict in the next century in some part of the earth, be it out of economic rivalry or as a consequence of colonial disputes.'[54] Nevertheless it was plain whom he meant when he spoke of 'a great naval power', and the ease with which 'a great naval power' could blockade Germany's few major ports and bring her sea trade and thus her economic life to a standstill at little cost to herself. It was even plainer when he compared the 42 cruisers which would be provided by Germany's Naval Law with the 206 already possessed by 'the greatest naval power'—in addition to its chains of coaling stations and naval bases commanding all the chief trade routes. His whole argument was designed to show how easily this 'great naval power' might succumb to the temptation to exploit Germany's defencelessness at sea; against such a danger the fleet provided by the first Navy Law would be impotent; as stated in that Law its value against 'greater sea powers' was no more than that of a sortie fleet. What was needed now was a deterrent.

It is significant that when the Bill was referred to the Budget Committee for detailed scrutiny Tirpitz, feeling that his wits were not quick enough to parry the questions which his explanation had left wide open, feeling perhaps that he might be manouevred into inadvertent admission of the *Mächtpolitik* (power-politics) he pursued, asked Bülow to argue the Navy's case for him. And it is a measure of the cynicism still felt about the Navy policy and propaganda, for as one speaker remarked, all that was lacking was a 'big Navy Opera', that Bülow felt it necessary to fabricate details of the English menace which Tirpitz's justifications implied. He felt able to do this as the debates were held in secret.

> In 1897, as the fleet measure was introduced, the possibility of a clash with England did not seriously appear to be at hand. But I dare not conceal that since then circumstances have so changed that today such an eventuality is within the bounds of possibility.[55]

He made a great point of the unique dangers of a war with England, reinforcing Tirpitz's arguments about the ease with which the mistress of the seas could strangle Germany's trade, cut off her colonies and 'throw back our economic and political development for generations', producing effects 'similar to the Thirty Years' War'; moreover, he said, the majority of English people viewed such a naval attack on Germany as a relatively easy task without dangerous consequences to themselves. He knew this to be absurd. Britain was dangerously isolated and was beginning hesitatingly to search for friends, not additional enemies. Germany and America were the most obvious choices, and an attack on Germany was the last thing British politicians considered. Bülow's impressions from his recent visit had left him in no doubt on this score and other German reports bore it out. Here is Count Metternich, soon to become German Ambassador in London:

> I have never believed that England harboured an aggressive purpose against Germany. I do not consider her capable of such sinister intentions—to descend upon our ships and destroy our commerce only to be rid of a competitor. English capital is too vitally interested in Germany to want to destroy German prosperity, and the game is not worth the burden of Germany's eternal enmity. Contrary to the opinion held by many clever men and by the majority of European Cabinets, I would like to make the heretical statement that English politics are not consciously aimed at laying plans for a European war. A Machiavellian policy of this kind is remote from the English mentality, and I cannot see why the English should consider it an advantage to see Europe go up in flames. They are very well off as it is.[56]

Nevertheless, Bülow's arguments, like Tirpitz's, were convincing enough to those who wanted to believe. To those who didn't they appeared just as dangerous, and after stormy sessions in which he was accused by the Socialist leader of wanting a powerful fleet so that when it was ready Germany could 'go for someone', the balance of votes was still held by the Centre Party. Dr Lieber was ill, much to Tirpitz's chagrin as he had spent a great deal of time on him, but his replacement made it clear that the Centre votes could be bought by a tariff on the import of wines—the Party was based on the wine-growing areas of southern and western Germany. When the Treasury Minister promised to impose a duty on foreign champagnes and other classes of wine the Bill passed the Committee with little amendment; in June it passed its second and final reading in the full house with a substantial majority.

The most remarkable passage in the explanation accompanying the new Law, and the part which came to be quoted most frequently in England in later years was the justification for the greater battle-fleet as a 'Risk Fleet'.

To protect Germany's sea trade and colonies in the existing circumstances there is only one means: Germany must have a battle fleet so strong that even for the adversary with the greatest sea power a war against it would involve such dangers as to imperil her position in the world.

For this purpose it is not absolutely necessary that the German battle fleet should be as strong as that of the greatest naval power, for a great Power will not, as a rule, be in a position to concentrate all its striking forces against us. But even if it should succeed in meeting us with considerable superiority in strength, the defeat of the strong German fleet would so substantially weaken the enemy, that in spite of victory he might have obtained, his own position in the world would no longer be secured by an adequate fleet ...

5

The Kaleidoscope Shifts

Sections of the British Press were quick to seize on the threat implied by the German 'Risk Fleet', but the Lords of the Admiralty were little more impressed than they had been by the first Law. The genius of the Royal Navy had always lain in attention to practicalities, not speculation, and it was in keeping that when—over a year after the passage of the second Law—the Director of Naval Intelligence raised the question of a German threat in the North Sea, the First Lord minuted that Admiralty policy was 'to be strong enough to beat France and Russia for certain. When this subject gives us no further occasion for reflection, it will be time enough to consider a new point of departure.'[1]

Beneath the surface phlegm strange things were happening; new men more in tune with the age, less hampered by the hard traditions of the sailing navy, and impatient to make their mark in a Service grown stiff from its century of superiority, were reaching positions of influence. Everywhere there was a spirit of change. One of the most remarkable manifestations was the new attitude to gunnery; although the battleships of the Royal Navy had been designed as great gun platforms, the practice of gunnery had fallen into comparative neglect during a century in which showy evolutions and smartly-painted ships had become the criterion of efficiency. In 1897 at the annual Prize-Firing a particularly impatient young Captain named Percy Scott had shown up the gap between outward show and real fighting efficiency by scoring a startling eighty per cent hits to rounds fired—against an average of just over thirty per cent for the Service as a whole. When he repeated the feat in his next command on the China station, the officers of the squadron were so enthused with his novel conception of 'continuous aim'—instead of allowing the ship to roll the sights on target—and with the telescopic sights and gunnery training machines his carpenters and electricians had extemporised that they copied his methods in their own ships. The following year their results were equally startling. From China the 'new gunnery' spread through the British fleet like wildfire; quite suddenly gunnery became a respectable preoccupation. And French officers noted, with astonishment, that their arrogant rivals were now scoring twice as many hits per minute as their own best ships.

At the same time Fisher was stirring the Mediterranean Fleet from its peace routines with evolutions designed to simulate the chances of a modern naval war; long-range firings, high speed passages from port to port, exercises to evaluate the battle fleet's chances against torpedo craft attack by night or by day, inspections designed to test the initiative and reflexes of his Captains and Commanders, all followed one another in rapid succession. Those officers who failed to reach his standards found themselves on their way to a distant station within hours; those with ideas, however subordinate their rank or short their length of service, found themselves drafted on to special committees set up to examine specific problems.

impossible to exaggerate the new ardour, the feeling of relief among younger officers who felt that the day had dawned when mere peace ideas and manoeuvres were about to give way to real war preparations ...[2]

Fisher brought the Admiralty into his schemes, bombarding their Lordships with his ideas on the strategy and tactics for Armageddon.

My submission is that the Fleet as now constituted in the Mediterranean is not prepared for war *and cannot be exercised for war,* because we have an insufficiency of cruisers and destroyers and practically no auxiliaries at all ... The special point I wish to make is that unless I have the use of these vessels to cruise with the Fleet during peace exercises, I cannot find out their deficiencies or the best way of applying them in war. They will come upon us crude, unorganised and unpractised in their duties at a time when all our energies are required in attacking the enemy. Our frontiers are the coasts of the enemy and we ought to be there five minutes after war is declared![3]

In lectures to his officers this phrase became, 'The frontiers of

England are the coasts of the enemy. We ought to be there five minutes *before* war breaks out!'[4] Similar aphorisms and exaggerations to drive home a point enlivened his most serious discussions on tactics and strategy. 'Prayer for the unready and unpractised fleet! Give peace in our time, O Lord!'[5]

Like Tirpitz, he chaired his special committees of bright officers as *primus inter pares*, drawing out their brains, never hesitating to admit that he needed further information himself, yet—egocentric to a degree, very conscious of his own will, used to getting his own way, his thick bottom lip curled like a pugnacious schoolboy. Like Tirpitz, no conception was too great, no detail too small for his attention: 'remember it is detailed minute attention to minutiae and the consideration of trifles which spell success.'[6] Like Tirpitz most of his waking hours were spent in thought or discussion about the needs of the fleet; at night he kept a pad and pens by his bedside so that he would not lose the ideas that might come to him in the small hours. Like Tirpitz his volcanic energy and will to succeed had few outlets apart from the Service; love of Navy and love of country had fused indissolubly in him, two facets of one consuming passion.

Comparisons can be stretched no further. Fisher's mind was infinitely more open, flexible and agile than Tirpitz's, his wits were quicker, and the steel in his soul was leavened by boyish zest and outbursts of spontaneous gaiety which could bring him waltzing in to a formal dinner or turn his table at a Banquet into the semblance of a gunroom mess. To the orthodox he appeared 'brilliantly insane, while he with more reason thought they were respectable imbeciles'.[7] While Tirpitz appeared a recognisable type, a compound of what Bülow liked to call the 'hard-working German Michael' and a machiavellian politician, gaining extra-ordinary force through the narrowness of his vision, Fisher was unconfined and indescribable.

> I have known personally a dozen of men who have been in my time the most remarkable and famous men in the world; Lord Fisher was the most fascinating of them all, and the least like any other man.[8]

For the Navy, Fisher was the personification of change. His mind reached out ahead over the rim of the technical horizon. The recent invention of the gyroscope as a controlling device for torpedos would extend their effective range beyond present effective gun range; what then of battle tactics based on artillery duel? What of the chase, the basis of British naval thought, if the enemy fired torpedoes astern? Wireless telegraphy promised to extend the vision of a fleet by enabling scouts and cruisers to report from well beyond visual range, would in time affect the strategic distribution of the fleets themselves. Submarines such as the French and Americans had pioneered and which the Royal Navy had started building—in order to gain experience in countering the menace— promised to render traditional blockade tactics obsolete. Everything was in flux. No hard and fast rules based on historical dicta or present classes of ships would do. There was really only one rule:

> *Whatever type the French have, we must go one better* ... if we build as quickly as we ought to build, we ought always to commence after they are well advanced and have the more powerful vessel afloat beforehand. *What I beg to impress on you* ... is that speed is almost the first desideratum in all types from the battleship downwards to meet the game England must play in a naval war ...[9]

As for the Admiralty, it had scarcely changed since sail gave way to steam; radical overhaul was decades overdue:

> What we want is an *additional naval member of the Board of Admiralty absolutely disassociated from all the administrative and executive work and solely concerned in the* 'PREPARATION OF THE FLEET FOR WAR'. Battenburg has invented a magnificent name for him, 'THE WAR LORD' ...[10]

And, because there was no 'naval von Moltke' free to pre-think the probabilities of modern war, the Admiralty's grand strategy was dangerously out of date.

> All round the compass we have no friends. It is truly a case of 'splendid isolation', but that being the case, surely we ought to consider the fundamental principle of war, which is to concentrate your force on the vital point of the war! *We are weak everywhere and strong nowhere!* We have dissipated our naval forces all over the globe ... Of what earthly use is it cutting off the legs and arms of your enemy in China and elsewhere if he pierces your heart in the Mediterranean![11]

97

Tirpitz, brooding in his Black Forest retreat on the next stage of the great plan, seeing the future as an endless extension of the present, visualising battleship following methodically on battleship in an inflexible line pointing at London, had no more inkling of the changes bubbling just under the glittering crust of the Service he sought to hold up with menaces than he had of the changes likely to result from the menaces themselves. Some of his staff officers were not so sanguine; in 1902 a memo headed 'War with England' pointed out that already, in peace, England frequently concentrated her European naval squadrons for training and manoeuvres; in war her first move would be to concentrate her forces. It went on to point out that in war it would not even be imperative for England to finish the affair quickly with her home fleet for 'the longer the war lasts, the more fundamentally would German trade be ruined. England has time slowly to crush us.'[12] This was an accurate reading of the situation which Germany, with her interior position, must face in any war with Great Britain. The inference was that Britain would not use the traditional blockade—on which Tirpitz's plans relied—if this proved too costly in ships, but would use her enormous strength to strangle German trade out of range of torpedo boats. In that case the German battle fleet, if it was to produce any effect at all, would need to sally forth to give battle while the British fleet was still intact, concentrated and superior.

This inference was not stated in the memo. Yet it was obvious enough for the Royal Navy to be moving towards it already. That same year, when the British home fleets were concentrated for the annual manoeuvres, the objects of their war game with real ships were 'to evaluate the risks involved in keeping such a close watch on a fleet in a defended port as to ensure bringing it to action if it emerges, or whether it is better to adopt some other line of strategy involving less risk to one's own ships but giving him greater chances of evasion.'[13]

Meanwhile France, with a century of experience and frustration at the game Tirpitz was trying to play decided—not for the first time—that it was ridiculous to continue allowing British naval strategy to dictate her own policy. 'France? will she always allow herself to be dragged along by English ideas? will she always leave to her great historic adversary the choice of arms?'[14] Of course it was to Britain's advantage to give the impression that nothing had

changed since the Nile and Trafalgar, that battleships were still
the dominating units at sea and that 'The Empire of the Seas' could
only be obtained with battle fleets either annihilating the enemy
battle fleets in pitched battle or neutralising them by blockade.

> And it is the part of all the rival powers with France at their head
> to applaud and precipitate themselves on the great English doctrine
> like a moth rushing to the light that dazzles it. There is not a
> naval programme which is not established upon this (English)
> model ... Never has England gained a more complete and decisive
> victory. In this she triumphs over the whole world, for her security
> and her power at the present time depend less upon her formidable
> squadrons than upon this universal spirit which she has created,
> and which is indeed the masterpiece of her policy ...[15]

The French argument went on to describe the English strategy in
terms that Fisher himself might have used:

> The sea is not to be looked upon as a means of transport between
> the different Continents, but as a territory, a British territory of
> course. The English fleet which owns the Empire of the Seas, places
> its frontiers at the enemy's coasts, and will dispose of all commerce
> behind that frontier just as an army disposes of the resources of a
> conquered province ...

Now, the French argument went, technical developments had
rendered it possible to puncture this conceit. France only needed to
construct the necessary number of submersibles and submarines as
an offensive arm to sink the British battleships and they would be
unable to risk themselves near French coasts—or even around their
own. The British might counter by building submarines, indeed
they had already started, but this scarcely mattered: 'submarines
cannot fight submarines under water. The problem is insoluble.'
The construction of submarines did not preclude building surface
commerce raiders armed with guns, indeed with British fleets thrust
back from the coasts by the submarine it would enable such vessels
to operate far more easily and effectively, and strike England on
her tenderest nerve.

Similar arguments were not lacking within the German Service;
Tirpitz ignored them all. Despite his grandiose objective he was
still on a very limited budget. Much smaller than Great Britain's,

smaller than the French, Russian or even American, and he refused to dissipate any money on experiments or projects which did not promise immediate returns in terms of the main plan. Besides, he was a disciple of Mahan, the most influential exponent of the 'English doctrine', the most convinced denigrator of cruiser warfare against trade, and enthusiastic admirer of the undeviating battle-ship building programme of Colbert. But the chief reason Tirpitz did not recognise the potential of submarines was that they lay outside the narrow focus of 'the plan'. Years later, when answering criticisms of his late start on submarine building, he let fall the revealing explanation:

> I refused to throw money away on submarines so long as they could only cruise in home waters, and therefore be no use to us ...[16]

While Tirpitz was playing into the hands of the superior battle-ship power by challenging them at their own game and refusing even to experiment with new weapons which might turn their flank—or defend his own waters effectively—Fisher, who took from Mahan only what he chose, was so enamoured of the possibilities of the submarine boats that he manoeuvred one of his most brilliant protégés, Captain Bacon, into the post of inspecting Captain of submarines. Within a few months Bacon reported:

> The risks of allowing a large ship to approach such a port (defended by submarines) are so great that I unhesitatingly affirm that in war time it should never be allowed ... A ship should not approach within twenty miles of an enemy's port with a view to remaining there ...[17]

The ground was slipping from beneath the tactical concepts on which the Tirpitz Plan rested. In the field of strategy things were far worse; what had seemed solid ground was revealed as a deli-cately-sprung trap-door which sank further the more pressure was placed upon it, meanwhile operating a whole series of balances and alarms.

The first hint of this came in 1901. Bülow, who had succeeded Hohenlohe as Chancellor the previous year, was still trying to steer a delicate course between Great Britain and the Dual Alliance of France and Russia while Wilhelm was doing his best to help by sowing suspicion between the Russian and the English Royal Houses at every opportunity. Lord Salisbury was well aware of these machinations and his suspicion of German motives was only surpassed by his dislike of Wilhelm's falseness. However, the faction of his party led by Chamberlain still—despite all Bülow's rebuffs—favoured an understanding with Germany, England's 'natural ally'. When in January, Wilhelm made a precipitate visit to England on hearing that his 'English grandma' was dying—surprising his hosts by his devotion and tenderness towards the old Queen in her last moments—he learnt of Chamberlain's hopes and wired Bülow that the English seemed to be coming 'as we expected they would'. Bülow replied:

> Your Majesty is quite right in feeling that it is the English who must make the advances to us. They have just had quite a drubbing in Africa, America proves to be uncertain, Japan unreliable, France full of hatred, Russia perfidious, public opinion in all countries hostile ... now it gradually dawns on the English that they can no longer maintain their world empire solely by their own efforts against so many adversaries ... Your Majesty would accomplish a real masterstroke if without Your Majesty's prematurely binding Yourself or making explicit declarations Your Majesty could produce the impression in responsible English circles that there was hope of a future solidly-based relationship with us ...[18]

Wilhelm followed these instructions with such success that, notwithstanding the deep distrust in which he was held by Lord Salisbury, those members of the Cabinet who favoured an Anglo-German alliance were encouraged to try harder to obtain one.

It was a short-lived 'master stroke'. Bülow's diagnosis of England's plight had been accurate, but his forecast of her patience and infinite gullibility was too optimistic. Although acutely aware of the danger that Tirpitz's overall plan, once discovered, would turn Great Britain against Germany, he had failed to take the inference that each battleship added to the German fleet was a part of the overall plan and would play a part in producing this effect—long before the whole plan could be realised. And he failed to allow for the possibility that each move Britain made away from Germany would be a move towards Germany's Continental enemies. When Chamberlain and others hinted at this he dismissed it as a bargaining ploy, 'a threatening apparition to scare us'.

The first move came in August that year. By then the hopes raised at Wilhelm's visit had been dashed by Bülow's refusal to follow up with any concrete agreements—despite great efforts on the British part—and the formerly pro-German faction in the Cabinet had become disillusioned, Chamberlain himself embittered as a rejected suitor. One of the most vital areas where agreement had been sought was the Far East, where all the European Powers, joined by Japan and the United States of America, hovered around the decaying carcase of the Chinese Empire. As each Power built up its squadrons in the area it had become obvious that Britain alone could not hope for her traditional naval superiority without denuding the Mediterranean or Home fleets, which were of course the foundation of her world strategy. It had become important to obtain allies. For this reason Japan had been invited to the Anglo-German talks; she had common interests with Britain in resisting Russian expansion, the most immediate threat to the status quo in the area and the traditional threat to all British eastern interests, especially India. When it became clear that Germany was not really interested in agreement, the Foreign Secretary, Lord Lansdowne, re-opened negotiations with Japan alone. These led to the Anglo-Japanese alliance of January 1902, in which both parties pledged themselves to remain neutral if the other found itself at war with one power, but to come in with their ally should a second Power join the enemy. Its avowed aims were to preserve free trade and the territorial integrity of China. More important it ended the isolation of both island Empires; for Japan, there was the immense prestige of being the first eastern nation to be recognised as an equal by a European Power—the first world Power at that—and the assurance that in any future conflict with Russia, the Royal Navy would hold the ring. For Britain there was the assurance that the Russian and Japanese fleets, the two most powerful in the area, would not be combined against her. And with the Japanese Navy effectively added to her own China Squadron, she had no need to weaken her home or Mediterranean fleets. In this respect the Agreement was very carefully worded. Japan had wanted her to maintain a force equal to any third Power in the area; this was amended to 'an effort to maintain such a force so far as may be possible *available for concentration*'[19] in Far Eastern waters.

The Alliance was the first crack in the strategy of the Tirpitz plan—not that it came as a result of the plan; it was a response to the general naval build-up outside European waters, in particular the growing squadron of Russian battleships at Port Arthur. To Britain, government and Admiralty alike, the German programme was only a part of a worldwide surge of naval building.

Wilhelm, Bülow and Tirpitz took the news calmly enough. Wilhelm made a marginal note on the report, 'At last the noodles have done it!'[20] His idea of the Japanese was a caricature entitled 'THE YELLOW PERIL', against which all European nations should set their shields; in any case Britain's attachment to this inferior race made the likelihood of her entanglement outside European waters more, not less likely, and seemed actually to strengthen Tirpitz's thesis.

This was the problem to which British statesmen turned their attention as relations between Russia and Japan deteriorated; both had ambitions on Manchuria. The obvious danger in the conflict that seemed likely to develop was that France, as Russia's partner in the Dual Alliance, would come in on Russia's side, thus drawing Great Britain in on Japan's side and precipitating a great war. On top of this spectre came growing realisation of the German aim to profit from just such a situation, as the meaning of the *Flottenverein* and *Flottenprofessoren* and Pan-German propaganda at last sank in. The annexation of Holland, the annexation of half the States in Europe—discovered in one Pan-German atlas to be shaded in the same tint as the existing German Empire!—the annihilation of part of the British fleet while her main squadrons were engaged elsewhere, even the invasion of the British Isles, on which several German officers effused publicly, all the most extreme Pan-German aims were 'discovered' by the British Press through 1902 and paraded as the aims of official Germany. Wilhelm's speeches, which had attracted little attention when made, were resurrected and used to show that the policy found expression in the very highest circles: 'The trident belongs in our fist' and 'Although we do not yet possess the Navy we ought to possess we have nevertheless fought for our place in the sun and won it. Our future lies on the water ...'[21] were two popular examples. Then there had been his extraordinary diatribe at Bremerhaven to the troops embarking for the Boxer War, perhaps the most damaging speech he ever made. Mounted on a wooden podium erected near the quay he had assumed his harshest tone and called on the assembled men to give the world an exhibition of Prussian steadfastness, virility and discipline:

> There will be no quarter, no prisoners will be taken! Just as a thousand years ago the Huns under King Attila created for themselves a name which still stands for terror, so may you impress the name of Germany on China that for a thousand years no Chinaman, whether his eyes be slit or not, will dare look askance at a German![22]

Before the speech was over, Bülow, who had been listening with mounting apprehension, had bound all journalists present not to transmit it for publication until he had provided an authorised version. One reporter who had been sitting on a rooftop taking it all down did not wait for the official draft and before many days the story had spread from his small Wilhelmshaven paper to the Press of the world; while the speech itself was forgotten soon Wilhelm's associations of Germany with 'Hun' and frightfulness were not.

In 1902 Kipling revived them in '*The Rowers*', an allegory in which the British crew, having come through the ordeal of the South African war, now had to exert themselves 'to league anew, with the Goth and the shameless Hun'.[23]

In the summer of that year of popular realisation of the German aims, the British Press featured yet another gaffe by 'Willy the Witless', which all Bülow's efforts failed to hush: after meeting the Tsar at Reval Wilhelm had signalled on parting, 'The Admiral of the Atlantic bids farewell to the Admiral of the Pacific!'[24] It was intended as pleasantry, but the British took it as a portent.

Far more alarming than the loose tongue of mad 'Billy of Berlin' or the flood of 'Big Navy' propaganda which Bülow could not control were Tirpitz's battleships themselves. As they slipped into the water and were completed on time with thorough German system they took on a far more threatening shape than they had possessed as paper projects. It was noted for instance that their steaming radius was too small and their accommodation too cramped and inconvenient for cruising outside the North Sea or Baltic. In August 1902, after the visit of an Admiralty official to Kiel and Wilhelmshaven a Confidential Memorandum was printed by the Admiralty, whose tone and conclusions were startlingly different from those drawn by Their Lordships only a year previously:

> An examination of the German shipyards, ships and shipbuilding establishments gives rise to some very serious reflections and suggests questions of the first importance. That the naval power of Germany is already formidable no one who has the slightest acquaintance with the German fleet will deny. That it is destined in the near future to become more powerful than it is at present is clear from the statements made by the Emperor and his Ministers, by repeated expressions of opinion in the German Press; and above all by the rapidity and certainty with which the formidable programme put forward by the German Admiralty is being put into execution ...

The paper went on to point out that the very large and very sudden increase in the fleet could have little importance against Germany's Continental neighbours; it could only be aimed at England.

> Against England alone is such a weapon as the modern German Navy necessary; against England, unless all available evidence and all probability combine to mislead, that weapon is being prepared.

The conclusion was clear; insufficient preparations had been made for 'meeting and defeating Germany on the sea'; it was imperative 'they should be made *now*'.

> In view of the fact that the whole of the German fleet is always within striking distance of our shores it is no longer safe to dispense with a modern and powerful fleet in Home waters. The maintenance of a large fleet in the Mediterranean and the China Seas does not guarantee us against German attack ... The danger from Germany is not immediate and can be guarded against if we act now, and do not wait until it is too late.[25]

The second crack in the Tirpitz Plan—the victim had woken and was about to alter his dispositions to meet the threat.

In one very important respect the dispositions had already altered. In advance of Admiralty policy, the British people themselves had swung around to face the new enemy. From the few men of real influence in the government, Foreign Office, Press, out to the mass readership of the new popular journalism the image of Germany by the end of 1902 was that of a nation systematically organising itself not only to infiltrate British markets overseas, but to overthrow the British Empire by force. In January 1903, the German Ambassador in London wired a confidential report:

> As long as I have known England, I have never observed here such bitterness towards another nation as at present exists towards us ...[26]

After all Bülow's and Tirpitz's manoeuvrings in the shoal waters between German apathy for the fleet and British awareness of danger, the inevitable had happened; Tirpitz's nightmare of a sudden British attack before his squadrons were ready seemed to be taking substance. Bülow, resting in his villa on the island of Nordeney, 'looked with anxiety on the dark and turbulent North Sea, our German Ocean',[27] speculating on the chances of carrying the fleet programme to its conclusion without 'a clash with Albion'; in the light of *Realpolitik* it seemed like squaring the circle.

Close by a sturdy English yacht named *Dulcibella*, formed in the mind of Erskine Childers, appeared from the mists, sounding her way slowly through the shifting channels between the islands and mud flats as her skipper, Davies and his Foreign Office friend, Carruthers, enveloped in oilskins and seaboots, sought an answer to *The Riddle of the Sands*. After many adventures they found it in preparations for an invasion of England with flat-bottomed barges drawn by tugs. And, half-burned in a villa on Nordeney, they found a copy of a Confidential German memorandum, suggesting that such an invasion would not be possible until the fleet was stronger—a decade at least—for while the barges might land their troops, once the British fleet concentrated across their supply lines their position would be hopeless. This was Tirpitz's view precisely. Davies and Carruthers and the little *Dulcibella*, her decks worn grey by the weather, the shelves in her steaming cabin lined with much-thumbed volumes of Mahan on Sea Power, established themselves in English literature and mythology—along with the German plans for invasion.

As the threat from Germany loomed former enmities paled. Fisher, who had been called to the Admiralty as Second Sea Lord, expressed a widespread view when he wrote in the summer of 1902:

The German Emperor may be devoted to us, but he can no more stem the tide of German commercial hostility to this country of ours than Canute could keep the North Sea from wetting his patent leather boots! It's inherent. Their interests everywhere clash with ours, and their gratitude for all our astounding beneficence to them is nil! It is a fact that at Hong Kong a body of German merchants assembled to drink champagne in gratitude for our reverses in the Transvaal, looking thereby to German ascendency there, through Holland, which they intend to annex. Mind, this is our colony, where we give them every freedom to oust our own merchants and our steamship lines from their former predominant position! If you turn to France—in absolutely nothing do we clash, *and never can clash*. We hate one another (or rather it is only they who hate us) because 'Perfide Albion' is taught in their nurseries, and the greatest cads in England now travel and take away our character by behaving like cads ... I am perfectly convinced, if the matter were properly engineered, and the Press of both countries interested in the subject, we should have a vast change, and both enormously to the advantage of France and ourselves ...[28]

A similar view had animated the French Foreign Minister, Théophile Delcassé, since before the turn of the century. Sharing a common border with Germany, France had felt the pressure of her expanding economy and ambition, and the physical presence of her great army long before England. When it became clear that she aimed to build up a powerful fleet as well Delcassé, plotting this new factor on the chart of French fears, came to the conclusion that the battleships were really intended for the Mediterranean; Wilhelm, in his view, foresaw the disintegration of the Austro-Hungarian Empire, and was just waiting to bring that ramshackle system under the wings of the Prussian eagle, and at the same time acquire an eastern Mediterranean base for his fleet. Trieste, it seemed to Delcassé, was the logical pivot for Germany's new world policy.[29] The prospects of such a central European colossus with a population over sixty millions, stretching from the Baltic to the Mediterranean and controlling that central sea was infinitely alarming, and from the moment he came to office Delcassé had sought to heal the old wounds with England and bring her weight into the ring against Germany. The chief instrument of this policy was the French Ambassador in London, M. Paul Cambon. As British hostility towards Germany grew, Cambon's chance came. Early in 1902 the German Chargé d'Affaires noticed him in long and intimate conversation with Chamberlain after a state dinner. 'I watched them and noted that they talked together for exactly twenty-eight minutes in the most animated manner. I could not, of course, catch what they said, and only heard two words, "Morocco" and "Egypt".'[30] Later, Cambon approached the Foreign Secretary, now Lord Lansdowne, and produced a list of subjects, chiefly in the colonial sphere, on which the two nations might come to an agreement. Lansdowne showed the list to King Edward VII, who invited Cambon to dine at Buckingham Palace and congratulated him on the approach. 'We must go on.'[31]

The next step was taken by the King himself. Like Wilhelm he was to a remarkable degree a personification of the dominant traits of his country. Theories held no fascination for him; he lived for the moment and did what seemed most commonsensical in the light of present circumstances. He was not clever in an accepted sense; he read no books. But during his long wait for the Crown he had learned well in the school of men and women of the world and, in complete contrast to Wilhelm, had acquired real wisdom and unerring judgement of men. Similarly in outward style the identification with his own countrymen and the contrast with Wilhelm could not have been more marked. Wilhelm lived—and the irreverent said slept—in uniforms and shining, plumed helmets, Edward usually in plain clothes and soft hats chosen not to impress but to suit the occasion or time of day or weather. Wilhelm struck poses and declaimed like a parody of an Elizabethan dramatist, Edward was the most natural of Kings abominating rhetoric and false sentiment. Wilhelm was excitable and nervous, quick to imagine offence, eager to meddle or display his knowledge, Edward was phlegmatic, not assertive, not half such a fascinating talker as Wilhelm on his day, but with a flair nonetheless for saying the right thing at the right time. Above all Edward was a master of simple geniality, not ashamed to indulge his tastes in things all Englishmen could understand, women and horses, good food, cards, cigars the size of capstan bars. His personality, well-knit and assured seemed to fit his people like a glove. It was no accident that as the British moved towards the idea of rapprochement with France, Edward chose to pay a State visit to Paris.

The Cabinet was not consulted in advance. Foreign Office officials, when they heard of his intention, were doubtful; the British Ambassador in Paris thought the idea mistaken in view of the Anglophobia endemic to the capital, and at first it seemed as though he were right. As the King drove through the streets from the Station, crowds cheered their own President seated with him in the carriage, but jeered at the carriages following with the Royal entourage, hurling witticisms and anti-British slogans, 'Vive Fashoda!' 'Vivent les Boers!' even 'Vive Jeanne d'Arc!'

The King, undeterred, made speeches expressing British friendship for France, hoping that the two countries, 'the champions and pioneers of peaceful progress and civilisation', could bury their past differences and develop for each other 'sentiments of the warmest affection and attachment'.[32] And on the third day his obvious sincerity had effect; he broke through the prejudice of centuries with a simple speech ending:

> Je n'oublierai jamais ma visite à votre charmante ville, et je puis vous assurer que c'est avec le plus grand plaisir que je reviens à Paris, où je me trouve toujours comme si j'étais chez moi.[33]

This received tremendous applause and sympathetic coverage in the Press, as did his impromptu greeting to a French actress whom he recognised one night at the theatre: 'Ah, mademoiselle, I remember how I applauded you in London. You personified there all the grace, all the esprit of France!'[34] It was exactly right. Afterwards he and his entourage were greeted with enthusiastic cheering wherever they went.

After the visit one foreign Ambassador in Paris reported home that there had seldom been such a complete change of attitude as that which had taken place in France towards England and her Sovereign. The German Ambassador in London reported:

> The visit of King Edward to Paris has been a most odd affair and, as I know for certain, was the result of his own initiative. I am far from assuming at present that King Edward meant to aim a blow at Germany by this visit. But the opinion now on both sides of the Channel was favourable; accordingly it was from his and his government's standpoint very wise to contribute their part to it ...[35]

He went on to repeat his conviction that the British government, in approaching reconciliation with France had no desire to create opposition to Germany. This was certainly true of the final act of rapprochement. For as relations between Russia and Japan deteriorated, threatening imminent war, the talks which Delcassé and Cambon had initiated to settle colonial differences assumed greater urgency. The possibility of being dragged into a Far Eastern war if France came in on Russia's side, and that just at the moment when it seemed as if the long-standing rift between them was about to be healed, was enough to quell any remaining British doubts. On April 8, 1904, the *Entente* was sealed in an agreement covering sources of friction between the two countries throughout the world. the most important areas were Egypt, which was recognised as a British sphere of influence, and Morocco, recognised as a French sphere. More important for Delcassé than any specific provision, the *Entente* was a step towards the isolation of Germany. This was perceived just as clearly at the British Foreign Office where a group of younger officials who recognised Germany, not France or Russia as the greatest threat to the British Empire, were reaching positions of influence. 'Our object ought to be to keep Germany isolated in view of her nefarious projects with regard to the Austrian Empire and Holland,' wrote one of these men. 'You are right,' his correspondent replied, 'she is false and grasping and our real enemy commercially and politically.'[36] About the same time the First Secretary of the British Embassy in St Petersburg wrote to his friend, President Roosevelt, that England was trying to settle her differences with Russia too, as with a strong German fleet in the North Sea 'if we were at war with Russia, Germany would either take Russia's side, or exact very hard terms from us for her neutrality. The German fleet has really revolutionised politics.'[37]

Meanwhile Wilhelm and Bülow, surprised by what they had regarded as an impossible friendship between England and France, assured themselves that it could not last. And to smooth their ruffled feelings and keep open the lines to Berlin King Edward decided to pay a State visit to Germany. Wilhelm was delighted. It would give him an opportunity of showing off his new fleet to his Uncle, and he sent a special messenger to intimate that he would like to receive the visit at Kiel during Kiel Week. Bülow and Tirpitz immediately guessed his intention—'Bragging,' said Tirpitz, 'is a vice Wilhelm will never be rid of.'[38]—and both tried to persuade him to keep the fleet away from Kiel during the King's visit. Wilhelm replied that it was childish to imagine that the British were not appraised of German naval strength from the smallest pinnace to the largest battleship. Tirpitz pointed out that there was a difference between seeing these things on paper and seeing the whole fleet manoeuvring before their very eyes; the English, especially, were open to direct impressions. Bülow supported him, but that same evening Wilhelm, as Commander-in-Chief, instructed his naval Cabinet to order all ships in home waters to Kiel for the visit.

When the great day arrived, Tirpitz looked on helplessly as almost all the German ships were flaunted before the British Royal party, including Lords of the Admiralty. To his heated imagination, the King exchanged many 'a meaningful glance' with the Sea Lords. To Wilhelm the glances could only mean admiration; at the Imperial Yacht Club, he let himself go.

'When as a little boy I was allowed to visit Plymouth and Portsmouth hand in hand with kindly Aunts and friendly Admirals, I admired the proud English ships in those two superb harbours. Then there awoke in me the wish to build ships of my own like those some day, and when I was grown up to possess a Navy as fine as the English.'[39]

Once again Bülow moved quickly to stop any reporters from leaving the building before he had got out an official version. The next day, after reading the cuttings prepared for him, Wilhelm said sorrowfully, 'You've made me another new speech. And you've left out just the best bits.' Bülow replied that if Wilhelm described the fleet, constructed at such heavy cost and sometimes danger, so sentimentally as the outcome of his own personal inclinations and boyhood memories, it would be difficult to obtain further millions for it from the *Reichstag*. Wilhelm grunted, '*Verdammter Reichstag!*'[40]

Neither the millions which would have to be obtained as Tirpitz moved towards his distant goal, nor the diplomatic and strategic moves against Germany which had resulted from the millions spent so far caused Wilhelm to re-examine his policy. His need for a fleet was too obvious to need analysis—indeed England's new-found friendship with France, which revealed her envy and malice towards Germany, was another reason why he must have it.

Tirpitz also failed to re-think the fleet plan. To have done so would have been to admit flaws in the great conception, perhaps destroy the basis for the Naval Law, *his* Naval Law, which he needed emotionally as much as Wilhelm needed the fleet. Reason was called in, not to analyse the plan in the light of the changing circumstances, but to serve it. The fleet Law over-rode everything. When Wilhelm sent him plans for larger, faster and more heavily-gunned ships than those he was building, enthusing about such battleship/cruisers as the type of the future, he judged them in the light of the Naval Law, and turned the idea down. They would cost too much: 'Money will always be the decisive factor'.[41] Already battleships were costing more than allowed in the Estimates; to inflate them by half again would be asking too much of the *Reichstag*, especially as he was planning another 'spurt' to keep the building tempo up to three large ships a year when it was due to drop to two in 1906—or even to increase it to four.

As if to justify this determination to sacrifice size, gunpower and speed to the Law, he argued that it was not the superiority of individual ships that would prove decisive in battle, but *numbers*. It is possible he believed this; it was a favourite dictum of the 'historical' school led by Mahan that the decisive factor in battle would be the total volume of effective gunfire, not the greater size of individual guns, nor the greater size or speed of individual ships. This 'historical' school, looking back to Nelson's time, when the 'hail of fire' from British line-of-battle ships had demoralised enemy guns' crews and given Britain mastery of the seas, argued that as medium calibre guns could be carried in far greater numbers than large calibre pieces and could be fired very much faster, their barrage would rout the enemy *crews* long before occasional large shells from the necessarily few great pieces could be effective. The only advantage of heavy guns was long range, but as long range fire from moving and rolling ships was simply throwing ammunition away, the extra size—therefore target area and cost—of the ships necessary to mount them was money thrown away—so the Mahan school argued. They were wrong—as was to appear. Tirpitz's battle-ships, which had a smaller calibre main armament than most and more medium calibre pieces, showed that he subscribed to this 'hail of fire' theory. It was convenient for him to do so; smaller battleships suited his comparatively small and hard-fought budget, and suited the shallower approaches to his North Sea harbours.

Yet Mahan, in earlier works, had described how the seventeenth century Dutch, prevented by sand bars at the entrances to their harbours from building ships as large as the English, and therefore unable to mount such powerful batteries had been defeated by the weight of English shot. In his Memoirs in 1919 Tirpitz pointed this out:

> In all essentials a naval battle is a fight of one ship against another; the decisive technical factor is rather the concentration of force in the individual ship than the actual number of ships. As the Dutch could not build their vessels very big owing to the course of their rivers, as the English were able to do, the latter obtained this superiority.[42]

In 1904 he used a totally opposite argument; probably he believed it then; perhaps he simply wished to prevent Wilhelm's grandiose ideas from wrecking the fleet Law. If so his argument need not have been conscious fabrication: Tirpitz was a master of self-deception. With his ultimate goal in view it was in character that he should bend all extraneous factors and conflicting ideas to suit it. As he wrote to Wilhelm's brother, Prince Henry of Prussia, the idea of a cruiser/battleship would endanger the Naval Law, not only on account of the cost, but because it would fuse the distinction between these two distinct classes of ship—thus the functions ascribed to them in the Law. This would 'entirely forfeit the confidence of the *Reichstag*.'[43]

Apparently blinkered to change, technological, strategic and diplomatic, Tirpitz retired to his mountain retreat and pondered various plans worked out by his departments for preventing the drop in building tempo due in 1906. Should he present a *Novelle* to add a 'Flying Squadron' for the Far East? Should he simply ask the *Reichstag* for a continuation of the 'three-tempo'—but that would kill the fleet Law idea as surely as Wilhelm's leviathans—should he throw caution to the winds and ask for a third double squadron of battleships for the Home Fleet? What would England do? Would it be better to shorten the life of the older coast defence ships and replace them with modern battleships at a 'four-tempo'? Should elements of each of these plans be combined?

While he wrestled with the problem and took soundings in private with *Reichstag* deputies Fisher, who had been chosen to succeed the retiring First Sea Lord in October, was at Portsmouth working out details of a sweeping reorganisation of the British fleet, ships, men, routines and strategic orientation.

I'll alter it all, and those who get in my way had better look out.

I've ruined about eight men in the last eighteen months, and I'll ruin anyone else who tries to stop me ... I'd ruin my best friend if necessary for the Service.[44]

His schemes, open-minded, flexible and forward-looking, could not have provided a greater contrast to Tirpitz's rigid programme: 'as regards the Navy, and more especially as regards the designs of fighting vessels,' he wrote in a preamble to the overall plan, '*History is a record of exploded ideas.*'[45] His thoughts on the capital unit expanded the theme:

All are agreed that battleships must for the present be continued, and that their characteristic features, distinguishing them from armoured cruisers, are more powerful guns and more armour. The armoured cruiser somewhat foregoes these two requisites to get more speed. No one can draw the line where the armoured cruiser becomes a battleship any more than when a kitten becomes a cat!

The battleship of olden days was necessary because it was the one and only vessel that nothing could sink except another battleship. Now every battleship is open to attack by fast torpedo craft and submarines. Formerly transports or military operations could be covered by a fleet of battleships with the *certainty* that nothing could attack them without first being crushed by the covering fleet. NOW ALL THIS HAS BEEN ABSOLUTELY ALTERED! A battleship is no protection to anything or any operation, during dark hours, and in certain waters is *no protection in daytime* because of the submarine. Hence what is the use of battleships as we have hitherto known them? NONE! Their one and only function—that of ultimate security of defence—is gone—lost! No one would seriously advocate building battleships merely to fight other battleships—since if battleships have no function that first class armoured cruisers cannot fulfil, then they are useless to the enemy and do not need to be fought.

Hence the history and justification of the type of new battleship now proposed; for *what else is she but a glorified armoured cruiser?*[46]

Tirpitz's world was about to take another kaleidoscopic turn.

6

Fisher

Fisher had asked that his appointment as First Sea Lord should run from October 21, 1904, the ninety-ninth anniversary of the Battle of Trafalgar. A day before this he handed his civil chief, the First Lord of the Admiralty, a memorandum outlining the changes he intended to carry through.

Although sixty-four years old, his wiry, cropped hair grey-white, Fisher had remained as young in spirit as any midshipman and quite as irreverent and impatient for change; his mind had lost none of its edge, nor his personality its frightening fire and force.

> The full eye with its curiously small pupil, the wide, full-lipped mouth drooping mercilessly at the corners, the jaw jutting a good-humoured challenge to the world, all proclaim a man who neither gives nor asks for quarter. He laughs, he cracks jokes, he talks with voluminous geniality; but behind all these breezy externals of the seaman are his three 'R's' of war—Ruthless, Relentless, Remorseless —and his three 'H's' of battle—Hit first, Hit hard and keep on Hitting.[1]

His talk still crackled with aphorism and biblical quotation and the sincerity that came from deep convictions. In writing he tried to reproduce the stunning effect of it all with different coloured inks, multiple underlinings, capitals, exclamation marks, in printed memos with sudden changes of type face and size, white spaces, whole phrases in capitals. The Admiralty felt his arrival as a 'tornado with a nib on the end of it.'[2]

His memorandum to the First Lord began:

> The Scheme herein shadowed forth must be adopted as a whole! The whole scheme could emerge next Christmas morning from the Board of Admiralty like Minerva from the head of Jupiter—full-

developed, full-grown, complete and armed like Minerva against all objectors! *and this is possible!*

The country will acclaim it! the income tax payer will worship it! the Navy will growl at it! (they always do growl at first). *But we shall be thirty per cent more fit to fight and we shall be ready for instant war!*[3]

There followed a quotation from Corinthians—'The eye cannot say to the hand I have no need of thee; nor again the head to the feet, I have no need of you'—to make the point that all parts of the Scheme were necessary 'for the perfection we must have if England is to remain the "Mistress of the Seas"'. It was essential she should remain so 'Supreme, unbeatable' as the British Navy was the best guarantee for the peace of the world.

So we must have no tinkering! No pandering to sentiment! No regard for susceptibilities! No pity for anyone! We must be ruthless, relentless, remorseless! And we must therefore have The Scheme! The Whole Scheme! And Nothing But The Scheme!!!

The scheme set out new types of fighting ships, in which speed, both for strategic combination and tactical deployment was to be 'the first desideratum'. 'It is the *weather gage* of the old days. You then fight when it suits you best. Some people don't want it for battleships *but they are wrong*, because both strategy and tactics demand speed.' A uniform armament in place of the main, secondary and often intermediate batteries of contemporary classes, was another prime object. The overall design philosophy was 'to divest our minds totally of the idea that a single type of ship as now built is necessary, or even advisable; then to consider the strategic use of each different class ...'

With the development of new types went the scrapping of older vessels kept in reserve or 'showing the flag' in distant stations. 'The most demoralising and expensive and inefficient thing in the British Navy is the mass of small, isolated vessels which are known as the "snail" and the "tortoise" classes, which can neither fight nor run away ... the chief calamity is the deterioration of the men who serve in them, and the frightful anxiety of every Admiral to get them hauled up on the beach or sunk before the enemy take them!' With the scrapping of obsolete ships went the redistribution of the scattered squadrons themselves. Their stations dated from the sailing era; now steam power, the intercontinental cable, and the wireless had made the rapid concentration of forces at any point a far simpler matter, and Fisher aimed to keep only five main British fleets to 'lock up the five strategic keys of the world'—Singapore, the Cape of Good Hope, Alexandria, the Straits of Gibraltar, the Straits of Dover. But the chief purpose of his redistribution was to meet the threat from across the North Sea. This was to be accomplished in two stages: first the Mediterranean Fleet was to be reduced from twelve to eight battleships and the Home Fleet increased from eight to twelve—made possible by the French *Entente* —and the Channel Fleet was to have more modern battleships. At the same time, in preparation for the second stage, the Home Fleet was to be renamed the Channel Fleet, the Channel Fleet renamed the Atlantic Fleet; behind these two a new Home Fleet was to take shape gradually as the most modern of the new types of warships were completed and came into commission. It was a subtle plan designed to transfer the main strength of the fleet to home waters quietly and without obvious provocation which might spur Wilhelm to retaliate with a larger programme.

Finally, to keep the whole strength of the Navy in instant readiness for war at all times—'suddenness is now the characteristic feature of sea fighting'—the scheme envisaged 'nucleus crews' for ships in reserve. The 'nucleus' was to consist of all the specialists and officers essential for fighting the ship—some two-fifths of the full complement—who would live on board and know their vessel intimately. On mobilisation the crew would be completed from shore establishments. This part of the scheme—'the cornerstone of our preparedness for war'—was made possible by the men released from all the obsolete vessels which were to be scrapped. It was to change the Fleet Reserve, then in the hands of small care and maintenance parties into the Reserve Fleet. This Reserve Fleet, stationed in three home ports was to be the nucleus around which the new Home Fleet was to take shape.

The First Lord read the memorandum foreshadowing such radical and momentous changes in the hallowed routines of the Service, made some marginal notes querying some more extreme conclusions, and handed it back to Fisher with his general approval the following day, October 21.

Meanwhile immediate events claimed attention. The war which had been threatening between Russia and Japan had erupted earlier in the year, and in the summer the Russian Pacific Fleet had been blockaded in Port Arthur by the Japanese, who thus gained the freedom of the sea for troop transport and supplies. To dispute this local command, the Russians started their Baltic Fleet, headed by their four latest first class battleships, on a long journey around the western coasts of Europe and Africa to the Sea of Japan. The Russians were notoriously unpractised and unskilled sailors and to add to the difficulties of their Commander-in-Chief, Admiral Rozhestvensky, they had been alarmed by rumours of Japanese torpedo boats lying in wait for them in European waters. Wilhelm had contributed to this. Although Germany was neutral he had been unable to resist intrigue; as one contribution to the Christian struggle against the 'Yellow Peril' he had offered to protect Rozhestvensky's squadron through the Baltic and North Seas—in token of which he had ordered his police to look out for 'suspicious Japanese with luggage'.[4] The German military attaché in St Petersburg had gone further, pointing out to the Russians the danger of an *English* surprise attack; the Japanese had started the war with a torpedo boat attack on the Port Arthur Fleet without a formal declaration—what was to stop the English doing the same with the Baltic Fleet as it passed through the North Sea and along the English Channel?[5]

With such auguries and news of constant reverses in the Far East on top of their own lack of confidence and training, it was not surprising that as the Russian fleet passed the Dogger Bank on the night of October 22 lights and flares from a British fishing fleet were taken as enemy recognition signals. Immediately Rozhestvensky's flagship opened fire. Taking their cue from her the other battleships also opened up; drums beat to quarters, bugles blared, rumours crystallised, the light quick-firers were manned in a panic and the port column found itself under fire from the starboard column. The 'Battle' lasted for some twelve minutes before order was restored; in that time one Hull trawler had been sunk, four set on fire, the battleship *Oryol* damaged and her Chaplain mortally wounded. Rozhestvensky steamed on into the night, offering no apologies, detaching no ships to aid the burning British boats.

News of the incident reached England on the 24th, and created an explosion of popular indignation which threatened war. British cruisers met and shadowed Rozhestvensky's fleet provocatively close, the Channel squadron battleships raised steam and cleared for action, while their Commander-in-Chief, Lord Charles Beresford, drew up a plan for battle of contemptuous simplicity, detailing only half his force for the engagement unless the Russians 'commenced to knock my ships about', when the other half would join in. Fisher wrote to his wife. 'Things look very serious. It's really the Germans behind it all ... that German Emperor is scheming all he knows to produce a war between us and Russia.'[6]

This was a reasonable theory. From the beginning Wilhelm had been backing the Russians in the hope of gaining the Tsar's gratitude and at the same time turning him against England. Despite reports from his military and naval attachés which contrasted the apathy and inefficiency of the Russian forces with the fanatical martial ardour of the Japanese, he had continued a policy of aid and advice to an extent which compromised German neutrality—never publicly declared in any case. His friend, Albert Ballin, head of the Hamburg-Amerika Line, had signed a contract to supply Rozhestvensky's fleet with 338,200 tons of coal for his voyage around the world—the best Welsh anthracite! This had been done without prior consultation with the German government, which had also been kept in the dark about the pessimistic reports from the military and naval attachés. Wilhelm saw the coaling contract as one more claim on the Tsar's gratitude, but it had become very clear that it was fraught with the most terrible dangers, especially in the light of Bülow's and Tirpitz's fears of a British preventive assault on the German fleet. The British might consider the coaling a violation of German neutrality, and stop supplying Ballin, or worse still declare war on Russia and apprehend the German colliers, bringing about an incident in which Germany was face to face with the greatest sea power, or the Japanese might seize the colliers and precipitate a similar incident in which Germany would find herself opposed to England's ally—all this without any guarantees that if the worst came the Tsar would come to Germany's aid.

When news of the Dogger Bank incident broke Wilhelm, Bülow and Holstein met in something like panic and, fearing the worst, hurriedly drafted a Defence Treaty with Russia; Wilhelm outlined the idea in a personal letter to the Tsar. The Tsar, also shaken by the aggressive British reaction, penned an equally hasty reply agreeing to the proposal, whereupon Wilhelm, Bülow and senior military, naval and diplomatic advisers met again to thrash out the details. The shadow of war seemed to loom over them. 'This evening,' Wilhelm wrote, 'a terrible drama may well begin, the consequences of which are unforseeable. God be gracious and spare us.'[7]

Tirpitz, called in to the talks, was horrified by the position in which Germany had become entangled. Even if the agreement were to be signed 'the military significance of a Russian alliance for us in a war at sea is practically zero',[8] while the fact of an alliance, once known, would further strengthen British hostility towards Germany. Bülow and Wilhelm were well aware of the 'Danger Zone' for the fleet, yet here they were persisting in politics which might have been designed to provoke a British attack!

An extension of the war in the Far East was the last thing the British government wanted, especially in view of all their feelers for an understanding with Russia along the lines of the French *Entente*, and when the initial shock had worn off and the Tsar had apologised for what was obviously a mistake, they allowed the situation to cool. On November 1 Fisher wrote to his wife, 'I've been with the Prime Minister all day, morning and afternoon. It has very nearly been war again. *Very near indeed*, but the Russians climbed down again ...'[9]

The Press followed the government's lead, swinging around again to face the main enemy. The German Ambassador in London reported to Bülow a story going the Club rounds that Germany had warned the Russian government of the dangers facing their fleet when it emerged from the Baltic in order to provoke an Anglo-Russian conflict.

> Germany is presented as the true enemy. The German Emperor is said to have the intention of waiting until his fleet is large enough to take on England ...[10]

This was Fisher's view. His answer to the threat was as simple as Tirpitz's fear—a preventive war before the German fleet had grown large enough to resist—a modern 'Copenhagen'. He mentioned the idea to the King and to the First Lord. The First Lord wrote a note to the Prime Minister:

> Fisher's intellectual flaws are on the same scale as his intellectual virtues. I told you his proposal about the German fleet at Kiel—

it was no love of paradox nor said to shock—He meant it![11]

The idea was echoed in *Vanity Fair* on November 10, and the *Army & Navy Gazette* on the 12th. The *Vanity Fair* article was headed 'The Shadow of the Kaiser's Ambition'; it warned its readers of Wilhelm's ambitions on Holland. 'The Texel, Vlieland, Terschelling and Ameland in the hands of Admiral von Tirpitz ... would enable the General Staff of the Army to prepare to embark a great expedition. It is worthwhile for anyone who is inclined to smile at the German peril to glance at the map of Holland. There is no getting out of the fact that with the Hague and Amsterdam in German hands we may write *Ichabod* over the ports of London, Liverpool and Glasgow.' It ended with an exhortation to the British people 'to make up their minds as to whether or not they mean to permit the rape of Holland by the Hohenzollern.'[12]

The *Army & Navy Gazette* was more explicit.

> Before now we have had to wipe out of existence a fleet which we had reason to believe might be used as a weapon to our hurt. There are not wanting those, both in this country and on the continent who regard the German fleet as the one and only menace to the preservation of peace in Europe. This may or may not be the case. We are content to point out that the present moment is particularly opportune for asking that this fleet should not be further increased ... People have been asking, what is the use of the British Navy? It might be replied that there is a very obvious use to which it might be put, with beneficial results to the cause of civilisation and the world's quiet.[13]

The following week one of Fisher's most intimate naval correspondents writing in the *Sun*, urged that the Copenhagen affair of 1807 should be repeated against the German fleet, and *Vanity Fair* returned to the theme under the heading, 'A Navy without Excuse'. Germany, it asserted, contemplated an attack on England somewhere between the years 1908 and 1913:

> Day and night Germany is preparing for war with England. She will strike only when she is ready to strike; that is to say at the exact moment when England is at the greatest disadvantage and Germany in the best position to obtain the initial successes indis-

pensable in naval warfare. If the German fleet were destroyed the peace of Europe would last for two generations, for England and France, or England and the United States, or all three would guarantee the freedom of the seas and prevent the construction of more navies which are dangerous weapons in the hands of ambitious powers with growing populations and no colonies.[14]

German officers had only themselves to blame for these articles; *Vanity Fair* was saying no more than they themselves had been arguing in public and private for years. They didn't see it like that. They saw Admiral Fisher, ruthless, relentless, remorseless; they heard of his suggestion to the King and they interpreted it in the light of what they would do in Fisher's position. Tirpitz and Wilhelm had the same reaction. When the German naval attaché in London reported an Admiralty war game in progress, Germany versus England, due to finish before Christmas, Wilhelm noted, 'Before spring we must be ready for anything.'[15]

But Tirpitz's concentration on the distant goal and the split between him and the operational planners and between these planners and the Great General Staff of the Army had left the Service ready for nothing. Naval 'Plans for the defensive against England',[16] formulated in December 1899 as Tirpitz expounded his 'Risk' theory against England to the *Reichstag*, called for an invasion of Denmark by the Army to seize control of the entrances to the Baltic and so prevent the British fleet from getting through to Kiel. General Schlieffen, Chief of the Great General Staff, had been unenthusiastic; against England alone it might be possible, but if England had one or more Continental allies the divisions required for Denmark would weaken the German forces unacceptably in the decisive theatre—which was of course France. Inter-Service discussions dragged on desultorily for four years—with the invasion of Sweden to secure *both* sides of the Baltic entrances added to the plan—but the Anglo-France *Entente* killed it so far as Schlieffen was concerned.

The sudden fear of war following the Dogger Bank incident blew fresh life into the Navy's case, and for a short time at the end of 1904 Wilhelm leant his supreme authority to the invasion of Denmark. Then Schlieffen's alarm at the weakening of his thrust into France, combined with Bülow's fears—when he was informed of the plan some months after it had been approved—that a seizure of the Baltic entrances would alienate Russia, caused Wilhelm to turn right round and support the Army. In February 1905 the Chief of the *Admiralstab* (which had replaced the *Oberkommando* as operational planning department in 1899) wrote to Tirpitz:

> HM the Kaiser has recently ordered that the Navy has not to count upon the assistance of the army in a strategical defensive ... on the one hand the Chancellor has recently expressed important doubts from a political standpoint while on the other hand the Army cannot provide the troops ... without making success in another place questionable.'[17]

The 'other place' was Luxemburg, Belgium and the corner of Holland through which Schlieffen intended to march on Paris. This flurry of argument in which five of Germany's small neighbours came under threat from one or other of the Services and in which the decision to spare the two northern countries came not from any realisation of the effects on world opinion of such violations of neutrality, but from purely military and power-political consider-ations provides a startling glimpse into the compulsions of the German Services and the nature of supreme decisions in Wilhelm's *Reich*.

Meanwhile recognition of Germany's continuing impotence at sea despite all that had been spent on the Navy, and the increased risk of conflict since the outbreak of the Russo-Japanese war brought more criticism of Tirpitz's policy; even von Heeringen, who had worked closely with him from the beginning, expressed his doubts about the Service getting through the 'Danger Zone' without war, and thought that the Navy had no choice now but to put 'preparedness for war ... above all other considerations. In every measure we take, we must ask ourselves not what will happen in the distant future, but what real increase in power it brings in the time immediately ahead.'[18]

Tirpitz's reply was revealing; he agreed that such things as coastal fortifications, overseas ships, experimental vessels like sub-marines had been curtailed to force the fleet programme ahead, but he was unrepentant:

> The idea that we must subordinate 'tomorrow' for 'today' is correct only with the greatest reservations. The danger zone for Germany is not just there today, but will in all probability also be there tomorrow, and we must reckon with these facts in the development of our Navy.[19]

When Bülow, realising that the fleet policy was not only failing to produce the expected diplomatic results, but was actually hazarding the ships and overseas trade on which Germany's future depended, asked Tirpitz if he expected to be through the 'Danger Zone' soon, the 'Master' replied, 'We are just going into it.'

This seemed to receive confirmation early the following year, when the civil Lord of the Admiralty, replying to a toast at a constituency dinner, and expanding on the results of Fisher's redistribution of strength in home waters and the reforms of the Fleet Reserve, let his enthusiasm for the instant readiness of the Navy carry him away: 'If war should unhappily be declared under existing conditions, the British Navy will get its blow in first, before the other side has time even to read in the papers that war has been declared ...'[20]

In German naval circles, taut with apprehension, there could be only one interpretation of such a bellicose statement; it was a declaration of intent to launch a sudden strike without warning in the Japanese style. Wilhelm, who needed no convincing that the British would take any opportunity to cripple his fleet, protested vehemently to the British Ambassador, afterwards writing to Tirpitz that he had insisted the 'revenge-breathing corsair' at the Admiralty be officially disavowed by his government and disciplined.[21] Excitedly he told his chief of the naval Cabinet that these continued English threats were proof of the need to accelerate the German programme.

They had the opposite effect on Tirpitz. The risk of an English preventive assault seemed so real that he decided to shelve the various schemes for a battleship *Novelle* which his departments had been working on for two years. At a meeting with Wilhelm on February 11 he explained that the idea of a third double squadron of battleships or a 'four-tempo' building rate was now out of the question.[22] It was financially impossible because the larger battleships needed to keep pace with constant British size increases would each cost thirty million marks and would necessitate widening and deepening the Kiel Canal; the *Reichstag* would not swallow an increase of that magnitude at the same time as an increase in the programme itself. It was politically impossible because it would rouse the English too much. Instead he suggested a cruiser *Novelle* which would both divert the *Reichstag's* attention from the increased cost of battleships and help persuade the English that

German naval expansion was not aimed at them, but was simply designed to protect Germany's growing overseas interests—as he had always publicly maintained. With such a *Novelle* the three-tempo could be kept up until 1912. Wilhelm agreed, as he always did when exposed to Tirpitz's powerful logic. On February 20 Tirpitz announced to the Budget Committee of the *Reichstag* his intention of introducing a *Novelle* in the autumn.

The same day the German naval attaché in London reported Fisher's latest shock, a battleship of 18,000 tons mounting no less than twelve 12″ guns, entirely dispensing with secondary and intermediate armament.

Fisher had been working on plans for such a vessel during his year at Portsmouth. At that time Percy Scott, the great gunner whose achievements at the turn of the century had set the gunnery revolution in motion, had been Captain of the gunnery training school, HMS *Excellent*. Scott's work on long-range gunnery had made it inevitable that Fisher's ship should have only one calibre of gun, that the heaviest practicable. For it had been clear that long-range fire had to be controlled from aloft, and 'spotted' on to target. The three different calibres of guns on the latest battleships, which had to be given different angles of elevation to reach the same distance, whose shells consequently passed through different levels of atmosphere and arrived at different times, made 'spotting' needlessly complicated, if not impossible. Besides this the lighter calibres were not so effective at long distance; they had to be angled higher and their shells, dropping at a steeper angle, had to be exactly on range to hit; heavier shells, with a flatter trajectory not only had more chance of hitting even if the range was not absolutely accurate, but they retained their momentum better and were thus more efficient armour-piercers; they also carried a far larger bursting charge. They had every advantage except rate of fire. But as Scott's work suggested that long-range fire would need to be deliberate, each round or salvo 'spotted' on to target from the results of the previous salvo, rate of fire would not be a vital factor. As the development of fire control instrumentation and 'spotting' procedures promised to make long-range fire effective, the 'all-big-gun' ship had become inevitable. In America, where one of Scott's most brilliant disciples, Lieutenant William Sims, had been made Inspector of Target Practice, work on plans for a class of 'all-big-gun' vessels was even further advanced.

Besides its single-calibre battery, Fisher's great ship was designed for speed, as he had made clear in 'The Scheme', the weather gage of the old days and vital for a Navy which meant to take the offensive. The vessel was to have a cruiser speed and a battleship armour and armament; it was virtually a new class of vessel. However, Fisher knew that such a radical departure would not be accepted easily and on becoming First Sea Lord he had set up a Committee of experts from outside and inside the Service to carry conviction when the inevitable protests started. It was from the deliberations of this Committee which Fisher surrounded with an exasperating blend of secrecy and advertisement leading to every sort of rumour that the German attaché finally obtained his information.

As more accurate details of the new vessel came into the German Navy Office there was mounting pressure on Tirpitz to re-think his attitude to the large, high-speed cruiser-battleships which Wilhelm had been urging him to build. However, Wilhelm's designs owed nothing to scientific gunnery or tactics; they were stimulated simply by a world-wide movement towards speed for *closing* the range and a few large guns for hammering at point-blank—really the opposite of Fisher's reasons, and at first Tirpitz refused to alter his ideas. In April Wilhelm visited the Italian Fleet at Messina and, shown plans for a 22-knot battleship mounting eight heavy guns, again wrote to Tirpitz comparing the small, slow, lightly gunned German battleships unfavourably with these vessels of the future. Tirpitz's reply indicated that he was still in the dark about the scientific gunnery revolution which had rendered the British and American plans essential, and the tactical ideas which guided Fisher. His whole scheme was still absurdly subordinated to the demands of the Naval Law: *numbers*, not the superiority of the individual ships was the deciding factor. In any case, he argued, it would be a tactical error to build larger ships and create an impression that Germany was taking the lead in the armaments competition! As for speed, the Italian ships were designed for the Mediterranean and would not be suitable for the rough conditions of the North Atlantic, and he repeated his old arguments about fast battleships obscuring the difference between battleships and cruisers, thus leaving the Naval Law wide open to a mauling in the *Reichstag*. And what of the cruisers? If they had no margin of speed over battleships they would not be able to fulfil their reconnaissance function.[23]

The self-deception was breath-taking. His budget was far smaller than Fisher's, but so was his investment in existing ships. While Fisher was preparing to speed the obsolescence of the entire British fleet with new types of fast battleships and even faster armoured cruisers with a similar all-big-gun armament for reconnaissance, battle and commerce protection, Tirpitz with far less to lose refused to depart from conceptions and classes of ships already out of date. He was not simply allowing Britain the choice of arms, but allowing her superiority in the arms she chose. With his unfavourable geographical position which made 'victorious' fleet battle—or at least a realistic threat of victorious battle—a necessity, this was folly. However, his arguments were reinforced by the chief of the Construction Department, who reported that Wilhelm's demands for eight heavy guns and twenty-two knots were impossible for a battleship which would need to steam through the Kiel Canal; the best that could be managed was twenty knots and six heavy guns—revealing once again that the *Reichsmarineamt* had no idea of the gunnery and tactical revolution under way, but was simply responding without understanding to outside trends.

Wilhelm's Marine Cabinet was no wiser; the chief wrote to Tirpitz:

> I prefer the possibility of strategic combination by means of the canal to tactical concentration in the large type, and only after the domestic situation has allowed us to enlarge the canal would I build the very big ships.[24]

It was at this point that Bülow decided to test the Anglo-French *Entente*. The time seemed right for a reckoning with Delcassé and his English collaborators for, with Russia fully engaged in the Far East and suffering loss after loss, the full weight of the German Army could be held over France; would John Bull prove a true friend in Marianne's need? It was a risky question to put—foolhardy in the light of his own advice to Wilhelm about never doing or saying anything which might endanger peace while the fleet remained in the 'Danger Zone', but Bülow trusted to his own skill to avert a general war. So it was that when the French, acting in the spirit of the North African agreements of the *Entente*, told the Sultan of Morocco that his troops should be placed under French officers and his customs under French officials, Bülow struck. Wilhelm was the chosen weapon; he was cruising in the Mediterranean at the time in the liner *Hamburg*, chartered from his friend, Ballin. He was to go ashore at Tangier and pledge Germany's support for the Sultan's independence—which was guaranteed under the Madrid Treaty of 1880, to which both Britain and France were signatories. At first Wilhelm demurred, but after several urgent promptings from Bülow he agreed—still most reluctantly for there was a heavy sea running off the port and the only way of going ashore was by launch through white breakers. When he had passed that ordeal safely he found another in the shape of a mettlesome Barbary stallion which the Sultan had provided for his journey from the landing stage. The beast would have been difficult at any time, but excited by crowds of Moors and Arabs, and in Wilhelm's report Italian anarchists, lining the route staring in astonishment at the magnificent uniform, plumed helmet and thunderous moustaches of the German Emperor, it provided a dangerous seat. It was not surprising that after it all Wilhelm's speech was a good deal sharper than Bülow had expected.

The European capitals hummed. King Edward VII, one of Bülow's targets in the operation because of the part he was supposed to have played in the *Entente*, was furious; he thought the carefully-managed incident:

> the most mischievous and uncalled for event which the German Emperor has ever been engaged in since he came to the Throne. It was also a political theatrical fiasco, and if he thinks he has done himself good in the eyes of the world he is very much mistaken. He is no more nor less than a political *enfant terrible*, and one can have no faith in any of his assurances. His own pleasure seems to be to set every country by the ears ...[25]

Having set the stage, Bülow stepped up the tension by making it known that the Imperial government could not recognise the right of France, England and Spain to settle the Moroccan question by themselves. He demanded a Conference of the original signatories of the Madrid Treaty, refusing however to negotiate with France so long as Delcassé remained responsible for foreign affairs.

The challenge was plain. Would the new-found *Entente* hold? Would Britain support France militarily over an affair that scarcely touched her own interests? If she did could her small army be of any assistance against the full strength of the *Wehrmacht*? But did

Wilhelm and Bülow really mean to force it to war, like Bismarck in 1870, or would they back down if the *Entente* stood firm? What in any case was the *Entente*? There was no military commitment in writing. Was there a moral commitment? Bülow maintained an inscrutable posture as the crisis mounted.

For those elements in the key positions in the British Foreign Office who were hostile to German ambitions the moment was right for a reckoning, but they feared that Wilhelm would not let it come to war while his fleet and his entire overseas trade and colonies were at the mercy of the Royal Navy. Fisher was filled with the same mixture of anticipation and fear lest the golden moment slip. With Admiral Sir Arthur Wilson Commander-in-Chief, home forces, and an incomparable tactician, he had made plans for the seizure or annihilation of the German fleet, together with troop landings at points in Holstein and Pomerania to draw units of the German Army away from their main thrust into France. And again he urged the politicians to strike now while the naval balance was so favourable. When asked what the Admiralty reaction would be if it turned out that Germany was really angling for a port on the coast of Morocco, he wrote to the Foreign Secretary:

> Without any doubt whatever the Germans would like a port on the coast of Morocco, and without doubt whatever such a port possessed by them would be vitally detrimental to us from the naval point of view and ought to be made a casus belli, *unless we get Tangier*, which perhaps (but only perhaps) would be a quid pro quo. For this reason the Germans will ask for Mogador and Mazagan ... This seems a golden opportunity for fighting the Germans in alliance with the French, so I earnestly hope that you may be able to bring this about. Of course I don't pretend to be a diplomat, but it strikes me the German Emperor will greatly injure the splendid and increasing Anglo-French *Entente* if he is allowed to score in *any way*—even if it's only getting rid of M. Delcassé ... All I hope is that you will send a telegram to Paris that the English and French fleets are *one*. We could have the German fleet, the Kiel canal and Schleswig-Holstein within a fortnight.

A Foreign Office official to whom Fisher showed the letter thought it 'stunning' and Fisher himself—who admitted to him that the gist of it was 'rot' and it would not matter whether the Germans acquired Mogador or not—was a 'splendid chap'; he 'simply longs to have a go at Germany'.[27] The Foreign Secretary showed the letter to the Prime Minister commenting that it would be amusing to confront their colleagues with the seizure of the German fleet, the Kiel canal and Schleswig-Holstein as a fait accompli at their next meeting, but 'we can't go as fast as that!'[28] Nevertheless he sent a telegram to Paris saying that Britain was ready to join France in offering strong opposition to a German demand for a port in Morocco, asking for full consultation between the British and French governments should such a demand be made, and offering Delcassé 'all the support we can'.[89] Similar verbal assurances of support carefully phrased without any specific commitments convinced Delcassé that Britain was actually making overtures for Anglo-French action against Germany, who he was convinced was bluffing. The French Minister of Defence, faced with the reality of the great German Army and no assurance of British support, nor any assurance that such help would be useful or in time, was doubtful. At a vital Cabinet meeting on June 6, 1905 the French Premier cast his deciding vote with the doubters. Delcassé resigned. Bülow's triumph was complete; the same day Wilhelm raised him to the rank of Prince.

The British Prime Minister wrote to King Edward:

> Delcassé's dismissal or resignation under pressure from the German government displayed a weakness on the part of France which indicates that she could not at present be counted upon as an effective force in international politics. She could no longer be trusted not to yield to threats at the critical moment ...[30]

As it turned out the temporary damage to the *Entente* was of less importance than the long-term effect of the crisis. At the Conference which met at Algeciras to consider the Moroccan question Britain and France held together against Germany and Austria and carried Russia and the other European Powers with them. Bülow, finding the Central Powers quite isolated, had to back down and allow France a dominant position in Morocco. Then it was the turn of the German Foreign Minister to resign. Wilhelm, who had in the meantime conjured the Tsar's signature to another Russo-German alliance, only to have it immediately repudiated by Bülow and the Tsar's own advisers who could not afford to offend the French, gave vent to his despair:

> all the miserable, decadent Latin peoples will be mere instruments in England's hands to fight German trade in the Mediterranean. We

have no friends any longer whereas the unsexed relics of the ethnic chaos left behind by Rome hate us ... all this romance catsmeat betrays us left and right and throws itself into England's open arms for her to use against us ...[31]

This, less picturesquely, was how it appeared to many people in Germany. Goodwill visits by the British Atlantic Fleet to Brest and the French Northern Squadron to Portsmouth; revelations in the French Press of joint Anglo-French military agreements against Germany—although this story was premature—; a visit of King Edward to Paris where he invited Delcassé to dine; Edward's failure to meet Wilhelm when he travelled through Germany for his annual cure at Marienbad, and a pro-French and violently anti-German tone in large sections of the British Press, convinced Germans that England had plotted to isolate them; Delcassé had been their tool—hadn't *The Times* always referred to him as 'the great Frenchman'? As so often in Imperial Germany, facts were reversed, other countries' reactions to the German goad were elevated into causes, and the honest German Michael saw himself the object of unsolicited hatred and envy from all sides—particularly from England. The Press had stressed England's envy and malice for a decade; now it was plain for all to see.

This attitude suited Bülow very well as it concealed the way his plan had miscarried: one tactical success in removing the firebrand, Delcassé, had been achieved at the cost of total strategic defeat. England and France were closer together than before, alerted to their danger unless they stuck together, warned of the need for co-ordination between their military and naval departments, actually conducting staff talks on joint war plans against Germany; although these talks were theoretically non-binding the *Entente* had become something very like an alliance.

The impossible position in which Bülow's *Realpolitik* had placed Germany is illustrated by a memorandum prepared for the Board of Admiralty by the Director of Naval Intelligence; it dealt with combined Naval and Military operations with France against Germany:

Great Britain in alliance with France would not merely be in possession of such overwhelming naval preponderance as would permit her under certain circumstances, to risk her ships to an extent not formerly contemplated, but also from the mere fact that she would have been fighting side by side with Russia's ally, she would have possessed an effective guarantee against Russian hostile action on the North West frontier of India ...[32]

The Anglo-French naval preponderance had been emphasised by the results of the war in the Far East. The Japanese had captured Port Arthur and destroyed the Russian Pacific Fleet, afterwards meeting Rozhestvensky's Baltic Fleet after its epic journey around the world and annihilating it off the Tsushima entrance to the Sea of Japan, wiping Russia from the list of naval Powers. After that there were no fleets with any possible 'Alliance' or 'Risk' value for Germany. However many ships the Royal Navy might lose in a clash with Tirpitz's battleships there was no one to take advantage except the United States of America or Japan; Japan was allied to Great Britain, the United States was friendly, sharing information on gunnery advances and working towards co-operation in the Pacific. Fisher had emphasised this after Tsushima by bringing home the China Squadron battleships and adding them to the Channel Fleet, which now totalled fifteen battleships and six armoured cruisers, the most powerful naval force ever under a single command, and unmatched in quality of *matériel* and leadership.

Tirpitz's policy lay in ruins; like Bülow's it had reversed the intended effect; had the main enemy pursued *Realpolitik* the entire German Navy, merchant marine and colonies could have been snapped up and German growth stunted for generations. Wilhelm and the Navy League reacted angrily by demanding more battle-ships, and a faster building tempo—*seven* a year to get the fleet quickly through the 'Danger Zone'! Tirpitz considered this a sure way to bring on the clash he feared.

It would also have led to a clash in the *Reichstag*; this was exactly what the extremists wanted. Social Democratic represent-ation had grown and seemed destined to continue growing in-exorably, the coalition of 'patriotic' parties and the Centre which had seen the first Navy Bills through was showing signs of strain and schemes for jerking the Empire violently to the Right, never far below the surface of Prussian official thought, were freely aired. All the recent setbacks in foreign relations contributed to the mood for 'radical' solutions; it was necessary to rally all patriotic elements and cut through the deepening ranks of external and internal enemies of the State. A provocatively large Navy Bill which the

Reichstag would be bound to throw out would give such an opportunity. By dissolving the House and holding elections during which the bitterness after Algeciras and the Anglo-French 'conspiracy' against Germany could be used to inflame nationalist sentiment, a suitably patriotic House might be obtained. And if not—the army could be used to suppress the Socialists by force. With the internal position secured it would be time for the armed reckoning with France; a popular foreign war would again consolidate the Empire behind the Crown, swing the European balance of power decisively back in Germany's favour, provide colonies and vast sums in indemnities from the beaten foe. The ensuing prosperity would lay the spectre of Socialism.

Bülow was attracted by some of these arguments; a provocative Navy Bill would tend to divert criticism of his own failure in foreign affairs; a dissolution and a 'patriotic' election campaign would similarly divert attention and, hopefully, produce a more reliable 'bloc' in the House for the government. Consequently he told Tirpitz that he could pitch his demands in the *Novelle* as high as he liked; he would guarantee their acceptance. In particular he thought Tirpitz over-estimated the difficulty of persuading the *Reichstag* that the Kiel Canal should be widened and deepened for the larger battleships which Wilhelm demanded ever more stridently since the details of Fisher's new ship had reached him. At this Tirpitz, most reluctantly and against his own judgement of what was possible with the money available to the Navy Office, withdrew his opposition to the large type; the Construction department was set to plan a ship of about 18,000 tons, mounting twelve 11" guns with a speed of nearly 19 knots, and the Financial Department was ordered to prepare estimates for the Canal widening scheme. He was being driven up strange and unforeseen, immensely costly paths.

But on the size of the *Novelle* itself he refused to move. It was evident to him that an increase in the size and armament of individual ships together with an increase in building *tempo* to four ships a year would be interpreted as a direct challenge to the British fleet, and he told Bülow that 'even a calm and rational British government *must* arrive at the conclusion to crush such an opponent before he has acquired the military strength to endanger England's world power position.'[33] He was equally pessimistic about the internal consequences of a provocative Bill: 'the majority of the

Reichstag would not follow the government if it strove for a German fleet of equal value to the British. What then?' His own answer was that with food prices already high because of the tarifs, and with events inside Russia and Austria encouraging Social Democracy in the *Reich*, the tremendous costs of a large increase in the Navy Law carried great political danger, the real possibility of failure in new elections and a consequent loss of prestige for the government both internally and externally. He doubted whether the *Reich* possessed the 'inner strength to come through (such) an era of conflict' as would result.[34]

Because Tirpitz's fleet bills had provided Wilhelm with the solid foundation of what he desired above almost everything else, he was one of the most influential men in the small circle of power around the Crown, and his refusal to fall in with the simple solutions of the violent men was decisive in preventing a 'major domestic and international crisis from breaking out'[35] in the aftermath of Morocco. Whether it was the internal or the external danger that weighed most heavily in his calculations, it was the threat of an English preventive assault which he used to clinch his arguments with Wilhelm and Senden and Bülow as they tried time and again to persuade him to use the bitterness against the *Entente* and violently nationalist Navy League and Pan-German agitation to increase his programme. A preventive war, he insisted, would destroy the patient work of a decade of naval development.[36]

Similar fears were expressed by the *Admiralstab* and the Staff of the Commander-in-Chief at Kiel; trying to devise operations against England and France with such hopelessly inferior forces as to render the task impossible, lacking support from the Army, and with no 'distant goal' to divert their attention from immediate danger they suffered serious attacks of nerves as war scares conjured from the violent nationalist propaganda and rumours—England had promised France 100,000 men to fight on the Continent—blossomed into fears that Fisher was coming. During one of these scares cautious parents at Kiel kept their children from school for two days. The Berlin stock market also reacted to Fisher stories. And in Carlsbad and Marienbad where Fisher annually took the cure, Germans gazed with horror and fascination at the arrogant features of their arch enemy; Catholics crossed themselves.

Fisher delighted in being the most feared and hated man in Germany; he took it as the greatest compliment.

I've got our Channel Fleet up the Baltic and cruising in the North Sea. Our drill ground should be our battle ground! Don't repeat that phrase, but I've taken means to have it whispered in the German Emperor's ear! The next move on the naval board will make you hold your breath when it comes! So get your heart ready for a shock! ! ![37]

H.M.S. *Dreadnought* was intended to shock. Having decided on the revolutionary all-big-gun cruiser-battleship, hence the relegation of all Britain's existing battleships to the second rank, Fisher knew he had to establish a lead in the new type to match his preponderance in the old. He had to keep the details of the design secret, then build her at great speed, carry out trials, learn the lessons, incorporate them in the next class, all before Tirpitz penetrated her secrets. He had to grasp and hold the strategic initiative. Above all he had to be Fisher, with:

a childlike joy in shocking or surprising people. He kept the heart of a child, and it was the secret of that amazing vitality and freshness that was always his. Had it not been so a man so strong, so grim of conviction, so forthright in action, would have hardened into iron.[38]

The Keel of H.M.S. *Dreadnought* was laid on October 2, 1905; by the 4th all the floors and lower frames were in position, by the 7th the armoured deck beams were in place and a month later the armoured deck itself had been laid and riveted home; the ship grew like a forced plant under Fisher's blend of drive and persuasion; on February 10, 1906, just eighteen weeks from laying down, she was launched with a mighty fanfaronade of publicity. That morning, as if in terrible portent, the dockyard at Portsmouth was lashed by a hurricane with driving rain. In the afternoon the sun broke fitfully through the still dark clouds as King Edward VII in the uniform of an Admiral of the Fleet performed the naming ceremony. Fisher, with his flair for the dramatic detail, stood beside him, and when it came to singing 'For those in peril on the sea' it was noticed that the two shared the same hymn sheet.[39] It was no accident that after the grey hull had taken the water the King decorated the two officers who had done most for the new spirit of straight shooting in the fleet, a Knight Commander of the Royal Victorian Order for Percy Scott, and Commander of the Victorian Order for the

Director of Naval Ordnance, John Jellicoe.

The great ship was fitted out with turbines—a new form of propulsion. barely out of its prototype stage—and with turret complexes originally ordered for the last two conventional battleships she steamed out for sea trials on October 3, one year and a day from her commencement. It was a breath-taking performance, epitomising Britain's heavy engineering, especially marine engineering strength, her lead in tactical and great gunnery theory, her will to maintain naval supremacy. The *Dreadnought's* looks asserted it: the stark simplicity of her great turrets spaced over the straight sweep of steel side marked the end of compromise. This was the ultimate conception of the great gun platform: after successful gunnery trials in which she fired full eight gun broadsides at thirty second intervals it was apparent than no earlier battleship could live with her; her name became the generic term for a new class of capital ship.

The *Reichsmarineamt* design for a large battleship to Tirpitz's specification did not match up to the new class; the speed of only nineteen knots, two knots less than the *Dreadnought*, barely a knot more than pre-Dreadnoughts gave her away as a reaction to outside pressures rather than a creation of tactical expertise; her six 11″ gun turrets arranged fore and aft and either side of her superstructure gave her only eight guns on each broadside, the same total as the *Dreadnought* achieved with her five turrets or contemporary American classes achieved with a super-firing arrangement of only four 12″ turrets. The main armament pattern, together with a secondary armament of twelve 5.9″ pieces revealed adherence to close-range 'hail-of-fire' theories of battle which Fisher—and the Americans—had moved way beyond. Wilhelm was not enthusiastic when he signed his approval of the design on March 3, 1906. Later the same month when Tirpitz's six-cruiser *Novelle* passed through the *Reichstag* with scarcely a murmur except from the Socialists, he gave vent to his exasperation with Tirpitz's attitude. 'One has not asked for enough, one feels now that the people who pointed this out were right! *Hinc illae lacrymae!*'[40]

When Tirpitz saw this note he submitted his resignation. It was the culmination of more than a year of disagreement over ship designs and political tactics; it was time to point out that without his own contribution Wilhelm would not even have a fleet programme to argue about. He wrote to say that he could not continue in office if he had lost his Sovereign's confidence. Wilhelm, who had recently returned a resignation from Bülow over his own attempts at personal diplomacy with the Tsar, knew that Tirpitz was equally indispensable, and apologised. Tirpitz asked permission to go on leave, and retired to brood in the Black Forest for the rest of that spring and summer.

It was not long before he was thinking about the next *Novelle* on the way to the 'Iron Budget'. Despite his moderation and statesmanship, his awareness of danger in the forceful solutions recently pressed, his ultimate goal was not negotiable. No matter that his policy had largely precipitated the hard-line solutions by forcing such a startling realignment of Powers against the *Reich*, no matter that his original justification of the fleet as a decisive power factor in the European balance had been demolished by the Anglo-French understanding—which left his fleet virtually alone on one side of the scales—no matter that England had raised the stakes by initiating a new and far more costly class of great ship that upset all his strategic and financial calculations, and that taxes to meet this escalation must exacerbate the already difficult domestic situation, no matter that already, long before he was near his 'distant goal' or making any way across the 'Danger Zone', the fleet policy had recoiled dangerously on both the external and internal relationships of the *Reich*, he refused to admit any flaws in the great conception. It made little sense in the changed circumstances it had brought about, but he deceived himself more easily than the English. And he had never expected plain sailing; now was a time for strong nerves and a cool head, not sudden changes of course or panic short-term solutions. In any case the national feeling he had created for the fleet as the essential expression of world Germanism could not be reversed; it pulled him on.

To the English it made no sense at all. Fisher was in the saddle. There was no lack of commentators to point out that Germany, after years of self-sacrifice in confident anticipation that Britain was on the down-grade and they had only to add to their fleet to gain control of the North Sea, now found that the British Channel Fleet alone was more than equal to the whole German active fleet.

(Germans) have been misled by the German Navy League and by leaders who have advocated an active naval policy. They find that while they have been borrowing largely year by year in order to pay for their new ships, Great Britain has shown no inclination to abdicate her historic position. The German people, as they look upon the powerful Channel Fleet cruising at their very doors, will be reminded that it is merely the advance guard of Great Britain. In the home ports are a dozen more battleships held on the leash, in commission and stored ready to sail at a few hours notice and fight. Within a few day's steaming are nine battleships of the Atlantic Fleet which can sweep up the Channel and into the North Sea. Owing to the wisdom which has been shown in the direction of British foreign policy, this country is now on the friendliest terms with France, Spain, Portugal and Italy, while evidences of a rapprochement with Russia are not wanting. For the present Germany stands alone. In southern waters the British fleet has no probable objective ... economically and geographically Germany is in a hole, and the ebullitions which lately appeared in the German Press were merely expressions of chagrin now that the German government realises that it has been checkmated.[41]

The hints of a Russian *entente* were surely founded. A Liberal government had taken office in December 1905 and the new Foreign Secretary, Sir Edward Grey, had made Russia one of his first priorities. Whether he shared the view of the War Office, Admiralty and permanent officials of his own office that 'Germany's avowed aims and ambitions are such that they seem bound, if persisted in, to bring her into armed collision with us sooner or later',[42] Grey clearly recognised the restlessness of German policy. Early in 1906, he wrote to the British Ambassador in St Petersburg that 'An *Entente* between Russia, France and ourselves would be absolutely secure. If it is necessary to check Germany it could then be done.'[43] And on May 29 the Russian Foreign Minister was invited to start talks with Britain aimed at settling the differences between them. Diplomatically and strategically Germany was sinking deeper in the hole Tirpitz had dug. *The Times* thought this must be obvious to the leaders of German naval policy and saw the small cruiser *Novelle* as a reassuring confirmation of this view, for 'if we are to discern in the growth of the German navy a deliberate menace to the naval supremacy of this country ... we must attribute to Germany a singular lack of intelligence and perspicacity in adapting the means to the ends.'[44]

It was not intelligence, but emotion, ambition and high pride that directed and supported German naval policy; intelligence was called in for justification.

Tirpitz schemed and fretted in the Black Forest. Alarmed by reports from England that Fisher was planning his next class of Dreadnoughts with 13.5" guns and bringing out a class of 'Dreadnought' cruisers, he ordered his construction department to plan their next battleships with twelve 12" instead of 11" guns, and to follow with cruisers mounting eight 12" pieces. Projected costs rose by 2 million Marks each battleship, 10 million for each heavy cruiser.*

Fisher wrote to a friend:

> It's so very peculiar that Providence has arranged England as a sort of huge breakwater against German commerce which must all come either one side of the breakwater through the Straits of Dover or the other side of the breakwater the North of Scotland. It's a unique position of advantage that we possess and such is our naval superiority that on the day of war we 'mop up' eight hundred German merchant steamers. Fancy the 'knock-down' blow to German trade and finance! Worth Paris![45]

---

* Cost of battleships rose from 24 to 38.5 million Marks (almost £2 million, or about the same as the early British Dreadnought classes) and heavy cruisers from 21.3 to 37 million Marks between 1905 and 1907.[46]

7

The Burden of Armaments

Fisher's success in pulling the Navy around to face the German threat, and frightening Tirpitz out of his battleship *Novelle*—at least for a time—had an equal and opposite effect at home. Socialists and the Radical or Left wing of the ruling Liberal Party, who had little idea of the dark warp of German thought, and who viewed Continental affairs in an optimistic and essentially *rational* light, regarded Fisher's belligerent attitude, and his appetite for ever larger ships, which must provoke foreign response and so step up the competition in armaments, as little short of a crime. The British fleet was already large enough to take on all the Continental Powers together; there was no need for such senseless provocation.

The Liberals had come to power on a pledge to put social benefits before arms, and many saw navalists and even the Admiralty itself as little more than the tools of the great armaments barons, who put their own profits before the conditions of their workpeople. The Prime Minister, Sir Henry Campbell-Bannerman, was far too shrewd an old dog to take such a simple view. He hated the idea of war, but while war was a possibility he regarded the efficiency of the armed services as one of the most elementary cares of a government and the strength of the Navy as one of the most elementary cares of a British government. Nevertheless, he also hated the 'jingo' expansionism of so many Britons, and he regarded the extravagance of the new imperialists and extreme navalists as the chief danger to the welfare of the ordinary people of the country.

> What is all our wealth and learning and the finest flower of our civilisation and our constitution—what are these and our political theories but dust and ashes if the men and women on whose labour the whole social fabric is maintained are doomed to live and die in darkness and misery in the areas of our great cities. We may undertake expeditions on behalf of the oppressed tribes and races,

we may conduct foreign missions, we may sympathise with the cause of unfortunate nationality, but it is our people who have the first claim on us.[1]

With the British Navy in such a dominating position, he was sympathetic to the idealists in the Party who wanted a part of the national revenue diverted from the 'ruinous waste' of armaments towards pensions and other social welfare schemes. And despite the fact that Fisher's programme of changes had been carried through with an actual reduction in the estimates, the Admiralty were asked for further reductions for 1906-7, specifically the dropping of one 'Dreadnought' from the four which the previous Conservative government had stated as the necessary annual output. Fisher agreed; while he had one 'Dreadnought' battleship and three battle cruisers in various states of construction, no European Power had even laid one down. As Campbell-Bannerman put it, 'The man who has had an ample dinner, as much as he can digest, does not make himself stronger by going on eating dinners in order to impress other people.'[2]

The leader of the Conservative Party, Balfour, attacked this cut-back, pointing out to a largely hostile audience in the House of Commons, that the British Fleet was for defensive purposes and theirs—implying Germany's but saying the 'Continentals' '—were not for defensive purposes alone.

'Why not?'

'Because their shores are unassailable, partly for geographical reasons and partly for the reason that they have great land armies which would make invasion by any maritime Power absolutely ludicrous and futile. Therefore their navies are not needed to defend their shores—not wholly or mostly needed to defend their shores, and if there is to be a diminution of armaments it must begin with those whose armaments are kept up for purposes not purely defensive ... This is the warning I give, I give it in all sincerity. If we, the late government, erred by having too large armaments, we erred in the patriotic belief that those armaments were necessary ... But do not, in answer to abstract reasoning, based on no consideration of the real necessities of the case, plunge into a reckless course of diminishing the forces on which your dignity and security ultimately depend.'[3]

This was, of course, Fisher's view. He regarded war as the

ultimate waste and misery with quite as much passion as the most pacifist Liberals, horrified as they were at his fierce-face solutions.

Meanwhile his reforms had provoked even fiercer arguments within the Service itself. For his onslaught on Tirpitz's strategy had been an onslaught on much that had seemed permanent in the routines and habits of the Royal Navy, and the changes had been forced through with few concessions to conservative opinion—indeed many of his moves had seemed designed to alienate the older hands; as in his time in the Mediterranean, he had sought ideas and results from whatever rank or age group could provide them most scientifically and had packed the Admiralty with a group of brilliant young officers known as the 'Fishpond'. Those who didn't fit or couldn't think in his terms were pitched out; senior Admirals were confronted with faits accompli instead of consultation. Worst of all he gloated over his methods, the officers whose wives he intended to widow, whose houses he would reduce to dung-heaps, and was unrepentant about the 'Fishpond': 'Favouritism is the secret of efficiency'. All this was most un-British and thoroughly unsettling to the senior and retired members of the finest Club in the world.

Besides the offensive manner of the reorganisation and of the man behind it, the changes themselves—which had not been explained—seemed to strike at the roots of the Service. The Jamaica base, known to generations of officers ever since there had been a Royal Navy, abolished, Bermuda reduced, Halifax and Esquimault closed, hundreds of small craft wiped out of commission at the stroke of a pen; where would the small ships necessary for protecting Britain's merchant shipping life-lines in war be found? Nelson had said that 'Frigates' would be found engraved on his heart when he died; had Fisher forgotten the despair felt by all British fleet commanders in the great French wars at the shortage of small craft? As for the 'Dreadnought' policy, it was madness. It cancelled out fifteen years of determined and costly battleship building, for by reducing to the second rank all those ships in which Britain had such a preponderance and allowing all nations to start level in the new capital ship stakes, Fisher was simply inviting a resurgence of naval competition. It was the part of the British Navy to follow, not lead—to watch other countries' building, then to use their own greater resources to overtake. To actually initiate change and spur others on was folly and absolutely contrary—so they argued with scant regard for history—to the policies which had guided British Boards of Admiralty throughout the last century.

There were other changes of emphasis, not so obvious, but equally subversive of the best traditions of the Service. Preparation for war instead of 'house-maiding' and other peace routines was admirable as an object, but the manner in which it was being promoted seemed to threaten the independence of Commanders-in-Chief and the spirit of their squadrons. This was particularly evident in gunnery. A new post, Inspector of Target Practice, had been created for the great gunner, Percy Scott—a leading member of the 'Fishpond'— so that gunnery innovations could be disseminated throughout the fleet, practices and competitions standardised and results usefully compared; previously each squadron had got on with its practices and prize firings as its commander thought best. The arrival of Sir Percy and his minions to watch and comment and report back to Fisher appeared to the fiercely individualistic Admirals as a system of centrally-organised spying. The introduction of the Press as an aid to competition was another malignant departure; the points each ship and squadron achieved in the annual prize firing and the new long-range test called Battle Practice were now reported in the national papers, and analysed; those ships and squadrons and gunnery officers at the top were held up for public admiration, those at the bottom exposed to public censure. The results were certainly astonishing: records in speed and accuracy of fire were set up and as quickly broken until shooting began to look too easy and harder conditions, longer ranges were demanded. But the wild rivalry created the feeling that results and ideas to improve performance in the artificial conditions of peace tests counted unduly in an officer's record, and especially the feeling that an élite of narrow-minded specialists was taking over the Service seemed to threaten the fraternity and esprit of the Navy. 'The game is more than the player of the game, the ship is more than the crew.'

It could have been argued that equally wild rivalry had animated the crack squadrons for such 'artificial' evolutions as mast and yard drill in the last decades of the previous century and had *enhanced* esprit—that centralisation, central dissemination of the latest technology, and specialisation were all inevitable in an increasingly technical Navy—that the *Dreadnought* herself was an inevitable product of gunnery specialisation. Rational argument was as little use against disaffected British Admirals as it was against Tirpitz. Underneath their splendid uniforms and Olympian hauteur were human beings with their whole way of life under threat; they reacted humanly.

The fires of resentment were stoked by an intellectual school of officers who looked to history for 'lessons' to guide them through the maze of technical change. Their prophet was Mahan; their conclusions were opposed to those of Fisher and his creatures, who they thought paid so much attention to nuts and bolts, all the facets of 'materialism', that they had lost sight of the real battle-winning factors.

> A man who had not pondered over the acts of the great leaders in wars of the past almost inevitably assumes the mental attitude of the bad workmen who complained of his tools. He naturally asks for better ships and weapons, and relies on large ships, on thick armour and on big guns ... It is only by study and reflection that an officer can come to know that victory does not depend on such things, but on the courage, the will, and the intellect of the Admiral, and on the spirit with which he inspires the officers and men of the fleet. If this be accepted as true, then the war value of a Navy is measured by the capacity of the Admirals who control it, and by the spirit which animates the Captains, officers and men rather than by the size or special characteristics of the ships.[4]

Thus wrote the leading British exponent of the 'historical' school. It was a seductive doctrine, for it had elements of truth and seemed to be supported by some of the most glorious episodes of British naval history—and even from such a recent battle as Tsushima, where Togo and his fanatically trained officers and men had annihilated a Russian Fleet deploying many more heavy guns. As the protest over Fisher's changes rose to a tumult, the 'historians' deployed their argument against the 'Dreadnought' policy. Neither speed nor heavy guns, nor the long-distance fire they implied were necessary; all detracted from the real fighting power of a ship which was measured by the volume of close-range fire from light guns carried in great numbers along the broadside, and fired rapidly in order to shatter the morale of the opposing men; it was not ships but *men* who were defeated in battle. The idea that the Royal Navy should 'play for safety' by firing at long range was 'diametrically opposed to the teaching of Nelson', and as Mahan had said, 'destroyed the mental attitude which keeps offensive power in the foreground.'[5]

This exaggeration of the moral factor came from a grotesque mis-reading of naval history and a desire—like Treitschke's—to compress the past into neat sets of universal laws. It got short shrift from practical men: Percy Scott saw no reason why the volume of fire from light guns should affect an action fought outside the range at which they would hit. His American colleague, William Sims, pointed out that as all guns, their crews and the bridge, conning tower and engine room personnel would be behind heavy armour impenetrable to light guns, neither the ship nor the men could be materially injured by small-calibre fire. Fisher's Director of Naval Ordnance reported that the *Dreadnought*, in her first Battle Practice, had thrown a total 21,250 lbs of shell in eight minutes against the top pre-Dreadnought's 15,200 lbs; more to the point she had thrown seventy-five per cent greater weight of shell into the target. British observers' reports from the Battle of Tsushima all suggested that 'the fate of the day had lain with and been entirely decided by heavy guns.'[6] And Percy Scott, commenting on the comparative ineffectiveness of long-range fire in that battle, pointed out that many people did not require such evidence to teach them that trying to conduct a fight at long range without the necessary tools for doing it with, was a useless expenditure of ammunition.[7] However, Scott's development of the tools for the job, and all the gunnery reports were highly secret and Fisher could not use any of these overwhelming arguments to sink the 'historical' school, who continued to give the emotionally dissatisfied or slighted Admirals much of their powder and shot.

One officer with a historical bent and a peculiar satisfaction with his own intellectual capacity was Captain Doveton Sturdee, Chief of Staff to Admiral Lord Charles Beresford, Commander-in-Chief, Mediterranean. Beresford himself had few pretensions to brains. He was an Irishman of a particularly gallant, capable and winning character, a splendid leader, hearty and breezy with a fund of humorous ancedotes and a charm which captivated all ranks and ratings and which had knit the Mediterranean Fleet into the 'Band of Brothers' of Nelson's ideal. He was also spoiled. His reputation and high position in Society, combined with his charm and spirit had allowed him throughout his career, to combine sailoring, socialising and political campaigning—usually against the Admiralty of the day—to a degree which would have been unthinkable for most officers. Beresford had not only got away with it, he had become a public idol; his was the sort of fighting and forthright character the British expected of their naval heroes. The Press had given him every excuse for believing he was another Nelson. He had few doubts of it. And he believed that he was destined for the supreme position in the Service.

His relationship with Fisher had never been easy. Fisher had envied his easy popularity and disapproved of his immunity to the ordinary restraints of the Service; he himself had worked and driven tirelessly to rise above the herd, and even then had been virtually unknown outside the Navy before he became First Sea Lord. Everyone in the land knew 'Charlie B'. Then both were large characters. Fisher had felt it necessary to make his own leadership quite clear when Beresford had been his Second-in-Command Mediterranean. Beresford, while allowing himself digs at the 'Asiatic' cast of Fisher's features and his yellowish skin—he was a 'mulatto', descended from a Singhalese Princess—had buckled down well and supported him enthusiastically in his campaigns for reform. But even that had created its difficulties.

> There is a good deal in what Beresford urges, but he exaggerates so much that his good ideas are unpractical, and his uncontrolled desire for notoriety alienates his brother officers ...[8]

So wrote Fisher—one of the 'brother officers'—in 1902. The differences between the two men were especially marked in their reasoning powers. Beresford altogether lacked Fisher's power of sustained thought, and his ability to grasp and hold firm to the essentials of a case; his mind was quick but not profound, and lacking capacity to separate the important from the trivial, was too often led up rambling byeways suggested by immediate impressions. His discursive fulminations about the Service gave it away; as Fisher remarked of them, 'The tongue is an unruly member, especially when it's an Irish member.'[9]

In the Mediterranean in 1905 one of Beresford's most immediate impressions was the dislike his Chief of Staff harboured for Fisher and all his works. His Second-in-Command, Sir Hedworth Lambton also disliked Fisher. He was a capable, but also a very social Admiral with a conservative outlook who put more emphasis on the traditions Fisher was outraging than on the changes the Service needed if it was to meet the challenges of the new century. Small wonder that Beresford began to feel that Fisher's reforms and the divisive partisanship he had introduced spelled ruination for the Service. In December his feelings were lifted to a more explosive personal level as Fisher was made an Admiral of the Fleet; this extended his active service and made it probable that by the time he retired as First Sea Lord Beresford would be too old to take over. Through 1906 the atmosphere in the Mediterranean flagships passed from discontent to open disaffection; the feeling percolated down to the other Captains. One of Fisher's protégés, Bacon, who had joined the fleet, reported in April of the want of loyalty among the Admirals, who 'thought they were justified in throwing discipline to the winds and agitating privately against their governing body.'[10] Fisher brought this to the attention of his First Lord 'in the interests of the Navy and its hitherto unquestioned discipline and loyalty.'[11] Among the incidents he noted were Beresford's canvassing of the Captains under his command whether or not they approved of the Board of Admiralty, and a speech he had made at an official dinner, pouring scorn on a new class of short-service men taken in to the Service for tasks that did not require a high degree of training; Beresford had proposed to parade some of these to show his guests 'the rotters their Lordships expected him to work with.' Fisher ended, 'the above needs no comment. I don't suggest any action at present, but I think it desirable the Board should be aware of what is going on.'

After the Mediterranean command the only post which Beresford could be expected to accept—apart from First Sea Lord—was Commander-in-Chief Channel, now the most prestigious appointment afloat and one which carried with it responsibility for all home forces in war. Failing this, Fisher was convinced that he meant to go ashore and lend his great reputation to the agitation against the Admiralty in the country and in parliament. Consequently, in the summer, Beresford was offered the Channel Fleet from March 1907 when Sir Arthur Wilson was due to haul down his flag.

However, in October 1906 the Admiralty announced a new distribution of home forces. Following the policy of a gradual build-up of the most powerful units to face Germany, the 'nucleus crew' ships in the three main home ports, together with six fully-manned battleships—taken from the Channel, Atlantic and Mediterranean fleets—were to be combined with six fully-manned armoured cruisers into a new Home Fleet based on Sheerness. Immediately there was a howl of protest from the forces arrayed against Fisher.

Already that summer the Admiralty had announced a reduction of one more capital unit from the Estimates in order to set an example in armaments limitation before a second Hague Peace Conference which was to be held the following year; together with the previous dropping of a battleship on the ground of economy this left only two from the four the Conservatives had thought necessary —although it had been agreed that the third ship would be restored if the Hague Conference proved abortive. Now that the Channel Fleet was to be weakened to provide for a new force composed largely of 'nucleus crew' vessels which the critics alleged could not be ready for instant action, and therefore constituted an 'unready fleet', Fisher was attacked as a creature of the Liberal 'Little Englanders' who were prepared to weaken the Navy for the sake of economy. And when another reorganisation was announced which further weakened the Channel Fleet by combining all home waters destroyers and submarines into an independent command, the anger rose to a crescendo. On the facts the alarm was ludicrous; as the German Naval Staff knew only too well the overwhelming British preponderance and concentration in home waters made any thought of attack insane for years to come. Nevertheless the criticisms mounted into a crisis of confidence for the Board—which was of course Fisher. Fisher's own policy of never explaining and treating his critics as if they were both incompetent and malicious didn't help. Viscount Esher, a confidant of the King and all men of real influence in the country, and an ardent Fisherite, wrote to counsel him and assure him of his support right or wrong.

> Just now it is *you* who are the national asset, not your opinions ... *But* I deprecate, if you will allow me to say so, your *method* in dealing with these opponents ... (who) should be answered and argued with. Not by you personally but by people properly coached to do it ... In a country like ours, governed by discussion, a great man is never hanged. He hangs himself. Therefore pray be Machiavellian, and play upon the delicate instrument of public opinion with your fingers and not with your feet ...[12]

Later, he met Fisher and discussed the issues in more detail, writing afterwards to his son:

> He (Fisher) expounded for my benefit his strategical plans, especially in view of a hostile Germany. They are too secret to write down.

He sits still under calumny, because to reply would necessarily entail revelation of our strength and the main strategical idea. In point of fact our power is six times that of Germany at the given point of battle. He discussed with me his own position, and the difficulties raised by his enemies, and his danger from their animosity.[13]

Beresford's animosity was by now at boiling point. Not only was Fisher occupying the only position he really coveted, but the Channel Fleet which he had accepted as a powerful force of sixty-seven warships of all classes was to be a mere twenty-one battleships and cruisers for his own tenure of command. He saw Fisher's enmity behind the reorganisation. In part he was right. Fisher suffered neither fools nor traitors. Beresford, once a fine sea officer, had passed his peak; his plan for battle against Rozhestvensky's fleet after the Dogger Bank incident had indicated to Fisher and the Board a dangerous failure to grasp the first principle of war; he could not match up to Sir Arthur Wilson. As he was also open in his contempt for the reforms which Fisher so vehemently believed in, it would have been surprising if Fisher had not sought to deal him a blow where it hurt most—in his overweening vanity. As a close observer of Fisher put it, 'I do not think we should exactly define him if we said he was vindictive in the ordinary, narrow, personal way. But that the spirit of vengeance was not absent from his composition during the naval controversies I think we must admit.'[14]

On hearing of the reorganisations proposed Beresford cancelled his previous acceptance of the Channel Fleet. Fisher would have been willing to let him go—with all the consequences for increased agitation that were bound to follow—but took advice that in the present situation, surrounded by a host of enemies, conciliation would be the better part. So he listened to what Beresford had to say about the unbalanced fleet he was to inherit, agreed that:

1. Lord Charles Beresford is a greater man than Nelson.
2. No one knows anything about the art of naval war except Lord Charles Beresford.
3. The Admiralty haven't done a single d—d thing right![15]

And having disposed of the preliminaries, he assured Beresford that he could have both the Home and Atlantic Fleets and forty-eight destroyers and attendant scouts whenever he wanted them for training exercises, although these would not normally be a part of the Channel Fleet. On these terms Beresford accepted. Before taking up his appointment he went on leave to America where his younger brother had died, leaving him a small fortune. Fisher commented on his absence, 'We can sleep quiet in our beds. That bolt from the blue can't be coming or "the one man on whom all depends" would surely ask that some other Admiral should take his place!'[16]

As thorns for Beresford's ample flesh Fisher produced Vice-Admiral Sir Reginald Custance as Second-in-Command Channel, and Rear-Admiral Sir Percy Scott for the Channel cruisers. Custance was a leading light of the 'historical' school, and had been firing envenomed darts, particularly against the 'Dreadnought' policy from the pages of *Blackwoods Magazine*. Fisher detested him and knew that Beresford also disliked him. Sir Percy was, of course, one of the strongest swimmers in the 'Fishpond', and one who enjoyed considerable popularity for the marvellous things he had done for fleet gunnery during his time as Inspector of Target Practice; the *average* percentage of hits to rounds fired was now above the *record* set by Scott's own ship at the turn of the century, while the top ships were making better practice at nearly four miles than Scott's had made at fourteen hundred yards. If anyone could be expected to steal some of the limelight from Lord Charles, it was Percy Scott. In this respect the appointment was to exceed Fisher's wildest expectations.

However, Custance's appointment proved a disaster. Beresford's hostility towards Fisher overrode all lesser feelings, while his ambition and vanity were ideal weaknesses for the intellectual Custance to exploit in his own campaign against Fisher and all 'materialists'. The two men and Doveton Sturdee, who came with Beresford as his Chief of Staff, were soon united in a common cause against the Board of Admiralty, which began to make the previous Mediterranean agitation seem half-hearted.

Beresford opened the campaign with a series of letters to the First Lord and to various men in high positions suggesting that the Home Fleet was a fraud on the public and a danger to the Empire, and that the unbalanced nature of the Channel Fleet and the lack of war plans constituted an equally grave danger. These ideas were common currency among Fisher's opponents, but the lack of written war plans was not public property and Beresford's use of it is evidence of the determined conspiracy Fisher was up against. In fact Beresford's illustrious predecessor had worked out plans with Fisher for the crisis that had arisen with Germany over the last few years, but neither had divulged them to a soul, regarding secrecy and surprise as 'the pith and marrow of war'. As for putting them to paper, this would have been unthinkable to either man. The Fleet was not like an army which required detailed staff work for co-ordination and supply; each ship carried with it everything it needed, and constant exercises in peace accustomed each Captain so far as possible to take his place in the overall scheme. However, to answer the criticisms of lack of war plans Fisher had set up a Committee in the summer of 1906 which had rushed out a set of printed Plans for War against Germany, and these were ready before Beresford returned from his extended leave in America to take over the Channel Fleet—some time *after* Sir Arthur Wilson had left.

These first documented War Plans against Germany suggested two chief strategies, either a distant commercial blockade carried out by cruisers and submarines cordoning off the Straits of Dover and the northern North Sea exits supported by the main battle fleet concentrated in an East Coast port, or if this did not bite sufficiently hard, a close blockade by cruisers and flotilla craft of the German coastline of the North Sea and Baltic, and the blocking of the mouth of the Elbe with hulks and older warships; to enforce close blockade the battle fleet would be divided so that both Baltic and North Sea blockading craft were supported by heavy ships within six to eight hours' steaming. This second alternative carried obvious risks; its merit lay in cutting off Germany's Baltic trade from neutral ships as well as all her Atlantic trade. A further Plan C envisaged even more offensive action, seizing two Frisian Islands off the mouth of the Elbe, and two Baltic Islands, bombarding Kiel, and finally attacking the German fleet inside Kiel.

These plans probably bore little relation to Fisher's. It is even possible that Fisher encouraged the idea of close blockade—which had been proved practically impossible under modern conditions—in the hope that the Germans would learn of it through their network of agents; it is even possible that he made sure they did hear of it; this was about the time he supplied them with false information on the battlecruisers of the *Invincible* class which caused Tirpitz's Construction Department to design and build an obsolete armoured cruiser, the *Blücher*.

Certainly the *Admiralstab's* own 1906 Plans for the war against England envisaged the British fleet making an immediate sortie into German waters—this despite the fact that German strategists were already questioning the Royal Navy's need for such a risky policy and suggesting that its wisest course, rather than separate her forces in an inevitably costly battle against German coastal defences, would be to decoy the German Fleet to sea and 'there to strike'. This was Sir Arthur Wilson's view. Commenting on the printed Plans, he said there were two courses open to the British Fleet, either to stop the enemy coming out of his harbours, or to tempt him out and try to catch him at sea. The first alternative would be difficult and costly to maintain, and if effective 'would bring us no nearer to the end'.[17] Fisher noted 'This is Admiral Yamamoto's secretly expressed opinion based on the Japanese naval study of the question of war between England and Germany'.[18] Wilson thought that the second course of tempting them out, if skilfully conducted with North Sea sweeps by the battle fleet in full strength at irregular intervals would prove the most effective in the long run.

The Preamble to the War Plans, written by the brilliant naval historian, Julian Corbett, said much the same:

> It is obvious therefore that since the flotilla has acquired battle power our old maxim of seeking out the enemy's fleet requires modification, and still more so the kindred tradition that the proper place for our fleet is the enemy's coast ... It would seem therefore that the old maxim should be varied somewhat in this way: *The first aim in a naval war is to devise some means of forcing the enemy's fleet to expose itself to being struck by our own, and that in waters as unfavourable to him as possible.*[19]

In view of all these pointers it cannot be doubted that the 'Plans' were nothing more than a rushed tactic against Fisher's British enemies. In this light the section of the Preamble devoted to the distribution of the British Fleet is interesting. Corbett was a seeker after truth who had little use for the dogmas of the 'historical' school critics of Fisher, and this section represents Fisher's own views.

> Strategical concentration at sea in time of peace is not the same thing as tactical concentration for battle ashore, as an unscholarly habit of thought is too often apt to assume. It does not mean

massing all your available forces in one body. It means distributing your fleet so as to ensure the greatest number of strategical combinations that there is any likelihood of your requiring. It means distributing it so as to ensure the best training, so as to give Flag officers the best opportunities of independent command and the Service generally the chance of getting familiar with as many probable battle grounds as possible ... it means the power of rapid and unostentatious massing of any force required at the moment relations become severely strained ... Though we cannot tell exactly where the first strain will come there must be a point where the tension is greatest, and there must the chain be stoutest. Hence the creation of the Home Fleet and its gradual and unostentatious increase of strength against which diplomacy is powerless to complain ...

As Fisher explained it to King Edward:

Our only probable enemy is Germany. Germany keeps her whole Fleet always concentrated within a few hours of England. We must therefore keep a Fleet twice as powerful concentrated within a few hours of Germany. If we keep the Channel and Atlantic Fleets *always* in the English Channel ... this would meet the case, but this is neither feasible nor expedient, and if, when relations with foreign powers were strained, the Admiralty attempt to take the proper precautions and move our Channel and Atlantic Fleets to their proper fighting position, then *at once* the Foreign Office and the government veto it, and say that such a step will precipitate war![20]

To Beresford, these arguments were simply excuses for relieving him of his ships; here he is writing to King Edward's private secretary a month after hoisting his flag in the Channel Fleet battleship, *King Edward VII*:

I am most distressed and alarmed at the complete absence of organisation and preparation for war in the Fleet. It is a danger to the State, and if Germany attacked us suddenly she would inflict terrible disasters on us and she might win. My predecessor had sixty-seven ships, although I can find no plans as to what they had to do: I have only twenty-one—at the moment thirteen. The Home Fleet is the greatest fraud ever perpetrated on the public and every single Admiral that knows anything about war is of the same opinion. I am very much perturbed in my mind whether I ought to remain here, struggling to get some sort of plan effected, or go straight out and tell the people the facts as I did before ... I am doing the best I can to help authority to get things right, but it will be absolutely impossible under the present allocation of ships and fleets ...[21]

Although Beresford's fleet, reduced as it was, could have taken on and should have beaten the total force of battleships and cruisers available to Germany, his Plans forwarded to the Admiralty involved more warships than the Royal Navy possessed! Egged on by Custance and Sturdee, who opined that they were 'living over a live mine', he declaimed to all who would listen that the Empire was in jeopardy.

Fisher fumed.

The truth is that such language on the part of Lord Charles Beresford and Captain Sturdee, besides being insubordinate, is perfectly preposterous, and when used, as it freely is, in general conversation, it is most baneful in its effects on the personnel of the fleet in fostering a spirit of disloyalty towards the Admiralty. It is certainly a great blow to discipline that such disloyalty should be overlooked. Our superiority over Germany is so overwhelming and the superiority of our personnel and gunnery practice is so great that the Germans know it would be madness for them to provoke a war. Captain Dumas, our naval attaché in Berlin, confirmed this opinion by a most convincing conversation yesterday. One-third of the crews in every German man-of-war are newly entered raw recruits, one-third are under two years' service ...[22]

However, with the Liberals disunited over the naval question, and under attack from the Conservatives for not building more Dreadnoughts Fisher found no support for dismissing Beresford. Instead a Conference was arranged at the Admiralty between the First Lord, Fisher and Beresford in an attempt to clear the air.

When they met in July Beresford was asked to explain his rambling letter to the First Lord that the Home Fleet was a fraud and a danger to the State. Beresford, without his two advisers, asked if the letter had been official, then explained that it had been merely a private letter; 'We have all written much stronger stuff than that on important questions of that sort. I suppose you all laughed at that and said "That is Stuff". It was only a term. If we went to war suddenly you would find it is true. If I had said officially that the Admiralty had created that, or if I had pitched into the Admiralty about it, that would be different ...'[23]

'What you want to say to us now is "You must not take my letter in this way, I was only doing it as giving you a friendly criticism, and not meaning you to take it as anything insubordinate"?'

'Certainly. That I had any notion of insubordination I absolutely deny. That letter of mine to the First Lord has absolutely no right to go before the Board ...'

Eventually the talk moved to Beresford's complaints of lack of cruisers and destroyers to train together as one force. Fisher pointed out that he had the destroyers whenever he wanted them for exercises, but nevertheless offered him another two armoured cruisers and two divisions of destroyers and attendant vessels. Beresford replied, 'On those lines I will let you know. If I have a fleet which is a striking force ...'

'It is no use haggling over terms and descriptions like this,' Fisher cut him short, 'The whole sea force comes under you as senior Commander-in-Chief and comes under you each year during exercises and as Sir Charles Hardinge said to me this morning, speaking of the Hague Conference, it is perfectly ridiculous to think that anything can happen in the shape of a sudden, treacherous attack on the Fleet without some preliminary strained relations.'

'That is a matter of opinion. It is most unlikely that this house in which we now are is going to be burned down, but it is possible.'

'I do not suppose that you are not working for the good of the State ...'

'Only we differ,' Beresford cut in. 'You are here doing your level best and I have got to go out and do war duty. I tell you what I think, the only thing I can do. I never go back on my opinion.'

The First Lord came in: 'If you had said what were your reasons, but to say without giving your reasons that our policy is a fraud and a danger to the Empire, that is pretty hot.'

'You have not got it officially. You cannot say that. If I said that officially you would say, "You can go!"'

So the discussion circled, Beresford refusing to admit the insubordinate language which he had committed to so many letters, unable to substaniate his charges of 'fraud and danger to the Empire', unable even to make up his mind about the extra cruisers and the destroyers he was being offered. 'I cannot see the thing straight off ... I never come to a conclusion myself without I think. On principle, being a public man I never say a thing straight off. Have those ships you are going to give me nucleus crews?'

'No, they are fully manned.'

At long last he accepted the additional ships and the meeting broke up on a note of forced geniality, Beresford insisting that he did not dictate to the Board of Admiralty for the Board was the constituted authority, and he had never written officially or privately except in the most respectful manner!

It was a short-lived truce. The same month the results of the annual Gunlayer's test were published. Pro-Fisher newspapers commented on the low position of the Channel Fleet, seventh out of the eight fleets or squadrons, and drew attention to the particularly low position of the Channel Fleet flagships, comparing their results with the good shooting of the Home Fleet flagships! The previous year the *King Edward VII* had come second in the Fleet in the heavy Gunlayer's test.

Percy Scott, taking up his appointment that month in command of Beresford's cruisers, found himself entering 'an atmosphere of suspicion, animosity and discord ... it was soon made apparent to me that I was expected to acquiesce in the views of the malcontents, and to join in the crusade against authority ...'[24]

Meanwhile the delegates to the second Peace Conference met at the Hague. As at the first Conference cynicism was more apparent than determination to grapple with the real problems of European peace. It could not have been otherwise; Germany and Russia had both refused to discuss limitation of armaments, Russia because she still had an enormous programme to make good her losses in the Japanese war, Germany because she intended to complete her Naval Law, and regarded 'limitation' as a diplomatic ploy designed to prevent it. The naval rivalry overshadowed everything.

The British Liberal government was sincere about wanting limitation. The burden of armaments was intolerable when so much was needed in the social field. The Foreign Secretary, Sir Edward Grey, thought the expenditure on armaments so great 'that in a sense we suffer every year that depression of national life which is itself one of the worst conditions of war ...'[25] The Prime Minister, Campbell-Bannerman, wrote a long article on armaments limitation which assumed that everyone recognised how futile and self-defeating was 'the endless multiplication of the engines of war'. If the struggle for sea power was continued, he could see no end to it but economic exhaustion.

> We have already given an earnest of our sincerity (in limitation) by the considerable reductions that have been effected in our naval and military expenditure as well as by the undertaking that we are prepared to go further if we find a similar disposition in other quarters. Our delegates, therefore, will not go into the Conference empty-handed. It has, however, been suggested that our example will count for nothing, because our preponderant naval position will remain unimpaired. I do not believe it. The sea power of this country implies no challenge to any single State or group of States. I am persuaded that throughout the world that power is recognised as non-aggressive and innocent of designs against the independence, the commercial freedom and the legitimate development of other States ...[26]

Such hopeful ideas were turned to good account in Germany; here is Tirpitz at his most cordial and subtle, talking to the British naval attaché, Captain Dumas, who had called his attention to the strong comments in German newspapers reflecting Britain's honesty of purpose in proposing limitation. Tirpitz agreed that the papers were wrong; the British government was perfectly sincere.

> But our people don't and will never understand such a scheme. I myself realise the puritan form of thought possessed by Sir Henry Campbell-Bannerman and that he is perfectly honest and feels it a religious duty, but look at the facts. Here is England, already more than four times as strong as Germany, in alliance with Japan, and probably so with France, and you, the colossus, come and ask Germany, the pygmy, to disarm. From the point of view of the public it is laughable and Machiavellian and we shall never agree to anything of the sort.
>
> Also look at the past year—what have you done? Why you have built faster than you have ever done before and we—why, we have gone quietly on with our programme of old construction and laid down nothing new at all. Which country has done anything, yours or mine? I am prepared to acknowledge it as a correct religious aspiration, but not for practical people who live in this world. We have decided to possess a fleet and that fleet I propose to build and keep strictly to my programme.[27]

Tirpitz did not, of course, reveal that the reason he had laid down nothing that year was because the *Dreadnought* had caught his construction department on the wrong foot, nor that he was preparing to introduce another *Novelle* to increase the ultimate size of the fleet. Nevertheless, he had a good point in the overwhelming superiority of the British Navy, one which he and Bülow, Wilhelm and the German Navy League and the German delegates to the Peace Conference played on endlessly. The British Admiralty tacitly conceded it in their own appreciation of naval limitation:

> From the selfish standpoint of pure opportunism it seems clear that our present relative naval position is so good that we might express our adhesion to the principle on condition that other countries were willing to do likewise.[28]

However, the Admiralty had not altered their opinion for the earlier Conference that the practical difficulties of limitation were likely to be overwhelming, and the chief of these was lack of force to enforce the decrees of Conference.

> The notorious hostility of Germany to any limitation of armaments is also a stumbling block which bids fair to effectually frustrate the pious intentions of the advocates of limitation. For how can this country, or still more France, agree to check the growth of her Navy while a potential enemy as enterprising and unscrupulous as Germany is adding ship to ship in this ruthless game of naval beggar-my-neighbour?[29]

When this was put to Tirpitz by Captain Dumas, who pointed out that many people in England felt that the German Navy was being prepared for a war with England, the great man became very excited.

'Good heavens! What have I ever said or done to give rise to such an opinion. If I had wished for or harboured such designs I could have doubled our Navy last year, whereas in fact I have done nothing of the sort. Besides, how could I dream of attacking England with a Navy less than a quarter the size. I have too high a respect for your officials to believe that such an opinion can be seriously entertained.'[30]

He went on to point out that such an attack would inevitably result in the temporary commercial ruin of Germany, and therefore be a crime and a bad blunder.

'I love England. My wife and daughter were educated there and I have numerous friends there. It is impossible to imagine that Germany and I or my countrymen could be suspected.' His brows contracted into a look of suspicion which the British attachés knew well. 'It would be easier to understand that Germany might fear the designs of England who—*I know*—offered to lend France 288,000 men last spring. But that help would have been useless against the four million men Germany can put in the field.'

The arguments were inevitably circular; the enormous British lead and the ruthless German ambition made them so.

Meanwhile another argument had been added to the German armoury. Bülow had given it official currency in a long speech to the *Reichstag* in November 1906 during which he warned London, Paris and St Petersburg of the danger of trying to encircle Germany. 'A policy directed at German encirclement, the creation of a ring of Powers around Germany to isolate and cripple her, that would be a policy dangerous to the peace of Europe.' Wilhelm, translating it into personal terms, was convinced that his Uncle Edward, was behind this baneful intrigue; it had all started with his visit to Paris. And reversing all facts in the peculiar, revealing style of Imperial Germany, Wilhelm fulminated on his Uncle's envy of Germany and spite, and his habit every morning at breakfast of searching the papers for news of his (Wilhelm's) doings so that he could scheme how best to outdo them. He wanted the newspapers to talk only of the King of England!

The idea that Edward VII was behind all Germany's troubles was convenient for everyone in Court and political circles; it provided a scapegoat for the collapse of German naval and world policy, and the bitter isolation in which they found themselves. It was accepted as fact. Bülow, caught as ever between the need to weld the Empire together with a strong, outward-looking policy, and the dangers which such a policy was bound to produce, appealed in the *Reichstag* for calm. 'In Germany we are all becoming nervous, both Right and Left, above and below.'[32]

As if to confirm this in the spring of 1907 King Edward VII only had to visit the King of Spain and rumours flooded Berlin that war was about to break out between England and Germany. The Berlin Stock Exchange dropped six points. Even foreign Embassies were not immune from the fever. The Belgian Ambassador reported:

> Like the Treaty of Alliance with Japan, the *Entente Cordiale* with France and the negotiations pending with Russia, the King of England's visit to the King of Spain is one of the moves in the campaign to isolate Germany that is being conducted with as much perseverance as success by H.M. King Edward VII ...[33]

The 'encirclement' legend provided Germany with a perfect argument for her naval policy, and it was used both internally to strengthen waverers and convert Social Democrats, and externally as a counter-attack on the British 'limitation' gambit at the Hague Conference. Here was England, intriguing to isolate and contain Germany within a ring of alliances—now planning to disarm her as well! England, who had just added the *Dreadnought*, the most powerful battleship in the world, to the most powerful fleet in the world—England was suggesting that Germany who had scarcely started to create her fleet and who had no naval allies of any consequence, should stop! The British could not be serious; it was simply a diplomatic move to shift the odium of refusal at the Hague on to Germany. The German Foreign Office made it clear to Sir Edward Grey that if the proposal for limitation of armaments were brought forward Germany would know that it was the work of her enemies and a plan to put her in an awkward position.

Grey could not understand the German argument. It seemed clear to him that 'encirclement' was a myth with 'no origin in truth';[34] the negotiations he was conducting with Russia were defensive, chiefly to settle the differences between the two nations in Persia and safeguard the Indian border. As for the great strength of the Royal Navy, it was as clear to him as to any navalist that it had to be superior as its defensive function required it to be able to take the offensive and drive an enemy off the sea! Britain could be starved into submission without a single enemy soldier landing on her shore. This was not the case with Germany; her equivalent was the greatest army in the world. He was willing to concede Wilhelm's and Bülow's repeated point that each State had the right to decide for itself the amount of force it considered necessary for the protection of its interests, but he considered the question not one of right, but of expediency. If Germany continued to take the high line that her naval expenditure concerned only herself, then Britain would be bound to go on building to keep ahead of her; the relative positions would remain the same but the cost for both would be ruinous.

Kaiser Wilhelm II, dressed as Admiral of the British Fleet.
Radio Times Hulton Picture Library

Bernhard von Bülow (*above left*) and Admiral Alfred von Tirpitz
(*below*), the pilots for the Kaiser's 'new course'. *Radio Times
Hulton Picture Library*

The dynamic 'Jackie' Fisher as a Captain in the years before the German challenge began. *Radio Times Hulton Picture Library*

King Edward VII. *Radio Times Hulton Picture Library*

With the launch of the *Dreadnought* in 1906, Fisher introduced a new element into the 'naval race'. *Radio Times Hulton Picture Library*

HMS *Dreadnought*, the ultimate great-gun battery. *Radio Times Hulton Picture Library*

British fleet reviews in the Solent in 1907 (*above*) and Spithead 1911 (*below*). *Imperial War Museum*

1. Lothringen	7. K. Karl der Grosse	13. Ersatz Sachsen	19. K. Barbarossa
2. Elsass	8. K. Wilhelm der Grosse	14. Zähringen	20. Hessen
3. Deutschland	9. K. Wilhelm II	15. Wettin	21. Hannover
4. Nassau	10. Ersatz Baden	16. Mecklenburg	22. Pommern
5. Ersatz Würtemberg	11. K. Friedrich III	17. Schwaben	23. Schlesien
6. Braunschweig	12. Wittelsbach	18. Preussen	24. Schleswig-H...

The Kaiser's Dreadnoughts: The German Battle Fleet as it Will Be in 1910

DRAWN BY DAVID B. WATERS

The naval 'scare' of 1908; the *Daily Graphic*'s prediction of the German fleet in 1910. *Radio Times Hulton Picture Library.*

The German pre-dreadnought battleship *Preussen. Imperial War Museum*

'A Signal Indiscretion': *Punch* cartoon of 1907 satirizing the Beresford-Scott feud. 'Now then, Charles, my boy, if you *must* box Percy's ears, you might wait till my visitor's gone.' *Reproduced by kind permission of* Punch

Charles William de
la Poer Beresford,
as a Captain.
*Radio Times Hulton
Picture Library*

Portrait of Percy
Scott as a Captain.
Courtesy of
HMS Excellent

The young Winston Churchill. *Radio Times Hulton Picture Library*

Two men struggling against a fate they could not resist: Edward
Grey (*left*), Bethman-Hollweg (*right*). *Radio Times Hulton Picture
Library*

Winston Churchill and Admiral Fisher going to the launch of
the Dreadnought *Centurion* in 1911. *Radio Times Hulton Picture
Library*

1914: Wilhelm II at Kiel with Archduke Franz Ferdinand of Austria; in the background Grand Admiral von Tirpitz (with forked beard). *Radio Times Hulton Picture Library*

The end of a dream: The German battle cruiser *Hindenburg* after being scuttled at Scapa Flow. *Imperial War Museum*

But he saw no point in causing unpleasantness or scoring quick but ultimately negative points in such a vital game, so he adopted an indirect approach. His instructions to the delegates at the Hague stressed that while the British government wanted limitation raised, the 'apparently final declaration of the German government that they would take no part in such a discussion'[35] meant that the question must be left untouched. Should the matter come up for discussion, however, the British delegation was to propose that the great Powers should communicate their programmes of naval construction to each other in advance. He hoped this would provide opportunities for negotiation before the governments were publicly committed to their programmes, bring home just how much each country's programme was dependent on others, and eventually achieve a pragmatic limitation.

In Parliament he again expressed his despair at 'what is almost the pathetic helplessness of mankind under the burden of armaments.'[36] And discussing the pressure from the Radical wing of his Party in favour of Great Britain setting a more vigorous example in disarmament, he said that while such courageous action might lead to reform 'there is also a chance that it might lead to martyrdom. We must proceed at such a pace as will carry the leading countries of the world with us.'

Social reformers were unimpressed; they cared as little for the trend of German thought as Tirpitz for British naval thought and what they had heard they dismissed as malicious propaganda from the Northcliffe Press. It was evident to them that reasonable men of goodwill sitting around a table could settle the question of armaments for the benefit of the whole of mankind—equally evident that Great Britain should and could well afford to take the lead. Grey, in Lloyd George's words, was a 'cold fish'. For some the conversion came later, but others never did realise that reason provided no arguments against men committed to force.

The German delegation, led by Baron Marschall von Bieberstein was even more arrogant in its determination to bring healthy realism to the hypocrisy and idealism of disarmament than its predecessors in 1899. It was not alone in its view. The British Foreign Office, Admiralty, and Conservative Party, the Russians, and the French were equally sceptical of the practicability of limitation; most thought, like Bülow, that the 'great diversity which characterises the geographical, military, economic and political positions of the

various countries'[37] made any outside attempts to dictate the amount
of force each nation required, not only impossible but likely to
lead to great friction. The Germans were not content to think this
to themselves. As crass in the logic of *Realpolitic* as so many British
Liberals in utopianism they made a virtue and a weapon of their
belief, openly treating the Conference as a diplomatic battleground,
terrorising the smaller European nations into supporting their view,
bringing home to moderate men the reality of the legend of a
'militarist Germany, steeped in the spirit of caste and of barrack
discipline, bowed under the absolute will of a Monarch, rigid in its
mighty armour ...'[38] They scorned the known British desire for a
reduction in armaments as purely selfish and hypocritical. As
Marschall wrote to Bülow:

> Freedom, humanity and civilisation. And the world is convinced.
> These three catchwords are not the common property of all nations.
> They are the monopoly of England; when they are employed by
> England they exercise an irresistible attraction upon large masses
> of people throughout the whole world. Herein lies one of the
> elements of British strategy. One cannot feel a grudge against
> Englishmen if they exploit the situation to the best of their
> ability ...[39]

The Conference was doomed before it started. In the event Grey's
proposal for prior consultation between the Powers on their naval
programmes was put by the leader of the British delegation after a
humanitarian speech dwelling on the hope among all nations and
'all poets, prophets and inspired souls'[40] for a return of a golden age
of universal peace. Marschall saw the proposal as yet another
attempt by England to 'retain by diplomacy what she was in danger
of losing by competition.'[41]

As for limitation, this was dismissed in deference to the German
view with the hope that all Powers would study the question.
Compulsory arbitration instead of a resort to arms, also opposed by
Germany, was agreed but only in principle; again the Powers were
asked to study the details further. The Conference proved a triumph
for realism; few illusions survived the experience. As one British
delegate noted, it had served to confirm 'the fact that the Powers
are constantly preparing for war. It has not given a greater sense of
security, but rather the reverse.'[42] The voting had followed the
pattern of European rivalries, Austria and Germany against the

Entente and Russia, now joined by the United States—a confirmation for the German delegation that the whole exercise had been a British plot to add to the ring around the central Powers. Before the delegates finally rose there came news of the signing of the Anglo-Russian Convention which Grey had been working for; it settled the spheres of influence of the two Powers in Persia, Afghanistan and Tibet, removing these areas from the list of political danger spots, and for Britain securing the North-West frontier of India and the northern flank of her Red Sea-Suez-Indian Ocean shipping route from Russian penetration. To Germans it was another success for King Edward's policy of encirclement.

The German Navy League made the most of it. Surrounded by such a host of enemies infected with England's envy and malice and dancing like puppets to her tune, Germany's pitifully small fleet (*Flöttchen*!) was totally inadequate for the dangers it might face at any hour. A larger programme was urgently needed, and a faster building *tempo*; six capital ships a year would scarcely be enough. The flood of articles and pamphlets representing England as the arch-enemy prompted the old Prussian, Holstein, to wonder that English distrust of Germany was not even greater.[43]

Tirpitz felt the time ripe for the next stage in his plan. A *Novelle* was necessary in any case as the need to keep up with Fisher's increases in the size and power of Dreadnoughts had added some 9 million Marks to the 1906 costs of each new battleship (now 47 million Marks as against 24 million Marks for the last pre-Dreadnoughts, an increase of 96 per cent) and no less than 14 million Marks to each battlecruiser (now 44 million Marks as against 21.3 million Marks for the pre-Dreadnought armoured cruisers, an increase of 107 per cent).[44] Once again he felt it expedient to draw attention away from his failure to keep within the financial limits of the law, and the consequent need for increased taxation, by altering the Law itself. One of the chief alterations still necessary for the 'Iron Budget' he was moving towards was a reduction of the life-span of each great ship from 25 to 20 years; he had been planning to introduce this about 1912 when the building *tempo* was due to drop to only two ships a year. Now, the feeling in the country and in the *Reichstag*, where the Social Democrats had recently suffered their first ever electoral reverses, convinced him that the political climate was right.

The chief danger in such a *Novelle* would come from England.

For a reduction in ships' life span to 20 years and the consequent replacement programme for existing older ships would mean raising the building tempo to four a year for the next four years—unless some replacements were postponed. Yet postponement might prompt sections of the *Reichstag* to ask whether, in that case, the ships were really necessary, while other 'patriotic' sections who demanded decisive action would feel the Bill totally insufficient to meet the dangers with which the *Reich* was faced.

As always, Tirpitz had been working on several different plans to meet the difficulties ever since the passage of his last *Novelle*. At first he had been against provoking England—and the *Reichstag*—with the four-tempo. As one of his close advisers put it in February 1907:

> If we go over to a four-tempo in the next few years without recognisable cause, we would not only have to bear the stigma of originating an unfruitful arms race and of being a menace to peace, for which the German Empire already has a sufficiently bad reputation, but what is far worse, the Liberal Ministry in England would be thrown out and replaced by a Conservative government, which, even assuming the best case, by vast expenditure on the fleet would take from us all prospect of catching up with English fleet power within the foreseeable future.[45]

Another large argument against the four-tempo had been the immense increases in the costs of the great ships themselves. Consequently in the spring of 1907 Tirpitz had decided to bring in the *Novelle* with some replacements postponed so that the building rate would remain at three a year. However, he had asked the Construction department if building *times* could be shortened: they had replied that the most economical rate of building was 42 months, but it would be possible, at increased cost, to complete a battleship in 36 or even 30 months. Krupp had confirmed that they could meet the demand for the heavier ordnance at such shortened building times.[46]

Speed of building had always been as much a part of Tirpitz's plan as regularity. For this was England's strong point. His earliest notes, made when he had taken over the Navy Office in 1897, had stressed it: 'The private dockyards must learn to build *quickly* in order to be competitive against *England*.'[47] Now German shipbuilding was—at least in theory—competitive.

And as soundings in the *Reichstag* through the summer of the Hague Conference revealed more enthusiasm for the fleet and fewer doubts about the necessarily higher taxes than he had dared to expect, the pressures grew on him to accept the necessity of a four-tempo, simultaneously cut down building times and quickly cross the 'Danger Zone'. Of course he was acutely aware that this might precipitate the very danger he feared; the possibility of a preventive strike by the British fleet never entirely left him. Yet the English Liberals were not the men to stage a calculated 'Copenhagen', especially after their humanitarian pose at the Hague. A more likely response would be that 'vast expenditure' which his advisers feared would destroy all prospects of Germany catching up within the foreseeable future. Against these external dangers he had to set the extremely favourable nationalistic climate within the Empire and within the *Reichstag*; such prospects for bold and patriotic measures could not be counted upon to last for ever. He felt the moment should be grasped. But above all, Tirpitz had caught a glimpse of the end of the tunnel. The Anglo-Russian agreement had buried his 'Risk' fleet notion as surely as the *Entente* and Tsushima had put paid to his 'Alliance-value' fleet, but since the *Dreadnought* it scarcely mattered. All nations started afresh in the new capital ship stakes and as each year passed the British predominance in pre-Dreadnought battleships would count for less and less. With the Liberal government in power in England the chance of shortening the Royal Navy's lead by accelerating construction was there for the seizing. As the Anglo-Russian agreement was signed and the whole nation wallowed in bitterness at 'encirclement' he made his decision to accelerate. Simultaneously Navy League agitation rose to a crescendo; against the *six*-tempo they demanded, his own four-tempo would seem moderate.

On September 21st, he visited Bülow at his villa on Nordeney to discuss the prospects. Bülow, faced with a crisis in the *Reich's* finances, due chiefly to the cost of the Navy, as well as the crisis in foreign affairs which the naval policy had provoked, was nonetheless in favour. The Bill would be popular with the 'patriotic' *bloc* he had created for government policies in the *Reichstag*, and the soaring expenditure implied might even persuade those patriots who had so far resisted paying higher taxes that they would have to bear their share of the costs of *Weltpolitik*. He recognised the danger of a massive English response cancelling out the increased rate of building, or even the possibility of war, but he hoped to lull the British government with a diplomatic offensive to persuade them that Germany sought an understanding on arms limitation and a neutrality agreement. This would be effected through informal talks, which would not be allowed to turn 'official'. So the British response might be controlled. Tirpitz agreed with the strategy.[48]

On the 29th Tirpitz had an audience with Wilhelm; a four-tempo, he explained, together with building times shortened to 30 months would give Germany a full *double-squadron* of Dreadnoughts by 1913. Wilhelm agreed to the plan enthusiastically.[49]

The scene was set for the greatest naval challenge the British had faced for over a century.

The Year of Decision

Wilhelm's relations with his Uncle Edward VII had never been cordial; his nervous desire to shine, childish vanity and shallow brilliance had always been most disagreeable to the older man, while for his part Wilhelm made no secret of his contempt for Edward's self-indulgence, especially with women. And anxious as any parvenu social climber to have his importance recognised, Wilhelm had constantly imagined that his Uncle was slighting him. Now that he also cast Edward in the role of deliberate encircler and mobiliser of world opinion against Germany, and gave free vent to his thoughts about Edward's 'Satanic' character, which inevitably found their way to Edward's ear, relations between the two men, as between their countries, reached a record low.

To try and dissipate the poisonous atmosphere, in the Summer of 1907, Wilhelm and his Empress were invited to visit Windsor in the Autumn. This suited Bülow and Tirpitz very well; the Kaiser himself would be able to open the 'peace offensive' to persuade the English that the forthcoming increase in German building tempo was not aimed against them! Accordingly Wilhelm accepted the invitation 'with much pleasure', looking forward to 'some good sport in the dear old Park we know so well.'[1] The German Press altogether lacked his enthusiasm, and as the time for the visit approached and agitation against it mounted, Wilhelm made attempts to put it off. But Edward was insistent.

So it was, early on November 11, the Imperial Yacht *Hohenzollern* approached Spithead, appropriately in dense fog; the morning was spent at 'hide-and-seek', the German pilots unable to find the Nab, British pilots sent out to guide them in unable to find the *Hohenzollern*. At last contact was made and the brilliant reception committee which had dispersed for lunch while the hunt was on, reassembled on Portsmouth South Railway jetty. Prominent among the high officials and officers glittering with rank and orders were the Admirals of the Channel Fleet—which was at Spithead to accord the Imperial couple naval honours—Lord Charles Beresford, Sir Reginald Custance and, at a suitable distance, Sir Percy Scott. Lord Charles was considerably agitated. A rumour, as it later turned out unfounded, had reached him that Custance and his Chief of Staff, Sturdee, and the Admiral commanding destroyers so recently attached to his flag were all to be transferred from his command—not only that but a story was going the rounds that it was prejudicial to an officer's career to be connected with him in Service matters. This was Fisher's doing. He turned over in his mind a stinging letter; as toned down later for official transmission it went:

> The removal of such important officers from my command at or about the same time, will add enormously to my already exceptionally hard work. Their removal cannot help me to add to the efficiency of the Fleet. It may not have been intended, but it most certainly has the appearance of a wish to handicap and hamper me in carrying out the responsibilities connected with by far the most important appointment within the Empire, that of Commander-in-Chief of the sea-going fleets and vessels in Home Waters in war time, whose duty it will be to defend the heart of the Empire ...[2]

As if Fisher's malevolence in seeking to strip him of his right hand men were not enough there was the case of his creature, Percy Scott, whose insubordinate thoughts about his Commander-in-Chief had been revealed very publicly in a recent episode christened 'the paintwork incident'; speculation about this incident had now spread from the Channel Fleet to the national Press. The morning's front pages were full of it: 'A NAVAL SENSATION', 'KAISER SLURRED BY A BRITISH COMMANDER ON EVE OF FORMER'S VISIT', 'ANGRY ADMIRALS', 'FLEET ASTOUNDED'.

> One of the most stinging public reprimands in naval history has been passed by Admiral Lord Charles Beresford, Commander-in-Chief of the Channel Fleet, on Rear-Admiral Sir Percy Scott, in command of the First Cruiser Squadron, Lord Charles has stigmatised a signal ordered by Sir Percy Scott as *contemptuous in tone and insubordinate in character*. This amazing episode ...[3]

It had occurred a week ago. The Channel Fleet had become separated in fog while steaming for Portland after tactical exercises—in which Beresford had made his contempt for the Admiralty clear by appointing Custance instead of the Commander-in-Chief Home Fleet to command the Second Division! Scott's cruisers had arrived at Portland before the main body of the Fleet, and one had anchored outside the breakwater to carry out gunnery exercises. As a memo from Lord Charles had instructed all ships to be externally painted for Wilhelm's visit, Scott made her a signal:

> Paintwork appears to be more in demand than gunnery so you had better come in in time to make yourself look pretty by the 8th inst.[4]

One and a half hours afterwards the Channel Fleet battleships under Lord Charles steamed in to harbour. Had the atmosphere in the fleet been normal nothing further would have happened. But of course Lord Charles' and Custance's flagships had already been criticised in the national Press for poor gunnery, Percy Scott, whom they both regarded as one of Fisher's 'spies' was bending all efforts to make his cruisers good shooting ships and the word 'gunnery' used by him as it was in the signal had contemptuous undertones— or so it seemed to Beresford's officers when they heard of it. So they had brought it to his attention. Beresford, inflamed by his bitter quarrel with Fisher, seeing one of his enemy's minions delivered into his hands, had sent for Scott and without allowing him a word had told him that his signal was 'pitiably vulgar, contentious in tone, insubordinate in character and wanting in dignity'.[5] After which he had ordered it expunged from the Log Books. Not content, he had followed up with a public signal rebuking Scott before every officer and man in the fleet, again characterising his 'paintwork' signal as 'contemptuous in tone and insubordinate in character.'

It was this public rebuke, on the face of it an absurd over-reaction to a perhaps ironic, scarcely insubordinate signal, which lifted the affair into the headlines and gave the public their first hint of disunity in the Navy. The *Standard* reported one Channel Fleet officer as saying that the signal was the culmination of several, and was 'a cheap sneer at Lord Charles'. Another opined that Scott had been 'put up to it.'[6] Beresford had asked that Scott be superseded; instead it seemed, his own officers were to go. As Beresford brooded

in the mist, Fisher was composing the Admiralty reply: Percy
Scott's signal was 'inexcusable' but in view of the 'grave public
censure' already administered, their Lordships had decided that
'the case will be sufficiently further dealt with by the conveyance
to Sir Percy Scott of an expression of their Lordships grave dis-
approbation', then the sting in the tail, 'it being a matter vital to
discipline and good order that perfect loyalty to superiors should
govern the conduct of all officers of the Fleet.'[7]

Saluting guns cracked and ship and shore bands struck up with
the German National Anthem as the shapely white hull of the
Hohenzollern closed the jetty. Wilhelm, in his uniform as a British
Admiral of the Fleet with his Empress, accompanied by the Prince
of Wales who had gone out to meet them wearing a German
Admiral's uniform, could be seen on the quarterdeck. When the
Yacht had made fast and speeches of welcome exchanged, Wilhelm
inspected a Guard of Honour with all his usual restless interest,
then boarded the Royal train waiting to take him to Windsor. As
it steamed out the bands struck up again, saluting guns fired, and
all the warships in harbour joined in. Beresford and Scott, watched
keenly by reporters, turned on their heels without a word and made
straight back for their flagships.

In Windsor every effort had been made to provide an impressive
welcome: everywhere along the route from the station the old-
world streets had been hung with gay bunting, flowers, evergreens
and mottoes in English and German; the station itself was a riot of
colour interspersed with Royal portraits and the German Imperial
arms. A reception committee of plumed officers in gorgeous uniforms waited on the platform and just before the train was due, King
Edward himself in the uniform of the First Prussian Dragoon
Guards, made his way to the rich red carpet laid for the Imperial
couple. Even a Thames valley fog which shut out everything beyond
the station lights could not dispel the sense of occasion and the care
lavished on the welcome. The citizens of Windsor joined in as
heartily, massed deep and cheering as—the formalities over—
Wilhelm and the King were driven in an open landau towards
the Castle, where a bold legend on a blue ground proclaimed:
'*Dem deutschen Kaiserpaar ein herzliches Willkommen*'

At the Castle, Wilhelm was greeted by the Prime Minister and
Sir Edward Grey before being conducted up the magnificent stair-
case lined with picked men from the Royal Horse Guards to the

State apartments. He was captivated; as ever the memories flooded back.

> Among these memories stands foremost the figure of my revered
> grandmother, the great Queen, whose image is imperishably en-
> graved on my heart, while the remembrance of my beloved mother
> carries me back to the earliest days of a happy childhood spent
> under the roof and within the walls of this grand old Windsor
> Castle.[8]

After good sport in the grand old Park on the second day, the high
point of the visit was a State Reception at the Guildhall in the City
of London; if the world, as he believed, was ruled from Windsor
Tower, this was the hub around which its commerce revolved.

The City had contrived a welcome more impressive even than
Windsor's: the staid buildings along the route to the Guildhall
had been transformed into a scene of carnival with floral festoons,
flags, streamers, evergreens, reds and russets of Autumn foliage,
long boxes of chrysanthemums, palm trees, statues and bright
Crowns, German Eagles, venetian masts supporting a tracery of
white flowers overhead, Royal portraits, quotations from Shake-
speare, 'Good Lady, no Court in Europe is too good for thee' crimson
banners bearing the words 'Hoch Lebe!' and artistic statues, one
showing Queen Victoria flanked by Edward VII and Wilhelm
himself, with the inscription '*Blut ist dicker als Wasser*'. The sun
was bright and the crowds deep along the sanded streets were in
holiday mood; Wilhelm's progress was marked by a continuous
rolling shout, swelling and sinking but never ceasing. Upright as
the points of his stiffened moustaches Wilhelm saluted to right and
left. He was deeply moved.

> Amongst all the magnificent decorations we were able to admire
> I saw one inscription in big letters saying 'Blood is thicker than
> water'. May this ever be so between our two countries, and may
> the City of London successfully develop under the auspicious reign
> of His Majesty King Edward VII, my beloved Uncle, whom God
> preserve![9]

His sincerity was patent, as it was when he replied to the Lord
Mayor's toast inside the Guildhall:

'When I made an address from this place sixteen years ago I said my aim is above all the maintenance of peace.' Cheers! 'History I hope will do me the justice that I have pursued this aim unswervingly ever since.' Cheers! 'The main prop and base for the peace of the world is the maintenance of good relations between our two countries, and I shall further strengthen them as far as lies in my power.' Cheers! 'The German nation's wishes coincide with mine. The future will show a bright prospect, and commerce may develop among the nations who have learned to trust one another.' Prolonged cheers![10]

It was noted that he had laid special emphasis on the words, 'my aim is above all the maintenance of peace'. Sir Edward Grey was visibly moved by this, and shook hands on the sentiment with the German Foreign Minister who was sitting beside him, both promising to do their utmost to make it good. The Press—the most anti-German among them—was similarly affected and paid tribute to Wilhelm's peaceable record since he had ascended the Throne, seeing his evident goodwill as a sign that official Germany sought reconciliation after the bad blood of recent years.

The German Press, 'informed' and otherwise, took up the refrain. The Berlin *Vossische Zeitung* thought the warmth of the exchanges 'clearly intended to frustrate the speculations of those who saw in Great Britain's manifold agreements with other nations a sign that King Edward and his government were bent on creating a great and warlike coalition against Germany,'[11] and it hoped that the peaceable and friendly expectations raised 'would be confirmed by facts'. The *Norddeutsche Allgemeine Zeitung* thought the London visit memorable not only from the extraordinary brilliance of the reception, but because friendly relations between the two countries were 'a matter of such weighty import for the development of the international situation' that Wilhelm's expression of resolve to live in peace and friendship was 'a highly momentous event'.[12]

Even in Paris where it had been feared that the visit might cause uneasiness about the *Entente*, the response was favourable. 'The importance of peace for the common development of economic and political relations of peoples—what a fine text for a Prince who knows, when he likes, how to be a charmer!'[13] The *Siècle* reported:

> The English see in him (Wilhelm) not only the scion of a dynasty which they venerate and the grandson of Queen Victoria whom they consider a great figure in their history, but they further see

and appreciate in him a Sovereign who is manifestly of a pacific temperament in the midst of the most formidable military preparations of all times. All those merchants and men of business need peace for the accomplishment of their task and they are thankful to such as maintain it. The Emperor is too well-informed and too acute not to express to those who have given him such an excellent reception the sentiments which they long to hear.[14]

Could the Darwinist model of European rivalries be giving way to views based on commercial horse sense? Not that realists, least of all the French, expected Wilhelm to translate himself into a disarmer. But his repeated emphasis on his own pacific intentions and record was encouraging. As Wilhelm left Windsor he could reflect that his visit had succeeded beyond Bülow's wildest hopes for détente with Britain. He had been perfectly sincere; England always affected him that way. Instead of returning directly to Germany he went to Highcliffe Castle, near Bournemouth, for a week as the guest of Colonel Stuart-Wortley.

The same day Tirpitz's four-tempo *Novelle* was published in the *Norddeutsche Allgemeine Zeitung*. The *Bundesrat* had been considering it while Wilhelm had been making his speeches. At once it was as if they had never been. For it needed no deep analysis to appreciate that Tirpitz was bent on creating a Dreadnought battle fleet in the shortest time. With three battleships and one battle-cruiser to be laid down each year from 1908 to 1911, and four Dreadnought battleships already started—two in July, two in August that year—he would have thirteen Dreadnought battleships by 1913—or earlier if construction was pushed through fast. As the British programmes provided for only twelve Dreadnoughts by late 1912, the threat was clear. What also became clear was that, whereas Tirpitz's 1900 Navy Law had provided for a total of thirty-eight battleships and twenty large armoured cruisers, the *Novelle* translated this into fifty-eight Dreadnoughts—for the new battlecruisers were regarded as capital ships.

'The dominant idea' the *Daily Mail* wrote, 'is to build a fleet which shall fulfil the hopes and desires of the Pan-Germans and be mightier than the mightiest Navy in the world.'[15] The Paris *Aurore* commented:

The announcement of the formidable increase of the fleet undertaken by the German *Bundesrat* is a curious commentary on the visit just paid by the Kaiser to his Uncle, Edward VII ... the exposé of the new naval programme of the Empire shows that the strength of the German Navy will be doubled between 1907 and 1914. There can be no doubt that this formidable fleet, the construction of which is being pursued with a tenacity that one cannot help admiring, is directed mainly against England.[16]

The British Conservative and navalist Press made full use of the threat in an outcry against the small Liberal programme; Wilhelm, enjoying the life of an English country gentleman, poured out his hurt feelings to his hosts at Highcliffe.

'You English are mad, mad, mad as March hares. What has come over you that you are so completely given over to suspicions quite unworthy of a great nation? What more can I do than I have ever done? I declared with all the emphasis at my command at the Guildhall that my heart is set upon peace and that it is one of my dearest wishes to live on the best of terms with England. Have I ever been false to my word? Falsehood and prevarication are alien to my nature ...

To be for ever misjudged, to have my repeated offers of friendship weighed and scrutinised with jealous, mistrustful eyes, taxes my patience severely. I have said time after time that I am a friend of England, and your Press bids the people of England refuse my proffered hand and insinuates that the other holds a dagger. How can I convince a nation against its will?

But you will say, what of the German Navy? Surely that is a menace to England! Against whom but England are my squadrons being prepared? My answer is clear. Germany is a great and growing Empire. She has a world-wide commerce which is rapidly expanding, and to which the legitimate ambition of patriotic Germans refuses to assign any bounds. Germany must have a powerful fleet to protect that commerce, and her manifold interests in the most distant seas. Germany looks ahead. Her horizons stretch far away. She must be prepared for any eventualities,' and he mentioned the coming rise of China and of Japan—'Only the Powers which have navies will be listened to with respect when the future of the Pacific comes to be solved.'[17]

Distant views of the Pacific and world wide commerce protection made little impression on the British Admiralty who knew that German battleships were not designed for such far cruises, that they could not possibly protect German trade or colonies unless they first smashed the British fleet, and that the vast expenditure on the fleet was at the expense of the German Army, the only weapon appropriate against her Continental neighbours. Therefore the fleet was for use against England. The design was rendered more ominous by the sacrifices Germany was prepared to make. The Admiralty knew as well as Bülow that naval expenditure was provoking a crisis in the *Reich's* finances. Unable to raise indirect taxation because of the clause Tirpitz had been forced to incorporate in the original Navy Law of 1898, and with the 'patriotic' *bloc* deadlocked on taxes affecting wealth and property, naval construction had been financed largely by loans. Already the Imperial debt was over £200 millions with an annual charge of £7½ millions, and it was evident that the increases now proposed must result in higher taxation if the Empire were to remain solvent.

Fisher refused to be panicked. He had been certain of Tirpitz's aims long since. But thanks to the lead he had gained with the *Dreadnought* and Tirpitz's pause to redesign, the Royal Navy would have four Dreadnought battleships and three battlecruisers ready before a single German Dreadnought had been launched, and there were another three battleships from this year's programme following on the stocks for completion by 1910. The danger was not immediate; he saw no reason to anticipate the building programmes which would be necessary as the German ships materialised—indeed there was every reason to husband resources, wait to see what Tirpitz built and how fast, and then go one better. Consequently he proposed a 'very modest' programme of one battleship, one battlecruiser for the following year's Estimates.

Even this was too much for the Radical wing of the Liberal Party and Cabinet led by Lloyd George. Fisher conceded that the British preponderance 'at the present moment' might justify dropping the battleship, 'yet with the full and absolute certainty (now afforded by the German programme just issued) of having to commence a larger battleship programme in 1909-10, it would be most unbusinesslike, and indeed disastrous to close down the armour plate industry of this country by the entire cessation of battleship building.'[18] Already the industry had been hit hard by the Liberal cut-back. Fisher's refusal to compromise led to a split in the Cabinet and threats of resignation, either the social reformers or the Sea Lords would have to go; if it was to be the Sea Lords,

Lloyd George told Fisher, Beresford was ready to take over and cut the Estimates by £2 millions.

Beresford was by now in almost open mutiny; he boasted that he had the Admiralty in the palm of his hand—the country was behind him and he was only biding his time to crumple them up. In touch with leading Opposition politicians, anti-Fisher journalists and lobbyists appalled at Fisher's 'so-called reforms' and retired Admirals including the redoubtable former First Sea Lord, Sir Frederick Richards, and entertaining lavishly with his newly-inherited wealth, he sought to provoke a Public Inquiry or Royal Commission into the policy of Fisher's Board; the main prop of his argument was that there were no proper war plans. Fisher not only had to defend his Estimates sum by sum against the economists in the Cabinet, but found it necessary to defend his whole policy anew to those like Grey and Asquith who supported him and a strong naval policy. As for the threatened Inquiry:

> The result ... would show the Navy to be so strong as to play into the hands of the very strong party in the House of Commons who want to reduce the Navy, but it would also so utterly shake the confidence of the Navy in the Sea Lords that we should have no option but to resign and that, in confidence, I may tell you, we have decided upon ...[19]

Beresford had also been planning resignation so that he could be more publicly vocal in his campaign to bring Fisher down, but the 'paintwork' incident dissuaded him. It had been resurrected in the middle of December as the Press learned 'fresh facts'; these were that Percy Scott's signal had been a private message between himself and one of his cruiser captains, that the rest of the Channel Fleet had not appeared until afterwards, and that Beresford's signal for all ships to be 'out of routine' for painting had been made two hours later. With this new light on the incident most of the Press swung round to Percy Scott's side, many wondering why he had been allowed no explanation before. In January 1908 the affair was inflated further by the scurrilous Horatio Bottomley; copies of an article purporting to be 'The Truth' about the Beresford-Scott incident, which appeared in Bottomley's journal, *John Bull*, were sent to every officer in the Channel Fleet, together with placards advertising this GRAVE INDICTMENT OF LORD CHARLES

BERESFORD in letters four and a half inches high. Who posted them all remains a mystery, but Beresford had no doubt who was behind it.

> The thing evidently emanates from Fisher as the concluding sentence in the *John Bull* article says that I would be prepared to please the government in order to get into Sir John Fisher's position. This must have reference to the conversation I had when I met casually the Prime Minister, Harcourt and Haldane ... There is no doubt that this is one of the most determined, audacious, treacherous and cowardly attacks on me inspired by the gentleman from Ceylon ...[20]

With the disunion in the Navy and within the Channel Fleet an open scandal, Beresford took advice not to resign lest it be construed as a purely personal matter between himself and Percy Scott or Fisher, and not as he had convinced himself 'a question connected with the state of affairs in the Fleet ... the absence of proper organisation and preparations for war.'[21] In a clumsy attempt to probe the Admiralty preparations in this respect he wrote to the First Lord asking that the Director of Naval Intelligence and his assistant should be sent to meet him at his London Hotel to 'fog out' a skeleton war plan he had conceived! When Fisher demurred to such a 'purely Hibernian proposition, that the Admiralty 'fog out' a scheme of war in opposition to their own plans which they know and believe to be the best',[22] Beresford joined his fleet to carry out manoeuvres, as he told Arthur Balfour, 'to prove our shortage of small cruisers and torpedo boat destroyers again, after which I shall reconsider my position.'[23]

Fisher was furious at the pusillanimity of his First Lord and the Cabinet in allowing Beresford to get away with open disloyalty.

> To me it is almost incredible that it should have been permitted to naval officers on full pay and holding high appointments to be heard against the Board of Admiralty.
>
> Se soumettre ou se démettre
>
> But that officers should be openly fighting against the Board of Admiralty, and be encouraged by an inquiry being held in consequence of their insubordinate conduct is intolerable—is unprecedented ... Plans of war imply secrecy—secrets which should be locked in the breast of the war director alone, as was the case in Japan—secrets which may involve the calling on colleagues

for measures and material which cannot fully be explained to them; but if all is to be opened out and the Admiralty not trusted, I cannot imagine the retention of office by any First Sea Lord ...[24]

Fisher was successful in preventing an Inquiry. Of the few men who really counted in the Cabinet and in the country, most were for him. King Edward, who had a sure judgement for men, was a staunch friend and constant supporter; Viscount Esher who pulled strings behind the public scene, was another; the Conservative leader, Balfour, despite or because of his correspondence with Beresford was 'strongly for Fisher', as were Campbell-Bannerman, Asquith and Grey. Even the young Winston Churchill, very much under the spell of Lloyd George, his imagination alight with schemes of social reform, was strongly for Fisher and 'simply boiling with fury at Beresford and company.'[25] While the humiliation of an Inquiry was resisted, Beresford was not disciplined. The First Lord, Tweedmouth, was a sick and dying man; the Prime Minister was also failing, and with his Party divided on the Estimates and Beresford and the discontented apparently commanding great support in the country and among Admirals, he declined to take positive steps to end the potentially mutinous campaign. Fisher wrote, 'My view of drastic dealing with unruly conduct is nervously received at present but will eventually prevail I think ...'[26]

Meanwhile attention had moved back to the main threat as Tirpitz's *Novelle* was debated in the *Reichstag*. It was apparent that he had not misjudged the political mood. His chief allies, the National Liberals, proclaimed themselves anxious that Germany should be in possession of a fleet of first class ships at least equal to those of other countries in point of size and armament (i.e. Dreadnoughts) as soon as possible, and even went so far as to suggest that Tirpitz propose a fresh programme after 1911 when the big-ship building tempo was due to drop. Tirpitz responded to the cue in his flattest tones; if the Liberals could secure him a majority in the House for such a programme he would give them his professional support. All this was to be expected; another *Novelle* to keep the shipyards occupied after 1911 had been freely predicted in sections of the German Press ever since the contents of the present *Novelle* had become known. More surprising was the dearth of technical or political criticism of the fleet from formerly hostile parties. When Tirpitz assured the House that the government's sole ambition was to make Germany so strong on the sea that an attack on her would be no light matter, even the Radicals applauded—for they too only desired peace with England. And the Radical leader professed himself greatly satisfied with Tirpitz's denial of any intention to rival England's naval armaments![27]

An assault on the basis of the Tirpitz plan had been launched the previous year by sections of the Press and Progressives who disliked the power politics and the heavy financial burdens which a battle fleet policy implied. They argued that submarines would be both cheaper and more effective as a protection for German coasts and ports. In the autumn of 1907 a retired Admiral, Karl Galster had published a book advocating cruiser and submarine warfare in the best tradition of the French school, and pointing out that the German fleet would never be strong enough to mount anything but a guerrilla campaign against Britain. In December one of the most progressive of the important newspapers, the *Berliner Tageblatt*, carried the same message:

> The tasks of our fleet consist of the protection of our overseas trade, the safe-guarding of Germans abroad, and the defence of our coasts. It will never be able to fulfil the first two tasks; for the last, however, our forces suffice. An improvement of our coastal fortifications, the creation of a strong submarine arm and numerous mines are enormously more commendable for the purpose than the over-hasty construction of our fleet of capital ships which will hardly come to action against the British.[28]

Tirpitz's view of submarines had always been that 'they can serve well in specific local and secondary purposes, but they will never bring about a great revolution ...';[29] as local and secondary or defensive craft had no place in his scheme, indeed ran away with resources needed for the battle fleet, he had resisted them as long as possible. The first German submarine had been built by Krupp at his own risk, and it had not been until 1906 that a sum for submarine development had been included in the Estimates—then only five million marks. However, the progress made in Great Britain—which had over fifty built and building—and the potential of the diesel engine for a larger cruising radius, hence an *offensive* role, had persuaded him to ask for more money for development in the present *Novelle*. It was still little more than a gesture to disarm his opponents; with his sights narrowed on Dreadnoughts, submarines were an annoying and costly distraction.

Tirpitz's refusal to practice the defensive policies he preached went largely unchallenged in the *Reichstag* debates, as did the failure of his battle fleet policy to bring Germany any nearer safety in naval or world-political terms. The navalist propaganda had done its work. And Tirpitz took great care to hide his political aims behind the mystique of professionalism. When he adduced arguments to show the *technical* necessity for battleships, none among the laymen in the *Reichstag* presumed to question them; he was the military expert.

One of the few who saw precisely what he was about and consistently raised his voice against it and the inevitable arms race which the majority refused to face, was the Socialist leader, August Bebel.

> The German government will never be able to eradicate from the minds of the English people the idea that the German Navy is directed against England if only because there is no other adversary against which it could be used. England, for her part, will strain every nerve to maintain her naval supremacy. But what if one day she wearies of her exertions and allows herself to be provoked into striking before it is too late?[30]

This brought a rare outburst from Tirpitz. With raised voice and a wealth of gesture he cried, 'We are building our fleet against no one. We have no grounds to build a fleet against anyone. We are strengthening our fleet because those who are our friends today might become our enemies tomorrow.'[31] He characterised fears that Germany sought to dispute the supremacy of the seas with Great Britain as 'products of the imagination'. The British Navy was immeasurably superior in technical and professional resources; England was in a position to build ships far more rapidly than Germany, and could therefore choose her own moment for any programme in the certainty that she would not be left behind. The German Navy which would take a generation to complete, had not yet been advanced to an important stage; he was consequently unable to understand Herr Bebel's misgivings and he begged him not to play with fire and excite uneasiness either in Germany or England.

The Navy Office and Navy League propaganda machines then turned Bebel's speech to their advantage, accusing him of advising

England that she ought to strike without further delay if she wished to anticipate German naval aggression.

Tirpitz, talking to the British naval attaché the following month, professed to deplore the alarm and uneasiness aroused by this treatment, and took the opportunity to point out how dangerous it was to suggest to a proud people like the Germans that they were not masters in their own house as regards what ships they might or might not build. 'Such remarks only increased the mad demands put forward by the Navy League and placed a weapon in the hands of the Chauvinists in both countries.'[32]

He asked the Englishman if he thought feeling in England any better.

'Yes. But at the same time, of course, the new Navy Bill—through the medium of the newspapers—has frightened many of the less instructed.'

Tirpitz replied that he was really at a loss to know what he could do; he could not believe that any thinking man in England could see any harm in the fleet Bill—after all it was not as if he was building any *more* ships than in the 1900 Law.

'It is not numbers, but the rapidity of construction of a Dreadnought type fleet that causes some uneasiness.'

Tirpitz evaded the point by suggesting that in view of England's alliances with France and Japan there were, from some points of view, more grounds for uneasiness in Germany.

Wilhelm also sought to disarm British fears with a typically impulsive letter addressed to the First Lord of the Admiralty, Lord Tweedmouth.

> It is absolutely *nonsensical* and *untrue* that the German Naval Bill is to provide a Navy meant as a 'Challenge to British naval supremacy'. The German Fleet is being built against nobody at all. It is solely built *for* Germany's needs in relation to that country's rapidly growing trade ...[33]

The immediate cause of this extraordinary letter was Wilhelm's annoyance at a phrase used by Viscount Esher in a letter published in *The Times*. The letter had attacked Fisher's critics, and ended, 'There is not a man in Germany from the Emperor downwards who would not welcome the fall of Sir John Fisher.' Wilhelm seized on this phrase as 'unmitigated balderdash' creating 'immense merriment in the circles of those "who know" here' ... after which he had complained at length of the 'perpetual quoting of the German danger' in the English Press.

> Once more, the German Navy is not aimed at England, and is not 'a challenge to British supremacy of the Sea', which will remain unchallenged for years to come ...

Edward VII was furious at this latest piece of gaucherie and sent his nephew a terse note:

> Your writing to my First Lord of the Admiralty is a 'new departure', and I do not see how he can prevent our Press from calling attention to the great increase in building of German ships of war, which necessitates us increasing our Navy also.[34]

Tweedmouth, however, was flattered by the letter and talked of it freely. So did Fisher. Meeting Esher at a Levee a few days later, he came up excitedly and said, 'You have had the greatest compliment paid you that was ever paid a man. The German Emperor has written to Tweedmouth nine pages in his own hand, full of abuse of you!'[35] It quickly became common knowledge in informed circles, and the following month, after Tirpitz's *Novelle* had sailed through its third and final reading in the *Reichstag* with the expected easy majority *The Times* made use of their knowledge. The British Naval Estimates were being debated in the House at the time and the Conservative opposition was making play with the fact that while the Liberal government had been reducing British capital ship construction from four in 1905 to three in 1906 and 1907, and now to only two, Tirpitz had increased from two in 1905 to three in 1906 and 1907 and was now up to four. *The Times*, anxious to keep the German danger to the forefront, produced Wilhelm's letter to Tweedmouth as evidence of an 'insidious attempt to influence the Minister responsible for the Naval Estimates in a direction favourable to German interests. If there had been any doubt about the meaning of German naval expansion before,' the editorial asserted, 'none can remain after an attempt of this kind.'[36] Although most other newspapers failed to go so far as this, and the government succeeded in playing the incident down in the debate following the revelation, the affair had the opposite effect to that Wilhelm had intended, generally deepening the suspicions which had been aroused by the publication of Tirpitz's *Novelle* immediately after his own protestations of friendship at the Guildhall.

As *The People* put it, the German Fleet could not be pacific.

> Germany's frontiers are on the land and can be adequately defended by big battalions of soldiers, as was amply demonstrated in 1870 when the French fleet was ten times as large as Germany's but was unable to inflict any serious harm upon its opponents, and was quite unable to delay by a single moment the capitulation of Paris and the crowning of the King of Prussia as German Emperor on French soil.[37]

This showed, *The People* continued with a phrase that gained notoriety some years later when used by Winston Churchill, that 'a German fleet is a luxury not a national necessity, and is not therefore a fleet with a pacific object.' It endorsed Germany's right to indulge any luxuries she chose, but 'what we have to do is to see we are sufficiently armed to meet our necessities.'

This view was not shared by many Liberal organs, nor by Radical and pacifist Liberals in Parliament, who took Wilhelm's and Tirpitz's protestations at their face value, and pointed to Britain's enormous superiority and enormous expenditure on her Navy in terms which must have delighted Tirpitz. There were, they argued in the Estimates debate, only four naval powers of consequence.

'Against which of these powers are we maintaining our present naval strength? Japan is an ally, France our friend, and the idea of war with the United States no man seriously entertains.' Cheers! 'Germany remains. Here I think a danger exists, but it is of such a character that I am convinced that if it were brought out into the open and frankly discussed it would disappear.' Hear, Hear! 'There are men in this country who assert that war between ourselves and Germany is inevitable and who say that Germany will be the attacking party. They are industriously engaged in the Press and on the platform spreading suspicions of the designs of that Power and by their action they are fostering the danger they profess to dread. In Germany there are also men who say that war between the two countries is inevitable. In their view we are to be the aggressors. What is the root of the fear entertained by the Germans that we might make an unprovoked attack upon them? Undoubtedly it is that we are maintaining a power in excess of our apparent requirements.' Cheers![38]

Government policy was ably defended against these attacks from its own benches by Asquith, soon to take over from Campbell-Bannerman as Prime Minister. He assured those who had 'spoken with so much force and feeling' that in their desire to reduce the growth of military and naval expenditure they had the complete sympathy of every member of the government.

'Among all the avoidable curses which in these days afflict the civilised world there are few I think that bring a greater sense of despair than the competition in armaments.'[39]

He went on to detail the reductions already made in naval expenditure and reiterated the government's intention to do all in their power to prevent a new spurt in competitive shipbuilding. But, he warned, future British programmes 'must depend upon the additions made to their naval forces by other Powers. Our naval position is at this moment, as I believe, one of unassailable supremacy, and such it must remain.' Opposition Cheers! 'The command of the sea however important and however desirable it may be to other Powers is to us a matter of life and death. We must safeguard it, not against imaginary dangers, but we must safeguard it against all contingencies that can reasonably enter into the calculations of statesmen.'

This was a paraphrase of the Admiralty view:

> The British Empire floats on the British Navy. It is our all in all. Victory at sea, desirable to foreign States is a sine qua non to our continued existence. We must win at sea or perish as a nation ... *Ententes* may vanish—battleships remain the surest pledges this country can give for the continued peace of the world.[40]

Asquith's implicit warning to Germany that the Liberal government meant to retain British naval supremacy whatever additions Tirpitz might make to his fleet was unequivocal. But it was not enough for the Opposition. The government spokesman explaining the Estimates had mentioned for the first time ever the possibility that Germany might accelerate her construction. If this proved the case and she built her Dreadnoughts in less than two years she might have thirteen Dreadnoughts by late 1911 against only twelve British—given existing British programmes and rates of construction. Balfour hammered the point home.

Asquith replied, 'Without in any way forecasting what the British shipbuilding programme for next year may be, I will say without the slightest hesitation that if we find at the time that there is a reasonable probability of the German programme being carried out in the way that the paper figures suggest, we should deem it our duty to provide not only for a sufficient number of ships, but for such a date of laying down of such ships that at the end of 1911 the superiority of Germany which the Rt Honourable gentleman foreshadows would not be an actual fact.' Cheers! 'I hope that is quite explicit!'[41]

Esher confided to his Journal:

> The event of the past few days has been the success of AJB (Balfour) in drawing from Asquith a declaration about the Navy, which would never have been obtained but for the Kaiser's letter. The net result of that famous epistle has been to force the government to give a pledge that in the next three years they will lay down ships enough to ensure our superiority ...[42]

Esher's view of German policy had long been as clear as that of the Foreign Office or Admiralty, as fatalistic as a Treitschkian vision.

> Nothing can prevent a struggle for life (between Britain and Germany) except the certainty that attack would fail. I am sure that the Germans are very patient and very bold. The sort of supremacy that Napoleon dreamed of for France, and nearly achieved—commercial as well as political—they desire as well as the former. And all their efforts are directed to that. The great obstacle is England. They do not want to conquer but to crush.[43]

His view was now shared by most men of real power in the Cabinet and the country. What other explanation *could* there be for Tirpitz's grandiose fleet plans and their constantly increasing pace? The possibility that the naval policy of a great nation like Germany was directed by the childish desire of the Monarch to shine as Admiral of a splendid fleet, and nursed by his Navy Minister's obsession with an inflexible battleship plan was too far-fetched to be entertained by the leaders of an Empire that felt its very existence challenged. The German Ambassador in London sent report after report on the hardening British attitude.

> Two different opinions are taken in England about the German fleet. One section of opinion holds that the fleet is being built for the purpose of attacking England; the supporters of this view point

185

to the assertions of the *Deutsche Flottenverein* and other Anglo-phobe statements. The other view is that our fleet is not a deliberate threat of aggression but a potential danger to England. Whether the threat is deliberate or potential, both sections of opinion, and all England agree that the danger exists ... The English are afraid of our fleet because we are their nearest neighbours and we appear to them more efficient than other people. We must pass by their land in order to reach the seas of the world ... A defeat in the North Sea means the end of the British Empire. A lost battle on the Continent is a long way from the end of Germany ...[44]

Wilhelm became exasperated with his Ambassador's insistence on looking at everything from the British angle: 'It is not our fleet' he noted in the margin of this despatch, 'but the absolutely crazy "Dreadnought" policy of Sir John Fisher and His Majesty' which had caused the mischief. 'Now they and the deluded Britons see that they have been totally mistaken, and that thereby they have destroyed their old past superiority ... They will just have to get used to our fleet. And from time to time we must assure them that it is not being built against them'.[45]

His brother, Prince Henry of Prussia, took the precept seriously and wrote to—of all people—Fisher.

Never mind *The Times*, never mind the Press! Let them be d—d like Admiral Farragut said at Mobile ... he who tries to prove that Germany is or will be a menace to England, or that Germany intends to be aggressive is certainly quite in the wrong and (pardon me) a lunatic! Germany wishes to be in a position to DEFEND her rights but *not* to *dispute* the rights of others![46]

When Fisher saw the King next he resurrected his suggestions that the German Fleet be 'Copenhagened'—as he put it 'treated like rogue elephants and, with tame females in the shape of British battleships on either side, hustled from Kiel Harbour as prisoners.'[47]

'Fisher,' the King said, after a moment, 'you must be mad.'

Prince Henry's next attempt at reassurance was in June. King Edward, on a voyage to cement the Anglo-Russian detente by a meeting with the Tsar, called in at Kiel on the way. The officers of his escorting cruisers were invited to dinner by Prince Henry, who made them a speech filled with every expression of friendship and disclaiming any aggressive intentions on the part of the German

Navy; he asked them to spread this good news throughout England. The report of the incident made by the Foreign Office representative with the King noted, 'It is thought by those who know Prince Henry that he would never have spoken in this strain without direct instructions to do so.'[48]

What impressed the British officers rather more was work in progress on enlarging the Kiel Canal for Dreadnought-size ships, and the smart appearance of the whole of the German North Sea Fleet lying at anchor in the harbour, 'while the intricate evolutions of the torpedo flotilla served as a useful object lesson of the efficiency of the German Navy.'[49]

After Kiel, the Royal Yacht steamed in brilliant weather to Reval where the King and his powerful suite which included Fisher and General Sir John French, were greeted by the Russian Imperial family and Ministers in speeches of welcome. Edward expressed a conviction that the Anglo-Russian Convention would not only draw the two countries closer together, 'but will help very greatly towards the maintenance of the general peace of the world.'[50] The Foreign Office representative enlarged on this to the Russian Foreign Minister:

Although the attitude of His Majesty's government towards Germany is and has been absolutely correct, it is impossible to ignore the fact that, owing to the unnecessarily large increase in the German naval programme, a deep distrust in England of Germany's future intentions has been created. This distrust will be still further accentuated with the progress of time, and the realisation of the German programme, and the increase of taxation in England entailed by the necessary naval counter-measures. In seven or eight years time a critical situation might arise, in which Russia, if strong in Europe, might be the arbiter of peace, and have much more influence in securing the peace of the world than any Hague Conference. For this reason it is absolutely necessary that England and Russia should maintain towards each other the same cordial and friendly relations as now exist between England and France ...[51]

To this end King Edward played his part as he had in Paris. Fisher wrote enthusiastically, 'The King has just surpassed himself all round. Every blessed Russian of note he got quietly into his spider's web and captured!'[52] Fisher played his own part with equal effect, whirling the Grand Duchesses with all his usual abandon and exuberant spirits. 'I said to my sweet partner in the middle of the dance, "How about Siberia for me after this!" which sent her into hysterics.'[53] She wrote to him after the visit.

> All our gentlemen—Ministers, Admirals, Generals—were delighted with you, as you brought such an amount of frolic and jollity into their midst. They couldn't get over it and spoke about you and your dancing, anecdotes etc, without end. I told them even if they tried their hardest they would never reach anywhere near your level ...[54]

Wilhelm viewed the unnatural festivities at Reval with the utmost suspicion; they marked the final stage in his wicked Uncle's deep-laid plan to throw a ring of enemies around the German Empire. The presence of Fisher and Sir John French was proof enough; the British denied it, but who could doubt that military and naval talks were under way—or even signed and sealed? Reviewing his troops at Döberitz, he gave vent to his frustration. 'Yes! It now appears as though they wanted to encircle us. We will know how to bear that. The Germans have never fought better than when forced to defend themselves.'[55]

When his London Ambassador sent him another report saying that the great mass of the English people only desired peace, and King Edward's policy was directed towards that end, he noted in the margin, 'Untrue. He aims at war. I am to begin it so that he does not get the odium.'[56] This was the trend of German Press comment. Although Bülow had given directions that the Reval meeting was to be reported quietly, readers of many newspapers received the impression that war might break out at any moment.

The British Foreign Secretary, Edward Grey, couldn't believe that Wilhelm or his government seriously believed the 'encirclement' theory: they must realise that if Germany had alliances, other countries needed them too. And believing the real point of friction to be naval competition he and Lloyd George made determined efforts to convince the German Ambassador, Count Metternich, of the British point of view: the German increase in tempo was self-defeating; every increase would be matched by a British increase, for the existence of England as an independent Power was bound up with the British Navy. 'Every Englishman would spend his last penny on maintaining British supremacy at sea.'[57] Metternich was already convinced of this, but he loyally maintained the official German line that it was the British 'Dreadnought' policy which had started the alarm. The English Ministers arranged another meeting and pointed out the dangers in the new tempo: taxation would have to be increased, they might even have to introduce conscription against the danger of German invasion; the public would become exasperated, yet the relative strengths of the two navies would not alter. Lloyd George insisted that a slight reduction in tempo would transform the whole situation. 'If Germany and Great Britain agree to cut down their programmes of construction by one Dreadnought a year there would be a complete change in public opinion.'[58] He also suggested that Great Britain would be prepared to re-interpret her 'Two-Power' standard of naval strength as a ratio of 3 : 2 against the German Navy.

When Metternich reported these conversations, Wilhelm became violent. His Ambassador should not allow himself, even unofficially, to listen to such shameless suggestions! He must be told that good relations with Britain were not to be had at the expense of the German fleet. It was 'measureless impertinence, a grave insult to the German Empire.' He should tell enthusiastic dreamers like Grey and Lloyd George to go to hell. He was 'too flabby.'[59]

Tirpitz was also opposed to the tone of Metternich's reports, fearing that Bülow and his Foreign Office might become entangled in their own web, succumb to the subtle blandishments of the British and trade *his* naval law for a loose political *detente* which would solve none of the vital questions for Germany, but leave Britain still mistress of the seas and arbiter of the world. And this just as he had come within sight of one of his goals. It needed only one more *Novelle* to add a minimum of two great ships to the fleet law when the building tempo was due to drop to two in 1912, and he would have reached the magic number of 60 great ships, each with a replacement time of 20 years; the three-tempo would be 'eternalised', the *Reichstag*, whatever its hue or temper powerless against the 'Iron Budget'. After this it was a matter of a few years only before the fleet achieved the 2 : 3 ratio with Great Britain which Lloyd George was offering. Then having sufficient strength to make a British attack a costly affair, Germany would possess a real world-power factor which England would have to acknowledge. On the other hand he was convinced that a retreat in the fleet question would mean abdication from Germany's world role.

189

And turning Metternich's arguments in his most accomplished style, he pointed out that the violent British reaction to the recent Novelle showed how essential it was to build up German fleet strength as rapidly as possible![60]

Grey was a man of calm judgement, who approached his task from a sense of duty; lacking the passion of many of his colleagues, preferring the solitude of weekends spent making long country walks or fishing to political or social activity, he sought, like Asquith, to reach detached conclusions based solely on the merits of each case. He knew a good deal of what he was up against with the German question; he had been forced to listen to Wilhelm inveighing against Jews during the previous year's Windsor visit and thought him not quite sane, and very superficial. Whether he had plumbed Tirpitz is less certain. In any case he had to keep trying. When, that summer, a meeting was arranged between King Edward and Wilhelm in another attempt to patch up the bout of ill-feeling since the Reval affair, he drafted his views on the naval rivalry in a memo for the King to use if the opportunity seemed ripe. This reiterated all the arguments which he and Lloyd George had used with Metternich; if the German Navy became superior or even attained a temporary superiority Great Britain would not only be defeated but occupied; for Germany with her great land armies, no such danger existed.

> Without therefore attributing any sinister motive to the German fleet it is a paramount need to increase British naval expenditure to meet the German programme, though we fear that this may be taken as a sign of increased rivalry and distrust ... On the other hand a slackening of naval expenditure on both sides would at once be followed by a great rebound in public opinion towards friendly feeling and security ...[61]

When the meeting took place at Cronberg in August, Edward mentioned that he had a paper on the naval question, but knowing Wilhelm's extreme sensitivity on the subject, left it at that. And Wilhelm declined to be drawn. However the Foreign Office representative with the King afterwards broached the subject to Wilhelm, telling him plainly that the speed with which German naval construction was being pressed forward was causing real anxiety in England, and unless the German government was willing to cut down its programme Britain would have to increase hers.

Wilhelm, in what seemed like a rehearsed statement, made it plain that there was no question of Germany altering her rate of construction; it had been fixed by law and would be completed to the letter; it had become a point of national honour. Discussions with a foreign government were contrary to national dignity and would give rise to internal troubles; he would rather go to war than accept such dictation.

His attitude came as no surprise, but it put an end to Grey's attempts at discussion; there was nothing for it now but to outbuild Tirpitz. To Edward, it was yet another example of the impossibility of his nephew. 'As if the law could not be altered by those who made it!'[62]

Wilhelm dwelt on the interview in fantasy, and the following day sent Bülow a long and detailed telegram describing how he had discomfited the Englishman and brought a look of 'speechless astonishment' to his face by refuting his figures. When the man had asked if German construction could not be stopped or slowed, he had looked him 'fairly and squarely in the face' and then said, 'Then we shall fight, for it is a question of national honour and dignity', whereupon the diplomat had 'flushed painfully, made a low bow and apologised for his ill-considered expressions!' That was always the way to treat Englishmen![63] Bülow concluded sadly that the time for obtaining real concessions from Great Britain and dissuading her from massive naval increases had passed. 'His Majesty sacrificed everything to his desire to build more and more battleships in the shortest possible time.'[64]

Edward travelled on from the meeting at Cronberg to Marienbad for his annual cure. On the golf course there he met Clemenceau, most vigorous, witty and savage hater of Germans and what they had done to his country in 1870. It was his conviction that they were now preparing for another war when they would march straight on Paris through Belgium and demand a huge indemnity as before. He remarked to the King that he had asked Grey what the British Empire would do in these circumstances; Grey had replied, 'undoubtedly it would create a great stir in Britain'. 'That,' Clemenceau said, 'would be a lot of use to France!'[65]

Clemenceau's estimate of Germany's mood to war was confirmed by numerous observers that summer. Colonel Trench, military attaché in Berlin, spent his leave touring Central and Southern Germany to find if the 'present state of tension of national feeling' and 'detestation of England was more or less limited to the northern States.' Contrary to his expectation he found it everywhere, and

> a conviction that Germany has a high mission to carry out with the right to Colonies for the expansion of its growing population and the hegemony of the world's trade, as well as—if the people will be willing to make the pecuniary sacrifices necessary to build a sufficient Navy—the command of the sea.[66]

Everywhere he found a strong current of irritation which he put down to the shocks received by German foreign policy, especially the meeting of Edward and the Tsar at Reval. Among officers of the Army he detected 'a growing weariness of the endless dreary routine of training', together with a belief in their Army's 'unquestioned superiority to any possible foe' and 'an intense desire to reap the harvest so carefully and patiently sown in preparation for war.' He concluded that 'so far as mental preparation for war goes, this country is mobilised, so that should it be determined to appeal to arms at any time before a relaxation of tension takes place, all that will be necessary will be to give the word to start.' He did not anticipate this coming immediately, indeed he guessed that the warlike preparations were designed to mature about 1915, but he feared that the feeling in the country was such that should German foreign policy receive another serious blow 'patient discretion would prove unbearable and Germany would strike even before she was ready.'

The British naval attaché had already reported in the same vein of a fretfulness and nervous irritation, 'known here as *nervös*', and of the Navy's warlike anticipation. German experts had come to believe that England would be content for them to have a fleet in the ratio 2:3 with England's; they expected to reach this position in 1914, and had high hopes that after that date England might be temporarily involved in some trouble abroad, leaving German ships temporarily in a majority in the North Sea.

> And I truly believe that the cry for an immediate attack on England might be too strong to be resisted. Certainly our risk would be enormous. So far as I have heard four such moments are looked for in Germany: (1) in case the United States and Japan should fight (2) if Turkey should be induced to fight England for the possession of Egypt (3) when the Japanese alliance expires (4) when

Japan has finished colonising Korea and her eyes might be turned to Australia.[67]

The attaché believed that reason would not deter the German people; they longed for revenge on England; the Franco-German war had whetted their appetites for enormous indemnities—some £750 millions were hoped for from England—'and above all Germany would be feared throughout the world.'

Incidentally I may remark, there is a sort of gleeful feeling among all classes that from about the same date (1914) owing to the necessary preponderance of ships which must be kept at home to balance theirs with a satisfactory margin, England's naval hands will be tied from active interference all over the world; and the tone is, as a naval officer said to me about eighteen months ago, 'You don't suppose that in ten years time we should allow you to have another Boer War do you?'

Analysing the feeling by class, the attaché believed that large merchants and manufacturers viewed any resort to arms with the utmost horror as possibly involving their ruin and a return to the comparative poverty of Germany in former days. The ruling classes, however, were ill-disposed towards England and 'would love to attack, but for the fact that they do realise the enormous risks in doing so'. The learned and professorial classes, anxious for a forward policy and aware that it must lead to a collision with the British Empire, he characterised as England's most dangerous enemies. As for the mass of people, they had been conditioned well by the Navy League and other propaganda organs; 'to make a quietly philosophical and home-loving nation such as Germany was prior to 1895 understand the benefits of sea power, the somewhat drastic method of making Germany envy England has had to be employed'; he believed they had now been whipped up to such an extent that it was doubtful if even Wilhelm, whom he thought basically peace-loving, could stop them.

I dare not finish without recording that I believe that at the bottom of every German heart today is rising a faint and wildly exhilarating hope that a glorious day is approaching when by a brave breaking through of the lines which he feels are encircling him he might even wrest command of the sea from England and thus become a member of the greatest Power by land or sea the world has ever seen.

9

Acceleration

In the Channel Fleet that summer more incidents in the Beresford-Percy Scott feud lifted public disquiet about the duel between Fisher and the Commander-in-Chief Home Forces in war to new heights. Since the Horatio Bottomley article Beresford had joined to his agitation to have Scott relieved of his command attempts to have *John Bull* sued for libel, and had engaged his eminent fellow-countryman, the barrister Sir Edward Carson to represent his criticisms of the Board in the House, writing him rambling letters filled with abuse of the 'vindictive Fisher' and the mess into which he had led the Board of Admiralty. 'As the American say, I shall "laff" when you begin on them ... you can slaughter them. You can point out that no wonder the whole Navy is in the state of unrest and disaffection it is reported to be in if the supreme authority will not support publicly Commanders-in-Chief in grave cases of insubordination and contempt ...'[1] As in his loud talk, free criticism of Admiralty policy for the Dreadnought, the scrapping of small ships, the lack of war plans, the faulty organisation of the home fleets always finished up in his letters as invective against his hated rival: 'I have nursed a "Hadder in my bossum". I wish that I was free and that this was not a personal question I could so thoroughly swab the floor of the House of Commons with Fisher & Co ... that grand old morale of the Navy is gone. All the good old comradeship disappeared. Admiral is set against Admiral—Fleet against Fleet.'[2]

To make the point clear, he went out of his way not to notice Fisher whenever circumstances forced them together. In May at the Royal Academy dinner they both attended Fisher had forced his presence on him and shaken him by the hand, but at a Levee a few weeks later, in full view of the King and several Cabinet Ministers he had turned his back as the First Sea Lord came up with out-stretched hand. The story had ripped through the Fleet and Society.

Rumours grew and were sedulously fostered by the 'syndicate of discontent' that the discipline of the Service was in danger and Fisher would have to retire if morale were to be restored. Later, news reached the Board from the Channel Fleet that Beresford was planning '*a great upheaval*' to force Fisher's resignation.

By this time Tweedmouth had been replaced as First Lord. In the Cabinet reshuffle following Asquith's succession as Prime Minister, Reginald McKenna had taken his place. Formerly a lawyer, he had a cool, analytical brain and precise judgement which exasperated some of the more political minds in the Cabinet. The Beresford affair was one of his first concerns. After studying the voluminous files of correspondence and transcripts of interviews and seeing Lord and even Lady Charles he reached the conclusion that Beresford was not the proper man to be given supreme command in war. In July he brought the matter before the Cabinet, suggesting two immediate steps, first the reorganisation of the Fleet in home waters by the absorption of the Home into the Channel Fleet, second the termination of Beresford's command. He found no support; the increased agitation against the Board that was bound to follow such a drastic step as cutting short the Navy's most popular Admiral would not bear thinking about. McKenna, believing there was no immediate danger, allowed his administrative judgement to be overruled by the political. He did, however, write to Beresford withdrawing Tweedmouth's engagement that he would have supreme command in the event of war; he had made up his mind, like Fisher, that if war threatened the right man to take over home forces was Admiral Sir Arthur Wilson.[3]

At the same time the Press came out with the latest Channel Fleet 'incident'. During manoeuvres after a visit to Christiania (Oslo) Beresford had become dissatisfied with the way Scott was bringing his division into cruising formation, and in the middle of the evolution had taken command himself, ordering the course they should steer. As Scott's flagship, *Good Hope*, had already come round some way on a different course she became separated from the rest of the division, steaming the same direction but some thirteen hundred yards abeam of the rear ship. To complete the evolution to bring Scott into the line again Beresford hoisted signals for the main body of cruisers to turn sixteen points (180°) to starboard, the *Good Hope* to turn sixteen points to port; if carried out this would have swung the *Good Hope* and the ship abeam of her in towards each other in much the same way as HMS *Camperdown* had swung into and through the side of HMS *Victoria* during a notorious and fatal evolution in the Mediterranean fifteen years earlier. Scott's officers looked at the distance between the ships, judged it too close, kept their answering pendant at the dip to signify they did not understand, and then ordered the helm over the same way as the rest of the division. Afterwards Beresford signalled to ask if *Good Hope* had taken in the signal to turn to *port*. Scott replied that his answering pendant had not gone close up because 'there was danger in such a turn. As the signal to turn to port was hauled down before *Good Hope* had answered it I concluded that the danger had been realised ...'[4]

It was a minor incident, just another symptom of the bad blood between the two, and neither thought much of it afterwards. Beresford even signalled that Scott was right in turning to starboard if he thought the ships too close. But the naval feuds were now a very public scandal and the affair was latched on by Press and Parliament as an illustration of the potential menace to the Service, thus the security of the country from senior officers in open discord. *The Times* carried a first leader well over a column in length stressing that it was the duty of all in the Navy to put aside personal opinions of Admiralty policy and follow the Service's 'noble habit of ready and cheerful obedience to all who are set in authority over them.'[5] If Lord Charles Beresford was at loggerheads with the Board of Admiralty, he was in *The Times*' judgement *ipso facto* in the wrong. 'If as is also alleged he is not on speaking terms with one of his flag officers, he is equally in the wrong, since it is his duty before all things to do nothing to impair the discipline, good order and good feeling of the fleet under his command.' He might have his grievances, and they might be legitimate grievances. 'But so long as he holds his present position he is not entitled to air them, let alone trade on them. It is his first and paramount duty to set a shining example of discipline.' He must, therefore be 'confronted with the historic alternative *se soumettre ou se démettre.*'

This was a favourite phrase of Fisher's; it was plain to those in the know who had inspired that burst of thunder. Meanwhile Beresford's allies were busy in Parliament. One particularly bitter and wrong-headed ex-lieutenant R.N. named Carlyon Bellairs asked if the government 'would impartially endeavour to arrive at a complete knowledge of the method of introduction and the changes in administration and organisation which originated this antagonism.'[6] Another suggested that while the dissension lasted the life of every seaman in the fleet was in peril, and another asked whether the changes the Admiralty had introduced, 'however valuable or valueless'[7] could ever justify this display of antagonism. Asquith replied shortly that the direction of naval policy lay with the government of the day 'and it is the business of naval officers on active Service not to discuss or criticise that policy but to carry it out with loyalty to their superiors, in harmony with one another, and with a single eye to the efficiency of the great Service to which they belong.' Cheers![8]

The next day it was the turn of Fisher's supporters to put down questions. As Lord Charles Beresford was not on speaking terms with the First Sea Lord or with his official subordinate, Sir Percy Scott, would the First Lord say what steps he proposed to take in the interests of discipline and fighting efficiency. And would he say whether the rules and regulations for discipline only applied to humbler ranks, stokers for instance, while Lord Charles was allowed to break them with impunity. Uproar!

The dispute dragged on through July and early August, gathering an overlay of lies, speculation and personal abuse which almost hid the original incident. The Beresford faction pressed for an enquiry, accused Fisher of sending the story of the 'manoeuvring incident' to the Press, and of dictating *The Times* leader! Fisher kept his head low, believing that Beresford was so maddened he would eventually hang himself; already he had confirmed that the Levee 'cut' had been no accident by stating that he would not shake hands with the First Sea Lord. 'Is it possible,' Fisher wrote to McKenna, 'that this state of affairs can be allowed to continue? Every trivial action has to be studied and even who one talks to considered as perhaps indictable! I think your advice is (as I understood it yesterday): "*Wait till October and the matter shall be dealt with! As to the lies, leave them alone.*" '[9]

In the meantime Percy Scott and the *Good Hope* were despatched to South Africa with a special squadron to show the flag at celebrations to mark the Union—and from thence to South America! McKenna officially buried the affair with a masterly statement in the Commons; the Board was satisfied that the manoeuvre was not dangerous. 'At the same time the Rear-Admiral, as he thought there was a risk in carrying out the order, was justified in turning the other way.'[10] A satisfactory conclusion for both parties. Inside was a hidden meaning; the manoeuvre was not dangerous—in the way it was carried out.

Presently the holiday season dispersed the contestants. As the great London houses emptied and Parliament rose a sort of silence fell over the dispute. Fisher travelled out to Carlsbad and threw himself thankfully into the international brilliance and intrigue of the Bohemian spas, as ever cutting a strikingly vigorous and spontaneous figure against the poise and calm of the fashionable English out there in force.

> I sat several times between Stolypin, the Russian Prime Minister and Isvolsky, the Foreign Secretary. I didn't begin it, but Stolypin said to me, 'What do you think we want most?' He fancied I should answer so many battleships, so many cruisers etc etc, but instead I said 'Your western frontier is denuded of troops and your magazines are depleted. *Fill them up,* and then talk of Fleets!' Stolypin looked hard at me and said not another word. I FELT I had got home.[11]

Fisher cut short his leave by two weeks after a warning from his ever staunch supporter, King Edward, that the mice were beginning to play. On his return, the over-riding problem was not Beresford, but the following year's Estimates. As he had confided to his intimates, this (1909-10) was to be the big year for building. A British Dreadnought preponderance in 1912, the danger year when Tirpitz's 'spurt' was likely to mature was *'vital to national existence.'*[12]

As the time approached to argue the programme through the Cabinet against the economists—who had already made their views very clear—signs multiplied that even six might not be sufficient. A remarkable expansion in German capacity to build the very largest ships had been evident for some time, as had a great expansion in Krupp's ordnance works; this last was the more alarming. The production of a battleship was an enormously complicated business requiring a host of ancillary industries capable of supplying and fitting specialised components to the tight schedules demanded by the honeycomb compartmentation of the hulls, which rendered spaces inaccessible to machinery once decked over; given this depth of industrial support for the shipyards the decisive factor in construction time was the production of the heavy guns and mountings. In the British industry a ship could be built in shorter time than her turret complexes. Consequently news reaching the British Director of Naval Ordnance in 1907 that Krupp had on order no less than six very large-base circular planes which could only be required for manufacturing the roller paths for heavy gun mountings was vital intelligence; it suggested that when Krupp's expansion was complete it would be possible for them to arm, and thus for Tirpitz to complete, more than six Dreadnoughts a year—more it suggested that Tirpitz might be planning something of the sort or why should Krupp, who had a monopoly in German heavy ordnance, invest so heavily in equipment?[13] Publication of Tirpitz's *Novelle* that November seemed to lend foundation to the suspicion: the later German Dreadnoughts only needed to be pushed through in two years each—Krupp would be able to arm them easily at the four-tempo—and Tirpitz could have seventeen Dreadnoughts at some time in 1912. British programmes, including the six Fisher intended to lay down in 1909-10, provided for only eighteen Dreadnoughts in 1912. Clearly this was an unacceptable margin. In December 1907, the Board had given Tweedmouth, then First Lord, a memorandum outlining the German capacity for sudden acceleration and warning that it might be necessary to lay down as many as eight capital ships in 1909-10 to meet it.[14]

When, shortly after Fisher returned to his desk in October 1908 German newspapers carried reports that two contracts for ships of Tirpitz's 1909 programme had already been placed it seemed that the spurt had started; as the British naval attaché in Berlin noted, this was six months before the usual time for the allocation of contracts and before the money had been voted by the *Reichstag*. His other reports revealed that the first German Dreadnoughts, laid down in the summer of 1907, were well advanced; *Nassau*, the first launched, was expected to be ready for trials in October the following year—an actual building time of some twenty-eight months only, although allowing for preparatory work and collection of materials before the keel was laid, an overall time of perhaps thirty months.[15]

A few weeks later the British naval attaché reported that premature awarding of *three* 1909-10 contracts had been 'partially confirmed' by one of his confrères who had been invited to attend the launch of a liner at the Vulkan Works, where one of the contracts was supposed to have been placed.

He states that he has reason to believe that the story is a true one, and that material is now being collected, and preparations being made to start building early in the new financial year. Assuming that Schichau (shipbuilders of Danzig) is acting likewise, and allowing thirty months for the completion of each vessel from April next, it is possible that Germany may have the following Dreadnoughts ready for sea by October 1911: ten battleships of the Dreadnought type, three battle cruisers of the *Invincible* type.[16]

The attaché's reports relied on hearsay because his own requests to visit German yards were refused. This in itself was suggestive. As British Naval Intelligence was without clandestine sources of information in Germany and regarded the various agencies purveying international military secrets from Brussels as dubious and their information probably worthless, doubts fed apprehension of Germany's increased capacity and produced real alarm. Grey himself sent an urgent cable to the Embassy in Berlin for verification of the stories.

Meanwhile news came from the Managing Director of Vickers that Krupp was buying outside the European Nickel Syndicate through whom orders were normally placed. 'The only inference to be drawn from that, as nickel was then almost entirely used either for gun or armament manufacture, was that Krupp was laying up secretly a large supply of nickel.'[17] This was confirmed from other sources. In December the British military attaché in Constantinople where German commercial and political interests were strong, sent a despatch on the menace which Krupps represented to England.

The management is entirely under the control of four directors, each of whom is devoted heart and soul to the interests of the Emperor. During recent years, (as can be proved) enormous quantities of heavy machinery have been purchased by Krupps, which can be required for no other purpose than that of manufacturing big guns and big naval mountings.

This present machinery is far in excess of any requirements for the existing naval programme of Germany. German naval mountings are simpler in construction than English ones, and are designed particularly with the object of being manufactured quickly ...

From information received it seems safe to say that it is, or was, the intention of the Emperor to secretly prepare all the mountings, ships' plates, ammunition etc at Krupps, and then suddenly to commence the creation of a number of battleships, sufficient to at least equal the naval strength of England ...[18]

Were these conclusions the result of British naval sensitivity? Could some of Krupp's extra capacity be for heavy field and siege, not only ships' guns? The very vagueness of the reports, 'from information received', 'partially confirmed by a confrère' deepened the fog, as did the German naval attaché's refusal to admit—despite the reports which had appeared in *German* newspapers—that any 1909 battleship contracts had been anticipated. Naval Intelligence tried to penetrate Tirpitz's intentions by comparing the sums of money provided for building programmes in the latest German Estimates; the first two instalments for the 1908 capital ships were almost fifty per cent up on the first two instalments for previous years; even allowing for the new four-tempo this meant something like £115,000 extra per ship, and they concluded that they were either building bigger or building faster. The probability was a size increase; succeeding classes of battleships had been growing larger for decades. Probability was not enough. For the first time since the ironclad revolution a foreign naval power had the capacity to build capital ships as fast as Great Britain, and her former assurance of being able to answer any foreign programme with a better one completed much more quickly was gone. With Germany's belligerent posture and undisguised Anglophobia, the hints of unnatural activity at Krupp's, Stettin and Danzig, and the official curtain that had dropped in front of attempts to discover the truth, probability faded before *possibility*.

The larger planing machines (for Krupp's). That is not the sort of story anyone would invent. It would never enter their heads to invent it ... Ordinarily speaking any firm would want only one of these to turn out a set of 13.5″ mountings, because you would take the different roller paths in succession, but if they ordered anything like four (or six), it showed they were going to have a big push suddenly. That was the point that was in my mind.[19]

By the end of December Grey had caught all the Admiralty's intense alarm. He told Count Metternich that the German Navy, using full power, could build twenty-one Dreadnoughts by April 1912; this figure was arrived at by assuming anticipatory ordering and building of both the 1909 and 1910 programmes, and in addition filling slips due to become vacant during the summer with four so far unscheduled vessels. He repeated the British offer of an exchange of information but stressed that, failing any agreement, Britain would have to base her 1909-10 programme on what Germany *could* build. Metternich, like the German naval attaché previously, assured him that the German naval programme was laid down by law, and would not be increased.

The repeated denials of anything untoward, contradicted as they were by all reports coming in to the Admiralty, convinced the Board that Tirpitz was preparing a sudden and secret 'spurt'. On January 3 Fisher wrote to the King, 'The outlook is very ominous. Herculean efforts of which we know secretly and *certainly*, are being made by Germany to push on their Dreadnoughts—so much so that McKenna, who was when he came here an extreme 'Little Navy' man, is now an ultra 'Big Navy' man, and Your Majesty would be astonished by his memorandum to Grey, and to the Prime Minister as to building more Dreadnoughts next year than intended, and we shall certainly get them!'[20]

The same day McKenna wrote to Asquith stating as fact that Germany was secretly breaking her shipbuilding Law of 1907. 'She will certainly have thirteen big ships in commission in the spring of 1911. She will probably have twenty-one big ships in the spring of 1912.'[21] It is not clear how the earlier 'possibility' of twenty-one had turned into a 'probability'; it was a large assumption. Had the fine balance of McKenna's intelligence been deranged temporarily by the magnitude of the danger signals coming in to the Admiralty and being amplified through Fisher? Or was his conclusion simply the most rational judgement on the evidence? His letter continued, 'German capacity to build Dreadnoughts is at this moment equal to ours. The last conclusion is the most alarming, and if justified would give the public a rude awakening should it become known.'

On January 14 the British naval attaché, Berlin, reported, 'I was informed "as a positive fact" that Messrs Schichau had commenced work on one of the battleships of the '09-10 programme ... My informant added that he thought Messrs Schichau could easily borrow the money until commencement of the new financial year. My informant had himself visited Schichau yard, for the firm were anxious to get an order from his government.'[22]

The following week the naval attaché reported that news had reached him from another source that Messrs Schichau were collecting material for a ship of the 1909 programme, also that Krupp had completed satisfactory trials for a 12" gun of fifty calibres; the first classes of German Dreadnoughts only mounted 11" pieces. McKenna also heard from a friend who crossed the ice at Danzig one night that the keel and first ribs of a Dreadnought were visible on one of Schichau's slips.[23]

With German acceleration of their 1909 programme in no doubt, the Sea Lords assumed that the 1910 programme would be similarly pushed forward and concluded it a 'practical certainty' that Germany would have seventeen Dreadnoughts by the spring of 1912—not the thirteen prescribed in the Naval Law. They drew up a memo for McKenna analysing the situation that year in the light of the current British programme for six Dreadnoughts to be laid down during 1909-10. Germany would have seventeen Dreadnoughts for certain (possibly twenty-one), and ten pre-Dreadnoughts, Great Britain eighteen Dreadnoughts, twenty-five pre-Dreadnoughts; giving a percentage value to the various classes of pre-Dreadnoughts this worked out at a ratio of strength of about 4 : 3 in Britain's favour—or only 5 : 4 if Germany completed twenty-one Dreadnoughts.

> Looking to the fact that our superiority of power over Germany will in 1912, even on the most favourable hypothesis, be dependent almost entirely on older ships, and that these ships will gradually fall out, when only Dreadnoughts will count as line-of-battle ships, we consider the situation is serious, and we wish to emphasise the point that Great Britain's eighteen to Germany's seventeen Dreadnoughts in 1912 is not considered in any way adequate to maintain the command of the sea in a war with Germany without running undue risk. We therefore consider it of the utmost importance that power should be taken to lay down two more armoured ships in 1909-10—making eight in all ...[24]

To the 'economists' and 'Radicals' in the Cabinet who were refusing to sanction even the six big ships McKenna had asked for originally, the demand for eight was madness. The leaders of the group were Lloyd George, now Chancellor of the Exchequer, and Winston Churchill, President of the Board of Trade. It was a strange partnership. Lloyd George, champion of 'the people' from whom he claimed to have sprung, was at heart as much a 'supreme navy' man as Grey or McKenna—he had made that clear in his conversations with

Count Metternich and others. He was also a supreme realist, his convictions dictated by political expediency. His chief concern was his own revolutionary Budget to be introduced that spring to provide pensions for the old by increased taxation from those who could afford it. This was what Liberals had pledged themselves to do, this and retrenchment in armaments. He feared that increased Naval Estimates on the scale proposed would split the Party in the House and in the country, and bring the government down. Moreover, he didn't believe the Germans *were* pushing forward their building programme; they were already in great financial difficulties, and he thought the alarm deliberately engineered by Fisher. On January 3, the day Fisher and McKenna had expressed their *certain* knowledge of German anticipatory building, he had written to Churchill:

> The Admiralty mean to get their six Dreadnoughts ... McKenna is now convinced we may have to lay down eight Dreadnoughts next year ! ! ! I feared all along this would happen. Fisher is a very clever person and when he found his programme was in danger he wired Davidson for something more panicky—and of course he got it. Can we not secure *reliable* information on this through the FO—or even the German Embassy as to what the Germans are really doing. Frankly I think the Admiralty are procuring false information to frighten us ...[25]

When, the following month, he was called to a meeting in Grey's room at the Foreign Office to hear from McKenna and Captain Jellicoe, Director of Naval Ordnance, details of Krupp's enormously expanded ordnance capacity—for this was the point which really disturbed the Sea Lords—he paced up and down by the windows fulminating on the Admiralty's extraordinary neglect in not finding out what was happening earlier. 'I don't think much of any of you Admirals and I should like to see Lord Charles Beresford at the Admiralty—the sooner the better.' McKenna, who heard some of this, immediately replied, 'You know perfectly well that these facts were communicated to the Cabinet at the time we knew of them and your remark was "It's all contractor's gossip"—or words to that effect,' and he drew his attention to the Sea Lords' memorandum of December 1907 which had given a clear warning of possible acceleration.[26] Lloyd George's annoyance was a measure of the weight of the evidence.

Churchill was another 'supreme navy' man at heart, but he had fallen under Lloyd George's spell; the quick-silver mind and political sophistication of the man fascinated him, above all perhaps the new vistas of Radicalism he had opened for him. Churchill's was an intellectual approach. Unlike Lloyd George, he liked to analyse and arrive at principles to which he could hold fast—great principles which he could see in bold colours and work at with all his ample resources of imagination and wit and astonishing verbal imagery. His mind was powerful and direct, almost ingenuous, 'full of ardour and surprise; eternal verities appeared to him as exciting personal discoveries.'[27] His latest discovery had been the poor. Quite as ardent a social reformer as Lloyd George and during his time at the Board of Trade quite as effective, he believed in the Liberal pledges, not only on grounds of principle and compassion but on national, even Imperial grounds: 'We are not going to measure the strength of great Powers only in their material forces ... the security and the predominance of our country depends upon the maintenance of the vigour and health of its population.'[28] He had also convinced himself that the talk of war between Great Britain and Germany as inevitable was nonsense. Germany had 'nothing to fight about, nothing to fight for.'[29] It was evident to him that 'a month of fighting would destroy more wealth than the successful trade of five years'; it must be equally evident to the Germans. As for Great Britain starting it, that too would be madness as Germany was among her very best customers. It was true that a *few* people in each country wanted to fight, but what of the rest of the hundred millions or so in the two countries?

'Are we all such sheep? Is democracy in the twentieth century so powerless to effect its will? Are we all become such puppets and marionettes to be wire-pulled against our interests into such hideous convulsions? I have a high and prevailing faith in the essential goodness of great peoples ...'[30]

Above all, he refused to agree that British naval supremacy was in danger; he believed four Dreadnoughts would suffice, for even if Germany had seventeen against sixteen British Dreadnoughts in 1912, the 'overpowering superfluity' of at least seventeen pre-Dreadnoughts assured British supremacy.[31] The technical details he had from two leading members of the 'syndicate of discontent', Admiral Custance—formerly Beresford's Second-in-Command, Channel—and the former Chief Constructor to the Navy, Sir William White; he it was who had established the classic form and built class after class of those pre-Dreadnought battleships in which Great Britain had such a numerical and technical lead. He detested the Dreadnought and all her spawn. Custance, of course, detested Fisher; the feeling was mutual, and when Fisher found out what was going on he jumped to the conclusion that the motive of Churchill's technical advisers was really 'a resuscitation of the Enquiry dodge'; he had already received warning that agitation was afoot. 'The baseness of it all is that Custance and White know that only four Dreadnoughts would compel my resignation! *That is the object and not the safety of the country* ...'[32]

When Churchill worked his details of pre-Dreadnought superiority into a memorandum for Cabinet consideration in February, Fisher primed McKenna for the fray:

> THE ONLY ISSUE is the number of Dreadnoughts! *Why?* Because as you yourself pointed out last night, no matter how many of the *Canopus* class, for instance, try to fight a Dreadnought, the Dreadnought at a range beyond the *Canopus* gobbles them all up! It's the armadillo and the ants—the armadillo puts out its tongue and licks up the ants—the bigger the ant the more placid the digestive smile! ... so I suggest to you that the controversy wants to be brought back to the number of Dreadnoughts, *and that we are fighting for our lives, and for a one-Power standard now*, when the pre-Dreadnoughts shortly go the way of all flesh and die out! And to ask the simple question that, though we build *six* Dreadnoughts, can we sleep quiet in our beds in view of the certainty that the Germans *can* have twenty-one against our eighteen in April 1912, *when they mean to fight?*[33]

McKenna, supported by Grey and other 'Big Navy' members of the Cabinet, argued the case for six staunchly against the Radical wing who would not concede anything over four, and the meeting ended in deadlock. Nevertheless Fisher believed he had the stronger hand; Churchill and Lloyd George were threatening resignation, but they had a poor and generally unpopular case and he didn't believe they would carry it through. Nor did he believe that Asquith, who was with him for the six, could go back on his pledges to maintain British naval supremacy made in the previous year's Estimates debates. As for the Sea Lords they were firm behind him and determined to resign if the government weakened; Asquith could not risk the national outcry that must follow such an exodus. After the Cabinet discussion Fisher wrote to the Editor of *The Observer*, a reliable ally:

> Well you want me to tell you, 'May I assume absolutely that the SIX are secured?' YES YOU MAY! I have had to hunt for the red ink so as to emphasise that! I nearly wrote it in my own blood! ... (N.B. The beauty of it is that though SIX are sufficient I am going for *eight* ! ! ! and if the Germans ... should have made the progress that is possible though not probable *we shall have the eight*! but don't allude to this). Really McKenna's conversion is almost up to Saul of Tarsus! ... now he's all with me for the eight though only to ask for six at first ... rely on me my dear friend & believe in the line of absolute trust in Asquith, Grey and McKenna is the one that will pay ...[34]

The next issue of *The Observer* carried the news under large headlines that well-informed Ministerial circles knew Asquith and McKenna to be adhering without reserve to their pledges so that the six Dreadnoughts required for the 'Two-Power' standard were 'absolutely secured'.[35] Churchill, Lloyd George and their followers would not agree, some from pacifist conviction, but not it was thought the two leaders. Esher met them, confiding afterwards to his Journal:

> I am bound to say that they are both attractive personalities. They take differences of opinion so well. Lloyd George, in his heart, does not care a bit for economy, and is quite ready to face parliament with any amount of deficit and to 'go' for a big Navy. He is plucky and imperialist at heart, if he is anything. Besides he despises the stalwarts on his own side ... (he) realises that in 1912 we shall be in danger of hardly having a *one*-power naval standard. Winston cannot see it. I pointed out to them that the great majority of the country is against them. That nobody goes into detail and that six Dreadnoughts—rightly or wrongly—stand for sea supremacy. To resign upon that point would ruin them ... Lloyd George, I am sure agrees; Winston trembles and would walk over a bridge, but his *amour propre* demands one. The question is can it be found?[36]

Churchill's refusal to compromise his opposition annoyed Asquith. 'For the first time he expressed deep disappointment in Winston. It was a personal wound because he had set such high hopes on him ... He said to me (his daughter) one day with great sadness, "I am

afraid that Winston is proving to be thoroughly untrustworthy." '[37]
On February 20, with the time for publication of the Estimates
nearly upon them and the argument still raging, Asquith wrote to
his wife.

> Winston and Lloyd George by their combined machinations have
> got the bulk of the Liberal Press into the same camp ... go about
> darkly hinting at resignation (which is bluff) ... there are moments
> when I am disposed summarily to cashier them both.[38]

Similar bitter arguments were disturbing the German government.
Bülow, primed with constant reports from Count Metternich about
British alarm at the new building tempo, British resolve 'to still
further immense financial sacrifices and effort'[39] to remain ahead,
had realised that the 'peace offensive' had failed. And convinced that
Tirpitz's inflexible plans, far from winning any freedom of action
at home or abroad, were driving Germany further into a corner, he
was making a determined attack on the Navy Office strategy. He
had opened the campaign by gaining an admission from Tirpitz
that he was not yet through the 'Danger Zone', and had then
adopted some of the arguments of Galster and the Progressives:
since Germany could not hope to outbuild Great Britain in battleships, why not concentrate on submarines and coastal defences and
drop one battleship a year from the programme? This would disarm
British suspicion, make for a smooth passage of the 'Danger Zone'
and result in a reduction in British building programmes, as it had
been made abundantly clear that British building was dependent
on German.[40]

Tirpitz refused to concede any points in the argument, for even
one ship dropped from the present programme would make it
impossible to justify *adding* the ships which he needed to complete
the 'Iron Budget' in 1912. So, against all Metternich's long and
detailed reports to the contrary, he maintained that it was trade
rivalry, not his naval programme which was provoking British alarm
and hostility. The *Flottenprofessoren* continued to publicise this
view. Whatever *their* real beliefs Tirpitz was patently insincere.
He knew from reports of German military and naval attachés and
from the British Press that his increased tempo was *the* central issue;
as he was building his fleet deliberately against England, deliberately
to circumscribe her freedom of political action he would have been
vastly surprised at any other result. The extent of British alarm

was the measure of his success. Already Grey was coming as a supplicant; as with home politics, it was no time to ease the pace, rather to increase the pressure and narrow the gap; he insisted to Bülow, 'Our duty is to arm with all our might.'[41]

To the Chancellor's argument that Britain might launch a preventive assault while she still had time, he replied that this danger was less than it had been in 1905—on what grounds is not clear. To the arguments for submarines, he repeated his answers to similar criticism in the *Reichstag*: 'Guerrilla warfare (*Kleinkrieg*) without a battle fleet is unthinkable,'[42] and he reversed Bülow's arguments about the increased tempo provoking an English attack by insisting that 'every new ship increasing our battle fleet means an increase in the risk for England if she attacks us.'![43]

Tirpitz remains an enigma. How much of this did he really believe, how much was conscious justification for his long-term goal? He knew that his Dreadnought fleet would not be safe from English attack until the Kiel Canal widening scheme had been completed about 1915; German operations plans conceded the virtually hopeless position of the fleet in a war with England, and he had recently been faced with a near revolt among the planners and front-line commanders, who suffered from the unpreparedness for immediate action caused by his concentration of all resources on the building programme for the distant goal.

What he did not know was that British operational strategy against Germany had changed in a way that fatally undermined the military, hence also the political goals of his long-term policy. Admiral Sir Arthur Wilson, British Commander-in-Chief designate, had determined in war to keep the British battle fleet concentrated to the north of Scotland—not to invest the German coasts.[44] This meant that the German fleet would need to act offensively to break a blockade. To do this successfully, on Tirpitz's own assumptions of the relative strengths needed for offence and defence, Germany would need a 3:2 *superiority* over the British fleet. Even if, as he believed, individual German ships and squadrons were more efficient, he would not need equality at the very least. Yet the rationale of his plan to forge a power political lever against England called in the first place for a fleet *inferior* to the British in the proportion 2:3. This was the external goal of the 60-Dreadnought '*aeternat*' he sought, for all the studies conducted by his office suggested that England would not be able to build, man and replace anything larger than a 90-Dreadnought fleet. Tirpitz assumed that once this 2 : 3 ratio had been reached, Germany would have such a good defensive chance that England would fear to attack—hence his power lever would start to operate.

This overlooked the very obvious point, which *Admiralstab* planners increasingly recognised,[45] that the British had no *need* to attack to achieve their purpose; they might use a wide blockade and still strangle German sea trade. Sir Arthur Wilson had decided to do just that. But Tirpitz refused to let the possibility affect his ship designs or his programme. He saw his struggle as political and economic; the goal was in sight; the violence of the British reaction testified to the economic strain they already felt. Long before his own fleet reached the magic 60 they would be forced to concede their present overwhelming supremacy.

But what of Germany, already heavily burdened with debt? His faith in her growing industrial strength was justified; on present rising trends she must overtake Great Britain. But the proportion of her defence budget—itself some 89 per cent of the total *Reich* budget—which went to the Navy hovered between 19 per cent and 26 per cent;[46] the rest went to the Army. In Great Britain some 60 per cent of defence spending was for the Navy, only 40 per cent for the Army.[47] While Tirpitz did not have to budget for a large cruiser force and world-wide presence like the Royal Navy, and could concentrate the greater part of his resources on the battle-fleet and supporting destroyers, and while the pay bill for the German conscripts was half that for the English long-term volunteer seamen so that he could concentrate a greater proportion on *materiel*, it must have been evident that to achieve anything like parity with the Royal Navy, either the German defence budget had to grow at least twice as large as that of the British Empire, or he had to wrest a much larger share of it from the Army. Even on these two large assumptions he could not expect much more than parity with the British fleet. In a shooting war this would not be enough to overcome Germany's hopeless geographical position and the naval allies his policy had forced on England. Even the absorption of the Dutch and Belgian ports, the undisguised aim of the Pan-Germans could not alter the position significantly; only the incorporation of France into a German continental system could do that—and yet any German attempt to achieve this must bring Great Britain in for the 'Copenhagen' war against her. And while Tirpitz appears to have convinced himself of the superiority of German ship construction, weapons and tactics, he was wrong. In most vital respects the British Service was several years ahead. Tirpitz remains an enigma. In his fight for the fleet he used so many specious technical arguments that his subordinates acknowledged him—respectfully— as 'the father of the lie';[48] now it is difficult to know which justification represented his real thinking at any time.

What is clear is that by 1909 Bülow had strong support for believing the policy mistaken. Among those who had once favoured it, the Foreign Office was most concerned with the astonishing way it had rebounded to limit German rather more than British freedom of political action, and was anxious for curbs on Tirpitz. So were important businessmen. One such was Albert Ballin, head of the Hamburg-Amerika line, influential not only through his wealth and wide contacts abroad, especially in England, but also because he was a friend of Wilhelm's. Once an enthusiast for a great fleet which would command respect in the world and strengthen Germany's commercial sinews, he believed that Tirpitz had, by great good fortune and remarkable restraint on England's part, safely negotiated the entrance to the 'Danger Zone' and acquired the foundation of such a fleet. Now was the time to bargain with England as one naval Power to another, not to persist in this uncompromising challenge to which Britain, by virtue of her greater need and resources would never yield, and which must ruin Germany. As he expressed it, an agreement on the naval question 'is a necessity for both nations, and this necessity should offer to practical men the basis for a fair compromise. Otherwise the life will certainly be knocked out of us, and in two years what will we have for this accelerated naval construction—a new financial catastrophe or a war?'[49]

Both possibilities were very real for Bülow. The debt financing of the Navy could not continue indefinitely. The previous November, in the wake of the *Novelle*, he had tried to raise the contribution from those who demanded armaments most vociferously by proposing an inheritance tax, only to have it thrown out by the *Reichstag*. But something needed to be done if the Empire's finances were to retain confidence. As for war, Ballin had returned recently from England, where he had talked with Sir Ernest Cassel, an intimate of King Edward. He had been told that someday Britain, joined by France and Russia, might have to enquire at what point Berlin intended to stop the naval building. Ballin had replied that Germany would resist such a 'Fashoda' with all her might.[50] This was just what Bülow feared. In such circumstances the hot-heads in the Army and the Conservative parties would never be restrained, and he knew that diplomacy would be powerless to prevent a European war. In November last there had been an incident in Morocco involving German deserters from the French Foreign Legion, trivial enough in itself, yet Wilhelm's eldest son, the Crown Prince, interpreting it in the light of the student's duelling code, had written to Bülow demanding that the 'insolent clique in Paris should be made to feel once more what a Pomeranian Grenadier can do ... the whole Army is longing to "get at 'em".'[51] If that was the attitude over deserters what would happen if German honour really were at stake! On that occasion Bülow had replied:

> It is excellent no doubt that the Army should not feel its sword has rusted in the scabbard; it is necessary even that the soldiers should be bellicose. But the task of a policy leader is to get a clear view of the consequences ... War today would be a serious matter, far more serious than it was in 1870. Moreover today it is improbable that we could ever fight France single-handed. We should have to fight England as well. And if we attacked France Russia would come in on her side. Consequently, and in view of the very difficult situation in Europe today, I feel that the main thing is to keep our powder dry.[52]

Bülow's analysis was correct. In London Esher noted in his Journal that although France had never asked Britain whether she would come to her aid in the event of war over the Moroccan incident, 'in point of fact Asquith, Grey and Haldane (of the War Office) had decided to do so. Haldane told Asquith that if we failed France he would not give ten years' purchase for the British Empire. This was very straight and courageous. Grey never wavered or doubted ...'[53]

In this respect Bülow's apprehension of danger was more realistic than Tirpitz's strange loss of caution. But above all Bülow wanted to retain some freedom of action for German diplomacy; while Britain felt imperilled by Tirpitz's programme they were all locked in immovable attitudes that must become increasingly tense as each German Dreadnought slid down the ways. Already British correspondents had noted they were engaged in a kind of financial warfare, while in the rival fleets the striving for efficiency, 'the strain and stress resembled closely the actual conditions of war.'[54] A way had to be found to reduce the tension and unlock the attitudes lest the military gain the chance they sought. Despite a threat by Tirpitz that he would resign if the idea for a reduction in building tempo were mentioned to Wilhelm, Bülow insisted that negotiations be opened with England to try and secure a neutrality agreement in return for a reduction of the German building rate. Tirpitz refused to consider altering his programme for any 'vague political agreement', but agreed grudgingly to a three-tempo for ten years if Britain agreed to no more than four a year. This was elaborate cynicism. He knew that no British government could accept such an abdication of naval supremacy and freedom of action. But Wilhelm supported his stand.[55]

That February (1909), with the argument inside the German government deadlocked, King Edward paid a State visit to Berlin, the first he had paid to his nephew's capital. Count Metternich had been recalled for the occasion and stood between Bülow and Tirpitz in the reception Committee at the Lehrter Bahnhof. As the train steamed in, he turned to Tirpitz and said, 'Unless you make it possible for Prince Bülow to bring off the naval agreement, this will probably be the last time that an English King comes here to visit a German Emperor.'[56]

Edward's hope that his visit might relax the tension between the two Empires was not fulfilled. The most elaborate arrangements on the German part and all Edward's flair for the right word could not disguise the depth of feeling. Edward's private secretary recorded:

> One felt that a few charming men really liked us, but with the majority I derived the impression that they hated us. The Germans never forgave the King for having, as they imagined, isolated them from the rest of Europe ... The Emperor for his part seemed to do all that he could to make the visit a success but was never at ease with the King. There were always forced jokes and the atmosphere seemed charged with dangerous electricity.[57]

Towards the end of February Winston Churchill laid his conciliatory 'bridge' towards the 'Big Navy' men, suggesting four possible ways for the two sides in the Cabinet dispute to meet. One of these involved building four Dreadnoughts immediately and two later if evidence proved them necessary. Fisher told McKenna he wanted no compromises on the six 'which we know in our hearts is too few, and jeopardising our national existence *and that we ought to build eight!*'[58] However, in a Cabinet meeting a few days later Asquith produced an ingenious compromise which appeared to satisfy everyone; four Dreadnoughts would be laid down during the coming financial year, and four more no later than April 1, 1910 if the necessity for them were proven. McKenna accepted this, but Fisher remained wary, insisting that the estimates should commit the government to the 'contingent four' more definitely. A footnote was therefore added giving the government powers to order guns and mountings, machinery, armour and collect materials for the 'rapid construction' of further ships during the year. Even so, Fisher remained suspicious; McKenna urged him to see Grey.

By this time more news of German shipbuilding activity had arrived at the Admiralty via an Argentinian naval mission which had been taken on a tour of inspection of the yards, during which they had seen twelve capital ships either building or having materials collected, and had counted a hundred heavy guns nearing completion at Krupps.[59] Fisher told Grey of this when they met, and his conviction that Germany would have twelve or thirteen Dreadnoughts by April 1911, and seventeen or twenty-one by April 1912. Grey assured him that he had been growing uncomfortable about German shipbuilding himself; what Fisher had said confirmed his own opinion that it was not possible to tell within six months when any German ship would be ready, and he thought it necessary 'to build as fast as we can until we have the situation well in hand.'[60] However, he went on, as McKenna had stressed that no time would be gained in letting more than four contracts at present, the first thing to do was to ask Parliament for the money for these four; the next thing was to give Parliament notice that contracts would be let in advance for four more as soon as it was considered necessary. It was up to Fisher and McKenna to tell the Cabinet as soon as the moment arrived when time would be lost by not ordering these 'contingent four'; if the Cabinet refused to give authority, *then* would be the time for McKenna and the Sea Lords to decide whether the action of the Cabinet was consistent with national safety. Put this way, Fisher agreed that the footnote met his needs for the moment, but he urged McKenna, when he presented the Estimates to the House, to 'remove all doubt that the declaration in the foot-

note that these four ships will be completed by 1912 is the determined resolve of the Board of Admiralty.'[61]

McKenna introduced the Estimates on March 16. The House
was packed but quite silent as he explained the difficulty the government found itself in; 'We do not know, as we thought we did,
the rate at which German construction is taking place.' He gave
the estimates of German progress which had been formed on the
evidence of acceleration and anticipatory ordering, and for the
first time in an official statement gave details of the building time
for battleships, passing on to an equally unique 'tribute to the
extraordinary growth in the power of constructing ships of
the largest size in Germany.'[62] This was the point which, from the
first, had impressed him; Germany now had fourteen slips capable
of carrying Dreadnoughts and three more under construction.
'What is true of the ships is true also of the guns, armour and
mountings. Two years ago anyone familiar with Krupps and other
great German firms would have ridiculed the possibility of their
undertaking to supply the component parts of eight battleships in
one year. Today this productive power is a realised fact.'

This was the point on which the opposition relied for their
attack. Balfour, assuming that Tirpitz had actually started to use
full capacity, asserted that Germany *would* have seventeen Dreadnoughts in little over two years time, by July 1911. McKenna
interrupted him, 'The Right Honourable gentleman is assuming that
another four ships will be laid down. The four ships of the 1909-10
programme will be laid down technically on April 1, 1909, but
the Right Honourable gentleman must not suppose that *another*
four ships will be laid down on April 1.'

'That is exactly what I do suppose,' Balfour replied. 'Having laid
down eight ships last year (the four of the normal programme plus
the four assumed from the reports to have been anticipated from
the 1909-10 programme), they may lay down four ships this year,
or they may do this year what they did last, and add eight ships. If
the Germans go on at this rate, which is more than possible, the
probability is that they will have on April 1, 1912, twenty-one
Dreadnoughts to our twenty (assuming the government's four
'contingent ships' would be built).'

Not content with this alarming figure, he went on, 'If the
Germans imitate the programme of the present government and
lay down not only their eight in the financial year but as well

demand a new group of four when the government propose to begin their new group of four, namely April 1, they will then have twenty-five!'

Asquith rose and assured him that such a number was a physical impossibility. The government, he said, had a most distinct declaration from the German government that it was not their intention to accelerate their programme—and they could only have seventeen Dreadnoughts in 1912 if they did accelerate; their stated programme provided for thirteen at that date. 'Thirteen is a certainty. It is because seventeen is a possibility that we are taking the power (to lay down four 'contingent ships'), otherwise we should not take it at all.'

Asquith had prepared the government disclosures of increased German capacity and apparent acceleration of the German programme to still the pacifist elements in his own Party who were bent on attacking the size of the Estimates.[63] He succeeded in this, but the speculation and suggestions conjured from the disclosures, so much more ominous on account of their uncertainty and the vagueness surrounding the 'contingent ships' left the government facing a far more serious attack from the other side for not building enough. By the following day when the Conservative former Civil Lord of the Admiralty, Arthur Lee, had piled on the horrors by asserting in the House that Krupp's annual output of guns, mountings and turrets exceeded that 'of our whole national resources put together'—no exaggeration according to Jellicoe, Director of Naval Ordnance[64]—the alarm grew into something like panic. The Conservative Press, the Navy League and patriotic speakers up and down the country vied to outdo each other in chilling prognostications and the careful distinctions McKenna and Asquith had made between what Germany could build and what she would build were lost to sight. All that seemed clear was that Germany had thrown down the gauntlet. She had been casting envious eyes on the British Empire for a decade; now she was ready to make her bid for the good places of the earth. The answer was simple: naval strength was measured in Dreadnoughts, therefore a maximum programme of Dreadnoughts must be laid down at once. 'We want eight, and we won't wait!' became the rally cry of Conservatives and navalists. Even such a balanced top insider as Viscount Esher was not immune from the fever. 'Unless the Board of Admiralty get their eight ships *at once*,' he wrote to his son, 'they ought to be hanged. I am going to try and put the fear of God into Jackie (Fisher) this morning.'[65]

Fisher was enjoying himself. At his desk by five or earlier each morning, firing off red-hot letters to the select band of editors and naval correspondents whom he trusted and used to disseminate and explain Admiralty policy, he was in the centre of one alarmist web. He believed the 'contingent four' were assured, but he had planned to make them 'Parliamentary sure'[66] by unleashing his Press friends and raising the public alert *after* McKenna's and Asquith's speeches to the House. Thus on the 19th he wrote to J. L. Garvin, Editor of *The Observer*, '*I myself feel secure*, but I don't want to allay the deep feeling in the public mind of all that is at stake—We have engineered eight Dreadnoughts this year. They can't be prevented! —We have engineered the great Radical majority into an obedient flock—Nevertheless don't desist!'[67]

Garvin responded with a fire-breathing article advising the country to 'insist on "the Eight, the whole Eight and nothing but the Eight" with more to follow, and break any man or faction that stands in the way', phrases unmistakably from the depth of Fisher's soul, so close were the two. 'We stand in a crisis of national peril', Garvin went on, 'such as for two hundred years has never threatened us in peace or war. By an act of moral treachery, which would justify us in armed reprisals now, a foreign Power has doubled its naval programme in secret, and has gained six months start in a conspiracy against our life ... We must fight before 1910—while we have a full margin of power in our hand, or build eight Dreadnoughts now. There is no third way.'[68]

At 5 o'clock on the morning this came out Fisher was writing to another of his intimates, the naval correspondent, Arnold White.

My dear Friend ... Don't check this wave of public emotion that will give us the eight Dreadnoughts a year! What a cold douche if I got up and said, 'Yes, the gradual, unswerving work of four years has now culminated in our having in home waters two fleets, each of which in all its parts is incomparably superior to the whole German fleet mobilised for war ... Look at the Battle Practice report. See the *Indomitable* hitting a target 14 times smaller than herself 13 times out of 15! At what distance? Five miles! ... 306 vessels went into the North Sea last year without a single breakdown or delay. That is the test of efficiency. "Sea-keeping and hitting!" SO SLEEP QUIET IN YOUR BEDS! It would be magnificent to say this but it would not be eight Dreadnoughts! Also I might say to them, "Don't boil over about the Germans! Believe me you don't understand their feverish haste in building Dreadnoughts. It is *not* to fight you! No, it's the octopus in the North Sea closing round it and the ever-present and daily increasing fear of a 'Copenhagen', which a Pitt or a Bismarck would not hesitate one second about! *Cease building or I strike!*"[69]

Meanwhile Count Metternich, who had wired Berlin before the Commons debate to obtain permission to contradict the acceleration stories, at last received a reply that he should admit prior allocation of two contracts for the 1909-10 programme; these had been given out in advance to prevent the private yards forming a ring to bid up prices. Tirpitz repeated this explanation in the German naval debates in the *Reichstag* on March 29, adding that the yards would not receive a pfennig until the contracts were signed on April 1, neither had the Navy Office helped them by arranging loans. But by letting out these two contracts early the two government slips which would become vacant in the summer could be played off against the other private builders to get lower prices. And he repeated earlier declarations that there would be no acceleration in building times, which would remain at three years for heavy ships. The German Navy would in 1912 have only thirteen Dreadnoughts.

Grey and McKenna, who had been pressing Metternich and the German naval attaché since the previous November for a true statement of progress wondered why it had taken so long to extract such an innocent admission, why Tirpitz could not have played off his government slips against the private yards without the two —or was it three—anticipated orders, and why the British naval attaché was still not allowed to see what was happening. Fisher tackled Metternich about it when the two found themselves by chance alone.

We two glared at each other for a second and then I got up from writing and spoke to him. I said, 'We are having a hot time, Ambassador about numbers of Dreadnoughts. Some say you will have 13 in April 1912, some say 17, Mr Balfour says 21.' Metternich: 'There will only be 13.' Self: 'Is that counting "Indomitables" (battlecruisers)?' Metternich: 'Yes—counting "Indomitables"'. Self: 'How all this scare would vanish, Ambassador, if you would let our naval attaché go and count them!' Metternich: 'That is impossible. Other governments would want to—*besides, something would be seen which we wish to keep secret!*' Just then Knollys came into the room and I left. My inference is that they are building bigger than they say they are.[70]

Despite the uproar from the Conservatives about the small building programme, Asquith refused to give a pledge that the 'contingent' Dreadnoughts would certainly be built, and on March 29 Balfour moved a vote of censure on the government for risking the safety of the Empire in its provision of battleships. The highlight of the subsequent debate was Grey's philosophical exposition of the great Liberal dilemma. His starting point was the awesome fact that 'half the national revenues of the great countries of Europe are being spent on armaments.[71]

'Surely the extent to which this expenditure has grown really becomes a satire and a reflection of civilisation. Not in our generation perhaps but if it goes on at the rate at which it has recently increased, sooner or later I believe it will submerge that civilisation ... Is it to be wondered that the hopes and aspirations of the best men in the leading countries are devoted to trying to find some means of checking it?'

He addressed himself to the pacifist aspirations. 'If we alone, among the great Powers, gave up the competition and sank into a position of inferiority, what good should we do? No good to ourselves because we cannot realise great ideals of social reform at home when we are holding our existence at the mercy, at the caprice if you like, of another nation. That is not feasible. If we fall into a position of inferiority our self-respect is gone, and it removes that enterprise which is essential both to the material success of industry and to the carrying out of great ideals, and you fall into a state of apathy. We should cease to count for anything among the nations of Europe, and we should be fortunate if our liberty was left and we did not become the conscript appendage of some stronger power. That is a brutal way of stating the case, but it is the truth.'

Moving to the central issue, he made the point once again that for Britain naval supremacy was a matter of life and death. It was not so for Germany. 'No superiority of the British Navy over the German Navy could ever put us in a position to affect the independence or integrity of Germany, because our Army is not maintained on a scale which, unaided could do anything on German territory.

But if the German Navy were superior to ours, they, maintaining the army which they do, for us it would not be a question of defeat. Our independence, our very existence would be at stake.'

The British government wished to come to an agreement which would end the naval competition, but here was the difficulty. It could not be on a basis of equality; it would have to be on the basis of the superiority of the British Navy. 'But it is another thing to ask the German government to expose itself before its own public opinion to a charge of having co-operated to make the attainment of our views easier. That is the difficulty which it is only fair to state.' Because of this, Grey again limited his suggestions to an exchange of naval information in the hope that it might lead to mutual confidence and eventual understanding.

In the meantime there was the question of the four 'contingent' ships whose uncertainty had provoked the censure. Grey had spent half an hour with Fisher before the speech, and he made it clear that while the government could not be bound to build them now—for one thing the Admiralty had decided to await the launching of the German ships before replying in case they were an improved type —they would not in any way limit the following year's programme. Further, although the German government had given a declaration of its building rate there was the possibility of a change of *intention*, and their declaration had said nothing about any collection of materials or manufacture of ordnance, armour or turrets prior to construction which would enable them to accelerate if they should change their intention. This was Grey's way of putting Fisher's point, 'The fact is that we must have a large margin against lying!'[72] and Fisher, listening intently, was delighted. He wrote to Esher:

> Grey rubbed in two great points ... 1. Lack of information as to German acceleration will be acted on as if acceleration were a fact 2. The eight this year won't affect next year. I watched Lloyd George and Winston with malignant glee as their two heads went together as he said those two things![73]

Asquith's speech which followed was equally moderate and firm. He repeated that there were only two ways of dealing with the naval competition, either by agreement on both sides to slacken the rate of construction or by the grant of reciprocal facilities for inspection of each other's progress. As both ways appeared to be blocked for the time being 'We are obliged by the most simple and elementary requirements of precaution to act as though the present intention of Germany may peradventure be subsequently modified, but to take also into account that their present productive facilities will certainly not be diminished.'[74]

Both sides of the Liberal Party came together in the voting to defeat the censure motion; both still believed their own views had prevailed. For the Liberal 'Imperialists' and the Admiralty the 'four' were assured before April the following year, for the 'little Englanders' there would have to be very convincing evidence of German acceleration before that came about. Churchill believed that even if they were ordered in the coming year they would still count for the 1910-11 programme. Fisher put his trust in Grey to 'keep the Navy right'; as he told the King, 'Your Majesty has one splendid servant in the Cabinet—the Foreign Secretary. He is as much above all the rest of them as Mr Balfour is above all his colleagues.'[75] McKenna was bitter about Churchill and Lloyd George, who he believed, put politics before the safety of the country, bitter too about Asquith's weakness. Esher told him twenty-five years experience had taught him that Prime Ministers—even the strongest— were called 'weak' when they tried to keep their Cabinet or Party together.[76]

The situation was resolved from an unexpected quarter. News reached the Admiralty that Austria was planning three or four Dreadnoughts and that Italy, anxious about these, was planning four in reply. Asquith, apparently genuinely alarmed at the prospect of eight more Dreadnoughts in the hands of the Triple Alliance lost any doubts he may have had about the 'contingent four', and McKenna was authorised to state that they would be ordered during the coming year without prejudice to the following year's programme. The Admiralty had their 'eight', the Radicals, although not convinced, had an honourable escape from the stand which they knew to be against the temper of the country at large, Asquith had a tolerably united Party, the Conservatives and navalists had a guarantee of naval supremacy over Germany—all in all a surprisingly satisfactory ending to what, despite the manipulation and intrigue, had been a real and justified cry of alarm.

In Germany meanwhile, Tirpitz's Estimates had been approved without debate in the *Reichstag* and the official contracts for the ships which had caused all the fuss—drawn up to stipulate a building time of *three years*—had been signed and the ships officially started. Tirpitz himself was simmering with indignation over the inferences which had been drawn during the 'scare', or so he made out to the British naval attaché. Growing very excited he said that his word had been doubted, in fact disbelieved and that despite his statement that the German programme was not being accelerated his word had been contradicted by the responsible British Minister. He had been tempted to speak his mind in the *Reichstag* but had handed the matter over to the Foreign Office instead; however, he wished to impress the attaché with the fact that he felt his personal honour doubted. After which he repeated that the contracts had been given out the previous autumn simply in order to secure better prices, and then launched into 'his usual harangue' about the German fleet being entirely defensive. 'Germany will never attempt to dispute the sea supremacy of England.'[77]

The following month, when the naval attaché again applied to visit the Schichau yard, thinking it would be 'interesting to see how far the Dreadnought had advanced in the seven weeks' since her official start he was refused.[78]

The question of honour loomed equally large in Tirpitz's struggle with Bülow. As Wilhelm told the Chancellor after discussing 'this whole filthy English naval and Dreadnought business' with Tirpitz:

> There has been no question of two equal powers discussing a suggestion, but always the same somewhat haughty demand of a stronger party to a weaker, who is not considered as an equal. Hence our refusal, since our personal honour was nearly always at stake ... they (Great Britain) always gave us to understand that it was in their interest that we should disarm, so that they, of course could maintain their advantage with as little trouble and expense as possible! That is a point of view we cannot accept either from the military or national standpoint of honour. Every English intrigue and machination is bent on forcing us to accept the two-power standard ...[79]

This, Wilhelm repeated after Tirpitz, Germany could not do without capitulating before the world and forfeiting national honour! Despite the powerful reinforcement the navalist pair gave each other, Bülow persisted in trying to bring reason and statecraft to bear, recalling Metternich from London to give his impressions of English feeling at a meeting on June 3 to which he called Tirpitz, the chief of Wilhelm's naval Cabinet, the Chief of the Great General Staff of the Army, the Foreign Minister, and the Minister of the Interior, Bethmann-Hollweg. Tirpitz refused to move an inch. His own personal observations, he said, contradicting Metternich, had led him to conclude that English hostility was not the result of the naval building tempo, but of German economic competition combined with the intrigues of Sir John Fisher, who was working against them with every underhand method. The stronger the German Fleet became the less prepared England would be to quarrel. He was forced to admit that Germany's chances in a war with England would be slender, and they would not be through the 'Danger Zone' until about 1914 when the Kiel Canal had been widened and Heligoland fortified. Bülow said this was all very well but how were they to get through their present difficulties; to bridge the gap between today and the achievement of the Fleet an understanding with England was necessary. And, referring to Tirpitz's proposal for a 3:4 ratio with the Royal Navy, he repeated that no diplomacy in the world could get England to accept a formula which appeared to her to menace her existence. Metternich had previously expressed his opinion that if they did propose such a ratio to England it would quickly lead to war. Tirpitz thought Metternich overstated the danger—he had just had a despatch from his attaché in London that a preventive war would *not* be declared by a Liberal government —but in any case the recent attitude displayed by the British government made it impossible for the approach to come from Germany. The meeting broke up on the rock of his obduracy.[80]

It was Bülow's last throw. He had started his pressure for an understanding with England the previous Autumn in the belief that he was in a strong position. Wilhelm had just created an international sensation by having the London *Daily Telegraph* publish a record of his remarks on Anglo-German relations made while a guest of Colonel Stuart-Wortley at Highcliffe Castle. Wilhelm's aim had been to dispel the English people's 'misconceptions' of his attitude towards them, and reassure them particularly about the German fleet. In the attempt he had surpassed all previous indiscretions, revealing among other things that during the Boer War when German public and Press opinion had been bitterly hostile to Britain he had not only refused to receive the Boer delegation which had been greeted rapturously in France and elsewhere on the Continent, but had worked out a plan of campaign for the British forces, had it checked by his General Staff and despatched it to England! 'As a matter of curious coincidence let me add that the plan which I formulated ran very much on the same lines as that which was actually adopted by Lord Roberts'![81] And insisting that he was still the friend of England, he had pointed to the difficulty of his task as the prevailing sentiment among large sections of the middle and lower classes in Germany was not friendly to England. He was, so to speak, in a minority in his own country. These extraordinary gaffes had produced the same reverse effects as the 'Tweedmouth letter'; to the British it had been confirmation from the highest source that the majority of Germans hated them, to the Germans it was the crowning folly of the 'personal diplomacy' by which Wilhelm had sought throughout his reign to bypass all normal diplomatic channels. The disclosure that he had actually helped the British to beat their blood brothers was a shock which displaced from the headlines the Balkan question, Sir John Fisher's machinations, even Prince Henry's ascent in a Zeppelin. In the *Reichstag* the criticism had bordered on abuse; demands had been made for constitutional guarantees against further Royal indiscretions, and even for changes in the Constitution which would make the government Ministers responsible to the *Reichstag*.

Wilhelm had broken down. Conditioned throughout his reign to believe himself the idol of his subjects—except Social Democrats—shielded from reality by the Cabinet system and the sycophancy of his entourage, the sudden discovery that his character and methods were widely disapproved even among the most patriotic elements had shattered him. He had taken to his bed with shivering fits and announced amid bouts of hysterical self-pity that he would abdicate. The Crown Prince, summoned to his bedside, had been shocked at his appearance: 'he seemed aged by years; he had lost hope and felt himself deserted by everyone ... his self-confidence and trust were shattered. A deep pity was in me. Scarcely ever have I felt so near to him as at that hour.[82]

In his discomfiture Bülow had felt his own position to be stronger than ever before, and had launched his attack on Tirpitz. But the moment had passed. By the spring of 1909 Wilhelm had recovered his will to reign and Bülow, whom he blamed for not defending him with sufficient vigour, had lost his trust. When the Chancellor had an audience to report on the meeting of June 3, Wilhelm took Tirpitz's part, refusing to believe in the danger of a preventive war; the English would never attack them alone. This was not the point Bülow was trying to make; it was the attack in concert with their continental enemies that he feared.

Without his Sovereign's confidence, and with the parties comprising his *bloc* in the *Reichstag* deadlocked on the new taxation he had proposed to overcome the financial crisis of the *Reich*, it was impossible for Bülow to continue as Chancellor; he resigned that year, as he had been appointed, amid the bustle of Kiel Week. Taking his leave aboard the *Hohenzollern*, he tried for the last time to impress Wilhelm with the prime importance of securing a naval agreement.

'Why must you end by harking back to that?' Wilhelm replied, annoyed and glancing at his watch like a spoiled child. 'Haven't I told you again and again verbally and in letters and marginal notes that I don't intend to let naval construction be interfered with! All such proposals are an affront to me and my Navy.'[83]

Bülow remonstrated that affairs of such importance could not be entirely decided by the student's duelling code, but Wilhelm only waved his hand towards the lines of battleships at their moorings nearby. 'Whoever looks out, as I do now, on the fruit of years of painful effort, has a certain right to feel proud of Himself', and then, 'I cannot and will not allow *John Bull* to give me orders on how many ships I am to build.'

While Bülow spent his last days as Chancellor in the shadow of Wilhelm's displeasure, Fisher was bearing with as much composure as he could muster the ultimate indignity of an enquiry into Admiralty policy. The previous December, while the 'acceleration' scare had been at its height within the Cabinet, McKenna had achieved his aim of having the Channel and Home Fleets merged into one and thereby terminating Beresford's command, which he thought, had become a danger to the State. Lord Charles' flag had been hauled down for the last time on March 24 at the height of the public 'acceleration' scare. Immediately the predictable had happened: his already swollen self-esteem puffed out by tumultuous demonstrations of popular affection in Portsmouth and London, his hatred of Fisher inflamed by the naval panic, he had thrown himself into the attack on the First Sea Lord with all his usual extravagance of language and assertion. There was no war plans, the organisation of the fleets was a danger to the State, morale was non-existent, training deficient, there were not enough sailors, cruisers, destroyers ... nothing it seemed was right with the Navy and the Empire was in peril. He had spent a long time with Balfour acquainting him with the lamentable situation and his opinion that the government could be turned out on the naval question—although he himself did not wish to make it a Party matter! Balfour had kept himself aloof from the attack on the Board and merely advised Beresford to see the Prime Minister about his allegations, and not to be too certain that the Admiralty had no war plans.[84] After which he had acquainted Esher of the rambling interview, sure that the message would be passed to Fisher.

Beresford had seen Asquith and put the principal points in his case to him, changing his main attack to the dispersion of the three fleets in home waters during his time as Commander-in-Chief—while the enemy had been concentrated—and the absence of supreme control. He had made it clear that if the government failed to take action he had a number of speaking engagements already booked and would make his revelations of Admiralty unprepared-ness public property. This had put Asquith in a difficult position, particularly as the public feud had been going on for so long and had been blown up by sections of the Press and Beresford's supporters into such a danger to the spirit and discipline of the fleet that many were calling for an end to it all, whatever the rights or wrongs, by the dismissal of Fisher as well as Beresford. Even *The Times* which had been violently *pro* Fisher, had ended its leader marking Beres-ford's retirement with the gentle hint that 'The period of service at the Admiralty ... ought not to be of indefinite duration.'[85]

After turning several compromises over in his mind, Asquith had decided to satisfy Beresford with a private enquiry into Admiralty policy by a sub-committee of the Committee of Imperial Defence. Although this unprecedented step suggested want of confidence by the government in its own Board of Admiralty it was less damaging than a public enquiry such as Beresford and his supporters wanted. Beresford was jubilant, and cancelled his speaking engagements. Fisher, whose first thought was instant resignation to register his disgust at the cowardice of the Cabinet's capitulation to indiscipline, changed his mind and resolved to hang on until he was 'kicked out'. He was strengthened by King Edward who ordered him to stay at his post and 'even under pressure', not to think of resigning.[86]

The sub-committee was composed of four Cabinet Ministers, including Grey, and was chaired by Asquith himself. Beresford, who had been applying Custance's brains to his case, and who kept him at hand to supply him with arguments throughout the hearings, opened with his chief allegation that throughout his period of command the fleet in home waters, instead of being one concentrated force under one supreme commander and complete in all types of vessel, had been divided into separate units under different Admirals. The Admiralty answer, ably put by McKenna, who cautioned Fisher to silence, was that this had been an interim measure because of the delicate political situation, and that the goal of one homogeneous force, which had never been lost to sight, was realised in the new merger of the Channel and Home Fleets. In any case the safety of the country had never been endangered, as Beresford alleged, as the forces available for concentration at home had always been far superior to those of the probable enemy; the Channel Fleet alone had always been more powerful in terms of weight of broadside than the German High Seas Fleet, even allowing for ships absent for refits, and the reserve strength of the British Navy had been 'immensely superior'. When Sir Arthur Wilson was asked for his views, he replied that there was much force in Beresford's argument, but all his objections had been met by the reorganisation recently introduced.[87]

Beresford's allegations about shortages of cruisers and destroyers and lack of training were soon disposed of by McKenna; it was pointed out that the Home Fleet under Admiral Bridgeman had done rather better than the Channel Fleet in gunnery! Most of Beresford's and Custance's other alarmist statements which they attempted to support, but often confused with historical analogies, were based on German naval *offensives* against the battle fleet and British trade; while the tone of much German comment seemed to suggest this, deeper insight into military and naval history might have suggested that a determined offensive with such a hopelessly inferior force as the Germans possessed was the last thing to be feared. As for Beresford's other main charge, the lack of war plans at the Admiralty, this was modified under cross-examination, indeed his original statement about it was shown up as a lie. And Sir Arthur Wilson supported the Admiralty case that rigid war plans such as Beresford appeared to want, where every ship was told off for its duty, were not only impossible but too inflexible for naval warfare; he was 'perfectly certain that any plan drawn up in peace would not be carried out in war.' There was also the question of secrecy, which both he and Fisher valued before all else, and which could not be preserved if War Plans were so generally known.

After fifteen meetings at which Beresford's inability to hold the thread of any consistent argument and Custance's malignancy became increasingly apparent to the Committee, the final Report was published on August 12:

> In the opinion of the Committee, the investigation has shown that during the time in question no danger to the country resulted from the Admiralty's arrangements for war, whether considered from the standpoint of the organisation and distribution of the fleets, or the preparation of war plans.
>
> They feel bound to add that arrangements quite defensible in themselves though not ideally perfect, were in practice seriously hampered through the absence of cordial relations between the Board of Admiralty and the Commander-in-Chief of the Channel Fleet. The Board of Admiralty do not appear to have taken Lord Charles Beresford sufficiently into their confidence as to the reasons for the dispositions to which he took exception; and Lord Charles Beresford, on the other hand, appears to have failed to appreciate and carry out the spirit of the instructions of the Board and to recognise their paramount authority.[88]

Beresford and his supporters were delighted, considering that the government could not have gone further in criticising the Admiralty without condemning themselves. Fisher was incensed; 'It's a cowardly document! It ignores Beresford's want of loyalty at the outset of the two years, and so how could the Admiralty give him its confidence ...?'[89]

He wrote to Garvin on the 'kernel of the matter' which had been omitted from the Committee's conclusions and most newspaper comment: 'Discipline! but I am still more disgusted with the Committee's Report which is not the least what it was when first composed and had then in it a splendid paragraph on discipline nor was there any stone at all cast at the Admiralty such as subtly done now more by innuendo than otherwise ...'[90] Fisher's supporters agreed that Asquith, in 'watering down' the Report as originally drawn up by the Committee had transformed it into a verdict in Beresford's favour. Esher compressed the essence of it in a note to Balfour:

(The Report) is couched in (Asquith's) usual cold, judicial language, and as you will note, contains no words of appreciation of the value of the naval reforms ... which lie at the root of the policy which CB (Charles Beresford) attacked. I imagine Jackie will be hurt at the want of direct support given to him, and CB will be furious. So I suppose the Report fulfils all 'political requirements'.[91]

The vindication of Beresford's campaign which his supporters read into the recent amalgamation of the Home and Channel Fleets and the innuendoes in the Report encouraged a resurgence of the campaign to oust Fisher. Beresford himself went stumping platforms throughout the country with speeches growing ever wilder, 'The plain truth is that we are face to face with a rivalry, not of one foreign power alone, but of *every* great naval power.' Yet, he insisted in his loud, nasal accents, the country was deficient in battleships, cruisers, torpedo boats, dock accommodation, reserves of coal, ammunition, seamen, marines, coastguard, training, organisation, war staff. The public was not only asleep but insensible. 'They have been drugged with falsehoods. Why are the Navy Estimates year after year so framed to be almost unintelligible? Why are official returns inaccurate? I tell you there is danger— now!'[92] Along with comprehensive criticisms of every aspect of Admiralty policy went a full-blooded attack on Fisher's system of favouritism and 'espionage in every fleet', and his 'intimidation' of officers who opposed his views—or were friendly with Beresford![93]

Fisher, still sustained by King Edward's faith in him, held on 'For the greatest of all things—*Discipline*',[94] but the enquiry and the vituperous agitation which had sought to obscure the real issues in the enquiry had weakened his position; in the autumn he told McKenna of his intention to retire in order to make sure that Sir Arthur Wilson, who was only two years his junior, could succeed him. McKenna accepted his decision with a heavy heart. 'You have been so good to me, so understanding of my differences, so skilful in teaching me, so brave in your support of my political anxieties, so affectionate in your personal relations that I have neither heart nor wish to go on without you.'[95]

He was made a Baronet in the King's Birthday Honours, and the following January, on his sixty-ninth birthday, turned over the post he had held for five tumultuous years to the one man he felt he could trust to carry on his policies. He found at the end that he had many more friends than he had thought. Congratulated on the reorganisation he had accomplished—so vast that it was difficult to comprehend it all—he replied, 'It was the splendid band who worked with me. "I have culled a garland of flowers, mine only the string that binds them" (Montaigne) ...'[96] To those who knew him best it was as if Nelson had stepped down from his column in Trafalgar Square.

The last large decisions he had been concerned with were increases in the calibre of armament for Dreadnoughts and in the speed of battlecruisers.

> Do you know that the ships we have just laid down are as beyond the Dreadnought as the Dreadnought was beyond all before her! And they will say again, "D—n that blackguard! Again a new era of Dreadnoughts. But imagine the German 'wake-up' when these new ships by and by burst on them! *70,000 horsepower!!! and guns that will gut them!!!* Oh my! that I was born too soon![97]

Tirpitz had just laid down the last two battleships of his 1909-10 programme, the *Kaiser* and the *Friedrich der Grosse*; against the ten all-centreline 13.5" pieces of the new British *Orions*, these had ten 12" guns arranged fore and aft and in echelon amidships.

The start had not been accelerated, indeed Fisher's information was that they had been deliberately 'set back' in order to mislead the Admiralty.[98] He and McKenna and others close to the original scare were still convinced that Tirpitz had started to accelerate and would have continued if he had not been 'discovered'. They knew that at least one of the 1909 ships had been laid down some months before her 'official' start in April; this had been common knowledge in Germany, and was freely admitted afterwards in the German Press; Wilhelm, when he heard of it, expressed his annoyance to Tirpitz as it was a 'justification, though only a formal one' for the British claim that building was being accelerated. Tirpitz denied this with an excuse that 'start of building' had nothing to do with 'delivery' and was solely a business matter for the firm, which had begun work at its own risk. He claimed, in any case, not to have become aware of the building start until the end of April—clearly a lie in view of the constant pressure from England for information since the previous autumn, for Tirpitz, whatever else he may have been, was thorough. As for the 'risk' he claimed, although the firm could have been confident that the *Reichstag* would pass the funds in April, its anticipation of this by at least five months was a considerable decision to take. Other reasons advanced for the early start were to prevent laying off workers and to beat an inflation of material prices expected in 1909; interest charges on the necessary loans must have eaten into any savings on that count.

It is possible that Tirpitz's explanations were so extraordinarily belated and, to the British, unconvincing simply because although true they were bound to lead to British suspicion—which was the last thing he wanted. The reason for his subsequent lie to the British naval attaché that it was not *possible* for Germany to complete a Dreadnought in under three years may have been similar. Or his intentions may have been preparatory—to wait and see the temper of Liberal England and whether the *Reichstag* would admit the increased price of acceleration. It is even possible, although most improbable, that he *meant* to cause a flutter at the Admiralty the more easily to get his own estimates through the *Reichstag*. When the British naval attaché congratulated him on their rapid passage, he replied, 'I have only to thank you people for that!'[99] And why, if secrecy was the object, did he allow Argentinians who had strong naval connections with England, through all his yards to count the ships on the ways and even the guns in the ordnance shops?

After all these years his intentions remain obscure. But there is no doubt, and was no doubt then that two Dreadnoughts at least were ordered before the start of the financial year and their materials were collected, that one at least was under way well before her official laying down date, that the German industry *could* build a battleship in two years, that Krupp *could* arm and armour them at more than four a year, and that the German Naval Estimates had a 'recurring marginal note' confusing exact budgetary control as it stated that the sums voted for construction in any financial year could be taken in any conjunction with sums voted for the same purpose in other years. Against the possibilities raised by these undoubted facts are another two: acceleration on the scale envisaged by the Admiralty would have cost Tirpitz an extra twenty million marks from his already very tight annual budget and would have cut into the many other already undernourished branches of the Service, and in the view of Tirpitz's Construction Department a building time of two years could only be achieved by getting *Reichstag* approval to reduce the annual instalments for the building programme from four to three.[100] Neither his 1908 nor 1909 Estimates sought this power.

Whatever Tirpitz's intentions, Fisher and McKenna and Grey rightly feared them; even today the only clear outlines in what must have been a deliberate fog are that accelerated starts *were* made, the power *was* there, Tirpitz *was* an intriguer to whom the end justified any means, any falsehoods—and his strongest compulsion was to traverse the 'Danger Zone' which successive British Liberal programmes and the Dreadnought policy had diminished.

The chauvinist Crown Prince of Germany, who found him a 'surpassing personality', wrote:

His life thoughts and activities were entirely filled with the determination to master the enormous task (of creating the Navy) for the good of the Empire and in spite of external and internal opposition ... He held firm to the conviction that the struggle with England for the freedom of the seas must sooner or later be fought out. His object was the 'risk' idea, that is to say he maintained that our Navy must be so strong that any possible contest with us must appear to the English a dangerous game.[101]

Panthersprung!

Wilhelm's choice of a successor for Bülow fell eventually on Bethmann-Hollweg, a Prussian of serious mind and forbidding exterior with a reputation for scrupulousness, tenacity, perseverance, patience, all the solid and reliable virtues which the delightful Bernhard was widely believed to lack. He had worked his way scrupulously through the ranks of the Prussian Civil Service to become Vice-Chancellor and Minister of the Interior under Bülow, who recommended him as a 'good plough horse', plodding slowly and steadily so long as there were no hurdles in sight.[1] Bethmann's own estimate of himself was not so very different, and he accepted the post from an ingrained sense of duty with much self-doubt, believing it suitable for a genius or a man driven by lust for power, whereas he was neither—simply an ordinary man.

Such a negative, yet realistic estimate was totally in character. Bethmann, known from his furrowed brow and pensive manner as 'the philosopher of Hohenfinow'—his family estate not far from Berlin—had a deep analytical, but scarcely creative mind. His tendency was to see present difficulties in greater detail than ultimate aims, hence to hedge decisions with a host of conditional possibilities, and hedge new departures in policy with so many compromises to existing circumstances that they fell flat between all parties, too Left for the regressive élite, far too Right for progressives and Socialists. The very depth and independence and scrupulousness of his judgement almost ensured his failure, for as he realised too well, it needed a touch of wilful madness to break out of the iron cage in which the Junkers had locked themselves and the *Reich*. This he could not supply; there were no wayward connections crossing the impeccable circuits of his brain; he lacked flair as he lacked eloquence or 'charisma'.

The problems he faced as he moved in to the *Reichskanzler*

Palace on the Wilhelmstrasse were daunting. The optimism of the turn of the century when the 'new course' had been charted to steer the *Reich* to world power between England and France/Russia, and to use the resulting increase in material prosperity and growth in national consciousness to bind all the separatist elements together under the Prussian/Hohenzollern banner had vanished, replaced by extreme pessimism. For the very opposite had been achieved. The drive for world power had only driven the other great Powers together to defend their interests; the appeal to national sentiment and envy of Great Britain, and the wide world hopes raised had turned sour on repeated rebuffs as the other Powers combined to check them; the tariffs on imported foods demanded by the landed elite in return for supporting the naval construction necessary to give the policy force had raised the cost of living for the masses', encouraging Social Democracy, and the huge expenses of the Navy had widened the rift between the established agrarian and the new industrial 'patriots' by creating a financial battleground on which to fight out their selfish aims and conflicting interests. The result of the conflict in which neither side had given an inch was financial crisis*, an internal defeat for the *Reich* which was quite as serious as her external setbacks.

The extent of the failure on all fronts was reflected in the violence of the excuses which put every checked ambition down to the enemies of the State, externally to King Edward VII and the financiers of Paris, internally to Social Democracy and—shades of the future—Jews; the nature of the excuses, hardening attitudes further, had led to an increasingly fatalistic belief in the simple and violent military solution for all problems within and without—which was in any case a part of Prussian thinking.

The *Reich* was set on a dangerous downward spiral which, by the nature of the beliefs and increasing desperation of the ruling elite,

---

* From 1901 to 1909 inclusive 2,444 million Marks (some £125 million) were spent on the *Reich* Navy; this was almost exactly matched by the sum of the loans, 2410 million Marks, raised during the same period to balance the *Reich* Budget. As a proportion of total *Reich* expenditure the Navy share had risen from 18 per cent to 26 per cent while the Army share had fallen from 58 per cent to some 55 per cent.[2] The total armed Services share of the *Reich* Budget (in 1909 c. 1600 million Marks or c. £80 million) varied between 88 per cent and 90 per cent. In 1909 the British Naval estimates were £35 mils rising to £40 mils in 1910.

had to end in violence—unless Bethmann could reverse the momentum.

Bethmann saw the problems clearly; he had watched the polarisation of the parties during his time as Minister of the Interior, had seen the Conservatives under their inflammatory leader von Heydebrand, regress further in their pre-industrial attitudes, refusing to compromise on tax or suffrage reforms which threatened their estates and hold on power; he had seen the National Liberals who had benefited most from the Navy's intense stimulation of heavy industry and commerce, intoxicated with the vast industrial momentum of the Empire, grow more stridently 'national' and expansionist, less Liberal—and at the other end of the scale Social Democracy feeding on the crassness of the patriotic parties, frightening them by its growth, driving them to brasher excesses of language and policy. Bethman saw these desperate internal problems more clearly than most. But while he despaired the stubbornness of his own class as much as he loathed the hysteria of the Pan-Germans and the revolutionary aims of the Social Democrats, he was still by birth and inclination a loyal Monarchist and broadly in sympathy with the existing power structure and expansionist aims on which the Empire had embarked, and he proposed no basic changes of direction; in any case his temperament ensured that he would attempt to heal the internal weaknesses without bold new departures, but with patience and perseverance, seeking to conciliate more moderate agrarian, industrial and middle-class elements by checking their lunatic fringes, meanwhile fostering practical co-operation in work for the common good.

Such pragmatism and determination steadily to face a long haul back to political health were just what Wilhelm needed as a balance to his habit of bending or soaring over details in pursuit of his personal, short-term whims. But Bethmann had neither the dynamism nor the personality to beat through the cushioning effect of the Cabinet system, nor to open windows on the 'stupefying atmosphere' of official Berlin.[3] His attempted checks were negative, his manner pedantic, and Wilhelm who found his lectures much more tiresome than Bülow's as they lacked all humour or wit, continued to oscillate on his own fantastic plane further from reach than ever. He had never wanted Bethmann in the first place, and had only been persuaded to appoint him after his own more forceful, hardline choices had been disapproved by his advisers, anxious about domestic politics. The temperamental distance between Emperor and Chancellor was increased by Bethmann's inability to communicate with or win the trust of the military who formed such a large and influential element of the Imperial entourage. In Court circles he was regarded as the ultimate bureaucrat. The Crown Prince interpreted his insistence on weighing every move as vacillation—'his hesitating heart had no wings, his will was joyless, his resolve was lame'—and thought him no match for the 'quick-witted and inexorable men whom England and France had chosen as the exponents of their power.' The adolescently chauvinist Crown Prince was not the person to appreciate the depth of the new Chancellor, but his estimate had point; even Ballin, who was no militarist, called Bethmann 'Bülow's revenge.'[5]

Apart from the domestic and financial crisis which the new Chancellor had been chosen to surmount, the most urgent task as he took office was to mend relations with England, and he immediately addressed himself to the naval question which Bülow had been unable to solve, and which he was advised on all hands lay at the root of the problem. Unofficial talks were already under way between Ballin, who was convinced that Tirpitz's uncurbed ambition was the chief cause of the trouble, and Sir Ernest Cassel, one of the financial barons of the City of London and confidante of King Edward VII. Ballin hoped that his explorations might lead to official negotiations in which Tirpitz, whose pretensions as a politician had grown with his success as an administrator, would deal direct with the British Admiralty. It was an ingenious plan; the British, he knew, would never yield their margin of superiority and Tirpitz would either have to admit failure as an international politician or make the kind of compromise he was not prepared to concede to his own government.

Bethmann would have none of it; Anglo-German relations were his province and they would be conducted through the proper official channels. Ballin found himself shut out, and Tirpitz also, after he had given the Chancellor his idea of a compromise; this was a slowing of the German tempo to three in 1910, then two from 1911 to 1914 on condition that the British matched it with four in 1910—thus foregoing their 'contingent four'—then three to 1914. This would have resulted in twenty-four German against thirty-six British Dreadnoughts built or on the stocks in 1914, thus the 3:4 ratio of strength which Metternich had feared to suggest to

Britain lest it provoke a preventive assault! Worse, from the British angle, it would have meant a ratio of 3·2:4 in *completed* Dreadnoughts over the years 1912-14—assuming that both countries took approximately the same time to build. This was closing the gap indeed! Tirpitz knew it would be unacceptable; he made certain of it by insisting that Dreadnoughts which had been promised to the British government during the naval scare by British Dominions overseas should be included in the British total.

Bethmann seemed to think it a real concession because it included a commitment that Tirpitz would not introduce a *Novelle* in 1912 when the tempo was due to drop to two big ships a year. Tirpitz, of course, had made up his mind that this drop in tempo *would* have to be prevented and there was general agreement in Germany that he would bring in a *Novelle* about 1911 or 1912—what, otherwise, would happen to the expanded shipbuilding and armament industries? Bethmann regarded a promise to forego this future increase as sufficiently attractive for Britain to forego the extra ships of her current programme; yet these were being built, not so much against the stated German tempo as against the possibilities inherent in increased German *capacity*. Criticised as Bethmann was for thinking all around a problem, this was one he viewed from an exclusively Prussian angle.

Tirpitz, meanwhile, was doing his very best to kill any remote chance of his 'concessions' being accepted by feuding with the British naval attaché, granting him only the briefest interviews, using them to repeat endlessly his complaints about British politicians doubting his word as a naval officer and a gentleman, refusing to arrange visits for him to German yards, deliberately obscuring ordering, laying-down, completion trial dates and building times for Dreadnoughts, and finally refusing to supply any information. He rung down the curtain on the performance by boycotting the attaché altogether. 'He is very angry,' his adjutant explained, 'about the statement made in England that the *Nassau* was built in twenty-six months.'[6]

His manoeuvres were quite unnecessary. At the British Admiralty, where a good deal of thought had been given to a standard of strength to replace the 'Two-Power' standard, now so obviously dead, sixty per cent over German naval strength had been adopted as an unofficial yardstick; this meant 38, not 32 British to 24 German Dreadnoughts. Besides this, Bethmann had determined to make it a condition of any naval agreement that it should be preceded by a political agreement—the kind of mutual neutrality pact that Bülow had been angling for. But as Metternich had already explained, Great Britain could scarcely agree to remain neutral if Germany were at war on the Continent without rendering her French and Russian *ententes* meaningless.

Grey made it clear that in the British view the naval question took precedence. Bethmann then agreed that both naval and political agreements could be concluded simultaneously. He didn't mention Tirpitz's specific proposals, but suggested a mutual 'relaxation' of building tempo for a few years. As this would not affect the total number of Dreadnoughts eventually to be built under the Naval Law the British reply was not enthusiastic. The negotiations never had a chance. On the British side suspicion of German motives was paramount; Grey thought the German Empire had reached that dangerous point of strength where they 'itched to dominate'; the Foreign Office thought their proposals designed to tie British hands while they overran France and established a Continental hegemony —after which it would be time to challenge Britain—and the Admiralty, certain that an attempt had been made suddenly to seize the trident, had no faith in any assurances that could not be checked by their attachés. As for Bethmann and his Foreign Office, they laboured under the impression that if Britain wanted a naval agreement she must pay a political price! It was a strange attitude, for it was Bethmann and the German Foreign Office who wanted the political agreement, who would, therefore, have to pay a *naval* price. Tirpitz was not willing to pay with his programme, but Bethmann's misjudgement was total when he assumed that Britain might pay with hers *and* sign a neutrality pact as well!

The inept proposals served, if anything, to increase British suspicions and were brushed aside at the first opportunity. The free-for-all building race, which both Admiralty and Navy Office believed to be safer than arbitrary political interference, continued. The German Estimates were passed without serious opposition in the *Reichstag*; in reply to their four the British Estimates for 1910 contained five new Dreadnoughts, together with sums for the 'contingent four'; meanwhile two colonial Dreadnoughts provided by the governments of Australia and New Zealand, had been laid down in British yards. Taken with the 1909 estimates, this meant a total of fifteen big ships either laid down or projected in one year. It was the answer Metternich had forecast. Inside the Liberal Cabinet, the Radicals were appalled, but Asquith stood by Grey and McKenna and, against news that Austria had laid down two of her proposed Dreadnoughts the Admiralty view prevailed. For, as McKenna said in the House, there was still doubt about what Germany might have in commission by 1912.

Churchill was still with the Radicals although his attitude towards Germany was not so uncritically optimistic as the previous year; he had peered at the tensions beneath the surface of Wilhelm's Empire and produced a memorandum for the Cabinet on its financial structure which concluded that the 'over-flowing expenditure of the German Empire strains and threatens every dyke by which the social and political unity of Germany is maintained.'[7] Increased taxation on every form of indulgence was strengthening the parties of the Left who were the chief opponents of armaments expenditure, yet the Imperial debt had increased during the past ten years by over £100 millions.

> These circumstances force the conclusion that a period of severe internal strain approaches in Germany. Will the tension be relieved by moderation or snapped by violence? ... one of two courses must be taken soon and from that point of view it is of the greatest importance to gauge the spirit of the new administration from the outset. If it be pacific it must soon become markedly so, and conversely.

To gauge the spirit of Bethmann's administration was difficult; his struggle to achieve 'pacific' results without really altering the external goals or internal balances tending towards violence, produced a more than usually confusing picture. Meanwhile the potent mix of overconfidence and desperation brewed during the Bülow years continued to ferment among the most influential and vocal sections of the community, giving off heady fumes which defied rational assessment.

'German industrial progress is overtaking that of England with giant strides', wrote Dr Schulze-Gaevernitz, a more moderate member of Wilhelm's academic garrison and described as 'a man of peace'. 'The day is now not far distant when the economic power of Germany will equal that of England mistress of the world and still its leading Banker and Creditor.'[8] After that the 'Two-Power' standard for her Navy would become financially impossible and

British sea dominion would 'melt away in the veritable sunshine of peace'. As if to counteract such un-German language Dr Schulze went on, 'Today perhaps, but not tomorrow New Germany rising, can be struck to earth by a mailed fist.' And repeating countless 'historical' analyses, he pointed out that British sea dominion had been built up in war with Spain, Holland and France—why not now with Germany? What made it even more tempting for her was the proffered alliance of Germany's Continental opponents: 'England's friendship it was that rekindled the desire of France for revenge and the hope of an English alliance has strengthened against Germany the Pan-Slavic races of eastern Europe.'

Pity the great German Empire!

It was clear enough, the Doctor maintained, that 'not Germany but Britain is today chiefly responsible for the overwhelming armament of Europe ... Figures prove it. By hundreds of millions British expenditure for Army and Navy have always exceeded those of Germany. The tension between the two nations has been still further strained by the latest British naval programme ...' He ended by looking forward to the day when there would be a balance of naval power between the great nations; 'The age of dominance at sea by any single nation is approaching its end.'

His message was essentially the same as those from more extreme organs like the Navy League Journal who never tired of proclaiming force as 'the decisive factor in the world'. Holding this belief together with a touching faith in the supernatural ability, unswerving direction and utter ruthlessness of British statesmen—in comparison with whom German diplomats were amateurs who had rings (literally) run around them—they looked on a British preventive attack as a real danger. Or, as another academic put it about this time: 'England will be content if by means of alliances she can reap the fruits of war without fighting for them ... But if they come to the conclusion that their trade, under the pressure of foreign, and particularly of German competition, is beginning a stage of decline ... should they see no other remedy, they will consider our destruction by war.'[9] To these realists the recent startling increases in the British Naval Estimates and the bellicose attitude of British navalists during the great 'scare', were proof of British preparations for just such an attack. To meet the threat the German building tempo had to be maintained. As for a naval agreement such as the British Liberals had proposed during the 'scare', Grey's speech on the matter was paraphrased as 'it must be an agreement which will allow us (Great Britain) to beat you easily, or to terrorise you into surrender without fighting, should any quarrel arise.'[10]

As with all good propaganda, none of the points lacked foundation. Overall it was false. Britain's seventeenth and eighteenth century wars, however analysed, were no evidence against her twentieth century Liberals. Above all the feeling created was negative and unhelpful. It was as unhelpful to Bethmann in his efforts for an understanding as Tirpitz's obstinate ambition. Founded on overconfidence due to sudden wealth and power combined with the dogma that force alone counted, the defiant mood went far beyond any rational assessment of chances; it was as if Germany's ruling and intellectual élite, crazed by the strains within the Empire and within their own changing yet rigid society, had turned against reason and life itself and were bent on carrying all with them to destruction.

To many observers at the time the explanation was much simpler. It was the age-old ambition to dominate and exploit the world. 'It is the old, old lust for power and glory and the old, old greed for trade and wealth', wrote the British Socialist leader, Robert Blatchford, who visited Germany at this time and wrote a series of articles for the *Daily Mail* warning Britons of the danger. 'World-domination-conquest! That was the dream of Babylon, of Persia, of Greece, of Rome, of Spain, and France and Russia. It is the dream of Germany today![11] 'The first of his articles was headed THE MENACE; it started 'I write these lines because I believe that Germany is deliberately preparing to destroy the British Empire ...' and because if this were accomplished 'it would be a misfortune for Europe and a blow to civilisation throughout the world.' He saw both economic and moral factors behind Germany's warlike preparations; she needed colonies for her expanding population, yet Britain had taken all those worth having, India, Australia, Canada, New Zealand, Eygpt and the most desirable parts of Africa; she needed coaling stations and bases to protect her growing trade, yet Britain had a world-wide chain at all strategic points already, and he echoed the German pamphlets, 'How many wars have been caused by commercial jealousy?' Hemmed in on the Continent, yet 'regarding world domination as her destiny' Germany was ready to 'strike out' for it, Blatchford asserted because she felt herself strong and believed that her rich and influential rival had grown 'fat and impotent' and would fall an easy victim to resolute assault.

German Socialists expressed themselves furious at the articles, accusing Blatchford of having his brain turned by 'plodding through reams of Pan-German twaddle'. Yet he was saying no more than August Bebel, respected leader and founder of the German Social Democratic Party, himself believed. Bebel believed it so passionately that towards the end of 1910 he took the extraordinary step of corresponding with the British Foreign Office—via the British Consul General in Zurich—to warn them of the danger England faced, and to pass on what naval and armament secrets he could glean from his position in the Budget Committee of the *Reichstag*. The similarity of the warnings expressed in these letters which lasted until Bebel's death in 1913, and those in Blatchford's articles, taken together with the short interval between the articles and the start of the letters prompts the suspicion that Blatchford obtained much of his material from the old German Socialist leader himself.

Bebel's clandestine correspondence started :

Though a Prussian myself by birth, I consider Prussia a dreadful State (*Schrecklicher Staat*) from which nothing but dreadful things may be expected; this England is sure to experience sooner than most people think. To reform Prussia is impossible; it will remain the *Junkerstaat* it is at present, or go to pieces altogether. The Hohenzollerns too won't change, and when the Kaiser speaks as he did at Königsberg lately, he does so as King of Prussia by the grace of God & with his Junkers behind him.

I cannot understand what the British government & people are about in letting Germany creeping up to them so closely in naval armaments. As a regular member of the Budget Commission I can assert that the German Naval Law of 1900 was directed against England & England alone ... The English Admiralty was caught napping again three years ago ... when a particularly veiled naval budget was submitted to us. What struck me immediately was that instead of the amount of 40 million Marks regularly asked in former years for exactly the same number of ships 47 million Marks were budgeted, from which I concluded that bigger ships and more powerful guns must be planned. I demanded an explanation but could not obtain a satisfactory one.

I am convinced we are on the eve of the most dreadful war Europe has ever seen. Things cannot go on as at present, the burden of the military charges are crushing people & the Kaiser & the government

are fully alive to the fact. Everything works for a great crisis in
Germany ...

The catastrophe will come, I believe, in 1912, if not earlier.
Prussia cannot hope to be ever in a better position for a sudden
attack on England than then, when the naval forces in the most
modern fighting units will be almost matched, whilst the land
defences of England will still be in a state of chaos ...[12]

Bebel went on to say that even if the Social Democrats attained a
majority in the *Reichstag*—impossible under existing electoral Laws
—'we could not prevent a war against England.' This passage was
underlined at the Foreign Office.

Blatchford's strongest evidence for Germany's intent to strike
was also the German Navy and the increased capacity of German
yards and arsenals which could now 'turn out a super-Dreadnought
a month, fully equipped and armed.' What could these feverish
preparations be for if not to try conclusions with the British Navy;
the fleet was 'built for the North Sea, exercised in the North Sea,
remains in the North Sea.' And it was well known that German
naval officers looked forward to a great battle with the British fleet
and drank a toast every evening to '*Der Tag*'.[13]

Despite all this, Blatchford saw France as the real danger point
for the British Empire. 'Unhappy France. The British Navy may
destroy the German fleet and ruin German foreign trade but nothing
on earth can prevent the German army from overrunning France
from Paris to Lyons and from the English Channel to the Mediterranean.' At the end of such a war Germany would not be satisfied
with an indemnity but would take possession of the northern provinces as well as Belgium, Holland and Luxemburg, then having all
the great Channel ports facing England would commence the construction of a fleet which Britain would be unable to match. 'That
is why I say the problem of British defence is the problem of the
defence of France.'[14] His conclusion was that Britain must increase
her army by conscription and be prepared to send it to Northern
France and Belgium.

His views might almost have been dictated by the British Foreign
Office; they represented in pamphleteering language the thoughts
of most influential Englishmen, and they carried great weight and
drew venom from Germany because Blatchford was no navalist
or imperialist, but one of the founders of modern British Socialism,

which was as utterly opposed as the German brand to armaments and nationalism.

Between the extreme suspicion, belligerence and high-spirited imperialism on both sides of the North Sea, Grey saw his task as one of gradual conciliation. Far more experienced than Bethmann, and with a subtler intelligence, he knew the differences between them were too fundamental to be solved at a stroke by any formulae, and he clung to his original hope that a simple exchange of naval information might be a stepping stone to better understanding of what he regarded as their *mutual* problem—the future of European civilisation.

> An agreement might be made, based on an understanding that the German naval programme should not be increased, accompanied by an exchange of information from time to time between the two Admiralties which, without revealing those details that are never disclosed, would satisfy each that they were being kept informed of the actual progress of shipbuilding in the yards of the other country ...[15]

This, he hoped, would remove the apprehension in Britain of future indefinite increases in the German Law, and would dissipate the suspicions in both countries that 'either government has hostile intentions or desires to steal a march on the other'. He thought that by limiting the anxiety in this way the political atmosphere might be cooled down with consequences possibly 'greater and more favourable than can be foretold.'[16]

Even this innocent proposal provided grist for German propagandists. The Navy Office was being asked to provide information which would enable Britain to keep her margin of supremacy but spare her either the pain of spending too much or the risk of spending too little —and what would Germany gain in return? Nothing! Wilhelm thought Grey's lack of interest in a political agreement suspicious; it confirmed the threatening nature of the *ententes* with which Britain had ringed him. Tirpitz was, of course, opposed to anything which might help Britain to preserve the 'Danger Zone' for his fleet; he explained to Wilhelm, the maintenance of Germany's world-power position—and he threw in for good measure 'and the maintenance of peace'—depended on making a British attack too great a risk.[17] If the British fleet could be kept permanently at such strength that an attack on Germany would be no risk, then the fleet policy would have failed. History would judge it a fiasco. He turned the detailed British proposals for an exchange of basic information like laying-down and completion dates, dimensions and for mutual inspection by naval attachés into another hard bargaining position by insisting that all information should be exchanged on the *same* day, and should include the next year's programme which would then be binding on both parties. As Sir Arthur Wilson, First Sea Lord, minuted, this was 'manifestly absurd'.

> In the first place the information is of no use unless it can be acted on, and in the second place it would act as a direct incentive to each government to exaggerate its estimates for fear of being called to account ... if, when both programmes were declared, their own might be found to be inadequate.[18]

Tirpitz cannot have expected his guessing game to be taken seriously. What he did expect—if anything—is obscure. Success and the legendary position he had won not only within the Navy, but within the Empire, where he was often compared with Bismarck himself, had wrought their decay; the young Tirpitz would have played the game more subtly. But now the fleet was an obsession, intrigue and the oblique approach compulsive habits—whether or not they served any useful purpose.

As Ballin had realised, his methods—like the fleet itself—were now counter-productive. They fooled no one except Wilhelm, who insisted on being fooled for his beloved battleships. At the British Admiralty nothing Tirpitz said or did or pretended was taken at face value. The replacement for the unfortunate British naval attaché who had been boycotted soon reported himself unimpressed with Tirpitz's sincerity of purpose and intention; he protested altogether too much about British aspersions on his honour and his word. This was particularly noticeable in early 1911 when McKenna admitted that the forecasts of German acceleration had not been realised. The attaché reported:

> In February and March 1911 Admiral von Tirpitz's volubility in asserting his own rectitude and veracity of statement as to the German Navy Law, and his general attitude towards the supposed admission of the First Lord of the English Admiralty that the English premises as to German naval progress had been wrong was noticeable to others besides myself. Further, the support given then to His Excellency by certain generally considered inspired Society talkers

in Berlin whose theme was 'if only you English would trust Tirpitz' was distinctly noticeable . . . as it was in the Press.[19]

The same report contained a number of other instances in which Tirpitz had been hostile to the British, or to his own officers who had been too friendly with English officers. Admiral Sir Percy Scott, for instance, had been shown inside the gun turrets of Prince Henry's flagship during a courtesy visit; when he heard of it Tirpitz had 'strongly attacked' the Admiral—Wilhelm's brother— remarking that Scott was 'a dangerously clever man'. Tirpitz's attitude on the British exchange of information proposals had lacked willingness to co-operate.

The attaché's report also confirmed that German shipyards would find themselves in difficulties in 1912 unless Tirpitz introduced a *Novelle* to prevent the tempo from falling to two—or unless they obtained orders from abroad. It ended with his assessment of the Navy Office's intentions over the last few stormy years.

Submitted that the factors which led to the acuteness on the naval question were (a) reduction of English Naval Estimates in two successive years which led to the ambition of Admiral von Tirpitz and the German Navy Party generally to think they had a chance of rivalling us by naval increases and political combinations (b) The attitude of alarm on the part of the English people and the somewhat peevish, weak-kneed tone adopted in the Press and generally, encouraged Germany still more, and made them feel that they had us beaten already and redoubled their naval activity (c) On these additional exertions being detected, a feeling of annoyance was present in the mind of Admiral von Tirpitz, and he seized the opportunity to whitewash himself and Germany, and to prepare for further naval efforts if England gave him reason or opportunity by first proclaiming the clean hands and intentions of Germany.

I submit that under the existing state of affairs in a growing nation like Germany, a similar reduction of naval estimates in the future can only lead to a similar state of things; that the only way to a good understanding between the two countries on the naval question is for England to steadily build ships yearly, or add to their naval strength until Germany realises it is hopeless to catch her up. I submit that it is the continuous strong programme that will depress the German naval parties rather than large increases follow- ing on reduced programmes.

The Attaché's conclusions were remarkably similar to those transmitted to the British Foreign Office by August Bebel in that same month of May 1911.

> ... *(it is) as certain as anything can be* that the Govt. will bring in a fresh big Naval Bill at the expiration of the present Law ... there is a way, but only one, to end the ruinous naval race between England and Germany, viz. the raising of an overwhelming special Loan for the Navy by His Majesty's Government. (That passage was underlined at the British Foreign Office.) This would so much frighten the commercial & industrial classes in Germany, who with the workmen have to bear the brunt of ever-increasing Imperial taxation, that the Liberals would refuse to vote supplies for a further increase of the Navy & probably the Centre Party too, in which case the German Govt. would have to give up the bid for supremacy at sea.[20]

Bebel's reason for sending a ceaseless stream of warnings and advice was not so much to help Britain deter the German government from its mounting armaments expenditure, nor to prevent the ruling classes in the *Reich* from unleashing the world war he felt inevitable, but to try and ensure that when the 'striking time' came Great Britain would not be defeated; that, he believed, would be as much a calamity for Germany as for Britain as 'all liberal and democratic ideas & institutions in Germany would be knocked on the head for a generation.'[21] Despairing of reform through the ballot box, knowing that his people would stand no chance against the army in an armed revolution—indeed that would give the army leaders just the chance they sought to suppress Socialism with a blood bath—he saw defeat in a foreign war as the only chance of breaking the Junkers' hold on power. It is ironic that while he was thus working for a massive increase in British naval armaments—at such great risk to himself and his Party—British Socialists, radical Liberals and pacifists strove in the opposite direction. To them, the Admiralty's admission that the Germans had kept to their stated programme was taken at face value—for it proved their point. McKenna's refusal to retract anything he had said during the 1909 debates, and his reiteration of the fact that acceleration *had* been started, but since abandoned, was taken as party propaganda, and the 'somewhat peevish, weak-kneed' tone of the radical attack on ever-increasing Admiralty estimates gathered volume in the country and within the government. Esher planned a Machiavellian manoeuvre to turn their flank, writing to Balfour's private secretary to ask for a Conservative assault on McKenna. 'If he is strongly attacked for neglecting to make us safe ... it will help him against those who ... want to eject him from the government and cut down the miserable number of new vessels which it is proposed to lay down this year'[22]—in fact five.

Grey, who could not reveal his Department's absolute suspicion of German and especially Tirpitz's motives, nor the evidence, had to reply to the pacifist attack during the Naval Estimates debates in general terms. It did not follow, he said, that one nation (Great Britain) could put a stop to the rivalry by dropping out of the race; it might very well be that this would have the reverse effect and cause others to give a momentary spurt in expenditure. He saw the way ahead rather in terms of gradual reductions in armaments as men's minds moved towards the idea of arbitration instead of war, and he looked forward to an eventual point in which national armies and navies were not in rivalry with one another, but were maintained as an international police force. This would need leaders with courage, but he found instances in history where public opinion had risen to heights thought impossible only a generation before; the abolition of slavery with all its vested interests was one such. His plea was for sanity.

> The great nations of the world are in bondage, in increasing bondage at the present moment to their armies and navies, and it does not seem to me impossible that in some future years they may discover, as individuals have discovered, that law is a better remedy than force, and that all the time they have been in bondage to this tremendous expenditure, the prison door has been locked on the inside.[23]

Grey's speech, with its emphasis on disarmament, taken together with a statement by McKenna that the Admiralty decision to lay down another five Dreadnoughts would give Britain thirty against the German twenty-one in 1914, was interpreted by the German naval attaché in London as a brilliant success for Tirpitz's programme: Britain was feeling the strain and she had dropped her vaunted 'Two-power' standard, evidently in favour of a ratio of something like 3:2 against Germany alone. Wilhelm was equally exultant, noting on the despatch, 'If we had followed the advice of Metternich and Bülow for the last four or five years we should now have had the 'Copenhagen' war upon us. As it is they respect our firm resolution and surrender to the facts. So we must go on building undisturbed.'[24] This was Tirpitz's view exactly. Discussing the situation with Bethmann he made it clear that it was now too late for any agreement with Britain to reduce the tempo which was due to drop to two next year; anything less would destroy the naval law—'indeed,' he said, hinting at the *Novelle* he had determined on to complete the 'Iron Budget', 'it might be necessary to *add* a few ships to remind the *Reichstag* that the three-tempo is the normal rate (for a fleet of 60 Dreadnoughts, each with a life of 20 years).'[25] Bethmann, confronted with Wilhelm's and Tirpitz's mutual reinforcement, at last reached the conclusion that an agreement with England was not possible. It was not only the navalist pair who forced his hand, but the powerful forces which they had generated and which still pushed them forward. As Bebel reported, the 'attempted "Disarmament-Entente" between England and Germany' was now 'buried altogether'[26]; the reason he gave was underscored at the Foreign Office.

... the article in the *Norddeutscher Allgemeine Zeitung*, approving in a way of Sir Edward Grey's speech, *caused such commotion & alarm in the military & colonial circles, that the Chancellor was obliged to revoke at the first opportunity* his former utterances, These people, of whom the Dynasty is absolutely dependent, would never permit to discuss the question of Disarmament seriously ...

But, attempting to salve something, Bethmann overruled Tirpitz's modifications to Grey's proposals for an exchange of naval information and agreed substantially the original proposals with the British government.

So far it had been Tirpitz and the German navalists who had obstructed Bethmann and his Foreign Office in their desire for agreement; now in the sectional chaos that served as a government under Wilhelm's free orbit, it was the turn of the Foreign Office to place Tirpitz's plans in jeopardy—and bind the ring around Germany even tighter.

The master mind behind this exercise in 1911 was the new Foreign Minister, von Kiderlen Waechter, an amoral, coarse-mannered swabian with a reputation for earthy wit and an over-estimate of his own abilities, perhaps induced by the generally poor level of ability in the Foreign Office—regarded by Ballin as a sealed cloister for aristocratic incompetents. That such a man should have been appointed to head the Foreign Office was either a reflection of the prevailing incompetence, or a grave reflection on Bethmann's judgement. Here is Bebel's report on Kiderlen to the British Foreign Office:

> He is a brutal fellow and looks it. His ambition is to imitate Bismarck, but there is every quality wanting in him to be compared to that Prussian statesman save the brutality; this the two have in common. Unfortunately Kiderlen possesses now the ear of the Kaiser, who originally did not like him. He got around his Imperial Master in a queer way, viz. by entertaining him with dirty stories, for which the Kaiser has a great partiality ...[27]

Kiderlen's scheme was a blatant return to the policy of hunting colonial successes in order to arouse national feeling and check the Leftward swing at home. Bebel referred to it as 'in the first place an election manoeuvre'[28] as the government feared large socialist gains in the forthcoming *Reichstag* elections. It was also a reaction to the total failure of Bethmann's attempts at moderate government 'above the parties'; in foreign affairs he had conspicuously failed to reach agreement with England, at home he had failed to move the Junkers on tax or electoral reform, hence failed to halt the slide to extremism of Right and Left.

Kiderlen's plan to strike out boldly to reverse the deteriorating cycle was inspired by a French move to quell native disorders in Morocco. French troops were sent to Fez—after the French government had notified Germany of its intentions—and Kiderlen, appreciating that this would take effective power from the Sultan of Morocco and thus contravene the agreement arrived at after the first Moroccan crisis, decided to trade German agreement to this new state of affairs for French territory in central Africa; his eventual aim was for a belt of German colonies across the heart of the Continent as a counter to the British chain from the Cape up to the Nile. To make his intentions brutally plain he decided to send warships to Moroccan harbours and land troops there. Wilhelm was sympathetic to the idea of seeking territory, but perhaps remembering his earlier adventures at Tangier and the baneful results, had no wish to send warships or take any steps which might precipitate war. However during Kiel Week Bethmann, who was in favour of those parts of his Foreign Minister's plans which had been divulged to him, persuaded Ballin to work on Wilhelm.[29] Ballin, strongly in favour of a 'livelier' foreign policy because the success of Social Democracy in various by-elections had convinced him that the Empire was already in the midst of a revolutionary situation,[30] succeeded in persuading Wilhelm to send ships, if not troops, and the following day Kiderlen was able to wire his office, 'Ships sanctioned.'

Immediately the gunboat, *Panther*, which was at Tenerife in the Canary Islands, was ordered to the Moroccan Atlantic port of Agadir, as were the gunboat *Eber* from the Cameroons, and the light cruiser *Berlin* from home. The *Panther* was the first to arrive in the evening of July 1. By this time a transparent excuse for the action had been delivered to the other signatories to the original Morocco agreement: German firms in southern Morocco 'and especially at Agadir and its environs' had been alarmed by unrest among the tribes in those regions and 'had requested protection by the Imperial government'. Everyone knew Germany had no important interests in Morocco, certainly not in Agadir, a small fishing port at the end of a caravan route, and according to the latest census there were not even any German nationals in the area! Evidently the stage had been set—but for what? Another attempt to split Britain and France—or to gain a part of Morocco, or naval bases in Morocco, or as Kiderlen had intimated earlier 'a decent mouthful' of the French Congo? Or was this the prelude to the assault on Paris for which the German Army had been waiting with unconcealed impatience? In the tradition of German *Real* diplomacy Kiderlen did nothing to limit the speculations.

Grey left the negotiations in the hands of the French government, but told Metternich that Britain intended to stand by her treaty obligations to France, and gave him a clear intimation of British interest: 'We cannot recognise any new agreement which is come to without us.'[31] He received no reply from the German government. In fact Bethmann could say little; Kiderlen was keeping him guessing as well as the French by asking for the entire French Congo! When Bethmann contrived to get him drunk to find out his real purpose, it seemed that he not only considered the possibility of war, but actually wanted one. As Bethmann himself was not against the notion that the *Reich* needed a war on idealist grounds to purge the petty self-interest of the Parties and unite them in a common great cause, he agreed that they should hold out and accept the 'risk' of war—while doing nothing to precipitate one.[32]

Meanwhile the German fleet was cruising in Norwegian waters; so was the *Hohenzollern* with Wilhelm and his Court, and the British Atlantic Fleet. This provided the only break in Germany's ominous silence towards Great Britain; Kiderlen suggested to the British Ambassador in Berlin that it would be diplomatic to avoid a meeting between the British fleet and the *Hohenzollern* lest the Kaiser be provoked into one of his notorious indiscretions. The Admiralty was already taking steps to prevent a meeting, but Kiderlen's strange warning prompted speculation; was it a ploy to conceal a planned German attack on the fleet—the 'bolt from the blue' which had occupied so many strategists during the succession of British naval scares? Tension was heightened by rumours from the Continent—many inspired by Kiderlen himself—that Germany was pitching her demands high because she intended to provoke war with France.

As the days passed and Grey still received no word from the German government Lloyd George and Churchill became converts to the view of German warlike intentions which Kiderlen, trying to force a submission from France, was doing his best to put about. Finally on July 21, three weeks after the *Panthersprung*, Lloyd George made up his mind; as he told Churchill before the Cabinet that day, Europe was drifting into war; it was time for Great Britain to make her voice heard. He was due to speak in the City of London that evening, and he had decided to insert a warning to Germany that if she forced a conflict she would find Great Britain on France's side. He asked Churchill how he thought Grey and Asquith would take it. Churchill replied they would be very much relieved; so far the Cabinet had been divided between Grey's uncompromising support for France and the Radicals' dislike of a Continental involvement. With the leading radicals committed to stand firm against Germany the government would be able to pursue a firm and united policy.

Before he went to the Mansion House to deliver his speech Lloyd George called in at the Foreign Office to show Grey his draft. Grey thought it excellent and salutary. Lloyd George was clearly associated with all elements in the country favourable to conciliation with Germany; a warning from him would carry far more weight than one from Grey himself, who was considered anti-German. It would indicate that Britain was united in active support of the French *entente*. The two of them called on Asquith who was equally delighted, and together they went over the precise wording to be used. As a result of the discussions Lloyd George was half an hour late for the dinner—an example of bad manners went the tittle-tattle to be expected from a radical Chancellor. He didn't give his reasons. And his speech made no undue impression on those present who were more concerned with his financial than with his foreign policies. But it was noted that at one point he drew a piece of paper from his pocket and read directly from it.

> I would make great sacrifices to preserve peace. I conceive that nothing would justify a disturbance of international goodwill except questions of the gravest national moment. But if a situation were forced upon us in which peace could only be preserved by the surrender of the great and beneficent position Britain has won by centuries of heroism and achievement, by allowing Britain to be treated where her interests are vitally affected as if she were of no account in the Cabinet of nations, then I say emphatically that peace at that price would be a humiliation intolerable for a great country like ours to endure.[33]

Few of the Bankers who heard the message realised it was addressed over their heads to Berlin and Paris. In Europe there was no mistake; the French took fresh heart, and in Germany where every imagined slight was felt as a blow to national honour, this real check came as a profound shock, particularly as no reply was possible—the fleet was still in the 'Danger Zone'. Tirpitz, who had not been consulted about Kiderlen's policy as the two detested each other, despaired of German diplomacy. Yet he and his advisers were quick to see that the anger against England which must result, and the feeling of German impotence against the British fleet could scarcely have been better timed for their proposed *Novelle* to raise the building tempo and secure the 'Iron Budget'. 'Whatever the outcome of this,' one of his colleagues remarked, 'it will work out for us.'[34]

This was ironic, for Kiderlen's aversion to Tirpitz stemmed from his belief that the Admiral had wrecked all chances of splitting the *Entente* by means of an agreement with England, and that his inflexible naval policy could lead to a fatal war.

In the meantime all that Bethmann and Kiderlen could do to salve some prestige from the setback was to try for Lloyd George's dismissal—as Bülow had accomplished Delcassé's—but even here they miscalculated. The situation was different. England was out of reach, Kiderlen's brutal tactics towards France had confirmed once again the newspaper image of Prussian militarism and Imperial ambition, and the mood was quite as defiant as Grey and his Foreign Office could have wished. When Lloyd George was summoned to Grey's room to hear the German complaint, he said to Churchill, who was with him, 'They may demand my resignation.'

'That would make you the most popular man in England,' Churchill replied.

The German note described Lloyd George's speech as a warning bordering on menace, and was itself couched in such menacing terms that Grey, whose apprehensions about Kiderlen's interest in the Norwegian cruises had not been stilled, sent for McKenna and advised him to have the fleet alerted against sudden attack. McKenna had the warning telegrams despatched; the subsequent activity in all home ports, noted by the German spy-ring in England, was interpreted in Berlin as preparations for the attack they feared. On board the *Hohenzollern* off Norway alarm bordered on panic; Wilhelm, seeing reality again for a brief space, remarked that it was not pleasant to think of war if one knew that one's sons would go to the front.[36]

In contrast to the *nervös* in high German circles, British reactions varied from relief that the challenge was at last out in the open to assurance bordering on phlegm. At the height of the crisis Sir Arthur Wilson, First Sea Lord, travelled to Scotland for a weekend shoot—dangerous nonchalance in the opinion of many including Lord Charles Beresford, particularly as the British Home and Atlantic fleets were then divided in some half dozen ports stretching from the North of Scotland to the south of Ireland. In contrast the German High Seas Fleet was concentrated and at sea—almost precisely the situation assumed for the opening of the most widely-read of all contemporary 'war-scare' novels, 'The Invasion of 1910'.[37] In that horrific tale which epitomised the fears of the 'Bolt-from-the-blue' school of strategists, surprise torpedo attacks on separated detachments of the British fleet had been followed by a North Sea victory for the concentrated German battle fleet. At the same time Wilhelm's soldiers had been landing on the East Anglian coast from Norfolk down to Maldon and Burnham-on-Crouch in Essex; Norwich had fallen within days; fierce fighting further south had culminated in the Battle of Purleigh (Essex), then the fall of Chelmsford, leading to the siege of London itself with the forces entrenched along a line Watford, Barnet, Waltham Abbey, Epping, Brentwood. The frightful tale had ended with the fall of London and the signing of an ignominious peace heralding the end of the British Empire.

To Arthur Wilson, the premises were ludicrous. While the British fleet was so much stronger than the German there was little danger of war, invasion was out of the question. Fisher shared his view. He wrote to Esher from Bad Nauheim on August 1.

> We are in the satisfactory position of having *twice as many Dreadnoughts in commission as Germany* AND A NUMBER GREATER BY ONE UNIT THAN THE WHOLE OF THE REST OF THE WORLD PUT TOGETHER! I don't think there is the very faintest fear of war! How wonderfully providence guides England! Just when there is a quite natural tendency to ease down our naval endeavours comes AGADIR!
> 'Time and the Ocean and some Guiding Star
> In High Cabal have made us what we are!'[38]

After his initial alarm at the unprecedented German response to Lloyd George's speech, Grey too thought the danger slight— although by no means gone. He put it down to the speech. His Private Secretary wrote to a colleague:

> Don't ever forget to teach your children to keep alive the memory of Lloyd George who by his timely speech has saved the peace of Europe and our good name. I shall never forget the service rendered by him. His courage was great as he risked his position with the people who have mainly made him ...[39]

The letter enthused over Lloyd George's continuing co-operation with Grey, ending 'We are sound that is the main thing'; this meant that all sides of the government now shared the Foreign Office recognition of German danger! Lloyd George himself, when asked if the German attempts to secure his dismissal could be made public, replied, 'Yes, it is just as well the nation should know what the German attitude of mind is. The policy of the jackboot won't do for us. I am all for peace, but am not going back to be jackbooted by anybody.'[40]

The most remarkable transformation wrought by the *Panther-*

sprung was that of Winston Churchill—yet it was not so much change as self-discovery. The revelation of Germany's hideous designs and the dark abyss into which lack of preparation or lack of courage could plunge the British Empire were themes to which his spirit responded like a swimmer rising from unnatural depths. It was the inspiration his imagination needed. 'Liberal politics, the People's budget. Free trade, Peace, Retrenchment and Reform—all the warcries of the Election struggle began to seem unreal in the presence of this new preoccupation.'[41] He was Home Secretary, yet it was Europe and the looming military struggle that engaged his mind.

His chief mentor was the Director of Military Operations, General Sir Henry Wilson, a remarkable soldier who had long been convinced that Germany was preparing another march on Paris, and who had sought passionately to move British strategical thought from simple dependence on sea power towards the military defence of France. He was convinced that the thrust, when it came, would be through Belgium; the German strategic railways, the siting of their marshalling yards and barracks left no room for doubt. Each year he visited Belgium several times with bicycle, maps and notebooks, to survey every route they might use, every position that might be held. He struck up a close friendship with the French General Foch, whom he saw as allied Commander-in-Chief when the 'big war' came, reopened liaison with the French General Staff begun during the first Moroccan crisis, refining it into a detailed mobilisation schedule whereby six British divisions would cross the Channel to stand on the left flank of the French Army to meet the main German thrust. One whole wall of his room at the War Office was covered by a huge map of Belgium with all roads useful to an advancing enemy standing out boldly. It was to this room that Winston Churchill came to drink in his profound analysis of the threat to France and via France to the British Empire.

The other room Churchill haunted was Grey's. Once he insisted on taking Grey to see Wilson; the talk was keen; as Grey recorded, Churchill's 'high-metalled spirit was exhilarated by the air of crisis and high events.'[42] Not content with pumping Grey, Churchill visited his Permanent Under-Secretary each morning to read the latest foreign telegrams; the Under-Secretary, sharply anti-German, formed the impression that both Churchill and Lloyd George who also visited him, were a little disappointed that war did not break out as the moment was 'exceedingly favourable'. He was 'struck by the determination of both of them not to permit Germany to assume the role of bully.'[43]

After Parliament had adjourned and most of the great and fashionable had left the capital sweltering under one of the hottest summers of the century, Churchill stayed on, calling for Grey in the early evenings for an eager quiz on the latest situation and whisking him off for a plunge in the Royal Automobile Club's swimming pool; 'there he would cool his ardour' while Grey revived his spirits, weary from the anxiety and his enforced vigil at a desk he longed to leave for his country home.

It was during this time on August 23 that Asquith called a secret meeting of the Committee of Imperial Defence to probe the preparedness of the armed Services in the event of war. The few Cabinet Ministers present—including Churchill and Lloyd George —found that the Army and Navy not only lacked a co-ordinated policy—which was common knowledge—but more seriously took quite opposed views of the general strategy for a European war. First, General Sir Henry Wilson, standing by his great map of Belgium specially transported for the occasion, lectured the Committee in detail on the need for the British Army to reinforce the French left flank as soon after the outbreak of war as possible in order to stem the high-tide of the German advance. Then Admiral Sir Arthur Wilson presented the Navy case for not allowing the British Army to become bogged down in a Continental war, but to hold it—in Fisher's term—'in the air' ready to strike anywhere around the German coast, where they would draw off many more enemy divisions from the main assault. This was Britain's historic strategy. But the Admiral carried less conviction than the General; for one thing he refused to divulge his plans, just as he and Fisher had refused to divulge their joint plan during the first Moroccan crisis for fear that once the Army and the politicians got hold of it all secrecy would be lost!

It is probable that he deliberately misled the Committee, particularly on the question of close blockade, for the same reason. And when cross-examined by the General on such fundamentals as the German railway system and the facility with which their divisions might be concentrated to meet the Navy's peripheral attacks, he made a poor witness. Afterwards the War Minister, Haldane, drew Asquith aside and said he could not continue to be responsible for the War Office unless the Admiralty consented to work with the General Staff of the Army and, moreover provided themselves with a staff of their own.

The situation was almost Wilhelmine with the roles of the forces reversed; in Germany the Army was the senior Service and brushed aside the Navy's phrenetic plans with little understanding; in England the Navy had been supreme for centuries and regarded the Army's detailed preoccupation with train time-tables and forage with scorn. What made the parallel with Germany even closer was the fact that most of the Cabinet had no idea that the General Staff—in fact Henry Wilson—had arranged joint war plans with the French down to details of the coffee-breaks en route to the point of concentration, thus virtually committing Great Britain to come in on France's side when the attack came—either that or lose her honour.

When Asquith learned the detailed plan he was against it, and was adamant that four divisions was the most that could be allowed the French. Many others were opposed in principle, believing the joint plans not only compromised the government's freedom of action in a crisis, but could even encourage the French to provoke Germany, and so plunge Britain into a war for nothing better than a Continental quarrel. McKenna still First Lord of the Admiralty, believed this, particularly as he was with Admiral Wilson, absolutely against the British Army being used as an appendage of the French in the main theatre.

With his Service chiefs at odds, but the Army appearing to have the better case, Asquith was forced to replace McKenna. Churchill was one obvious choice. His enthusiasm and unbounded drive, his fervid imagination which had caught 'on the idle hill of summer' the sound of distant drums 'drumming like a noise in dreams', his sympathy with the Army's point of view, which bubbled out of him in memos and long letters urging that the *ententes* be converted into military alliances, Belgium's neutrality guaranteed, and Holland's and Denmark's, all pointed to the irresistible force the Navy needed to revolutionise its thinking department as Fisher had revolutionised its *matériel*. Perhaps as the deciding factor, Lloyd George approved; he trusted that Winston would be able to reduce McKenna's ever-increasing estimates!

The appointment was sealed on a golden afternoon the following month during a game of golf at Archerfield, the house on the east coast of Scotland where Asquith retired for the summer recess. His daughter saw the two of them walking in after the game. Churchill's face was radiant. Immediately he asked her out for a walk with him.

> We were hardly out of the house when he said to me with grave but shining eyes, 'I don't want tea—I don't want anything—anything in the world. Your father has just offered me the Admiralty ... He was tasting fulfilment. Never before or since have I seen him more completely and profoundly happy. The tide of happiness and realisation was too deep even for exuberance ... 'This is the big thing—the biggest thing that has ever come my way—the chance I would have chosen before all others. I shall pour into it everything I've got.'[44]

As they walked down towards the darkening sea, two battle-cruisers became visible far away steaming from the Firth of Forth. To Churchill the sombre silhouettes were invested with a new significance.

Tirpitz, meanwhile, had lost little time in using the humiliation of Lloyd George's speech for his own purposes. As the Anglophobia of the Boer War had blown in the Navy Law of 1900 and the first Morocco crisis the *Novelle* of 1906, so the bitter 'storm of public opinion'[45] following the Chancellor of the Exchequer's open threat at the Mansion House had to be used for a *Novelle* to reassert the normal building tempo for the fleet.

Although some of his closest colleagues thought at first that only a renewal of 'the four-tempo against England' would satisfy honour lost over the 'Fashoda' Lloyd George had inflicted,[46] Tirpitz, who was just as incensed, had regained his fear of a preventive assault and was determined not to be unnecessarily provocative. He went to Bethmann with proposals for additional heavy cruisers—in fact Dreadnoughts, although not so obviously anti-British as battleships —to bring the building tempo up to *three*, and also proposed to meet one of the most constant criticisms of his policy by increasing the immediately battle-ready proportion of the total fleet. As for the extra cost, he suggested meeting most of it from loans, at the same time increasing the inheritance tax.

Bethmann knew that any increase in the fleet law would be disastrous from every point of view. At home it would bring on a fresh financial crisis, give added strength to Socialist criticism of high arms expenditure and indirect taxation and lead to further Social Democratic gains in the forthcoming elections. At the same time the proposed inheritance tax would alienate the Junkers, who had already thrown the idea out several times and were growing increasingly restive about the Navy's vast expenditure and totally negative results. In consequence they were moving back to their old 'continental' position of reliance on the Army as the basis of German power, and there was growing agitation for a halt to naval expansion in favour of Army increases. A new Naval Law, therefore threatened to strain the already difficult patriotic 'bloc' for government policies, besides providing perfect ammunition for the Left and Progressives.

In foreign affairs the vital question was still an arrangement with England, whose fleet, despite all Tirpitz's efforts, held the balance in Europe. As Bethmann confided to a colleague, had he directed Moroccan policy towards the war the military wanted, the army would be somewhere in France, most of the fleet would be on the bottom of the North Sea, the commercial ports blockaded, 'and the entire nation would ask me, "Why this?"' and, he added, would quite rightly string him to the nearest tree.[47] Besides his general anxiety over the sharpening of relations with England which must follow any increase in the naval law, Bethmann had a specific interest in maintaining the drop in building tempo due in 1912; he hoped to use this considerable slowing of construction as a bait to bring the British to the conference table again and achieve the agreement which had eluded his earlier negotiations, thus beginning the separation of England from her Continental *Ententes*. Kiderlen and the Foreign Ministry supported him fully on these grounds as the Minister of the Interior and the Treasury Minister supported his domestic and financial objections to Tirpitz's proposal—indeed the Treasury Minister, Wermuth, determined to apply economic sense to the runaway expenditure of the *Reich*, had already demanded cuts in Tirpitz's existing budget!

For all these reasons Bethmann was determined to fight the *Novelle*, and he told Tirpitz that his proposals would not only add to the governments economic difficulties, already under severe attack from the Social Democrats, but would amount to public recognition of the failure of Kiderlen's Moroccan policy, and moreover increase the danger from England.

However real his view of the English danger, it was felt acutely by all high naval officers outside the *Reichsmarineamt*: Admiral Holtzendorff, Commander-in-Chief High Seas Fleet, Admiral von Heeringen, formerly Tirpitz's chief of publicity, now head of the *Admiralstab*, and Admiral von Müller, chief of the Naval Cabinet, all feared a 'Copenhagen' if England were pushed too hard while the Moroccan business provided her with such a perfect chance to strike. None of them was able to visualise Great Britain remaining a passive onlooker while Tirpitz laboured so obviously to close the naval gap.

Despite all the arguments, domestic, foreign, strategic, Wilhelm himself backed Tirpitz, accusing Bethmann of being a hopeless weakling, and insisting against all evidence of British determination to overtrump every German increase that respect from England could only be obtained by a stronger fleet, 'downright anxiety about which brings Britain to an understanding.'[48] The first public intimation of this attitude came in a speech he made at Hamburg on August 27; he claimed to understand the 'enthusiasm of the people of Hamburg' as a wish to 'strengthen our Navy, so that we can be sure that nobody will dispute with us our place in the sun which belongs to us!'[49]

The Berlin Stock Market provided a different interpretation. As August drew to a close without any halt to the war rumours a vast number of amateur investors who had been speculating on the continuing rise in Germany's economy began to panic and switch their holdings into American shares. On Monday, September 4—'Black Monday'—selling orders pouring in from the provinces had completely unhinged the market and industrials dropped up to twenty per cent, in some cases thirty per cent. The British consul in Frankfurt, reporting on the extraordinary collapse, thought the investing public had entirely lost what little confidence remained after the Mansion House speech.[50] For a while Wilhelm's nerves were similarly affected and he listened to Bethmann's argument that the *Novelle* should be postponed until the following autumn, or even 1913 when the Kiel Canal scheme would be nearing completion. Von Müller was delighted, reassuring him that 'no one could, at the present time, accept the responsibility of a war with England.'[51]

It was not for long. On September 2, the German naval attaché in London, an uncompromisingly anti-English officer who believed that an eventual war for the mastery of the seas was inevitable, had reported his opinion that there was little danger of an immediate attack. Tirpitz was able to use this to work Wilhelm back to his own point of view. By September 12 Wilhelm was again declaring that the German people were furious with England, therefore in the best mood for a *Novelle*.[52] Von Müller remonstrated with him. The fleet was in a particularly unfavourable position *vis-à-vis* England, without sufficient submarines or mines to prevent a blockade or a 'Copenhagen' attack, with the fortifications to Heligoland incomplete and without any means of transferring Dreadnoughts from the Baltic to the North Sea save by exposing them all around the Danish peninsula. Wilhelm cut him short.

'The unfinished state of the Navy is always brought up when things get critical. This is certainly the time to move. The people demand it. If the Chancellor and Kiderlen and the Treasury Minister won't co-operate they will be sacked!'[53]

Müller, not usually outspoken, replied that he was convinced a conflict with England could not be avoided in the long run, but he was equally convinced that the present was the most unfavourable moment imaginable. 'The anger against England will also be there later to be used as a sure means of getting the Bill accepted.'

Wilhelm would not be diverted, and wrote to Bethmann insisting that a *Novelle* be introduced; both France and Japan had announced naval increases and England would accept it because of her guilty conscience over Morocco. Bethmann thought the excuses childish. As he had the support of most of the government, imperial entourage and high naval officers in believing the proposal mistaken at such a delicate point in Anglo-German relations, and as the vague dissatisfactions at the huge expense and impotence of the naval policy were beginning to coalesce in an alternative strategy for world power by stages, using the Army to secure the continental base as the first essential step, Tirpitz knew that he faced the most determined opposition of his career. He was equally determined —both to attain the 'Iron Budget' which would secure his fleet for all time, and to prevent the present Law's drop to only two ships a year between 1912 and 1917 lest the *Reichstag*—and the *Bundesrat* —became accustomed to two as the 'normal' tempo and made difficulties when it came to finding the extra money for a three-tempo at the end of the period. This was the internal rationale; it had been occupying Tirpitz since 1898, and now so near of achievement, it had become an obsession. Externally, he held to the conviction that Germany could not back down before England's attempts to keep her in a hopelessly inferior naval position without renouncing her claim to world power status. For in that case 'our policy must always show consideration for England and our sacrifices for the Navy will have been vain.'[54]

He put these arguments to Wilhelm at his hunting lodge at the end of September, together with an ingenious scheme to deal with the dangerous coalition of internal opposition: Great Britain should be offered an agreement on the basis of a 3:2 ratio of strength with the German fleet; this ratio would give Germany a sufficiently good defensive chance to deter an English attack. If England agreed, a three-tempo *Novelle* could be introduced the following year in order to reach this level; if she refused—and Tirpitz knew that she must refuse—she would incur the *odium*, a potent expression in the German book, and internal opposition to the *Novelle* would melt away. As always when confronted with one of the 'Master's' impeccable presentations Wilhelm allowed himself to be persuaded, and wrote to Bethmann outlining the new idea: the 'Risk-Fleet' theory, he explained, had fulfilled its purpose and been discarded; what was needed now was a new goal like England's 'Two-Power standard' clearly intelligible to the man in the street; such was the 2:3 ratio in capital ships. 'If in spite of it the English go ahead with excessive construction, they saddle themselves with the *odium of provocation* and hostile *intention* towards us before the world ... We will have done our share in showing them we have nothing frightful or underhand up our sleeves.'[55] Tirpitz, worried lest the favourable moment of intense anger against England slip away and the internal opposition mount, also wrote to Bethmann suggesting an early intimation to the British of the 3:2 proposal; when Bethmann expressed his migivings about such a 'provocation' he explained that the whole purpose of the naval policy was to secure political independence from England and a good chance of successful defence against an English attack. For this it was necessary to diminish the military distance between them, not to increase it by *voluntarily* sinking to the two-tempo. And he repeated an earlier argument with Wilhelm that if they did not succeed in diminishing the distance then the whole naval policy of the last fourteen years had been vain.

Bethmann maintained his opposition. Wilhelm, quite as impatient as Tirpitz for an immediate *Novelle*, vented his annoyance at his entourage: the Chancellor, he expostulated, was completely obsessed by his fear of England. 'But I will not allow England to tell me what to do. I told the *Reich* Chancellor to remember that I was a successor to the Great Elector and Frederick the Great, who never hesitated to act when the time seemed to have come.'[56] When Tirpitz had his next audience he repeated his threats that Bethmann would either have to introduce the *Novelle* or go. But Bethmann saw him shortly afterwards and calmed him, and in accordance with the delaying tactics with which he was hoping to kill the *Novelle*, persuaded him that the approach to Britain should await a more favourable climate in their relationship.

Fisher, in Lucerne, was still keeping in close touch with events within Germany and firing off letters retailing what he heard. To Esher he wrote:

I suppose if a Pitt or a Palmerston had now been guiding our destinies we should have war. They would say any peace would be a bad peace because of the latent damnable feeling in Germany against England. It won't be France any more, it will be England that will be the red rag for the German bull! And as we NEVER were so strong as at present, then Pitt & Co. would say the present is the time to fight! Personally I am confident of peace. I happen to know in a curious way (but quite certainly) that the Germans are in a blue funk of the British Navy and are quite assured that 942 German steamers would be 'gobbled up' in the first forty-eight hours of war, and also the d—d uncertainty of *where* and *when* a hundred thousand troops embarked in transports and kept 'in the air' might land! NB There's a lovely spot only ninety miles from Berlin![57]

Of Kiderlen's attempted coup at Agadir, he exulted that Lloyd George's speech had 'upset the German applecart in a way it had never been upset before! I suppose they were "*written-out*" words and Cabinet words, and they were d—d fine words!' He had heard via a Bremen multi-millionaire that the most optimistic assurances of peace were emanating from official quarters in Berlin.

This was correct. Confronted with a French government determined not to yield and with a British government which he believed was only waiting for the call to stand with the French, Kiderlen backed down, and in return for a parcel of virtually worthless acres on the Camaroons-Congo border, recognised the French protectorate over Morocco.

The obvious setback to German methods of diplomacy and the relaxation of war tensions led to a renewed outbreak of Anglophobia which surpassed all previous waves. Bebel reported to the British Foreign Office:

> You cannot imagine the bitter feeling now prevailing amongst our military, colonial & higher classes generally against England. I cannot in my long experience remember anything like it. No such general animosity existed either against Austria or France at any time. Our official classes feel thoroughly humiliated & are thirsting for revenge. *Everything is shaping itself for a war with England* (*Alles spitzt sich auf einem Krieg mit England*) ...[58]

Alarmed by the thought that a sudden German fleet strike against the Royal Navy might be successful, he continued in a later message:

> I ought not to tell you these things but I feel I must give you this hint, that we were told in secret by the Govt. our (Germany's) only chance against the more powerful English fleet would be to be 'two months in advance with our preparations at the moment of striking. The Minister added that they were straining every nerve to be thus prepared.[59]

Large sections of the German Press reflected the frenzy for revenge, and no longer content with tendentious slanting of reports or quotations from the most extreme British views, resorted to pure fiction. Wholly imaginary speeches were put into the mouths of British diplomats or senior Ministers. The most flagrant example was perpetrated on McKenna. At the end of September he was reported even by Progressive German papers, as having pronounced the thoroughly Treitschkian sentiment in an oration in North Monmouthshire, 'I take my stand on the unassailable proposition that peace is not the most necessary good of mankind; in the first rank stands the material interests of the British Empire!'[60] From there, went the reports, he had gone on to accuse Germany of transferring to Morocco 'those attempts at intimidation with which she has triumphed over the Russians in Persia and even over Great Britain in the East.' And he had explained the fundamental differences between British and German diplomatic tactics: in Germany 'much is demanded in order that a little may be obtained. Great Britain chooses her position at the first move and struggles there to the end.' The whole fictitious farrago was extraordinarily revealing of German thinking: 'Intimidation'—'triumph over Great Britain'—'much is demanded'—'the material interests of (*der Gross-Staat*) as a higher good than peace'.

Having reported the nonsense, the Editorial columns commented; here is the *Münchener Neueste Nachrichten*: 'It is characteristic of the state of feeling dominant in England that McKenna could hope to create an effect and find applause among his audience by means of a speech in which he emphatically baited Germany.'[61] The *Münchener Zeitung* went further: it was 'a *malicious* baiting of Germany and a wanton attempt to prevent a peaceable solution of the Morocco question at the last moment.'[62] The *Nachrichten* had that point as well: 'It would seem incredible that such a speech could be made in England at the moment when the Moroccan difficulty has been smoothed away, if we did not see in it the expression of a policy whose end and aim consist in prolonging the tension of relations with Germany and in an attitude of hostility towards her everywhere, and at all times, and under all conditions. Since this is incontestably the case, Germany will be grateful to McKenna for his public declaration.'

The following day the *Nachrichten* had a paragraph tucked away in an obscure corner: 'Mr McKenna made no statement in the least resembling that with which he is credited, and he made no allusion either to Morocco or to Germany ... the English daily papers of the 27th contain no such expressions, and the whole thing must have been a simple invention.' The *Zeitung* gave more prominence to the retraction, and went on to wonder at 'the incredible wantonness with which German papers reproduce, without criticism the information of dubious telegraphic bureaux, although such a sensational report, the strong political effect of which is obvious, stood in urgent need of conscientious verification.'

But it was the real Mansion House speech and the real blow to German prestige that continued to fester within the Empire after the fictions were forgotten. In November, after Kiderlen had signed the new Morocco agreement, the Conservative leader in the *Reichstag*, von Heydebrand, allowed himself a full-blooded reply to Lloyd George.

'Now we know where our enemy stands. Like a flash of lightning in the night these incidents have revealed to the German people where is the foe. The German people now knows, when it seeks expansion and the place in the sun which is its right and its destiny where is the State which thinks it can decide these matters!'[63]

The strategy for tackling the adversary was not so clear-cut; within the government the dispute over Tirpitz's *Novelle* gathered force. Bethmann mused, 'the German people have so frivolously played with war this summer. This is serious. This I must oppose.'[64]

Churchill

~~~~~~~~~~

Winston Churchill took over from McKenna as First Lord of the Admiralty on October 24, 1911. Almost his first act was to ask Fisher to meet him. The quarrel between them over the 'acceleration' estimates had been made up and Fisher, eager to return to the fray, and feeling younger after his long holiday than when he had retired, hurried back to England from Lucerne and spent a weekend at Reigate Priory with Churchill, Lloyd George and Haldane among the guests. He felt guilty about condoning the shabby trick played on his ever-loyal friend McKenna who had fought for the Navy so courageously, but convinced himself that duty to Navy and country came before personal considerations, and entered into the spirit of the discussions as if it had been October 1904 and his own time again: 'I had no sleep for four nights—when I wasn't talking I was writing. My brain was buzzing like a hive of bees! They all fell on my neck and kissed me ...'[1] He was as unaffectedly excited as a lieutenant over his first command: 'Winston Churchill, Lloyd George, Lord Haldane and Sir Rufus Isaacs—about as clever, each one, as you will find anywhere all the world over! However, I was in excellent form and got on splendidly.'[2]

The trip was made in secret so as not to rekindle the hatreds which the very mention of his name would have reawakened, and afterwards he retired directly to Lucerne. Whispers of his keen talks with Churchill crackled through the London Clubs, but not a murmur appeared in the newspapers. Churchill himself, inspired by the old Admiral's vision and certainty of judgement and youthful fire, was very tempted to ask him to come back as First Sea Lord, but knowledge of the bitter Service feuds that were bound to recur dissuaded him; instead he used him as his very secret, but principal adviser on all the great tasks that confronted him.

First of these, as he saw it, was to bring naval strategy into line with War Office ideas, and give the Navy a thinking department like the General Staff of the Army. Here, he found himself in absolute disagreement with Sir Arthur Wilson, McKenna's First Sea Lord. Wilson refused to revise his own very personal and very secret war plans for a maritime instead of a Continental strategy, and refused to admit any similarity between the two Services' need for a War Staff; the 'thinking department' of the Admiralty, he is supposed to have said, consisted of every soul in the building from himself down to the charwomen who emptied the wastepaper baskets full of the plans of amateur strategists. Fisher's own views were identical, and he found Churchill's and Lloyd George's involvement with the soldiers disquieting: 'It's the most extraordinary incident I ever knew of for these two special men to have become practically aiders and abetters of conscription, because that's the end of it ...'[3] But unlike Wilson he was a political animal, and he compromised on the War Staff Churchill was determined to inaugurate in order to get other essentials through. He rationalised it:

> The argument for a War Staff is that YOU MAY have a d—d fool as First Sea Lord, and so you put him in commission, as it were. But if there's a Barham as First Sea Lord, he'll run the war, and no one else! I never told anyone my real plan of War; no more would AKW (Wilson) ...[4]

Wilson had to go; even Fisher admitted he was no good ashore. His successor was chosen so that Prince Louis of Battenberg, Fisher's real choice for First Sea Lord, would be able to take over in 1914, when both he and Churchill anticipated the inevitable German challenge. A similar strategy was employed in the home fleets. Fisher wrote to one of his closest Press colleagues:

> I tell you (AND YOU ONLY) the whole secret of the rest of the changes. *To get Jellicoe Commander-in-Chief of the Home Fleet prior to October 21, 1914,* which is the date of the Battle of Armageddon. He will succeed Callaghan automatically in two years from December 19, 1911, so will have all well in hand by the before-mentioned date! Nunc dimittis! *Everything revolved around Jellicoe!*[5]

He wrote to McKenna's wife exulting over the triumph, this time giving *September* 1914 as the date 'that suits the Germans ... Both their army and Fleet then mobilised, and the Kiel Canal finished, and their new building complete.'[6] And to another friend, he explained that Jellicoe would be about the same age as Nelson at Trafalgar, 'and possesses all Nelson's attributes except Lady Hamilton, and there I sympathise with him!'[7]

As for *matériel*, he was insistent that the lead acquired with the *Dreadnought* be maintained by further *plunges*. 'Plunge is progress! Foreign Admiralties pause, while the British Navy, like John Brown's soul goes marching on! and splendid patriots like Sir William White, Custance and others make foreign Admiralties pause still more with arguments for small battleships ...'[8] Now Tirpitz had caught up in size of ship and Krupps were rumoured to be making a 14" naval gun, it was time to move up to a larger, faster class of battleship mounting 15" pieces. He told Churchill:

> The most damnable person for you to have any dealings with is a naval expert! Sea fighting is pure common sense. The first of all its necessities is SPEED, so as to be able to fight—
> > *When* you like
> > *Where* you like
> and *How* you like.
> Therefore the super-*Lion* (battlecruiser), the super-*Swift* (destroyer) and the super-Submarine are the only three types for fighting ... No armour for anything but the super-*Lion, and there restricted.* Cost £1,195,000; *speed over thirty knots*: all oil; ten 'improved' guns and you'll make the Germans '*squirm*' ...[9]

Churchill could not take the advice to such extremes, chiefly because Fisher's views on speed and long-range guns as the equivalent and offensive superiors of armour were not shared by many naval officers—indeed there was much criticism of the very weak armour of the battlecruiser type. If anything Churchill had to increase armour weight against the likelihood of heavier German guns; a speed of thirty knots was consequently out of the question without a gigantic and politically impossible increase in size and cost. But on the other points he followed Fisher's advice, *plunging* for a 15" main armament without ordering prototypes—there was no time for a prototype—*plunging* for oil fuel instead of coal to obtain high speed, although coal was plentiful and cheap within the British Isles and oil had to be imported by sea—subsequently *plunging* the government into buying a controlling interest in the Anglo-Persian Oil Company, a stroke which has been compared to Disraeli's purchase of Suez Canal shares the previous century. Results justified his boldness; the *Queen Elizabeth* class of battle-ships, laid down in 1912, proved almost as superior to previous Dreadnoughts as the *Dreadnought* to her predecessors; with a speed of twenty-five knots, belt armour impenetrable by German ordnance, and guns which threw a shell twice the weight and effectively very much further than the German 12" pieces, they were in a class by themselves, 'the most perfect example of the naval constructors art' of their time.[10]

Fisher was delighted with Churchill: *'he's a genius without doubt! ... and he is brave, which is everything! Napoleonic in audacity, Cromwellian in thoroughness!'*[11]

His impact on the Admiralty was similar to Fisher's own seven years before. Inspired by a feeling of imminent danger, hence by the urgency of his mission to re-organise and hone the Service to instant readiness for the trial that lay close ahead, and driven by the im-patience of his own genius to learn at first hand and master every detail of the vast fleets and shore establishments he had taken over, he was often careless of protocol, and in his enthusiasm outraged custom or forced his strong opinions on officers and members of the Board with an eloquence they could not match. Jellicoe, who admired his ability and the 'wonderful argumentative powers' with which he put the Admiralty case in Cabinet, found it a 'positive danger' when he turned his powers on to his colleagues on the Board, who were not trained to argue a case; 'his fatal error was his inability to realise his own limitations as a civilian.'[12] Despite violent storms on the Board and at sea caused by this confidence in his own 'civilian' judgement, and the imperious zeal with which he, 'the image of bubbling, ambitious youth',[13] over-rode experi-enced sailors, his clarity of purpose and intellectual power—combined with constant advice from Fisher—forced a second era of rapid progress in the war-readiness of the Fleet. And an equally exciting one. 'No man', wrote one observer, 'seemed to live in such a state of perpetual mental excitement or to be able to entertain so many vital and jostling ideas at the same time, or to be so honest and brilliant about them all.'[14]

His most constant image was of the menace overhanging Great Britain, and one of his first innovations at the Admiralty was to have hung on the wall behind the chair in his room a large wooden case in which a chart of the North Sea was fixed. On it a Staff Officer marked the position of the High Seas Fleet each day with flags. Churchill made it a rule to look at this chart when he entered the room each morning. 'I did this less to keep myself informed ... than in order to inculcate in myself and those working with me a sense of the ever-present danger.'[15] His intellect was informed by imagination. 'To discuss a question with Churchill was to see him dramatise it in successive scenes with effective lights and colours and then at the end choose the scene which was best dramatised and most effectively lit.'[16] What grander backdrop for the role in which destiny had cast him than the sombre gun platforms facing each other across the grey wastes known until recently as the German Ocean! Never before had the British Empire faced such deadly peril, never before had so little stood between it and military overlordship. McKenna, like Grey, had fought the good fight with facts and remorseless, sometimes arrogant logic; Churchill carried his with the fire of imagery. To many solid Englishmen he appeared no more than a posturing and ambitious publicity seeker—especially as his conversion had been so sudden; to others his images were irresistible. Esher, after lunching with him one day in November, confided to a friend, 'There are many rocks ahead for this country. Fifteen ships alone stand between Great Britain and conquest, and the annihilation of Empire.'[17]

The construction programme Churchill inherited from McKenna was for four capital ships to match the two of Tirpitz's fallen tempo, but in his first month in office in the aftermath of the *Panthersprung*, reports from Germany made it plain that if Tirpitz had his way the tempo would not remain at two, and the British naval attaché reported that without foreign orders or an increase in the annual programme from 1912 through 1917 Germany's naval shipbuilding industry would face dislocation. With the probability of having to raise his own programme to five to preserve a sixty per cent margin over a three-tempo, Churchill lent himself to yet another attempt at mutual limitation. The signs were not auspicious, the precedents even less so, and many thought it a dangerous course and likely to encourage Tirpitz by suggesting that the financial strain was proving too great. However, Lloyd George had backed him for the Admiralty in the expectation that he would bring the Estimates down—not raise them—and the two of them were still the closest collaborators. And while Lloyd George was bitter about the German attitude and their continued attacks on him personally,[18] he felt that no avenue which promised any possibility of reconciliation—however unlikely—should be left unexplored. Perhaps, above all, and before the whole Cabinet lay the bleak prospect of an unending commitment to five capital ships a year, with continually increasing annual Estimates as each batch came into service to swell the total fleet which had to be manned and maintained and replaced with larger, costlier units if recent history were a guide, with the eventual establishment standing at the staggering—indeed unthinkable—figure of some ninety-three Dreadnoughts (Sixty per cent above the fifty-eight of the existing German Law)!

This was the card Tirpitz was playing in his struggle with Bethmann, the Treasury Minister Wermuth, and the Foreign Office. Great Britain could not possibly maintain such a fleet; his principal assistant, Eduard von Capelle, whom he relied on for his financial wizardry, had produced studies showing that Great Britain building at a five-tempo, would be out of breath financially as early as 1918 or 1919. And she would not only find it impossible to replace her aging pre-Dreadnoughts, but—as Tirpitz had always maintained—would be unable to man her inflated fleet. The manning difficulties also posed financial problems; whereas the German ships were crewed largely by short-service conscripts, the British Navy employed only long-service volunteers with a rate of pay well over double their German opposite numbers. To Tirpitz, Capelle and Wilhelm it seemed impossible that Great Britain, with her world commitments and volunteer sailors could meet the concentrated threat their construction posed; she would have to come to them—or fight. To most high naval officers she had blundered badly by not forcing the conflict that summer when their own naval position had been virtually hopeless.

Bethmann, meanwhile, was attempting to turn the emerging 'continental' strategy—which was of course a reversion to traditional Prussian strategy—into a formal weapon against Tirpitz. At the end of November, in a desperate bid to head off the *Novelle*, he wrote to the Prussian War Minister to say that the government needed to know the Army's requirements in the coming year before a decision could be reached on the Navy Bill—a transparent invitation to the Army to put in for large increases which would sink the *Novelle's* chances. The Treasury Minister supported him, arguing that the Navy had already taken too large a share of the budget from Germany's 'first line of defence'; he disputed the Tirpitz/Capelle forecast of Britain's economic exhaustion by pointing to the vast sums she had raised to fight the Boer War; she would regard the struggle for the North Sea as far more important than a colonial skirmish. All reports from Metternich in London confirmed this view. He had spoken to Churchill and was struck with his determination to lay down two keels or more if necessary to every extra one from Tirpitz; Great Britain was 'ready for any sacrifice' to maintain her position on the seas. The German naval attaché stressed the same point: 'The policy of a superior Navy and of opposition to any fleet which is held to be a menace to England, is still demanded by the Board of Admiralty and will be supported by the Nation whether the First Lord's name is McKenna or Churchill.'[19]

About this time, at the end of 1911, word reached Wilhelm that the British government was prepared to help Germany acquire further colonies in return for concessions on the naval question. This was the line that Churchill and Lloyd George, in consultation with Grey, had decided upon: 'We were no enemies to German colonial expansion and if aiding Germany colonially would produce a stable situation it was a price we were prepared to pay.'[20] Wilhelm, interpreting the conciliatory approach as another stratagem to destroy the *Novelle* and keep his fleet permanently inferior, was furious. But Bethmann went to work on the chiefs of his Cabinets, convincing them of the potentially tremendous political advantages of an agreement with England, beside which the few extra Dreadnoughts Tirpitz wanted would be poor compensation; the Cabinet chiefs then convinced Wilhelm, who swung 180 degrees and became enthusiastic about the grand colonial agreement in prospect.

However, neither government was prepared to initiate formal talks for fear that they would appear the suppliant, unable to bear the strain of the competition, and once again Albert Ballin and his friend, Sir Ernest Cassel appeared on the scene as informal conciliators. Cassel had lost much of his influence at Court with the death of King Edward the previous year, but he was a long-standing and close friend of Churchill's; Ballin was as deeply concerned as he had been in 1909 about Tirpitz's insatiable ambition and the ruin to which it was leading Germany. In early January 1912 he sent a letter to Cassel—whether as the result of earlier prompting from Cassel, or indeed from Bethmann will probably never be known; the letter suggested that when Cassel came to Germany in March, Churchill should accompany him to negotiate on the naval question. Churchill would have been delighted to exercise his powers of argument on Tirpitz and Wilhelm, but wiser views prevailed and a note was drawn up for Cassel to take to Berlin in person. This suggested that in return for recognising British naval supremacy and not adding to the present Navy Law, even reducing its tempo where possible, Germany could expect not only Great Britain's help in the colonial sphere, but discussions towards a pact in which both sides would agree not to take part in aggressive combinations against the other.

Cassel arrived in Berlin on the morning of January 29 and met Ballin who went immediately to the Chancellery to notify Bethmann, and from thence to Wilhelm, telling him with some excitement of the Englishman's arrival on a matter of great importance. Cassel was then summoned, and handed his note to Wilhelm. The words had been carefully chosen by Grey, Lloyd George and Churchill, but swayed by Ballin's optimism that they represented an offer of alliance with Great Britain, and with his appetite for colonies whetted by the earlier hints from London, Wilhelm saw the vision of a great German *MittelAfrika* carved with England's help from the decaying Empires of Portugal and Belgium. He called Bethmann to the Palace and, retiring into his Adjutant's Office, they drafted a cordial but careful reply, stipulating that Tirpitz's latest *Novelle* which had already been drawn up—although not yet presented to the *Reichstag*—must be considered as an established part of the Navy Law in any negotiations. It was a forward bargaining position. For his part, Bethmann was quite prepared to sacrifice the extra ships of the *Novelle* as bargaining counters. Afterwards Cassel rejoined them and was handed the reply, together with a résumé of the *Novelle* which had been prepared by Bethmann. Both he and Wilhelm appeared delighted by the British overture—or was it the British response to Bethmann's overture via Ballin?—Wilhelm 'enchanted almost childishly so.'[21]

There was no enchantment in London when Cassel returned. The précis of the *Novelle* which he brought seemed to confirm all suspicions.

In fact it was not so stiff as Tirpitz had intended originally.

Bethmann's and Wermuth's intensive campaign and the threat of several high-level resignations from the government had persuaded Wilhelm that Tirpitz's proposal to fill all six of the existing 'two-tempo' years, 1912-17, with an additional large ship was politically impossible. The Army, while refusing to join Bethmann's campaign for putting financial obstacles in Tirpitz's path, was not prepared to support him actively. And as the final stroke January elections resulting in the Social Democrats more than doubling their votes to become the strongest single Party in the *Reichstag* had made a provocative Bill impossible. Tirpitz had been forced to drop three out of the six additional Dreadnoughts over the coming six years and settle for the three-tempo in alternate years only. Building tempo was not the only consideration, however; in response to the continuous criticism from the fleet about the Navy's unpreparedness for immediate war, Tirpitz meant to increase the proportion of ships in full commission by manning one reserve squadron, so that three instead of two battle squadrons would be ready at all times.

The significance of this was immediately apparent in the British Admiralty:

> The creation of a Third Squadron in full commission is a serious and formidable provision. At present, owing to the fact that in the six winter months the First and Second Squadrons of the High Seas Fleet are congested with recruits (because of the short-service conscript system) there is a great relief from the strain to which we are put by German naval power. The addition of the Third Squadron will make the strain continual throughout the year. The maintenance in full commission of twenty-five battleships, which after the next four or five years will all be Dreadnoughts, exposes us to constant danger only to be warded off by vigilance approximating to war conditions ...[22]

As Churchill put it in a paper for Cabinet discussion, 'The spirit may be good, but the facts are grim.' Against Tirpitz's 3,2,3,2,3,2 building programmes he proposed 5,4,5,4,5,4. 'This maintains sixty per cent superiority in Dreadnoughts over Germany alone. It will also be two keels to one on their additional three ships.'[23] He estimated that it would cost an extra £3 millions a year.

Against this sombre background the Cabinet was reluctant to abandon any attempt to probe possibilities of easing the competition and the War Minister, Haldane, was chosen as an informal emissary to Berlin. He spoke German fluently, was well-known to Wilhelm as an admirer of German literature and philosophy—which he had studied as a young man at Göttingen University—and although he knew little of naval technicalities it was felt that his enthusiasm for the spiritual aspects of *Kultur* and his previous acquaintance with Wilhelm more than made up for it. A telegram was drawn up by Grey, Churchill, Cassel and Haldane himself, suggesting that a Cabinet Minister should visit Berlin for private and unofficial talks. But it was made clear that if the German government were determined on their naval increases negotiations would be rendered 'difficult if not impossible.'

> If on the other hand German naval expenditure can be adapted by an alteration of the tempo or otherwise so as to render any serious increase unnecessary to meet the German programme, the British government will be prepared at once to pursue negotiations on the understanding that the point of naval expenditure is open to discussion and that there is a fair prospect of settling it favourably.[24]

Cassel sent the telegram to Ballin who, as before, took it directly to Bethmann, and the two of them went to see Wilhelm, who was still so enraptured by the prospect of colonial gains and an entente with Great Britain which would leave him master on the Continent of Europe that his reaction to the obvious British designs against his construction programme was uncharacteristic; he told the chief of his Naval Cabinet to enquire, secretly whether the *Novelle* might be further modified. Von Müller was now sceptical about the British approach, thinking Wilhelm had read far too much into the original note, whereupon he was told that they *had* to negotiate or it would be war in the spring—moreover war on three fronts. Müller thought this unlikely; if the British had wanted war they could have had it the previous summer. No mere reasoning could damp Wilhelm's enthusiasm. Müller noted in his diary that the Kaiser saw himself 'already as the leader of the United States of Europe and of a German colonial Empire right across Central Africa.'[25]

Tirpitz prepared himself to resist yet another political attack on his Fleet Law—and probably the most subtle yet. He reminded himself of the words of one American observer: if the leading English and German statesmen were brought together at opposite ends of a conference table he would be surprised if, at the end of the negotiations, Germany still retained even Potsdam. He need not have worried. Haldane's negotiations never had a chance. As Ballin wrote to Cassel, Germany's acceptance of naval limitation depended upon a 'strongly enunciated neutrality agreement', not vague expressions like 'reciprocal assurances'. For Bethmann was quite as determined as Wilhelm or Tirpitz that if Germany voluntarily limited her Navy it could only be on the condition that Great Britain agreed not to intervene in any Continental war in which Germany became involved. As this would have rendered worthless the French and Russian *ententes* with which Britain had sought to protect herself against Germany's growing ambition and strength and, in the opinion of practically all men of real influence in the country would have led to German domination of the Continent of Europe, it was a condition that no British government could have accepted.

Haldane set out on his mission without illusions. It was a great challenge, and if it succeeded, it was the greatest service he could render his country and, he believed, European civilisation, but he was 'far from sanguine of success'.[26] As he left London newspapers carried reports of the opening of the new session of the *Reichstag* and Wilhelm's speech from the Throne, 'It is my constant duty and care to maintain and strengthen on land and water the power of defence of the German people which has no lack of young men fit to bear arms. Bills which pursue this purpose are to be presented to you with proposals to cover the increased expenditure.'[27]

Although Haldane was visiting Berlin with his brother, a Reader in Physiology at Oxford University, ostensibly to study German educational methods, his real purpose was very apparent to the German Press. The frenziedly chauvinist *Post* bristled; if he came to try and divert the German government from its planned increases this was unthinkable. It was the dangerous policy of England, 'a policy of the utmost menace to peace, which has occasioned the necessity of such preventive measures of defence.'[28]

He met Bethmann for lunch at the British Embassy on his first day, and told him frankly of the dangers ahead. Of course the German people had the unfettered right to increase their armaments as much as they wished. But it was inevitable that as they did so other nations would draw together for mutual defence—and this was what was happening. He assured the Chancellor that Great Britain had no aggressive designs and no secret military treaties—

which appeared to relieve him—but warned him that if France were attacked he could not count on British neutrality. For one thing, Britain's naval position would be seriously affected if the northern French coast and ports were in German hands. For his part Bethmann gave an equal impression of frankness; he understood the British position. *But* he had his Generals and Admirals to contend with, and they were 'pretty difficult'. Haldane was left with the impression that he was an 'honest man struggling somewhat against adversity.'[29] In a sense he was right. But Bethmann's sincere desire for peace with Great Britain went far beyond a détente or entente which would put obstacles in the way of the expansion his 'difficult' military departments demanded; his determination for a rock-bottom guarantee of British neutrality whatever might happen on the Continent of Europe was the political counterpart of the 'Militarists' strategy.

The following day Haldane had what he expected to be the crucial interview with Wilhelm and Tirpitz at the Schloss. The German need for a political agreement before they could consider retarding their construction programme was made plain. In reply he pointed out that any agreement made while the *Novelle* still stood would be bones without flesh, for the British government would have to reply to its increases with increases of their own which were bound to strain relations. The only way towards a better understanding was by a fundamental modification of the German naval programme. Tirpitz said that Britain's insistence on the 'Two-Power standard' was a hard one for Germany, and he could not make any admission on it, to which Haldane replied that it was not a question of admission. Germany was free to do as she pleased; so was Great Britain. But as his government would lay down two keels to every extra ship Germany built, the initiative to ease the competition lay with Germany. Tirpitz, naturally, refused to admit that Germany could start the process of limitation while she was so inferior on the sea and unable to protect her interests. Eventually a compromise was agreed. Haldane was to assume that the *Novelle* would be carried through, but once a political agreement were signed Wilhelm would show his good intentions by announcing a slowing down in the rate of building the extra ships. Wilhelm was jubilant. Haldane, whose chief impression was of Tirpitz's stubbornness, was not encouraged.

The next day he had a final meeting with Bethmann which was

equally discouraging. The 'political' agreement the German government looked for was one which bound both parties not to join any
combination directed against the other, and:

> 3. If one of the high contracting parties comes to find itself
> involved in a war against one or more powers, the other of the
> High contracting party shall observe at least a benevolent neutrality
> towards that Power, and shall use all its efforts for localisation of
> the conflict.[30]

He told the Chancellor that this would stand no chance of acceptance by the British government, and together they re-drafted it,
arriving at a formula providing that neither Power would make an
unprovoked attack on the other or join in any combination against
the other for the purposes of aggression. This stood no chance of
acceptance by the German government, although Bethmann again
gave Haldane the impression that he would do all in his power
against the military.

As Haldane left Berlin the papers were filled with a speech by
Churchill, which was compared with Lloyd George's notorious
effort at the Mansion House; it was interpreted as being similarly
inspired by the British Cabinet. In fact Churchill had not consulted
anyone: determined to back up Haldane's mission with a strong
public affirmation of British naval policy, he had read a report of
Wilhelm's *Reichstag* speech announcing armament increases, and
the phrase about the German people *'which has no lack of young
men fit to bear arms'* had stood out vividly and given direction to
his thoughts.

'There is no doubt whatever that the nations of Europe are at the
present time pressing forward and pressing each other forward into
an avenue of almost indefinite naval expansion and expense. We
may have our own opinion as to how far future generations will
compliment the present age upon the wisdom, the Christianity, and
the Civilisation which have made that sterile and dangerous competition so large a feature of our lives. But there it is and we shall
have to meet it, and I am glad to tell you that there is no need
whatever for alarm, there is no need for the raising of any excited
panic and there is no need for despairing the resources of our
country ... We were never in a better position and the country was
never more united in its resolve to see the supremacy of the British
Navy maintained.' Cheers![31]

Great Britain, he went on, had sufficient money, and the resources of additional taxation should it become necessary: she had the warships, and she had the building capacity to build 'as fast and faster, cheaper and on a far larger scale than any other Power in the world.' Cheers! 'So if the money is all right, the shipbuilding plant is all right. But what of the men?' And he went on to detail the Navy's strength in long-service personnel trained from boys and the great reserve of seamen behind them in the country as a whole.

'Whatever may happen abroad there will be no whining here, no signals of distress will be hoisted, no cries for help or succour will go up. We will face the future as our ancestors would have faced it, without disquiet, without arrogance, but in stolid and inflexible determination. We should be the first to welcome any retardation or slackening in naval rivalry. We should meet any such slackening not by words but by deeds. But if there is to be an increase, if there are to be increases on the Continent of Europe we shall have no difficulty in meeting them to the satisfaction of the country.' Cheers!

Some German papers likened his words to the British Music Hall ditty of the previous century, 'We've got the ships, we've got the men, we've got the money too.' But it was another part of the speech that was seized upon most avidly. Churchill had compared the purposes of British and German naval power: 'The British Navy is to us a necessity and, from some points of view the German Navy is to them more in the nature of a luxury. Our naval power involves British existence; it is existence to us, it is expansion to them ...' The use of the word 'luxury' provided a convenient focus for resentment at the frank and in many eyes 'threatening' nature of the speech and it was quickly divorced from its context and interpreted as another goad and insult to the German people. The *Times* Vienna correspondent reported:

> It is doubtless difficult for British Ministers to remember that in seeking tersely to convey an idea to an audience they may be providing German writers and politicians with material for one of those legends which in modern Germany do duty for facts. Half the difficulty in improving Anglo-German relations lies in the tenacious faith of the German people in the perverted notions with which it is sedulously plied.[32]

So '*Luxus-Flotte*' joined '*Einkreisung*' (encirclement) and the French desire for '*Revanche*' (after 1870), and 'Lord Fisher of Copenhagen' in German Press shorthand on world affairs. Only the Social Democrats and their allies who already opposed Tirpitz interpreted the speech in the sense intended: 'The English government,' *Vorwärts* commented, 'wishes there to be no doubt left that it will still further overtrump the German increases. Disarmament or continuation of the senseless competition in armaments on a larger and stronger scale, that is the alternative with which the German government is faced.'[33]

But for the Pan-German, Colonialist, navalist and industrialist Press the speech and the motive for Haldane's visit were turned to use to whip up support for the proposed Bills to increase armaments by land and sea. It was not only British *Einkreisungspolitik* on the Continent of Europe that the German people had to fear, the island Empire's malevolence was apparent over the world; the Japanese Press was hostile, the United States was seeking an alliance with her against Germany! The Navy League Journal, *Die Flotte*, warned that 'only a determined combination of all our powers can prevent the possibility of having to maintain ourselves alone against a world of enemies and the jealous.'[34]

Fisher, still keeping out of the way on the Continent, wrote to Churchill of the extraordinary extent to which public opinion in Germany was being roused and congratulated him on his speech which, he thought, had counteracted the '*most damnable effect*' of Haldane's visit. While the backstairs approach by Haldane had left the impression that Great Britain was afraid, 'your Glasgow speech was as straight as a die. It said *We'll fight to the finish and mean to win—make no d—d mistake, dear friends.*'[35]

> Don't imagine I'm warlike ... I do earnestly pray that the government will not allow the Navy trumpet to give an uncertain sound, and the German then will not prepare himself for the battle ...

Churchill needed no encouragement. His next major speech which introduced the Naval Estimates to the House of Commons, was straighter and blunter. He dropped all pretence of building to the 'Two-Power' standard and revealed that the British programme was aimed at Germany alone, and was intended to provide a sixty per cent superiority in Dreadnoughts and a larger superiority in smaller craft. And for every ship that Germany added to her present Navy

Law, Great Britain would lay down two. She intended to be able to meet at her 'average moment' the full naval strength of an enemy at his 'selected moment'. Nothing so direct had been heard in a public statement in the lifetime of those present.

> Let me make clear, however, that any retardation or reduction in German construction will, within certain limits, be promptly followed here ... by large and fully-proportioned reductions. Take as an instance of this proposition which I am putting forward for general consideration, the year 1913. In that year Germany will build three capital ships (under the *Novelle*) and it will be necessary for us to build five in consequence. Supposing we were both to take a holiday for that year ... The three ships that she (Germany) did not build would therefore automatically wipe out no less than five British potential super-Dreadnoughts, and that is more than I expect them to hope to do in a brilliant naval action.[36]

The speech received a rapturous ovation. The *Times* called it 'perhaps the best exposition of naval policy which has been made since Lord George Hamilton's famous statement (inaugurating the "Two-Power" standard) in 1889.' Viscount Esher wrote, 'My dear Winston. In my time—extending now over thirty years of public life—no speeches have been made as yours—so straight and so daringly truthful.'[37] Even the Opposition spokesman on naval affairs welcomed it as the first speech by a First Lord to which he had listened with pleasure since the Liberals came to office.[38] Only the few Labour and pacifist Liberals objected, repeating their old arguments that reductions in armaments expenditure, not increases, were the way to friendly relations with Germany; once friendly relations had been established disarmament would follow of itself.

They were not living in the same world as Churchill and Grey. The negotiations begun by Haldane were being continued between London and Berlin with ever-increasing misunderstanding. For the British government the actual text of Tirpitz's *Novelle* had been the first shock. Haldane had been given a copy by Wilhelm and had brought it back for Admiralty scrutiny. The increases proposed in the active battle fleet strength together with an eventual doubling of the destroyer force ready for instant action and large sums provided for U-boats were more than Churchill had expected from Bethmann's précis, and appeared more menacing even than the three extra capital ships. It was plain that no political agreement could be concluded under this threat which would have to be met by British increases and probably by the withdrawal of British Mediterranean battleships to the North Sea. Grey had put these points to the German government in a series of notes towards the end of February. They came as a great shock for Wilhelm. He had set such hopes on his African Empire and the understanding with Haldane about construction tempo that the sudden introduction of personnel increases and the proportion of his fleet in full commission struck him as a deliberate attempt by Grey to repudiate Haldane— and himself—and yet another ploy to prevent him from doing as he wished with his own fleet. 'In the name of the German people as Emperor, and in the name of my armed might as supreme commander I must reject out of hand such a monstrosity as being incompatible with honour'.[39] And when he heard of Churchill's intention to call home the Mediterranean Fleet his first reaction was to instruct the British government that he would regard such a move as a *casus belli* to be answered by more additions to the *Novelle* and mobilisation! Second thoughts prevented this note being sent, but he relieved his feelings on Bethmann, who was still fighting against the *Novelle*, writing him a letter filled with such astonishing crudities that von Müller assumed he wanted the Chancellor's resignation. It duly came, with an expression of Bethmann's despair at the course of German policy.

> If we are forced into war, then we shall wage it and with God's help not perish. But to cause a war ourselves without our honour or vital interests being threatened, that I would regard as a sin against Germany's destiny even if we could expect complete victory. But that, too, is not the case, at least at sea.[40]

Tirpitz, meanwhile had been arguing that the sooner the *Novelle* was published, the less chance there would be for England to make even greater demands, and he threatened to resign if Wilhelm believed what he represented as Bethmann's claim that one extra ship every other year would bring on the danger of war. Wilhelm jibbed at taking either resignation seriously, and arranged a temporary truce: Tirpitz was to omit one of the extra Dreadnoughts from the six-year schedule and hold it for some indeterminate date after 1917; Bethmann was to continue his efforts for a neutrality agreement.

These were doomed to failure. The furthest Grey was prepared to go was 'England will make no unprovoked attack upon Germany and pursue no aggressive policy towards her.' When Metternich tried to add a phrase that would bind each party to 'benevolent neutrality' should the other 'become entangled in a war with one or more Powers in which it cannot be said to be the aggressor' Grey told him that the word 'neutrality' would inevitably offend the susceptibilities of Britain's other partners in the *entente*. Metternich already knew this; he had been representing the position in numerous long despatches to his government since the beginning of the year, together with his conviction that the *Novelle* was at the root of the trouble and should be abandoned.

> The world in general will draw the conclusion from another naval Bill—as consequence and answer to last year (the *Panthersprung*)—that we are arming for war; and will revive the unjustified reproach which represents us as disturbers of the peace. However that may be England will make ready for the war of decision to which we appear to be driving her, and which today and she still does not desire. In such a case she could not, in spite of her need for peace, let any favourable opportunity for the war of decision go by, without hurting her vital interest. The favourable opportunities, however, are to be found in the next few years before our fleet is built and before the first ship that the new naval Bill can bring us is on the water ...[41]

Many other long reports similarly opposing Tirpitz's policy caused Metternich's recall a few months later. As one Progressive newspaper put it, Wilhelm was tired of hitting the barometer to make it rise; he had replaced it instead.

Bethmann heard of Grey's rejection of his neutrality agreement and the reasons, which included both the *Novelle* and the need to preserve Britain's existing *ententes* on March 18, the day that Churchill made his Estimates speech. The tone of that speech confirmed the rebuff. For all practical purposes negotiations were at an end, although the Foreign Minister, Kiderlen—whom Wilhelm had left out of the original negotiations with Haldane—persuaded him not to stop talking altogether. Wilhelm was relieved at the British attitude. Now they knew where they stood. After his wild hopes and alternating rage at Grey's perfidy, after the in-fighting between his government and Service chiefs, the threatened resignations, the Socialist landslide in the elections, the compromises and the constant pressures from all sides, at last the choices had been narrowed and the decision made—by the British. Now even Bethmann must see that the *Novelle* had to go through. It was unthinkable to allow Grey and Churchill to dictate how many ships in full commission Germany should be allowed. As Tirpitz had maintained all along, the only way to achieve respect from England was to build more. Bethmann, at last, agreed. Long afterwards he excused himself for not carrying out his original intention to resign by saying that had he done so Tirpitz would have taken his place as Chancellor—which would have meant war.

The *Novelle* was sent to the *Reichstag* in April with the Bill for increasing the Army; Bethmann gave both his blessing in noticeably low key: the present European situation gave no cause for unease; he was convinced there was no government which either desired or was seeking to bring about a war with Germany. But strong armaments were needed not only for warding off possible attack, but for guarding their position in peace—for prestige and welfare in time of peace and as a measure of their value as friends and allies. Tirpitz followed him and in his low, barely audible tones gave his usual technical dissertation. The *Novelle* was required to remove two defects, the weakness caused by the dismissal of reservists each autumn and the disproportion between the total strength of the Navy and the portion ready for use at any time, and he explained how the increased complexity of modern ships made it difficult to mobilise quickly. The debate was colourless; the Centre Party had been bought off with concessions to their views on taxes and tariffs and the resignation of the Treasury Minister, Wermuth; with the Conservatives and National Liberals an impregnable 'bloc' had been formed against the Social Democrat and small Radical Party opposition. The Socialist leader made a predictable attack on 'militarism' but the result was foregone.

The bitterest attack on Tirpitz came from the leader of the Radical or Progressive party: he pointed out that for years the Secretary of the Navy had been building his Service upon the 'International Danger'. 'On the water the name of the danger is England. The Navy Office has grown into the conception "War with England is inevitable and so we must deliberately arm for it".'[42] He accused Tirpitz of systematising propaganda and organising a Navy League 'to blow wind into the sails of the Admiralty'. The League's appeal for the last ten years had been the propagation of fear of England and antagonism to England. But although it had been the naval policy of Germany that had produced the *Entente*, the hemming in of Germany and everything connected with the phrase 'Morocco troubles', Tirpitz had extracted from every setback new capital for his naval Bills. Tirpitz was dangerous; 'his policy is a defective circle without end and without breathing space.'

It was a small voice. Amidst the clamour of Germany arming reason was only heard in support of war. General Bernhardi's book, *Germany and the Next War*, found a wider audience than the Radicals. It was the ultimate, brutal statement of the biological view of politics. War, Bernhardi repeated by rote after the academic garrison, war was the essential mechanism through which human progress worked itself out; it was the first law of nations as 'the struggle for existence' was the first law of nature. After Hegel and Treitschke, he repeated that the first duty of the State was to itself, the first duty of the German State was to increase its territory and its power to spread its superior *Kultur*. This was a moral duty. War was a moral duty, but it was no use conducting an unsuccessful war; victory was a duty. Victory meant choosing 'the most favourable moment' to begin. This was, of course, the first tenet of the German armed Services, and the reason for the Navy's astonishment that it had not been 'Copenhagened' long since. Bernhardi, after Treitschke, saw the British Empire as the chief obstacle to Germany's break-through to world power, thus, after Tirpitz, the defeat of the British Navy as the most decisive task for Imperial Germany. His was only one amongst a flood of books, pamphlets, broadsheets and articles carrying the message that an 'inevitable' war of decision lay close ahead. Whether this was because, as in the General's exposition, it was a moral necessity for Germany to attack and expand, or as in so many others because England/France/Russia were gathering strength to fall upon her from all sides at once—with American and Japanese help—must have mystified anyone who retained independent judgement.[43]

Mystification would have been greater had they been admitted to the secret conclaves of the *Reichsmarineamt* and *Admiralstab*. How was the war of decision against England to be fought? In Tirpitz's view, unchanged since the turn of the century, the German fleet was to 'strive for the chance to fight a battle not far from Heligoland'.[44] This area would be fortified with shore batteries, minefields and nests of torpedo boats and, for the future, submarines; it was the ideal spot for the High Seas Fleet to fight the decisive battle. Why, in that case, should the British come? Was it necessary? It was a psychological necessity; their traditional offensive doctrine and the pressure from the British government and people to fight a battle as soon as possible would bring them off the German coast. But in case all the preparations made for their reception proved inadequate and their power was overwhelming, Tirpitz went on, 'we have in that area the fully guaranteed retreat ... into the mouths of our rivers.'

His old colleague, von Heeringen, now Chief of the *Admiralstab*, when asked about Germany's chances against England, replied, 'Not great'.[45] He based this less on the incompleteness of the Kiel Canal widening scheme and the defences of Heligoland than on 'the overwhelming superiority of the English fleet over the German.' In his view the best that the High Seas Fleet could hope for was to postpone the decision if circumstances should require it.

As ever, the hopeless position of the fleet was turned to use in the propaganda for the *Novelle*; once more *Die Flotte* sounded the tocsin.

> ... on the fifth day of mobilisation at the latest, 38 hostile battle-ships and 24 armoured cruisers can be assembled in the North Sea against the 17 battleships and 4 armoured cruisers of the High Seas Fleet. Any further word is superfluous.[46]

Yet Churchill had made it plain that further expansion in the German Navy Law would be doubled by the British, and this must widen not decrease the present gap between the fleets. Tirpitz regarded it as bluff. The British would not be able to keep it up, whereas Germany by virtue of her expanding economy, cheaper naval manpower and concentration of effort would have little difficulty in maintaining her fixed Law. Sooner or later the British would realise this; they would either come to terms or fight.

His public attitude was very different. As at the time of the acceleration scare he made much capital from the British reaction to his *Novelle*. At a reception following a large *Reichstag* dinner towards the end of April he grew vehement about her threatening attitude. 'The English cannot treat Germans as if they are Spaniards or Portuguese! If they continue threatening they will arouse the old Prussian spirit! I am a Prussian!'[47] Churchill's

'*Luxus-Flotte*' and Estimates speeches came in for repeated complaint as bluntly 'threatening'. He himself was for a good understanding with England, but Churchill's policy made that impossible —why he, Tirpitz, was held up as the bogey of England! As in the earlier scare he appeared to simmer under a sense of personal resentment.

In May the *Novelle* obtained its expected majority in the *Reichstag* and became Law; his tension eased. He was able to look back on his life's work with immense satisfaction. His record of success was unbroken. He had accomplished what had seemed almost impossible at the start, bringing the German people to full realisation of their need for sea power and ensuring them an eventual naval establishment of sixty-one capital units to be replaced after 1917 at a perpetual three-tempo which would be secure against any changes of heart within the *Reichstag*. It was Law. He saw his enormous achievement stretching into the future of the Greater Germany— of which he was the principal architect. He was the Bismarck of the world Empire. A large following encouraged his dreams and backed him for Chancellor in place of Bethmann.

The British naval attaché, trying to pierce the enigma of his policy described him in a despatch to the Admiralty: 'extremely ambitious and clever, suspicious of a more open policy towards England as likely to impair his chances of getting further Naval Estimates out of the *Reichstag*, very full of his own importance, reported to have ambitions beyond his present position, continually evolving new, larger schemes; when doing so he became something of a dreamer; he had great ideas for Germany's future. He was vain and somewhat suspicious.'[48] Although there was growing criticism of him within the Navy, the attaché continued, and he was accused of being behind the times, of having become a politician out of touch with naval affairs, of allowing the English to get ahead in designs and gunpower and of having held his post for too long, his critics usually found *themselves* replaced. Other officers spoke of him in reverential terms, comparing him with Bismarck.

The attaché had also noticed a new trend among senior naval officers close to the great man; some had ceased to be content to build up to a ratio of 2:3 with the British Navy and were openly calling for *parity*. He submitted his own analysis of German naval expansion:

1) A period when they state loudly that the German fleet is not intended to compete with the English, and England so strong that it is impossible to do so 2) Create a confused circle of arguments on relative naval strengths which makes it impossible to pin them down on any clear policy ... 3) The period now with us, thinking they have whittled down British supremacy sufficiently they show their hand somewhat and claim that England can no longer claim the superiority she has claimed in the past. Reason appears to be to encourage the German people to further increases ...[49]

A similar conclusion was reached at the British Admiralty. A Staff appreciation for the Cabinet drew attention to the remarkable expansion of the German fleet under a single minister, von Tirpitz, and suggested that the Law of 1900 and all subsequent amendments had been a single plan; further, there were already signs 'similar to those which have appeared on former occasions of increases, that even the mighty fleet which Germany will possess in 1920 (sixty-one Dreadnoughts) is no final limit to her naval aspirations'.[50] The memo pointed out that for protecting overseas possessions aiding commerce and showing the flag cruisers would have been more appropriate, while for coastal defence 'every development of mine, submarine and torpedo renders (her shores) more inviolate.'

> The whole character of the German Fleet shows that it is designed for aggressive and offensive action on the largest possible scale in the North Sea or the North Atlantic. The structure of the German battleships shows clearly that they are intended for attack in a fleet action. The disposition of guns, torpedo tubes, armour, the system of naval tactics which the Germans practise and the naval principles which they inculcate upon their officers leave no room to doubt that the idea of sudden and aggressive action against a fleet of great power is the primary cause for which they have been prepared.

The appreciation went on to point out that German torpedo boats were constructed for attack, not defence, and German submarines were all of the larger type capable of 'sudden and offensive action' at a distance from their bases; it was impossible to resist the conclusion that 'the German Fleet exists and has been created for the purpose of fighting a great battle in the North Sea ... against some other great naval Power.'

As for the German claim that she had no expectation of victory over the greatest naval Power, but was simply building a 'Risk Fleet', the Staff found this 'scarcely respectful of the sagacity of the German government ... Whatever purpose has animated the creators of the German Navy, and induced them to make so many exertions and sacrifices it is not the foolish purpose of certainly coming off second best on the day of trial.'

The memo concluded that the purpose of the fleet might be unconnected with the desire to use it. 'Still the German Empire has been built up by a series of sudden and successful wars ... Her military strength renders her alone among the nations of Europe free from fear of invasion. But there is not a State on her borders, nor a small State in Europe, but has either suffered at her hands or lies under the impression of her power. From these anxieties Great Britain and the British Empire, sheltered by the Navy of Great Britain have hitherto been free.'

The technical appreciation mirrored British beliefs. Some Liberals still believed in the defensive nature of the German Navy and attributed its expansion to British foreign policy and British naval provocation in a manner that must have delighted Tirpitz and his Publicity Bureau, but they were in a minority. Where power lay there were few illusions. The reputedly pro-German Haldane had been struck during his visit to Berlin by 'the tendency to swelled-headedness in the nation'[51] due to its extraordinarily rapid increase in economic strength; his knowledge of the General Staff convinced him that once the war party got into the saddle it would be war, not simply for the overthrow of France, but for the domination of the world. Asquith, weary of the negotiations started then, had come to realise that nothing short of a British promise of neutrality would meet Bethmann's purpose. And, ominously, Bethmann had raised his earlier demand to 'unconditional neutrality'. The talks died.

Balfour found it impossible to make sense of German policy unless they meant to make offensive war. Their system of strategic railways, many leading to small States which were no threat, the increases in naval and military power and preparation for instant readiness when they already possessed the greatest army in the world and the second largest Navy, and the 'assiduous, I had almost said the organised advocacy of a policy which it seems impossible to reconcile with the peace of the world or the rights of small nations',[52] left him in no doubt that she intended to redraw the map of Europe and the world. After studying Churchill's papers on the naval question, he wrote to him, 'A war entered upon for no other purpose than to restore the Germanic Empire of Charlemagne in a modern form, appears to me at once so wicked and stupid as to be almost incredible ...'[53] But no other interpretation seemed possible. And of reports from France that a war in May appeared inevitable, he wrote, 'imagine it being possible to talk about war as inevitable when there is no quarrel and nothing to fight over.'[54]

In July, Churchill announced his Supplementary Estimates to the House of Commons as the British answer to Tirpitz's *Novelle*. 'Taking a general view, the effect of this (new) Law will be that nearly four-fifths of the entire German Navy will be maintained in full permanent commission ... Such a proposal is remarkable and so far as I am aware, finds no example in the previous practice of modern naval powers.'[55] and pointing to the eventual strength of the German fleet as 41 battleships and 20 battlecruisers, supported by 'an ample proportion' of flotilla craft including 72 submarines, he announced that the British reply would be an increase in the rate of Dreadnought construction from 3,4,3,4,3 to 5,4,4,4,4 over the coming years.

As he had told Fisher earlier in the year:

> Nothing, in my opinion, would more surely dishearten Germany than the certain proof that as the result of all her present and prospective efforts she will only be more hopelessly behindhand in 1920. She would know it was not bluff because if a Liberal government could propose it a Tory government would *a fortiori* carry it farther ...[56]

But he warned the Commons, 'The strain we shall have to bear will be long and slow.'

As the race gathered momentum significant developments were taking place behind the public scene. The British and French naval Staffs, who had been discussing co-operation in case of war since the spring agreed on joint signal books and areas of command. Churchill, anxious that the planning should not *bind* either party to assist the other, stressed that 'no discussion between naval or military experts could be held to affect in any way the full freedom of action possessed by both countries.'[57] But as with earlier joint military planning no formulae could disguise the increasing moral commitment for Britain to support France in a Continental war. This was particularly evident in September when the French

Northern Squadron was moved from Brest to concentrate with their Mediterranean Fleet in Toulon. Combined with Churchill's movement of British battleships out of the Mediterranean to strengthen the home fleets its effect was to place the defence of the Mediterranean against Austria and Italy in the hands of France, leaving Great Britain to deal with the German fleet—at the same time protecting France's northern coasts. So ended the process of concentration started with the Japanese alliance and the withdrawal of capital units from the China Seas.

In fact the new dispositions would have been the best for both Britain and France even without the joint talks as France's Northern Squadron was no match for the High Seas Fleet and was better placed protecting her vital Mediterranean communications. And the Royal Navy could not afford defeat in the North Sea. But the significance of the movements was plain to Germany, who assumed a secret naval convention between the *Entente* Powers—further evidence of *Einkreisungspolitik*—added reason to hasten preparations for the inevitable war of decision.

During the winter war fever quickened. Fighting in the Balkans threatened to draw Austria-Hungary in against Serbia, who was supported by Russia. In that case France would be drawn in to support her ally, and Germany—as all military experts knew— would march on France. Was this the scenario for Armageddon? The British government learn from Bebel that Krupp's workers were extremely busy, working regular overtime; as foreign orders were slack Bebel drew the conclusion that Krupp was working for the government. He also reported the greatest activity and severity in drilling the new recruits for the Army: 'the young soldiers had daily four more hours of fatiguing drill than in ordinary times— of course to get them ready for the field at the earliest possible moment.'[58] Asquith and his senior Ministers grew increasingly anxious; believing that the British position should be made clear as a restraining influence, Haldane told the German Ambassador, now Prince Lichnowsky, that in the event of the conflict spreading to the Great Powers, England would find it impossible to remain neutral. She had formed links with France and Russia to preserve the European balance of power and no British government would be able to withstand pressure to come in on their side.

Lichnowsky sent a report of the interview home. When Wilhelm read it, he erupted; it closed the circuit on all his nervous tensions and frustration at Grey's perfidious policy during the Haldane talks. Was he to accept dictation from England at every step— Morocco, the Fleet question, African colonies, now Austrian prestige in the Balkans and the 'balance of power' in Europe! The principle of the balance of power was nonsense; *he* was the balance of power in Europe; if England disputed this it would make her Germany's eternal enemy. He scribbled in the margin of Lichnowsky's report, 'The final struggle between the Slavs and the Teutons will see the Anglo-Saxons on the side of the Slavs and the Gauls!'[59] And repeating the sentiment in a note to Kiderlen, told him that this must now form the basis of German policy. Military agreements must be made wherever they could be found, with Bulgaria, Rumania, Albania, Turkey, even Japan—'Every Power we can get is good enough to help us.'[60] His brother, Prince Henry, was instructed to write a letter to King George of England, warning him that the British position as outlined by Haldane would lead to an increase in German armaments unless it were rescinded. And his naval chiefs, Tirpitz, von Müller and von Heeringen were summoned together with General von Moltke, head of the Great General Staff, to an immediate meeting at the Palace. Bethmann, Kiderlen and the War Minister were not called—what could they know of war against England!

When the four had assembled Wilhelm opened with an excited account of how Haldane, speaking for the arch-hater of Germany, Sir Edward Grey, had informed his Ambassador in London that in order to preserve the balance of power, England would *unconditionally* support France in a Continental war; at least, he suggested, this was a welcome clarification of the British position! Moving on to the immediate situation in the Balkans he pointed out that Austria could not back down to the Serbs without losing control of all the Slavs within her own Empire; as Germany must support her ally any Russian move in support of Serbia would render Continental war unavoidable. The diplomats, he went on, had been instructed to find allies wherever they could; if Rumania and Bulgaria could be persuaded to come in on Austria's side, Germany would be free to fight 'with full fury' against France. Naturally the fleet must prepare itself for the war against England —he suggested submarine warfare against British troop transports to the Continent, mine warfare in the Thames, a hastening of U-boat construction.⁶¹

Von Moltke took the argument further by insisting that as the Continental war was, in his opinion, unavoidable, *now* was the best time to launch it before either France or Russia had completed their military preparations. There had never been a better time since the formation of the Triple Alliance. Tirpitz objected that the Navy was not ready. He would prefer it if the conflict could be postponed for eighteen months when both the Kiel Canal works and the U-boat base in Heligoland would be finished. Moltke retorted, 'The Navy will not be ready even then!' Meanwhile the Army's position would be growing progressively worse as French and Russian military programmes matured. 'War,' he declared, *'je eher je besser!'*⁶² His eagerness did not extend to the Bismarckian conclusion of an immediate declaration against Russia and France. Nor did Wilhelm play his own Bismarck; the weight of naval opinion was too pessimistic about their chances against England. Instead it was agreed that Bills for further increases in the Army and Navy should be prepared and that both General and Admiralty staffs work out plans for the invasion of England. Meanwhile Bethmann was to be instructed to use the Press to prepare the people for the European War, so that on the outbreak they would not question the cause for which they were fighting. Tirpitz guaranteed to do the same through his own agencies.

Naval opinion at this counsel seemed to correspond exactly with the British Admiralty expectation of war in the summer of 1914— when the Canal would be ready. Yet none of the Admirals present really wanted it, least of all Tirpitz. Their chances would be slim; the patient work of fifteen years would, in all probability, be thrown into England's lap. Small wonder that British Naval Intelligence, which had not penetrated the extent of the chaos at the summit of this most highly-organised nation, retained some puzzlement about Tirpitz's notion of a 'Risk Fleet' which could never be more than second best; the puzzlement was mirrored at the counsel: Wilhelm's priorities were for submarine and mine warfare; Moltke was openly contemptuous of the Navy's role and Tirpitz, in his concern for his battleships, had to fall back on the unreadiness of the U-boat bases; he might have added of the U-boat fleet itself after his delayed start.

* 'The sooner the better!'

In contrast to the naval doubts, the army was confident. They evidently interpreted the result of the Conference as a decision to strike out and gain the European continent directly the various conditions had been fulfilled, for a few weeks later, as the campaign mounted to alert Germans to the threat from the *east* the contingency plans for war in the east *only* were discarded. The Great General Staff left themselves with just one plan; this was for the war on two fronts, the mass of the German armies taking the initiative *west* with a decisive hammer blow through Belgium to Paris. Meanwhile a Bill providing for the largest ever army increases in peacetime was worked easily through a 'patriotic' *Reichstag*.

On the other side of the North Sea Churchill was enjoying his task hugely. He revelled in the advanced technology of his *matériel* departments and in the power and glory of his ancient office, its incomparable traditions and splendid symbols; the Admiralty yacht, *Enchantress*, was enchanting; the ensigns of the Lords of Admiralty, the glittering uniforms, pipes for the gangway, sailors statuesque with raised boathooks, white holystone decks, gleaming brasswork of the steam launches, rituals hallowed by centuries joined to the most advanced creations of the constructor's art and armourers science provided the utmost stimulation for his eager mind.

Fisher was still his chief adviser; he had caught all the old Admiral's uncomplicated tactical notions, and his mind was filled with ideas of chasing, blasting and shattering from enormous ranges. During his summer cruise in the *Enchantress*, leaning on the rail and gazing with Asquith's daughter at the sun-bathed Adriatic shore, she remarked, 'How perfect!'

'Range perfect,' he replied, 'visibility perfect. How easily we could bombard!'[63]

He shared all Fisher's delight in over-trumping Tirpitz. After the 15"-gun *Queen Elizabeths* had been designed he told a golf companion that he had knocked Germany sprawling in naval construction—as he had. He had never worked so hard, he added, nor been so happy. And to Lloyd George he said, 'Whatever life holds in store for me—even if I become Prime Minister—I think I shall never be happier.'[64]

Above all the intellectual delights, and sharpening them, was his ever-present sense of the drama in which destiny had cast him.

He saw his great fleet as the single chain binding the scattered British Empire and alone preserving it and its beneficient aims from the 'iron grip and rule of the Teuton and all that the Teutonic system meant,'[65] himself as the one chosen for the high duty of ensuring that the chain would hold when the strain came on. Certain of his inspiration and Fisher's heady advice, he fired off peremptory instructions and memoranda which, together with his natural impatience of opinion which did not coincide with his own, exasperated his Board to the point of mutiny; when told of the enormity of his offences he broke down and wept and pleaded ill-health; when the First Sea Lord's health began to break under the onslaught, he pensioned him off and promoted Prince Louis of Battenberg in his place—an able officer, but not a strong one. And in the Cabinet, his impassioned advocacy of the Navy's case for more money, not only for *matériel* to meet the German challenge, but for improvements in the pay and conditions of ordinary sailors, threatened his intimacy with Lloyd George, and the patience of other Radical members. He even upset the King, who in any case distrusted his flamboyance, by proposing to call one of his new super-Dreadnoughts *Oliver Cromwell*, turning his dialectical powers to the case for that Regicide's 'share in the strength and greatness of the Navy'!

As the time came to finalise the naval Estimates for 1913-14 the effects of Wilhelm's December War Council and the reversion of German strategic thought towards dependence on the Army to secure a great *Mitteleuropa* as springboard for world power became apparent to Continental observers. While the German Press and nationalist Leagues renewed their warnings of imminent danger with particular reference to the Slavs in the Balkans, and repeated the necessity for further military increases to meet the double onslaught being prepared in St Petersburg and Paris, Great Britain was allowed to sink more and more into the background. Kiderlen had died in December, but it was apparent that his successor, von Jagow, was continuing his policy of attempting to detach England from her Continental *Ententes*. Speaking in the *Reichstag* in February he stressed not only the 'common interests' of Germany and Great Britain, but also 'the points of interest of a sentimental kind'. Nothing could have been more calculated to alarm the British Foreign Office!

For once Tirpitz was forced to pursue the same aim as his diplomats. Although Wilhelm had pressed him to reintroduce the three heavy ships dropped from the previous year's *Novelle* and his estimating departments prepared a Bill to accomplish this, Bethmann's veto on foreign and financial grounds and the immense increases demanded by the Army convinced him that he would have to wait for a more favourable opportunity. Making a virtue of this during the Budget Committee debates on the Naval Estimates he went so far as to accept publicity the ratio of strength Churchill had proposed the previous year—although he expressed Churchill's sixty per cent superiority in terms of battle squadrons, five German to eight British. He would be content with such a ratio, and he gave the specious excuse that it would give Germany sufficient power to make an attack difficult. His reasonableness was even more alarming than Jagow's smooth speech. And the British Ambassador in Berlin wrote to Grey suggesting that his reasons for referring to Churchill's new standard—without however mentioning Churchill's specific reservations that Dreadnoughts being provided by Britain's colonies would *not* count in the British totals—might be to provoke further agitation in England among those Liberals in favour of naval economies. Tirpitz, he wrote, knew very well that public attention in Germany was concentrated on the Army and he would be unable to obtain further naval increases; 'Under these circumstances it would be perfectly natural that he should hope that Great Britain might be induced to mark time also, and abstain from taking advantage of what might appear to be the psychological moment for forging ahead.'[66] He added that he was under the impression that the German government was not anxious to have Tirpitz's statement taken as the starting point for further naval negotiations. Grey replied that he had no intention of proposing a naval agreement. 'I agree that what Tirpitz said does not amount to much, and the reason of his saying it is not the love of our beautiful eyes, but the extra fifty millions required for the German Army.'[67]

The estimate was confirmed in the next message from August Bebel:

'I was present at the secret sitting of the Budget Com. when Great Admiral von Tirpitz made his famous declaration, which came like a bomb to the general surprise of everybody. The Admiral laboured under great excitement & it was evident that he spoke absolutely *"contra coeur"* & under compulsion; at times he was quite bitter against England. We all guessed that the military party had once more prevailed & forced the hands both of the naval people & the Kaiser, in spite of the fact that the Navy is the latter's hobby. Next day it was already an open secret, that the General Staff had indeed peremptorily demanded, that no new credits should be asked for the Navy and that it was now the turn of the Army, neglected too long in favour of the former. It also became clear that the financial advisers of the Crown had stopped the further ambitious plans of Tirpitz & his party.

'We Social Democrats shall oppose the increase of the Army tooth and nail, but it will be voted by the *Reichstag* with unanimity against our votes & those of the Poles and a few Alsatians and Danes ...

'For the naval people the game is up altogether & England ought to realise this. Of course the German government now tries to cajole public opinion in England and to represent as a free resolution what is simply a bitter necessity. We cannot compete any longer with England for the naval supremacy, & if England now increases her naval armaments in any way she likes Germany cannot follow any longer. We cannot neglect our army in favour of a mad naval policy any more. We have not got the money & the govt. at last realises the fact ...'[68]

Churchill, in his own Estimates speech in March, replied to Tirpitz in his bluntest vein, as if following Bebel's implications: the colonial and Dominion ships were additional to the requirements of the sixty per cent standard; as the British pre-Dreadnought superiority lost its value over the years, it might even be necessary to increase the sixty per cent margin, or the shipbuilding programmes of other countries might render it necessary to increase the British programme above the margin. In any case he intended to lay down two keels for every extra ship Tirpitz proposed. As if this were not clear enough, he went on:

'I was present at the secret sitting of the Budget Com. when Great ever allow another naval power to approach her so nearly as to deflect or restrict her political action by purely naval pressure. Such a situation would unquestionably lead to war ... It would mean that instead of intervening, as we do now in European affairs, free and independent to do the best we can for all, we should be forced into a series of questionable entanglements and committed to action of the gravest character, not because we thought it right, but as a result of bargains necessitated by our naval weakness. Margins of naval strength which are sufficient when the time comes to compel a victory, and insufficient to maintain a peace.[69]

Then, calling Tirpitz's bluff and appeasing the Radicals in his own Party and the Cabinet at the same time, he repeated his proposal for a mutual holiday from naval building for one year; it would involve no alteration in the relative strengths of the navies, no abandonment of any Naval Law, but *would* greatly relieve the finances of each country.

To Wilhelm and Tirpitz the 'holiday' proposal was a device to break their hard-fought Navy Law, disrupt the orderly flow of work to their shipbuilding and armament industry, allow Churchill to increase his lead with the Colonial ships or by accelerating existing construction, thus thrust upon Germany the *odium* of refusal! The suggestion from Count Reventlow that Churchill take a year's holiday from speaking expressed their feelings exactly. Nevertheless the public response was in a low key; progressive papers were not unfavourable to the idea, even navalist organs and the Navy League itself, while deploring this latest outrageous attempt to 'infringe the sovereignty' of Germany, significantly did not call for increases in the battle fleet as a result. In the *Reichstag* Bethmann was not encouraging about the practicability of the proposal, but the tone of his speech was deliberately cordial, and he left the impression that his government awaited official proposals.

Although both Tirpitz's 'acceptance' of a 5 : 8 ratio and Church-ill's 'holiday' proposal had been made publicly, neither were followed up officially; Grey had no faith in Tirpitz's sincerity, Bethmann no wish to expose Anglo-German relations to the hazards of naval debate yet again.

The uneasy calm was disturbed from an unexpected quarter. In May the Canadian Senate rejected the Bill which was to provide three of the Colonial Dreadnoughts Churchill was relying on for his margin of supremacy, and in June he announced to the Commons that it would be necessary, in view of this, to accelerate three of the Dreadnoughts of the current British programme—an embarrassment so soon after his eloquent proposals for mutual reductions which Wilhelm and the German Press enjoyed to the full. Wilhelm had already given the British naval attaché his opinion of Churchill as a man who could not be trusted; he turned sixteen points to starboard too often!

But neither Wilhelm nor Tirpitz were amused by reports that

Churchill intended to use the debates on acceleration to repeat his public proposal for a shipbuilding 'holiday'. Prince Lichnowsky in London was instructed to make it plain that this would not be welcomed by the German government. And sending for the British naval attaché, Wilhelm told him that if Churchill made another reference to a naval holiday he would not answer for the state of opinion in Germany. He repeated his usual complaints about British attempts to wreck the German Navy Law, and went on 'I am no longer able to enter into a fleet agreement with Britain',[70] warning that if the efforts to cut into his Navy Law were continued, or if proposals came from England for a naval holiday he would give them a very rough answer. He urged the attaché to get these views *privately* and *quietly* represented in the right quarters at once', for he did not want a big fuss.

The attaché complied:

> I am perfectly convinced on one point, namely that if His Majesty's words as to the extreme undesirability of further reference to a naval holiday are not carried into effect, there will be further bother and a very great deal of it, probably resulting in an increased shipbuilding programme in Germany ... It is therefore best to go round the end of the wall and avoid all further reference to the idea of a naval holiday and *very, very* baldly state that a vote is necessary to accelerate the building of British battleships to replace temporarily the Canadian ships.[71]

He went on to warn Churchill that the German naval dialecticians 'of whom you know the chief' were just waiting to take up his words and make capital from them. The only way to silence the naval party was to avoid *all* comment.

Churchill thought it wrong for Wilhelm and the German government to stress privately that they would resent further proposals while maintaining in public that they had *received* no firm proposals from the British government. Grey agreed, but the number of confidential reports on the strength of Wilhelm's feelings and the probable repercussions from German navalists persuaded Asquith that Churchill should say nothing.

With Tirpitz and the German Navy League also quiet and the 'inspired' German Press following Bethmann's and Jagow's direction to concentrate hostility on the Slavs while avoiding it with the Anglo-Saxons, the tension between the two countries eased to an extent which would have seemed impossible only a year previously, and the naval dispute was allowed to fade into smaller print than at any time since the law of 1900. It began to seem as if Bethmann had achieved the détente in Anglo-German relations which had eluded Bülow.

When, in October the British naval attaché ending his tour of duty, called on Wilhelm to make his farewells, he was treated to a display of Royal charm and given a repetition of all the proofs of Royal friendship for England which had been detailed in the notorious *Daily Telegraph* interview. 'I wish you English could remember that I am bound to England by family and personal sympathetic ties, and that I would introduce sentiment into my international politics with England. It is forgotten in England how I broke all sorts of State and National obligations to go to England on the occasion that my dear Grandmother died in my arms.'[72]

Afterwards Wilhelm passed on to the naval question, repeating what he had said to the attaché during the summer: his naval increases were in answer to the programmes of his uncomfortable neighbours, France and Russia. It was absurd of people in England to complain of the Navy Law; it went on automatically. And warming to his subject, 'It is the result of England always threatening Germany. My people have got tired of it. Your great mistake was when you withdrew your ships from foreign stations and brought them into the North Sea because then Germany realised it was a threat to her. But it was also a mistake strategically because it was an upsetting of carefully balanced strategical conditions. In 1904, when Fisher withdrew the squadrons from abroad my Chief of Staff remarked to me on the strategic unsoundness of the movement and said at once, "This means war, perhaps in four or five years time!" War did not come, but what has resulted? Ten years of mutual recriminations and an increased German fleet and German resolve to have a fleet.'

He reminded the attaché in detail grown richer with the passing years of how the English Foreign Office representative with King Edward had once told him that he, Wilhelm, must stop building ships, and his crushing retort, and how afterwards one of his Generals, hearing of the Englishman's impertinence, had asked whether he had left the room by the door! Finally, he seemed to remember his original tone and concluded the interview by repeating that what England and Germany both needed now was a period of quiet development of their relations. The attaché left with a signed photograph, 'something for your writing table, so that you can show your friends what that dangerous person to England looks like!'

The increasingly friendly relations between England and Germany and reduced tension over the naval question encouraged all Radical and pacifist elements in Great Britain to renew their campaign against armaments, particularly naval armaments. They were joined by Chambers of Commerce, particularly in the North of England, other businessmen's organisations and influential sections of the Liberal and financial Press. Rallies and marches on Downing Street were organised, and scapegoats prepared to focus indignation; chief among these were the 'Armaments Barons' or 'MERCHANTS OF DEATH' with their powerful lobbies in parliament, and Winston Churchill, whose 'foolish and incomprehensible' notion of building two ships for every additional German had provoked and encouraged German navalists. For Churchill the situation was serious. His policy rested on a steady building programme which would crush Tirpitz's spirit and persuade the more rational elements in Germany that they could never hope to whittle away British sea supremacy. This was even more necessary in view of the cancellation of the expected Canadian Dreadnoughts, together with recent Italian and Austrian Dreadnought programmes. Any slackening in Britain's resolve was bound to be interpreted within Germany as a sign of weakness, and would encourage Tirpitz to greater efforts. Besides, he had learnt from what proved to be the last of Bebel's letters that the Navy Office had prepared a *Novelle* to be launched at 'a favourable moment.'

Knowing that the struggle for next year's Estimates—which would have to rise—would be hard and bitter, he decided, with Grey's backing, to repeat his 'holiday' proposals, and did so in a speech in Manchester on October 18—this time 'in the name of His Majesty's government'. His suggestion was that in the coming year, 1914, 'apart from the Canadian ships or their equivalent, apart from anything that might be required by new developments in the Mediterranean', Great Britain should put off building her scheduled four ships and Germany her scheduled two ships for a space of twelve months. 'That would mean that there would be a complete holiday for one year so far as big ships were concerned ... There would be a saving spread over six years of nearly six millions to

Germany and of nearly twelve millions to this country, and the relative strength of the two countries would be absolutely unchanged.'[73]

There were many practical objections to the proposal, which left either country free to spend the money saved on Dreadnoughts on submarines or any other warlike purposes—and even in England it was recognised that Germany was not likely to agree to a distinction between British Dreadnoughts built against Germany and colonial or other Dreadnoughts built for use against her Mediterranean allies! The German Press condemned the speech on all these obvious and usual grounds, but above all for its timing—just as better relations were ripening. And both the British Ambassador in Berlin and the German Ambassador in London made it clear to Grey that the German government would not welcome any further discussion of the matter. While hinting in public that Churchill's proposal was not designed to be taken seriously as it was aimed at the Radicals in his own Party and, in the event of discussions, at placing the *odium* of refusal on Germany, the German government's real reasoning was much more fundamental. Why should they allow England a breathing space just as the naval policy was beginning to bite? She was feeling the strain; that was clear from Churchill's successive approaches and the considerable agitation in England, especially among businessmen. It was no time to ease the pressure.

Wilhelm took the view to extremes, exulting that Churchill's successive approaches were 'a more brilliant justification of the German Navy Law'[74] than either he or his advisers could have dreamed of or expected. The over-reaction was a symptom of the more than usually nervous state to which he had been reduced by the bitter tug of war between his Service departments, and between them and the Civil departments of State. Totally unable to weld their opposed views into a consistent policy or to assert his supreme authority in any one direction for any length of time, agreeing one moment that England should be bought off with a neutrality agreement, the next moment demanding more battleships which would make any agreement impossible, depressed at the acknowledged failure of his naval policy, yet refusing to admit it, he alternated more wildly than ever between deep depression and misplaced elation. His response to the intractable domestic problems caused by the Junkers' refusal to bend before any of the strong

democratic winds blowing through the *Reich* was to rage at Bethmann and inform him that unless he were tougher he would send
one of his generals into the *Reichstag* and abolish it.[75] Yet it was
evident he lacked the will for this logical solution to the *impasse*.
Bebel heard from people in his immediate entourage that they
doubted his sanity at times.

> ... he talks incessantly from morning till night & nobody can get
> in a word; when he is alone, he talks to himself. When he became
> Kaiser I said in a speech, that he would destroy what his ancestors
> have built up & I am still of this opinion. Nobody outside Germany
> can realise the great apprehensions we are all under in this respect.[76]

Now Wilhelm convinced himself that Churchill's 'holiday' proposals were a sign that England was coming as a suppliant—'a
grandiose triumph for Admiral Tirpitz before the whole world!'[77]
—and he again called on Tirpitz to reinstate the three heavy ships
dropped from the 1912 *Novelle*. Bethmann thought an increase
would be madness, and Tirpitz, persuaded of the political and
immense financial difficulties now that the Army had the bit in its
teeth, concluded that the matter would have to wait. But he did
not give up hope.

The 'holiday' issue lay dormant until the following February;
then another of Grey's speeches deploring the waste of the armaments competition provoked Tirpitz into mentioning it briefly
during a Budget Commission debate on his Estimates. His tone was
friendly and, as always thoroughly reasonable. He thought public
opinion in England and Germany thoroughly different from what
it had been a few years ago; the two governments had mutual
confidence in one another; there was an increased feeling that they
could co-operate and work side by side on many points. As for the
naval question, he had nothing to add to his acceptance last year
of the ratio of 16 : 10 offered by England, although the idea of a
'holiday' year—which had only been mentioned in an election
speech—could not be realised. Unwisely, he elaborated on this by
saying that positive proposals had not yet reached Germany; when
they did they would be examined with goodwill. Jagow, who
followed him, left the same impression that the German government
was still waiting for official proposals.[78]

All this drew a quick note from Grey asking what was meant by
suggesting in public that Germany was awaiting proposals while

intimating in private that such proposals would 'be unwelcome and impair good relations.'[79] Jagow, instructed by Wilhelm not to reopen the 'endless dangerous chapter of armaments limitation'[80] side-stepped by suggesting that if the British government wished to begin negotiations on the basis of eight British to five German battle squadrons, the proposal would be examined carefully. He and Tirpitz knew that this approach would place the *odium* of refusal on Churchill! Grey refused to take the offer up; he distrusted Jagow; besides there were alarming indications from within Germany that the British approaches and the growing number of government speeches on the 'Burden of armaments' and Radical speeches on 'Merchants of death' were being taken as signs of weakness, and that the very obvious improvement in Anglo-German relations was being represented to the German people as a brilliant success for the naval policy: Tirpitz's ships were *forcing* a better tone from England.

Churchill, meanwhile, had joined battle with the Treasury and almost the entire Liberal Cabinet on the size of his 1914-15 Estimates; the fight was proving—as he had anticipated—stiffer even than McKenna's struggle for the 'eight' of the acceleration year for there was no immediately recognisable danger or provocation—indeed Bethmann, Jagow and Tirpitz could scarcely have been making sweeter sounds.

His Estimates, which he had worked up in elaborate detail to justify every sum, amounted to almost £51 millions, £3 millions up on the 1913 Estimates which had been £8 millions up on McKenna's in 1912. He outlined the chief reasons as the increased number of ships which had to be maintained in full commission because of the last German *Novelle*, the increases in pay and in numbers of personnel, increases in the size, speed, therefore cost of warships of all classes, the development of new services, particularly the air service, wireless telegraphy and oil fuel reserves (for the new super-Dreadnoughts and destroyers), and the general increase in prices and wages in the country. And he dwelt on the remarkable way that Admiralty finance was governed by previous decisions; thus his predecessor, McKenna, had ordered sixteen super-Dreadnoughts with a total of 152 13.5" guns, but not one of these had joined the fleet before he took over, and now all had to be maintained.[81]

His arguments made no impression. The 'monstrous size' of the expenditure contemplated and the implied abandonment of the basic Liberal principals of retrenchment and reform at a time when the international scene had never looked more rosy roused the more Radical elements in the Cabinet to fury. A number of them, led by Sir John Simon, united in an attempt to drive him from the government,[82] and worked on Lloyd George and McKenna to provide them with the technical and financial ammunition. Neither of these two wished to join in the campaign to 'down Winston', although both opposed the size of the Estimates; Lloyd George in particular, thought that Churchill could be persuaded to give up something for the sake of Cabinet and Party unity. It soon became apparent that he had nothing to give. And as the Radical Press and Liberal members of Parliament built up a great agitation for *cuts* in naval expenditure with personal attacks on Churchill for a speech he had made at the Guildhall giving notice of *larger* Estimates, it began to look as if he would be forced to resign.

By mid-December his position in the Cabinet had become critical. Lloyd George, asked by a colleague if he thought his friend would be forced out, replied, 'Not now, but I think he will later on. If he is wise he will try and fall in with the views of the Cabinet, and if I were you I should advise him to do so. His Guildhall speech was a piece of madness. The public will not stand provocative speeches of that sort. They are quite unnecessary. Winston has been a loyal friend to me, but there comes a time when one cannot allow oneself to be influenced by considerations of that sort.'[83]

McKenna, too, thought that Churchill would be forced to resign, but felt that he would be wiser to go on the Irish question—also erupting under the Liberal conscience.

Asquith, preserving an air of impartiality as he chaired bitter Cabinet arguments postponed what seemed an inevitable showdown by refusing to allow the debate ever to come to a conclusion; whenever it seemed as if total disagreement had been reached and a vote must result in Churchill's defeat, he switched the discussion to another matter or adjourned the meeting. He knew Churchill's case was impregnable. He could not drop two Dreadnoughts as the Radicals urged because he had given Germany notice of his building programmes to match the *Novelle*; the Cabinet was equally committed as it had approved the statements before they were made. To go back on this firmly expressed intention would not only encourage the German naval party, but would make any future expressions of naval resolve by a Liberal government meaningless.

In any case dropping the first year's instalments on two Dread-noughts would not affect the Estimates significantly; for a sizeable reduction work on existing ships would have to be stopped or money taken from the submarine or air arms, both of whose counterparts in the German Service had received substantial boosts from Tirpitz's latest *Novelle*.

During the Christmas recess—on Christmas Day!—Churchill wrote to Grey:

> I see my duty quite plainly and am willing to pay any forfeit that the fates may exact while on that path. But I hope in these weeks you will turn over in your mind the effect which the abandonment of programmes, definitely matched against the series in the German Navy Law, would have upon the position of England in Europe. My statements on the subject were not made without consultation and agreement; and such as they were they were spoken in the name of Britain ... and now it is suggested—seriously—that we should do for nothing what only last October we said we would not do except they did the same. The country will be made ridiculous before the whole world. I can clear my reputation by immediate resignation. But what happens to an individual Minister is of very small importance compared to the public interest.[84]

He also prepared a memorandum to put the wider issues before the Cabinet, illuminating them with his own brilliant imagery.

> We are not a young people with an innocent record and a scanty inheritance. We have engrossed to ourselves, in time when other powerful nations were paralysed by barbarism or internal war, an altogether disproportionate share of the wealth and traffic of the world. We have got all we want in territory, and our claim to be left in unmolested enjoyment of vast and splendid possessions, mainly acquired by violence, largely maintained by force, often seems less reasonable to others than to us.[85]

He made no concessions to his many opponents who accused him of having lost touch with Liberalism; against their mixture of lofty idealism and domestic anxiety he presented a thesis of Treitschkian starkness: British diplomacy depended for its effectiveness on the Navy, 'the one great balancing force' Britain could contribute to her own safety and the peace of the world; she was deeply involved in the European situation with responsibilities in many quarters, and had intervened regularly in the affairs of the Continent. It was only two years ago that the Chancellor of the Exchequer had gone to the Mansion House to deliver a speech which, in saving Europe from war, had brought Great Britain to the verge of it.

> The impression which those events produced on my mind is ineffaceable. I saw that even a Liberal government, whose first and most profound resolve must always be to preserve peace, might be compelled to face the gravest and most hateful possibilities.[86]

Before the Cabinet had time to tackle Churchill on this higher ground, Lloyd George had fanned contention by coming out publicly on the Radical side in an interview for the *Daily Chronicle* during which he made a pointed reference to Winston's father, Lord Randolph, who had resigned his post and wrecked his career on the issue of 'bloated armaments'. The effects were not as he might have expected. For a senior Minister to make public capital against a colleague while the matter was still under discussion behind the closed doors of the Cabinet room offended many in the government who sympathised with his case; Grey in particular was furious, refused Asquith's efforts at reconciliation, and moved towards Churchill. While outside the government Conservatives and navalist Liberals increased their campaign of support for the First Lord.

The controversy raged through January without a sign of compromise from either side. Both Churchill and Lloyd George, who had taken over naturally as spokesman for the economists, felt committed to the positions they had taken up; Asquith—committed to Churchill's public declarations of the previous year—tried to have the affair settled between the two of them outside the Cabinet, but Churchill refused to move and Lloyd George for all his skill in negotiation, could find no formula. Gradually the force of Churchill's detailed arguments against each specific economy that was suggested, together with the realisation that he would command great support in the country if he resigned on the issue of naval supremacy began to undermine the economists' more general charges of 'unprecedented' Estimates and 'unexampled increases at a time of international calm'. By the middle of January the relative strengths within the Cabinet had altered so remarkably that it was Lloyd George's turn to talk of resignation.

'The P.M. must choose between Winston and me. Our meeting (Lloyd George and Churchill) yesterday was quite friendly. We came to no agreement. None seems possible. What the issue will be I don't know. It looks as if Winston or I will have to go.'[87]

Churchill was equally tense. The following day he told a friend, 'I don't know how much longer I shall be here. The position is acute. I cannot make further economies. I cannot go back on my public declarations. David will find the Cabinet with me. The P.M. is committed to the expenditure up to the hilt. I can make no further concessions.'[88]

When told of his remarks Lloyd George said, 'I can see things are going to be very awkward. Probably I shall have to go.'

Asquith made it plain that he would dissolve the government if Lloyd George resigned, and continued his efforts to get the two together outside the Cabinet. The issue between them had by now been fined down to the number of ships kept in full commission. McKenna, the technical brains behind the economists in the Cabinet, considered it unnecessary to keep as many as twenty-nine capital ships ready to meet twenty-two German. Churchill was adamant that any less would reduce the strength at their 'average moment' dangerously close to Germany's at her 'selected moment'. Perhaps on account of Bebel's warnings his assumptions about German strategy were as wildly out as Tirpitz's about British strategy. The High Seas Fleet, which appeared to *Admiralstab* officers hopelessly inadequate for an offensive against Great Britain was, for him, the image of danger. He refused to move. 'David is accustomed to dealing with people who can be bluffed or frightened. He says that some of his Cabinet colleagues will resign. Let them resign!'[89]

By the end of January the position was still deadlocked with Lloyd George and McKenna maintaining that 'Winston will have to give way', Churchill maintaining that the Radical wing had no stomach for a real fight and would not resign if Lloyd George would only back him. Cabinets on three successive days at the end of the month seemed to confirm his optimism. 'I have made a smashing case! General statements as to extravagance are worth nothing. Let them go into details and I will meet them. I am confident I shall win.'[90]

Finally on February 10 Lloyd George capitulated. In return for a saving of £1 million obtained by omitting three light cruisers and twelve coastal torpedo boats from the new construction pro-gramme and cutting out the Summer Manoeuvres in favour of a test mobilisation of reserves—together with a pledge from Churchill that he would reduce his following year's Estimates—he gave his blessing to the full programme of four Dreadnoughts, three of which were to be accelerated in place of the Canadian ships—and the full fleet in commission. The following day the Cabinet endorsed the compromise. There were no resignations.

'Winston,' noted an observer, 'is in high spirits, and well he may be!'[91]

On March 17 he introduced the Estimates to the House. He made no mention of a naval 'holiday', but addressed himself to Tirpitz's acceptance of an 8 : 5 ratio, stressing that he had intended the ratio as a standard for home waters only. He proposed to station six Dreadnoughts in the Mediterranean when the replacements for the Canadian ships had been built, and neither these nor any other ships Great Britain might be forced to build by the actions of other naval Powers could be included in the ratio. Nor could any fixed ratio be binding; it might need revision one way or the other as circumstances altered. 'I have always guarded myself against any inference that it could be made an absolute standard.'

The hunt for mutual limitation was over. The race was to take its natural course. As Grey had said the previous month, it was not of England's choosing. 'The ships which Germany is going to lay down are being laid down under a Naval Law which cannot be altered, which was laid down many years ago by the *Reichstag*, and which cannot be altered by anything we do. If we shut down our programme altogether and desist from building anything this year, or if we were to build nothing the year afterwards, I don't think it would cause any alteration in shipbuilding in Europe.'[92] While deploring, once more, the wastefulness of it all, he had concluded to cheers that for Great Britain to make an enormous reduction in naval expenditure when there was no certainty that it would affect shipbuilding in Europe would be staking too much on a gambling chance.

Wilhelm's reaction to the breakdown of all pretence at negotiations was to renew his call for another *Novelle*. But Tirpitz thought it politically impossible; the Chancellor would never agree, the *Reichstag* would not vote the additional taxes; Germany's financial bow was already over-strung. Besides Churchill would use any further increases as an excuse for even more building. The message had gone home. All Tirpitz wished to do was keep the peace with

England and consolidate within his existing Law, allowing the rising tide of German industrial power to carry his fleet inexorably up to and beyond the strength of the Royal Navy.

At the Admiralty in London the Second Sea Lord's department prepared projections for personnel requirements in 1920 when the British fleet would amount, on present programmes, to the extraordinary total of at least 79 capital ships—perhaps 86—at least 63 in full commission, 62 of them Dreadnoughts.[93]

Summer, 1914

Early in the morning of June 23, 1914, lookouts at Kiel saw two great columns of smoke to seaward. Presently the funnels and tripod masts of four British Dreadnoughts appeared from the misty grey, and slightly astern three light cruisers. This was the Second Battle Squadron of the Home Fleet coming, as a tangible sign of the remarkable détente in Anglo-German relations to attend Kiel Week. Leading was H.M.S. *King George* V, flying the flag of Vice-Admiral Sir George Warrender; following in the line came the *Centurion*, *Ajax* and *Audacious*, the Royal Navy's latest and most powerful class of 13.5″-gun battleships. They passed Friedrichsfort firing a salute of twenty-one guns, which was answered by the battery and, in perfect order steamed in suddenly brilliant sunshine past flotillas of beflagged yachts and launches and the moored warships of Wilhelm's Navy to their allotted positions near a line of the five latest German Dreadnoughts, watched on all hands and by spectators deep along either shore with breathless curiosity.

Their dark grey paint looked almost black beside the light grey of the German ships and enhanced the effect of their greater guns and the more menacing disposition of their turrets arranged in superfiring pairs fore and aft with one additional on the centreline between the funnels and the after pair; by contrast the German fleet flagship, *Friedrich der Grosse* and the four other 'Kaisers' astern of her retained an arrangement of one foreward turret, one on either beam in echelon and one superfiring pair aft which had long been discarded by British—and even longer by American—constructors.

On board the British flagship a German officer, von Hase, who had been appointed ADC to Sir George Warrender for the duration of the visit, made mental notes for the detailed report he would need to make: Sir George had an aristocratic face and fine blue eyes; he was evidently a distinguished man of the world of the true English type; he was self-possessed and decided. Particularly impressive was his calm and easy relationship with his officers and men; military formality was almost non-existent, yet efficiency had not suffered. The squadron was in immaculate condition; the ships had come to their moorings simultaneously with quiet panache and a minimum of orders delivered in a most laconic manner. Von Hase was reminded of the story about a dinner aboard the cruiser *Breslau* the previous year; officers of ships from many navies had been invited; a British Admiral had sat next to the German Captain; at one point, raising his glass and gazing straight into the German's blue eyes he had whispered a private toast, 'The two white Nations!' Among the excitable and untrustworthy Latins and Slavs 'intellectually, morally and physically inferior', these two had recognised each other as 'representatives of the two greatest seafaring Germanic nations ... originally members of one and the same noble family'.[1] It was a deeply-held sentiment. Earlier that year Prince Henry of Prussia had made a similar comment to the British naval attaché: 'Other large European nations are not "White Men".' The attaché had reported the conversation in a despatch: 'I could not help feeling that His Royal Highness had voiced in a peculiarly British way a view that is very prevalent in our own Service.'[2]

Although von Hase was impressed with Sir George and his officers and the immense professionalism of the squadron, he was surprised to notice that the tall, fair Teutonic type was not so prevalent among the crews; many were small, of poorer physique than their counterparts in his own Service, even Jewish-looking. He had always thought Jews had an aversion to sea-going.

Later in the day, after formal, rather cool introductions between the British and German officers on board the *Friedrich der Grosse,* von Hase met the German naval attaché to London, who warned him to be on his guard against the English officers. 'England is ready to strike. War is imminent the object of this visit is only spying. They want to see how prepared we are.'[3] He was particularly warned against saying anything about the U-boat service. Elaborate precautions had already been taken to make it impossible for the British to count the number or estimate the size of the U-boats in harbour; they had been placed in the most inaccessible berths, their wireless aerials struck and guards mounted to keep away the curious.[4] The attitude was not confined to the youngest arm; when

Sir George Warrender offered to open his ships to German officers so that they might see everything they wished, the Commander-in-Chief of the High Seas Fleet declined the invitation; there were parts of German ships which were not allowed to be shown to *anyone,* he apologised. Later he relented slightly and Warrender's men were allowed aboard the pre-Dreadnought 'Deutschlands', while German officers visited the *King George* V and her consorts; the only parts the Germans were not allowed to see were wireless installations, director firing gear and fire control units aloft and in the turrets; these had been boarded over.

The day after the British squadron's arrival, the *Hohenzollern* made a ceremonial entry into the harbour through the new locks at Holtenau to inaugurate them and the whole scheme, now practically complete, for widening and deepening the Kiel Canal. She made a splendid sight in the sunshine, patterns of water reflected from her brilliant white sides, her gold decorative paintwork and yellow masts and funnels agleam, the Imperial standard floating above. As she left the lock the warships in the harbour thundered their salute. She steamed down the lines, each ship's band striking up as she passed, ensigns dipping, marines clashing their arms, crews lining the rails, the British sailors roaring 'hurrahs' and waving their caps high in time. Dominating the scene from the platform above the yacht's navigating bridge, Wilhelm stood bolt upright and alone, receiving the ovation; as he passed the *King George* V's bridge he turned and waved to Sir George Warrender. Overhead a Zeppelin, L3, drifted towards a flight of seaplanes.

The following day the Regatta started; the initial reserve between British and German officers began to melt in the round of sailing races, sports, garden parties, dances, banquets and private hospitality which followed each other in breathless succession from morning to early morning. The U.S. naval attaché reported on the great efforts the German officers were making to welcome their visitors, although he thought that the 'underlying hostility' especially on the British side, made any permanent results doubtful.[5]

Meanwhile another party of British sailors led by Vice-Admiral David Beatty, handsomest and most dashing officer of the day, whose rise to Flag rank had been quicker than any for over a century, was being entertained with even more unrestrained hospitality in St Petersburg. Beatty's itinerary had been planned to prevent the affair at Kiel from alarming Britain's *Entente* partners.

Earlier in the year he had taken his battlecruiser Squadron to Brest; now it was the Russian's turn to marvel at the great ships and the style with which this élite cavalry of the sea was taken through close-order manoeuvres at twenty-five knots; for their part, the British sailors marvelled at the Russian capacity for food and drink. While Beatty and his Captains were driven in gilded coaches with powdered footmen to lunch at the Tsar's country palace, other officers and men were entertained aboard Russian warships, their hosts making up for the obsolescence of most of the vessels with a surfeit of caviare, goose, salmon, trout, sherry, claret, champagne and vodka, knee dancing and high spirits. 'Every five minutes everyone clicked their glasses and had to empty them.'[6]

Beatty, not to be outdone, arranged a Ball on an even grander scale. Two thousand guests were invited, caviare and a hundred dozen bottles of champagne provided; the battlecruiser *New Zealand*, was secured alongside the flagship to provide a dance floor, and red and white striped awnings, coloured bunting, flowers and even fountains were arranged to transform the two warships into the setting for Viennese romance.

At the height of the festivities on June 28 came news of the assassination at Sarajevo of the Archduke Ferdinand of Austria-Hungary and his wife.

At Kiel Wilhelm received the news late in the afternoon while racing his yacht, *Meteor*. The race was stopped, the *Meteor* towed in, a state of mourning proclaimed, the grand functions to mark the final days of the British visit cancelled. On the next day Warrender, after giving a subdued lunch aboard his flagship for several of the German Admirals including Tirpitz, led his battleships out past the half-masted flags of the German fleet and the armada of small craft and headed for the Skagerrak and home: von Hase watched the squadron steam away with genuine feelings of regret; 'the fatherly, affectionate hospitality of the English Admiral I shall never forget.'[7] A farewell message flew from the German ships, PLEASANT JOURNEY.

Warrender replied, FRIENDS TODAY FRIENDS IN FUTURE FRIENDS FOR EVER.

Meanwhile his three cruisers took the shorter route home through the Kiel Canal, the officers noting with interest the increased width, the increased number of places where great ships could pass each other, the large size of the new locks at Holtenau and Bruns-büttel.

As the British squadrons made their return passages, sinister preparations were afoot in Berlin and Vienna. The assassination of the Archduke was the excuse the central governments needed to set in train the long awaited continental war of decision. The opportunity to settle the Balkan question, restore Austria's waning prestige and command over the disaffected Slavs within her Empire, and at the same time allow the Prussian armies to strike and smash France and Russia before the military preparations of the *Entente* matured was there for the taking. If the dream of a great continental 'bloc' under Prussian domination stretching from the Atlantic coast of France and the low countries right across Europe to the Caspian Sea, and an associated great African Empire were to be realised, now was the time. The moment was ripe. So many moments had been let slip in the past this one had to be fastened on and nurtured.

The conditions agreed at the war council during the previous Balkan crisis in December 1912 had been, so far as possible, fulfilled; allies had been sought, a few found; the German and Austrian peoples had been alerted by constant, intensifying propaganda to the imminent danger of a Slavic descent on their homelands; they would know what they fought for. The Austrian government had been stimulated to prove itself worthy of its stronger ally and Wilhelm had guaranteed German support when the moment came for them to uphold their rights in eastern Europe. During discussion of 'the anticipated war on two fronts' at the most recent joint staff talks in May, Moltke had assured the Austrians that they would not have to face the Russian armies alone for long; 'We hope to be finished with France within six weeks from the commencement of operations, or at least to have got so far that we can transfer our main forces to the east.'[8] Jagow and the Foreign Office, even Bethmann, had been convinced by the unrelenting pressure of the military that unless Germany provoked the conflict *soon* in these most favourable circumstances before the French or Russian military preparations were complete they would stand no chance when the Dual Alliance chose its own moment to strike—probably about 1916. This was as silly as most of Tirpitz's justifications for the course he had wanted to steer: the German armies and people fighting on interior lines for the Fatherland could have stood for ever on the defensive against the whole world in arms. But Moltke—like

Tirpitz—was the expert, his opinions were expert opinions, not to be criticised by mere civilians.

Besides this, and perhaps decisively, relations with England were set fair. It was difficult to imagine her pacifist government, already torn by rebellion in Ireland, going to war over a dispute so remote from her ken and vital interests as the Balkans. Even so, the strategic situation was not so hopeless as it had been in 1912; the canal was negotiable by the fleet, the Heligoland defences were ready and U-boat strength growing by the week. Tirpitz did not agree. But, then Tirpitz would *never* be ready.

And yet the conspiracy in Berlin was more than a desire to use apparently favourable circumstances for a preventive strike, more than the simple, long-cherished dream of conquest. For the military and the Foreign Office, for Wilhelm and Bethmann it was release. They had come to the end of their emotional resources; war was the lightning discharge from the strains within the Empire and more particularly within the 'government' where every faction tugged a different way, scarcely knowing what the others were about or why, and where supreme policy, embodied in Wilhelm, veered between them all like the restless needle of a galvonometer. In their separate, overheated perceptions, conditioned and unbalanced as they were by Treitschke's confusion of morality and necessity, war was the one direct and final solution to all problems of direction and to all difficulties, internal and external. It had become a psychological necessity.

Above all, Wilhelm had reached the crisis of his own fantasies; it was the moment his overweening and contradictory policies had made inevitable. His response was equally inevitable. Irresolute and timorous, in this military climax he had to prove the opposite —to his Generals, to his civilian government, to his Austrian allies. He urged them in his most bellicose idiom to smash Serbia once and for all.

Emotion and conspiracy crystallised. For Serbia, centre of the Pan-Slav movement, was already a 'raw, *direct* area of friction'[9] between Austro-Hungary and Russia. As relations between the central powers and Russia were so tense *before* Sarajevo that Bethmann had been prompted to warn his ambassadors that 'any number of secondary conflicts of interest between Russia and Austria might light the torch of war',[10] and as the Russian Foreign Minister had made it plain that Serbian integrity was for Russia *'une question de vie et de mort*',[11] and that an Austrian attack on Serbia would be a *casus belli*, encouragement for just such an attack, and promises of German support, come what may, were direct provocation for the war of decision.

Having chosen the moment and the means, the plot was hatched in the utmost secrecy. The ultimatum that would force the just war on Serbia and place the odium on Russia when she came as she must to Serbia's aid, was held back so that it could be delivered on July 23 when the French President and Premier, due to visit Russia, would be at sea and out of touch for several days, and when the forthcoming British test mobilisation of reserves would, hopefully, be ending. In the meantime, while discreet soundings were taken from British Ministers and political observers about her attitude in the event of a Balkan conflict leading to Continental war, the approaching crisis was concealed with every outward demonstration of normality. Ministers and senior naval and military commanders of both Powers left their capitals and commands for their usual summer retreats or spas; the High Seas Fleet was prepared for its annual manoeuvres off Norway, the *Hohenzollern* for Wilhelm's annual Baltic cruise, for which he sailed—as scheduled —on July 7.

Behind the deceptively placid surface of events high excitement prevailed. German Ambassadors in the major capitals were briefed on their role when the bombshell burst; the fleet was mobilised in secret; coal and oil stocks at Wilhelmshaven, Kiel, Heligoland and Danzig brought up to 'the prescribed war stock';[12] completion of the new Dreadnoughts, *König, Grosser Kürfurst, Derfflinger* and a new light cruiser were hurried forward and ships' companies for them assembled from the training ships; the Asiatic squadron in the Carolines under Vice-Admiral von Spee was ordered to keep 'in certain and constant communication' until the political situation clarified; in the Mediterranean the battlecruiser *Goeben* was ordered into Pola for boiler repairs and men rushed from Germany to speed the work. The chief of the *Admiralstab* wondered whether he should return from vacation and whether it was wise, in view of the coming British test mobilisation, for the High Seas Fleet to cruise so far from its base while the British fleet was virtually mobilised for war; it would be better he thought to hold the High Seas Fleet off the Skagerrak until the 23rd and see how matters developed. The Foreign Office, however, was determined to avoid premature 'political arousement';[13] no change was made in the scheduled Norwegian cruise.

Tirpitz, taking the cure before going to St Blasien, and kept informed of the preparations and daily rumours from Berlin and Wilhelmshaven, could only hope that the 'thunderstorm would pass'.[14] In April he had stated that he needed a further six to eight years to prepare the fleet completely for war. Now, it seemed, von Moltke was pressing on with his plans without the Navy, while Bethmann foolishly and unrealistically wooed England. He wrote to the section chief at the Navy Office who was keeping him informed:

> I am completely convinced that this wooing of England must lead to war with Russia. One only needs to remember what sort of a policy Bismarck, as an Englishman, would carry on against Germany and Russia. The *Reich* Chancellor is completely wrong and in love with his ideas of wooing for the favour of perfidious Albion. It is completely a question of the fate of the German people. Cost what it may, we must come to an understanding with Russia and put the whale against the bear. All sentimentality has to be silent.[15]

His protests were futile. As Germany reached her self-appointed crisis of decision with the Russian bear he was left outside the counsels; his policy had failed; there was no prospect of it ever succeeding. It was up to the Army and the diplomats to break through the ring of enemies and fulfil Germany's destiny.

As the date for the ultimatum approached the secret tension mounted. On the 18th, the Foreign Secretary, Jagow, requested details of the *Hohenzollern*'s itinerary after the 23rd so that he could keep in constant touch, and suggested that Wilhelm should continue his cruise exactly as planned lest a sudden return 'alarm the world'.[16] Wilhelm, of course, was in a high state of nervous excitement by this time. On the 19th he directed the High Seas Fleet to keep concentrated until the 25th so that it could break off its cruise quickly if ordered to do so; he also required the Managing Directors of the two great North German Shipping Lines to be told of the coming ultimatum so that they might make suitable arrangements for their vessels.

Jagow passed the message on the 20th. To the representatives of the *Admiralstab*, who were becoming increasingly anxious about the position of the fleet exposed to British attack off the Norwegian coast, he maintained that he had no detailed knowledge of the contents of the Austrian note, although his Under-Secretary said he believed from private information that 'Serbia could not swallow it.' When Tirpitz received this news he underscored the words 'not swallow'.[17]

By the same post he received an even more disturbing despatch from his 'ears' in Berlin. Jagow had been questioning the acting head of the *Admiralstab*, Rear-Admiral Behnke, on Wilhelm's reasons for keeping the High Seas Fleet concentrated at sea until the 25th. Behnke did not know; he could only guess that His Majesty was reckoning on a decision by the 25th on the position the Triple Alliance would take up; he doubted Jagow's suggestion that it had anything to do with the British test mobilisation, due to end by that date. But this evidently concerned Jagow, for he went on to ponder the question of English participation.

'How would it be,' he suggested, 'to threaten England that if she declared against us we would occupy Holland? How would the *Admiralstab* evaluate that?'[18]

I (Behnke) pointed out to him shortly that the occupation of Holland would make English operations during the war more difficult, and that the possession of Holland after a victorious war—if the war were being made full use of by us militarily and economically—would mean a very decided threat to England. I think, therefore, that a threat to occupy Holland could influence the resolve of England in the wished-for sense. Perhaps (on the other hand) it would give her a reason immediately to take sides against our party if she was already inclined to take part from general military considerations. Jagow declined that view, and thought that England would wait for a few days and make her behaviour dependent on the outcome of events. I took the view that England would side with the others against us. From the absolute military standpoint, that would be the right thing to do. His excellency, von Jagow, from political considerations, would not accept this view. We must then always reckon with a hostile England. His Excellency Jagow described the threat as bluff. I (Behnke) pointed out that with respect to the management of the war at sea, it would be right to threaten, in addition, the occupation of Denmark.

When Tirpitz read this he must have wondered if the whole of Germany was not in the grip of some fatal insanity. As it was. His reply is lost.

By this time the British test mobilisation of the Home Fleets had gone forward smoothly and there was concentrated in Spithead under the supreme command of Admiral Sir George Callaghan a vast armada of twenty Dreadnought battleships, four battlecruisers and nine of the most powerful pre-Dreadnoughts which, together with cruisers and destroyer flotillas, formed the First (later Grand) Fleet, thirteen older pre-Dreadnoughts of the Second (later Channel) Fleet, and fourteen other pre-Dreadnoughts of the Third (or Reserve) Fleet, together with all home defence cruiser squadrons and destroyer and submarine flotillas. The state of instant readiness of this immense force, beside which the High Seas Fleet of thirteen Dreadnought battleships, three battlecruisers and eight pre-Dreadnoughts, all with inferior gun-calibre and cruiser cover, had no hope of success, continued to prey on the *Admiralstab*, and on the day before the ultimatum was due to be delivered Behnke warned Jagow of the danger of a sudden attack by the British; the High Seas Fleet had to be recalled directly there was possibility of war with England.[19] Jagow replied, as he had before, that a premature recall of the fleet might cause general unease and be regarded as suspicious, especially in England. But the next day, the 23rd, he did transmit the *Admiralstab* fears to Wilhelm.

The chief of the Naval Cabinet, von Müller, with Wilhelm aboard the *Hohenzollern*, noted in his diary: 'the excitement grows. Fleet has established radio contact with us. Today the ultimatum is going to be handed over.'[20] The next day Wilhelm ordered the Commander-in-Chief, High Seas Fleet to commence coaling in Norwegian harbours, but to organise shore leave so that the men could be recalled at short notice should it become necessary to shorten the stay.

In Great Britain all attention was concentrated on the Irish problem. The affair at Sarajevo was, it seemed, being treated as an internal matter for the governments concerned. The European situation had never looked so fair or so settled. On the day that the Austrian note was delivered, Lloyd George spoke of the new feeling on the Continent and saw the signs as hopeful for future economies in armaments.

Take a neighbour of ours, our relations are very much better than they were a few years ago. There is none of that snarling which we used to see, more especially in the Press of those two great—I will not say rival—nations, but two great Empires. The feeling is

better altogether between them. They begin to realise they can
co-operate for common ends, and the points of co-operation are
greater and more numerous and more important than the points
of possible controversy.[21]

On the same day, the combined exercises which had followed the
test mobilisation of the home fleets were completed, and Admiral
Sir George Callaghan reported to the Admiralty that he was dispersing the Fleet; the ships of the Reserve departed to their home
ports to pay off their crews while the First and Second Fleets concentrated at Portland for a Flag Officers' Conference.

A few hours later, as the battleship, *France*, with the French
President and Premier aboard, set course westward through the
Gulf of Finland after farewell displays of friendship from Kronstadt,
Austria delivered her ultimatum to Serbia. Its harsh terms spelled
out the end of Serbian independence. Although it arose from the
murder of the Archduke in another country almost a month
previously, it gave the Serbian government only forty-eight hours
in which to reply. It was too obviously a recipe for Balkan war, and
the next morning as Europe awoke to the sudden crisis, German
Ambassadors in the major capitals hastened into action with urgent
requests to the Powers to help localise the conflict. The German
government, they said, had known nothing of the ultimatum before
hand. Now, it only sought to prevent intervention from other
Powers, which would 'as a result of the various alliance negotiations,
bring about the most inestimable consequences.'

The British Cabinet was debating the Irish question with all the
heat and hopeless divergencies this always provoked when a Foreign
Office messenger handed Grey a note giving the precise terms of the
Austrian ultimatum. As Grey read it out to the Ministers, the
unprecedented demands following each other in remorseless succession, possibilities of 'inestimable consequences' began to form in
their minds; it seemed unthinkable that any State could accept it.
For Churchill, tired after the protracted debate, Fermanagh and
County Tyrone faded back into the mists and squalls of Ireland
'and a strange light began immediately but by perceptible grad-
ations to fall and grow upon the map of Europe.'[22]

After the meeting he went back to the Admiralty and wrote out
a list of measures to take if the crisis developed: at the head of the
list was 'First and Second Fleets. Leave and disposition.' Fortunately

they were still at Portland for the Flag Officers' Conference, and would remain there for the next two days before breaking up into squadrons and dispersing.

That evening at dinner he sat next to Albert Ballin who had been sent over by Bethmann, probably at Wilhelm's instigation, to sound out the likely British reaction if the Balkan conflict should lead to European war. The previous evening before news of the ultimatum had reached England Ballin had dined with Grey and Haldane and a pacifist member of the Cabinet, Lord Morley, and had come away with the impression that Great Britain, with her concern for the balance of power in Europe, would only intervene in a Continental war if Germany were to *swallow up* France.[23] This was probably a measure of Ballin's natural fear of war with England, for Haldane's impression of the conversation was rather different; he thought they had made it clear that Britain's neutrality could not be counted upon if Germany *attacked* France. When Ballin tackled Churchill on the question Churchill replied that it would be a great mistake to assume that England would necessarily do nothing; she would judge events as they arose. Ballin, not to be put off, continued very earnestly, 'Suppose we had to go to war with Russia and France, and suppose we defeated France and yet took nothing from her in Europe, not an inch of her territory, only some colonies to indemnify us. Would that make a difference to England's attitude? Suppose we gave a guarantee beforehand?'[24]

Churchill only repeated his earlier reply; England would judge events as they arose. But it would be a great mistake to assume that she would stay out whatever happened.

When Ballin returned to Berlin he was able to report that no British Cabinet Minister had come out with an unequivocal statement that the British government *would* support France if she were attacked. And misled by the almost aggressive pacifism of some of the Ministers to whom he had spoken, and the general feeling throughout England that a Balkan war was none of their concern and it would be silly to become embroiled over such a remote dispute, he concluded that the British decision would turn on Germany's intentions towards France; if Germany made it clear that she had no intention of annexing French territory, particularly along the Channel coast where England was particularly sensitive, he was hopeful that the British would remain aloof. His simple faith in the efficacy of German 'assurances' was shared by Bethmann, who called the British Ambassador to the Chancellery on July 29 and put this very proposal to him. Germany had no desire to 'crush' France in any conflict that might arise, 'provided that the neutrality of Britain were certain, every assurance would be given to the British government that the Imperial government aimed at no territorial acquisition at the expense of France ...'[25] When the British Ambassador asked him about French colonies, he said that he was unable to give similar guarantees. However, he was prepared to respect the neutrality of Holland if Germany's adversaries did the same, and while it depended upon France what operations might be necessary in Belgium, 'Belgian integrity would be respected if she had not sided against Germany.'

Grey read the Ambassador's note of the conversation with a feeling of the utmost despair. It was evident that the German Chancellor felt a general war to be near. But what sort of a man could he be, seriously to propose a bargain which would reflect such discredit not only on the British government's honour but on its common sense and instinct for preservation! He replied that His Majesty's Government could not for a moment entertain the Chancellor's proposal ... it would be a disgrace for us to make this bargain with Germany at the expense of France—a disgrace from which the good name of this country would never recover.[26]

Meanwhile Wilhelm, dismissing Bethmann's pleas for caution in warship movements, had directed the High Seas Fleet to return home; the Dreadnoughts of the First Battle Squadron and the Scouting Group spearheaded by three battlecruisers returned down the Danish coast to Wilhelmshaven; the rest of the fleet including the five latest Dreadnoughts of the *Kaiser* class, went through the Belts to Kiel, where Wilhelm himself arrived during the night of the 26th-27th—despite Bethmann's plea that he, too, keep away!—and immediately ordered all approaches to the harbour secured against Russian torpedo boat attack. Then he entrained for Potsdam.

By this time Serbia had replied to the Austrian ultimatum with a masterpiece of appeasement; while escaping total abasement, it appeared to concede most of the Austrian demands and so sweep the ground from beneath the Austrian war party who, disconcerted by such an unforeseen hitch in the grand plan, had kept it secret even from the German government while they pondered the next move. Jagow, who had learned the terms of the reply direct from Serbia, also kept it secret. So it was not until the late evening of

Wilhelm's return to Potsdam that he and Bethmann were able to read the text of the reply when it was at last released by the Austrian government. Both were impressed. 'A brilliant performance for a time limit of only forty-eight hours!' Wilhelm exclaimed. 'This is more than could have been expected!' And venting his infinite relief at such an unexpected end to the intolerable nervous tension of the last few days he exulted, 'A great moral victory for Vienna! But with it every reason for war disappears.'[27]

This was not the view in Vienna. Another telegram that evening informed Bethmann of the Austrian government's intention to declare war on Serbia on the morrow—or the day after that—to cut the ground from under any attempts at intervention. For Grey was already busy trying to convene a Conference of the Powers to solve the dispute. At the urgent instigation of the German government the declaration was made the next morning.

Russia, meanwhile, had made her support for Serbia clear, backing the words with general mobilisation. And although the Tsar countermanded the order after receiving a personal appeal from Wilhelm to keep the dispute localised and treat it, not as a political matter, but as punishment for regicides, the Austrian declaration against Serbia resulted in a renewal of the general mobilisation.

Just before news of this decision reached Germany, there were startling indications from London that Ballin's assessment had been too optimistic. Prince Lichnowsky reported a conversation with Grey in which he had been told that if Germany and France became involved in the Balkan crisis, the situation would immediately be altered. 'The British government would, under the circumstances, find itself forced to make up its mind quickly. In that event it would not be practicable to stand aside and wait for any length of time.'[28] The warning was clear.

It was all too much for Wilhelm; when on the night of 30-31st, he read a report that the Russian general mobilisation could not be reversed, the awesome consequences of a great European war with England on the side of his Continental opponents stared him in the face. For if Russia mobilised he had to follow suit lest they gain too long a start and ruin his Great General Staff's plan—its only plan, its single, sacred, inflexibly time-tabled, long-matured, impatiently up-dated, grand plan for the grand war on the two fronts. Wilhelm's nerves cracked. After the brief reprieve from his image of continental war to be confronted suddenly with a yet more monstrous vision of conspiracy—and a conspiracy aimed at Germany's life. For it was suddenly evident to him that England, Russia and France had agreed among themselves to *compel* him to support Austria, thus to use the Serbian crisis as a pretext for waging the war of *annihilation* against Germany. He broke down, and seizing pen and paper allowed his agony to spill out:

> ... we are either basely to betray our ally and *leave her to the mercy of Russia*—thereby breaking up the Triple Alliance—or as a reward for keeping our *pledges* get set upon and *beaten* by the Triple *Entente* as a body, so that their longing to ruin us completely can be finally satisfied. That is in a nutshell the bare bones of the situation slowly but surely brought about by King Edward VII ... so the celebrated *encirclement* of Germany has finally become an accomplished fact in spite of all efforts by our politicians to prevent it. The net has suddenly been closed over our head, and the purely anti-German policy which England has been pursuing all over the world has won the most spectacular victory ... A magnificent achievement which even those for whom it means disaster are bound to admire. Even after his death King Edward VII is stronger than I, though I am still alive ...[29]

As all the wasted years of total misgovernment, of whim and infantile vanity and moral hollowness broke around 'Willy's' head —as those who had known him best had always predicted—Grey sought to pull Europe back from the very edge of catastrophe. His task was rendered impossible by the strong pacifist wing of the Cabinet. Even if he had wished to give France the dangerous guarantees she desired—or more important give Germany the un-equivocal statement of British intent to intervene which she feared, he could not. For he knew that neither Cabinet nor Parliament in its present mood, would back him. Instead he tried to put pressure on Germany to pull back her weaker partner—to stop at least in Belgrade—while the Powers *talked* the dispute out around a table. It was too late. While 'Willy' was locked in crisis—and his Chief of the Naval Cabinet heard from the *Admiralstab* that war had been decided on!—Bethmann followed the military time-table for that war like a lawyer in a trance, proceeding from the briefest ulti-matum to Russia to stop her mobilisation to German mobilisation in reply, to a German declaration of war against Russia.

The Chief of the Naval Cabinet, after reading the evening papers, noted in his diary, 'Brilliant mood; the government has succeeded very well in making us appear the attacked.'[30] Even the Social Democrats who had published an appeal for *international* workers' solidarity and 'Down with War' as lately as July 25, were caught up in the frenzy of enthusiasm which swept the country at the prospect of breaking through the ring of their enemies. When Wilhelm proclaimed, 'I no longer know Parties—only Germans!' the Socialists had realised, quite suddenly, that they *were* Germans.[31]

But there was still the matter of France before the government. The mobilisation order was swinging the great mass of the German armies into position for the swift thrust through Belgium that could crush France within six weeks of the outset of war, leaving the Russian borders thinly guarded until the troops could return. Yet Germany was not at war with France! It was a difficult situation. Bethmann solved it by dashing off a peremptory note to the French government, and followed it shortly with a declaration of war. But why? Tirpitz asked him. This must bring England in. Why these sudden declarations by Germany right and left? Bethmann raised his thin arms to heaven. 'It is necessary because the Army want to send troops over the frontier.' Tirpitz was reminded of a drowning man.

> Through all these days Bethmann was so agitated and over-strained that it was impossible to speak with him. I can still hear him as he repeatedly stressed the necessity of the declaration of war, with his arms uplifted, and so cut short all further discussion.[32]

By this time the Fleet had abandoned its posture against Russia and concentrated at Wilhelmshaven, prepared for imminent war with England. The orders for the Kiel squadron to traverse the Canal had been issued on the night of the 30-31st as Wilhelm became convinced of the *Entente* conspiracy against Germany. The Dreadnoughts of the Third Battle Squadron had gone through first —after lightening themselves by off-loading the coal that had been taken on as recently as the 29th—and the pre-Dreadnoughts of the Second Battle Squadron had followed more easily. By August 2, defensive minefields had been laid off the North Sea approaches, and cruisers, destroyers and U-boats with live warheads to their torpedoes were patrolling the 'defensive perimeter' centred on the fortress of Heligoland—waiting for the British to come—screwing their courage for *Der Tag*.

Churchill had no intention of obliging them. He had decided on distant blockade two years since. Now all was prepared. He had ordered the First Fleet to its war station to the north of Scotland as early as the 28th, before Germany was certain of British intervention—for the British Cabinet itself had been uncertain, indeed overwhelmingly pacifist at that time. While Germany still hoped that Britain would keep out of her Continental affair there was less danger of a surprise torpedo or submarine attack. The fleet had sailed from Portland in the early morning of the 29th, passing through the Dover Straits that night in mid-Channel and without lights 'like dark, shapeless monsters of another world through the myriad lights of the crowded Strait',[33] ships' companies at action stations lest the decision had already been taken in Berlin, lookouts tense, fingers close by the triggers of quick-firing anti-torpedo boat guns, then still darkened across the busy traffic of the Thames Estuary and northwards to the Orkney Islands beyond the range of most German small craft, steaming in single file which stretched over fifteen miles past the rocky outposts of Pentland Firth to anchor by divisions in Scapa Flow—a great, grey-steel armada holding more power in its long guns than any fleet before it, prepared by years of intensive training to hitherto unknown precision in gunnery and fleet manoeuvre, its officers and men conditioned by three hundred years of history to believe their proud Service *unbeatable*, like Beatty longing for war so that they might repeat the deeds of their forefathers.

Churchill was in similar condition:

Everything tends towards catastrophe and collapse. I am interested, geared up and happy. Is it not horrible to be built like that? The preparations have a hideous fascination for me. I pray to God to forgive me for such fearful levity. Yet I would do my best for peace and nothing would induce me wrongfully to strike the blow. I cannot feel that we in this island are in any serious degree responsible for the wave of madness which has swept the mind of Christendom ...[34]

During the first days of August as the despatch boxes brought increasing evidence of the failure of Grey's attempts to halt the madness, and it became clear that Germany would not be dissuaded from marching on France through Belgium, and that Belgium intended to resist to the utmost if she were invaded, all but the extreme pacifist wing of the Cabinet moved towards the idea of British involvement. Grey had felt all along that they were committed to France morally and by self-interest, and he had made it clear that he would not continue in office if the government let France down. But it was the issue of Belgian neutrality and Britain's 1839 Treaty obligations to guarantee it that persuaded the majority. When on Monday, August 3, they received an appeal from the King of the Belgians to uphold the sanctity of Belgium all but the most committed pacifists realised that they had no choice. Grey was at last able to speak to the country.

> I was myself stirred with resentment and indignation at what seemed to me Germany's crime in precipitating the war, and all I knew of Prussian militarism was hateful, but these must not be our motives of our going into the war ... The real reason for our going into the war was that, if we did not stand by France and stand up for Belgium against this aggression, we should be isolated, discredited and hated; and there would be for us nothing but a miserable and ignoble future.[35]

His speech to the House was in his iciest vein. Characteristically and deliberately he shunned emotion, not even divulging the ignoble bargain Bethmann had proposed at the expense of France lest it create fury. 'I would like the House to approach the crisis in which we are now, from the point of view of British interests, British honour, British obligations, free from all passion as to why peace has not been preserved.'[36]

He dwelt at some length on the undefended northern French coasts and the possibility of German warships in the Channel bombarding and waging war on shipping, on the French being compelled to bring their main fleet up from the Mediterranean, leaving that vital focus of British shipping routes insufficiently defended against the Austrian and possibly Italian fleets; he dwelt on the British Treaty obligations to preserve the integrity of Belgium, and read out the appeal from the King of the Belgiums. Then he came to the central issue.

> I do not believe for a moment that at the end of this war, even if we stood aside and remained aside, we should be in a position, a material position, to use our force decisively to undo what had happened in the course of the war, to prevent the whole of the West

of Europe opposite to us—if that had been the result of the war—
falling under the domination of a single Power, and I am quite sure
that our moral position would be such as to have lost us all respect.

The House, packed and silently attentive as it had not been this
century, felt the depth of the passion Grey was dredging. His
sincerity was more powerful than eloquence.

After pointing to his most strenuous efforts for peace right up to
and beyond the last moment, he concluded that a new situation had
arisen. Now, it seemed to him, Great Britain was forced to take a
stand upon the issues he had outlined. 'I believe, when the country
realises what is at stake, what the real issues are, the magnitude of
the impending dangers in the west of Europe, which I have en-
deavoured to describe in the House, we shall be supported throughout ... by the determination, the resolution, the courage and the
endurance of the whole country.'

Grey carried the House. Afterwards he composed a simple
ultimatum to Germany stating that unless the invasion of Belgium
were halted she would find Great Britain in arms against her; it was
timed to expire at midnight, August 4.

In Scapa Flow the ageing Commander-in-Chief of the First or
Grand Fleet was superseded by a younger Admiral, Sir John Jellicoe,
the outstanding professional whom Fisher had chosen and groomed
for supreme command at Armageddon. Early the following morning,
after intelligence that Germany intended to get commerce raiders to
sea before the ultimatum expired, he took his great fleet from the
Flow to sweep the northern exits they might use.

At the Admiralty there was little more to be done. All was ready.
The long period of strained relations consequent on Tirpitz's fleet
programmes and the ruthless trend of German foreign policy had
given sufficient warning; since Agadir Churchill had presided over
a type of anticipatory thinking and staff work that was quite foreign
to the Service. In co-operation with the War Office, Foreign Office,
Home Office and other important departments of State a *War Book*
had been prepared which itemised what each department had to do
at every stage in the period of strained relations which might
precede the outbreak of war, or in the event of a sudden 'bolt from
the blue' attack. The telegrams which were to set in hand the
different levels of preparedness had been made out and arranged in
order of priority, the notices, orders, proclamations either pre-

printed or set up in type, the necessary envelopes addressed and arranged in order. Everything that could reasonably be anticipated had been; there were failures which were pointed up during the subsequent months, more especially in Intelligence, anti-submarine measures and mines, but these were of a type inevitable after a century of peace and in the midst of a gale of technical change. In the main areas, where the chief threat was expected, the pre-thinking had been of an order never achieved, never attempted in England before.

Churchill sat in the War Room at the Admiralty in the calm after the last preparatory telegram had been despatched, listening to the clock ticking away the minutes before the ultimatum expired. His latest intelligence was that the High Seas Fleet had not stirred from its base where it lay surrounded by minefields and patrols of destroyers—awaiting the British fleet attack?

Grey, Asquith, Lloyd George and a few other Ministers waited nearby in the Cabinet room at 10, Downing Street, in touch with the Foreign Office, but mournfully aware that events had moved too far for recall. Outside crowds were massed outside Buckingham Palace and along Parliament Street gripped in the fever of momentous events; like the German crowds who had waved and cheered deliriously before the Imperial Castle in Berlin, few were aware of what lay beyond this long-expected hour of decision for them or for the world.

As the hands of Big Ben reached 11—midnight in Berlin—and the first stroke boomed across London, the National Anthem broke out from massed throats before the Palace and rolled like a wave to the silent Ministers. From the Admiralty Building the War Telegram was flashed to all stations. Churchill went out into the warm summer night and walked the short distance to 10, Downing Street to report that the fleet was under war orders.

'I thank God I could also feel in that hour that our country was guiltless of all intended purpose of war.'[37]

Epilogue

Great Britain's entry into the war came as a shock to Berlin, more profound for the tortuous hesitations that had preceded it. Everyone had known that she had to come in but all, except the Service departments had tried to persuade themselves that the spirit of pacifism and non-intervention which had distinguished so much British Liberal and even Conservative opinion at the start of the crisis might prevail, at least until France had been crushed. When the optimism proved false it was harder than if the issue had been clear-cut from the start; those who had been most optimistic were hardest hit.

Wilhelm was crushed. One long-standing confidant thought he had never seen such a tragic and disturbed face as the Emperor wore during the first days of August.[1] Bülow, recalled to the Palace after his years in disfavour, was 'moved by his pallor, his haggard, almost unnerved look. He looked excited and yet exhausted. His eyes blinked restlessly.'[2] As of old, he put his arm around Bülow's shoulders and began to pour out his version of the 'terrible events' of the past weeks.

Bülow passed on from this pitiful interview to meet Bethmann. 'Well,' he said after a long pause at greeting, 'tell me at least how it all happened.' Bethmann 'raised his long, thin arms to heaven and answered in a dull, exhausted voice, "Oh—if only I knew." '[3]

Ballin was equally stricken. A Norwegian shipowner who called on him on the day of Grey's ultimatum was shocked by the change that had come over him: 'he had had no sleep and ... radical changes to his face had made him an old, bent man.'[4]

After Jagow's warning of the possibility of war on July 20, Ballin had stopped the departure of several of his liners from German ports, and had redirected many ships to return home instead of stopping at their scheduled ports of call. Even so, when Grey's ultimatum expired on August 4, only half his fleet was at home, most of the rest lay abroad, the majority in America. Where-ever they were, they were no use to him. They could neither sail over seas controlled by the *Entente* navies, nor would the government allow him to sell them to neutrals in case they were used for bringing food and raw materials to England. The vast Hamburg-Amerika organisation came to a sudden halt, half the employees were called to arms, half the rest to civilian emergency duties and only a skeleton staff remained for care and upkeep. 'My life's work', he wrote to a friend, 'lies in shreds.'[5] The other great German shipowners were in similar plight.

The famous preamble to Tirpitz's 1900 Navy Law rang hollowly on their ears.

> no State could be more easily cut off than Germany from all sea intercourse worthy of the name ... To effect this it would not be necessary to blockade long stretches of coast, but merely to blockade the few big seaports. In the same way as the traffic to the home ports the German mercantile marine on the high seas would be left to the mercy of an enemy who was more powerful on the sea ...[6]

To protect this sea trade, Tirpitz had continued, there was only one means: 'Germany must have a battle fleet so strong that even for the adversary with the greatest sea power a war against it would involve such dangers as to imperil his position in the world.'

Now the battle fleet he had spent his life's energy creating lay passively at Wilhelmshaven. The sailors were excited by the prospect of the inevitable battle of decision with the English fleet, and were convinced that their own ships, guns, armour and discipline were superior, but neither the Commander-in-Chief, nor the *Admiralstab* shared their confidence. Against Jellicoe's Grand Fleet of 21 Dreadnought battleships, 8 powerful pre-Dreadnoughts and 4 battlecruisers, not to mention the numerous pre-Dreadnought reserves, their own 13 Dreadnought battleships, 8 pre-Dreadnoughts and 3 battlecruisers seemed inadequate. Against Jellicoe's 13.5" and 12" guns their own 12" and 11" seemed weak; against the Royal Navy's long and triumphant tradition, its *habit* of superiority, their own Service seemed a parvenu. They feared to leave the safety of their defensive position. The British must come to them. British naval doctrine indicated that they *would* come; were not the frontiers of England the coasts of the enemy!

Tirpitz was in despair. In every direction he saw confusion and the triumph of the forces against which he had struggled so long, but hitherto successfully. The Great General Staff of the Army was too confident of quick victory over France; they had not assessed the meaning of war against England; they did not appreciate the slow strength of sea power; they had brushed aside his most recent pleas to wait for a further six to eight years when the fleet would be ready because they thought in Continental, not world terms; to them the British involvement meant little more than a handful of those 'Aldershot tommies' with little caps and swagger canes who had been hard put to beat a few farmers in South Africa; 'If they come across,' the Army had maintained scornfully, 'they will be arrested!'

The General Staff obsession with the French and Russian military build-up, and the need to strike before the Russian strategic railways threatened their master plan had blinded them to the need for a strategy to take account of the war on *three* fronts. Confident that they would be in Paris by September and the war would be won before the following spring, they had disregarded England. There had been no combined planning with the *Admiralstab*. Ideas for thrusts to the Channel ports or the Danish Belts to aid fleet strategy had been treated as lightly as the idea that the German fleet could *ever* be ready to tackle the Royal Navy.

The politicians saw no further. Neither Bethmann nor Jagow appreciated the need for real power at sea; both had sought to win England's neutrality at the *cost* of the German fleet. And having failed, they had been rushed in to the war by military arguments without giving a thought to the naval consequences. When he had asked Jagow what he would do if the Army beat France and Russia, but not England, the little man had replied, 'If you had only brought us a little naval agreement with England, this war would not have been necessary,'*[7] thus revealing his total incomprehension of all that was at stake. With her industries cut off from world markets by the British blockade, and her colonies taken from her, what future lay ahead for Germany? Had the politicians only had the strength to resist the General Staff, in a few years everything would have fallen into their laps from the natural increase in German economic strength. He wrote to a colleague somewhat jealously about the Army's initial successes.

* We only have Tirpitz's word for 'necessary'. What did Jagow mean? But since Tirpitz's statements on matters of this sort are usually lies, what was the phrase Jagow actually used?

if these were not triumphant, but merely glorious, then would the other view break through—that we must have a fleet as strong as England's. *This natural and only goal of the last two decades* could never be spoken aloud, but could only be held in view for when Germany's trade and industry and colonies expanded further.[8]

But the bitterest blow of all for Tirpitz was the attitude within the Service itself. On July 29, he had suggested to the Chief of the Naval Cabinet that the *Admiralstab* should be merged with the Navy Office in the event of war to create a unified high command under single control; he had put himself forward as ready to assume this supreme responsibility. The response had been deeply wounding.[9] All the inter-departmental jealousies which he had used ruthlessly for his own ends during the preceding years, all the criticisms of his one-sided building policy, the weakness of German Dreadnoughts in gun-calibre and turret disposition in comparison to the British, above all his rigid concentration on the single 'long-term' aim at the expense of so many immediate necessities like U-boats or torpedo boats with sufficient range to take the offensive, all the hostility to his long and autocratic rule welled up. And this time he could not call on Wilhelm's support. For Wilhelm intended to be his own Supremo. Tirpitz had used this ambition often enough in his own struggles, flattering, encouraging his master's vanity and, if ever he weakened, holding before his eyes the image of the vast fleet of battleships which only he, Tirpitz, could give him; like Bismarck, he should not have been surprised at the outcome.

But the glimpse into the hollowness of his own position was sudden and shocking. He had created the fleet, but now the time had come to use it the *Admiralstab* was supreme, *their* policies would dictate the strategy, the Naval Cabinet's choices for active command would dictate the manner in which it was carried out.

The sole concession he obtained was that the *Admiralstab* should *consult* him. On July 30, he was shown their Operations Plan for a war with England. It was entirely defensive. Sorties outside the Heligoland Bight were ruled out until the British fleet had been reduced to equality with the High Seas Fleet by '*kleinkrieg*'—a submarine and torpedo boat war of attrition as the British blockaded or attacked. Wilhelm agreed. The fleet, *his* fleet must be preserved without loss so that it could be used as a bargaining counter at the peace conference after the swift, Bismarckian war his Great General Staff planned. Thus, unwittingly, he gave his final approval to the divergent aims and totally opposed strategies of the two Services under his overall command.

Although Tirpitz's own ideas on strategy had always assumed fighting the great battle in the most favourable conditions within easy reach of German submarine and coastal torpedo boat bases, and with the prospect of retreat behind coastal fortifications, he objected to the extreme defensive posture outlined in the Operations Plan and adopted by von Ingenohl, Commander-in-Chief, High Seas Fleet, particularly as it was argued on the grounds of qualitative as well as numerical inferiority of the ships he had built. Afterwards he wrote:

> We were defeated by the old traditional English naval prestige which had never been put to the test in modern times. This prestige made our leaders fear to send our fleet to battle while there was still time.[10]

In the Mediterranean the Austrian Fleet was similarly blockaded by the French while the German cruiser squadron fled through the Dardanelles to become locked in the Black Sea. In the Pacific von Spee made a bid for home via Cape Horn, leaving a handful of commerce raiders to confuse the pursuit; he won a shattering victory over the first British squadron to find him at Coronel, but was later annihilated by two battlecruisers at the Falkland Islands soon after he had rounded the Horn. Nearer home British troops to support the French left wing were allowed across the Channel without challenge; Beatty was even allowed to enter the Heligoland Bight with his battlecruisers and blow two German cruisers out of the water without being engaged by heavy ships. The High Seas Fleet remained at its moorings. After this Wilhelm's caution *increased*. His fleet was not to fight, even within the Heligoland area, if the British forces were stronger.

Tirpitz despaired. He wrote letter after letter to the chief of the *Admiralstab* complaining that the fleet was whiling away its time uselessly while the Army fought for Germany's existence. The orders to hold back and avoid serious losses would deny it any chance of decision by battle; opportunities to attack detached units of the British fleet or harass portions by night torpedo attack must be *made* not passively awaited. The use made of the powerful German fleet, he repeated again and again, in no way corresponded to its relative strength.

The English fleet, on the other hand, is achieving the full effect of a 'fleet in being'; extraordinary and increasing pressure on the neutrals, complete destruction of German seaborne trade, the strictest possible blockade, steady transport of troops to France. With all this is connected the isolation of Germany as regards news, and the incitement of the whole world against us.[11]

He warned that if the High Seas Fleet continued to remain in its 'withdrawn position', its moral strength and efficiency would decline.

There were signs of this before the winter was out. 'Deep disappointment mingled with boredom is rampant',[12] one sailor noted in his diary in March. To keep the men occupied as the ships swung idly in Wilhelmshaven Roads the days were filled with meaningless drills, marching, exercises, even unpacking their seabeds for inspection several times a day. The spirit and camaraderie of early August gave way to an embittered atmosphere in which quarrels were frequent and officers and men grew apart. All had a sense of the tremendous power of the fleet being wasted while the army fought and suffered the grim war of attrition in France. Von Ingenohl was jeered openly in the streets of Wilhelmshaven.

'*Lieb Vaterland magst ruhig sein,*
Die Flotte schläft im Hafen ein'*

Meanwhile the Grand Fleet under Jellicoe, after initial surprise that the High Seas Fleet was not living up to its aggressive pre-war image, settled down to more arduous but in no way demoralising routine sweeps across the northern North Sea in support of blockading cruisers, in the hope that one day von Ingenohl might venture out from the safety of his minefields.

Pictures rise to memory of scenes that will never be repeated. I can see the whole horizon covered with warships as the Grand Fleet moves at seventeen knots in a SE'ly direction on one of its periodic sweeps. The battle fleet is in four divisions in line ahead, disposed abeam, the columns being about a mile apart, and a mile or two ahead is a division of old battleships known as 'mine bumpers' since their function was to indicate, by blowing up, the presence of mines. Each division is screened by destroyers, and the cruisers are far ahead, almost out of sight. The fleet sweeps forward in perfect station, moving as one under one controlling will.[13]

---

* 'Dear Fatherland rest in peace, the fleet is sleeping in port.'

A gunnery officer in the battleship, *Colossus* addressed some verses to the High Seas Fleet:

> We know you love your home dear
>   Somewhat narrow though it be;
> But when daddy spends his days dear,
>   Up at Berlin on the Spree
> It isn't fair to keep you
>   Shut up by lock and quay—
> You ought to see the world dear,
>   So *do* come out to sea.[14]

When a more aggressive Commander-in-Chief, Reinhard Scheer was appointed in 1916, and instructions were relaxed to allow him some initiative it seemed for a brief space on May 31 as if the issue might, after all, be fought out. Scheer made a sortie up the coast of Denmark in the hope of luring Jellicoe through a submarine trap and perhaps catching a detached part of his fleet with the full force of the High Seas Fleet. In the event his U-boats were not effective and he was himself lured by Beatty right up to the guns of the Grand Fleet, concentrated and deployed in a vast line of battle right around his eastern and northern horizon off the coast of Jutland. Fortunately for him the hour was late and the evening hung with mist and the gun and funnel smoke of a hundred ships; he was able to swing his battleships around together, send his destroyers in to the attack and his battlecruisers in a suicide charge to cover his retreat and lose himself in the gathering darkness. The following morning he steamed safely into his own waters and all but one of his shattered battlecruisers limped home after him while Jellicoe and Beatty searched vainly out at sea.

Although Scheer and the Navy propaganda machine claimed a victory at Jutland because three British battlecruisers were destroyed (as it turned out by magazine explosion caused by inadequate precautions in the loading cycle to the turrets) against only one German battlecruiser and one pre-Dreadnought battleship, it was a strange victory that left the vanquished in possession of the field and caused the victor to break off and make for home in desperation by the shortest possible route. No thinking German officer could consider challenging the Grand Fleet again; with the completion of the four 15"-gun 'Queen Elizabeths' the British advantage in weight of metal was overwhelming; their advantage in effective range was equally great; the German 12″ battlecruisers had been helpless when engaged by the 15″-gun squadron. Von Hase, now gunnery officer of the *Derfflinger*, wrote of this part of the action: 'highly depressing, nerve-wracking and exasperating. Our only means of defence was to leave the line for a short time when we saw the enemy had our range ...'[15]

After Jutland the *Admiralstab* pressed for an all-out, unrestricted U-boat campaign against merchant shipping supplying England as the only means of bringing the war to a successful conclusion. The Great General Staff, bogged down on two fronts, supported them. The slow, strangling effect of sea power had been brought home; with a failure of the potato crop added to the effects of the British blockade it seemed that Germany could scarcely stand another winter; food-rationing was already severe; turnips had replaced potatoes on common dinner tables; it was essential to break through to a quick decision with England. And against the pleas of the politicians, who feared the effects on neutral opinion, Wilhelm supported his Service chiefs, and the 'unrestricted' U-boat war was declared. Within a few months it came very close to achieving all that the *Admiralstab* had predicted, but the mobilisation of neutral shipping and particularly the American entry into the war, which the politicians had feared most, finally made success impossible.

Meanwhile the British blockade bit deeper. The calorie intake of civilian workers dropped to half the amount calculated to keep them at a productive level, and by the summer of 1917 to a third—a bare 1,100 calories a day.[16] The wounded soldiers and shore-workers who hovered around the ships of the High Seas Fleet to beg for scraps of turnips from the sailors' more generous but still unsatisfying diet, grew more numerous. Officers, who suffered relatively little from the shortages, sought to stem growing disaffection by harsher punishments, more intensive drill; the germs of revolution bred; whispering enclaves of young sailors exchanged Bolshevik slogans in the idle ammunition chambers.

Finally in October 1918, as the officers ordered the fleet prepared for one last, suicidal engagement with the British to retrieve the honour they felt they had lost while the Army and the U-boat Service fought for the Fatherland, mutiny flared in the open; stokers refused to feed the boilers, petty officers were locked in their cabins, sailors rampaged around Wilhelmshaven, Imperial ensigns were replaced by the Red Flag. And the ships remained in harbour.

When they finally sailed out to meet the British it was after the Armistice had been concluded; the light-grey Dreadnoughts for which Tirpitz had laboured steamed with guns trained fore and aft between two columns of the Grand Fleet to internment in Scapa Flow; the following year their skeleton crews scuttled them as a belated act of defiance.

So ended the *Tirpitz Traum.*

Neither Wilhelm nor Tirpitz learned anything from disaster. Both wrote books of reminiscences after the war which might have been written in 1914, repeating and exaggerating the lies, evading the issues which had brought them and the whole civilised world the most evil harvest. The four years' sacrifice of blood and treasure might never have happened; their own part in untold human waste and misery might have been blameless; not they but England had fashioned Armageddon. Their pages, open to all to read provide a more revealing exposé of moral and intellectual poverty than the most eloquent indictment.

For Tirpitz the *causa remota* of the war was English commercial jealousy—an argument which English Liberals and an odd combination of American savants and naval men found so attractive that, despite conclusive evidence to the contrary, it is *still* well regarded.* The immediate cause of the outbreak of war was, in Tirpitz's view, the stupidity of Bethmann Hollweg. The High Seas Fleet served no useful purpose because of the stupidity of the *Admiralstab* and the timidity of successive Commanders-in-Chief; nearly always in history, Tirpitz insisted, smaller fleets had beaten larger ones. It was a remarkably selective approach to history, worthy of his great master, Treitschke, and even if the few obvious examples are accepted, left out a vital qualification—*if* the smaller

---

* On this question here are the comments of Prince Lichnowsky, German Ambassador to London during the two years prior to the outbreak of war: 'What has Great Britain to gain from a war with us? The destruction of our *trade?* British trade itself depends to a large extent on ours. In 1913 the value of British imports from Germany amounted to £80½ million, British exports to Germany £59½ million. Great Britain's trade with us exceeds that with any other European country, and if the U.S. and the British colonies are excluded, it holds first place in the *total* British exchange of goods. Furthermore, the British market needs certain German products ...' The full memorandum by Lichnowsky on the outbreak of war can be read in John Röhl's admirable book '*1914: Delusion or Design?*'[17]

fleets had the technical and moral ascendency, as Jervis's, Howe's, Nelson's or Togo's had. If, like Tirpitz's fleet, they appeared to be inferior in such a vital department as gun calibre, and lacked any experience of moral superiority there was little chance of them being taken into battle against a larger fleet, let alone winning.

Tirpitz had not only been outbuilt, but out-thought and out-designed. As the challenger, his part was to build the new type, the *Dreadnought* first, then to keep the technological lead with successively more offensive designs and more sophisticated fire control so that his inevitably fewer ships might hold the long-range advantage over many more obsolete enemy and annihilate them. Yet he allowed Fisher the initial advantage and was forced thereafter to follow in his tempestuous wake, never catching up, let alone overtaking. And although his position *vis-à-vis* the British break-water across all his exits to the oceans demanded an offensive strategy and offensive tactics—to which he paid constant lip-service —all his ships were designed defensively with more weight to armour than guns or speed. It was quite as meaningless to build *weaker* ships as it was to build a *weaker* fleet. He did both with consummate, totally misplaced skill. The *Admiralstab* did nothing with the fleet because there was nothing for it to do save be beaten or wait for peace. The material results of the Battle of Jutland tended to obscure this, and were used thus by Tirpitz. Yet the major British losses, none of which were battleships, were all caused by magazine explosion—subsequently guarded against—and occurred before the main battle fleets engaged. When they did come together Jellicoe's masterly deployment and his gun-weight, fire control and numerical advantages left Scheer in no doubt about the result unless he could disengage—which he did as rapidly as possible. In the brief main fleet actions the score of hits on major units in the line of battle was in the order of 70-17 in Jellicoe's favour.[18]

It is true that German night-fighting techniques proved immensely superior to the British during the brief night actions, true also that during the first months of the war only a portion of the British fleet had Percy Scott's director firing system while all the German ships had a partial director firing system, which would have given them an advantage. But none of this was permanent; by 1916 the entire Grand Fleet was fitted for director firing, and an action fought in anything but the calm conditions at Jutland must have proved its immense advantages over the low gunlayers' sights of the

German ships. After Jutland, British night-fighting techniques, magazine protection, shell penetration and other disappointing features which had emerged in the battle were taken in hand so that by 1918 the Grand Fleet's effective power was double its 1916 level. Meanwhile British ship construction had increased, while German construction on major units had slowed almost to a halt as the Army and the U-boat Service gained the priority.

For all these reasons it is difficult to imagine the German fleet, under the most favourable circumstances and the most aggressive Commander-in-Chief doing more than win the first battle or the first few battles in a campaign they could never have brought to a successful conclusion. And even one victory may be thought doubtful against the weight of metal and the calibre of Commander-in-Chief they were up against.

As for the High Seas Fleet's frequently quoted effect as a 'Fleet in being' which denied the British access to the Baltic or to the German U-boat bases, this is fallacy. Jellicoe would have been delighted to enter the Baltic if he had thought there was a chance of meeting and beating the High Seas Fleet there; what he dared not risk were the U-boats, torpedo boats and minefields with which the *Admiralstab* could have made his passage of the Belts too costly. Again it was not the High Seas Fleet which caused Jellicoe to declare the south-eastern portion of the North Sea out of bounds to his battle fleet, but the unseen threat of submarine and minefield, and by night destroyer attack. In the Mediterranean it was submarines that thrust back the French battle fleet from the Adriatic, *one* German submarine that caused the recall of the new *Queen Elizabeth* from the Dardanelles and dispersed the rest of the bombarding battleships.

Tirpitz's fleet was not only useless, but quite as counter-productive in the stress of war—diverting scarce resources from more potent arms and breeding disaffection and finally mutiny—as it was the diplomatic tussle leading up to the war, when it first alerted the British, then forced them into the opposing camp. His mistake was not to *start* the fleet programme—in all the circumstances of 1897 that was inevitable and correct—but to continue it long past the point of military or diplomatic effectiveness or economic sanity. With his eyes fixed on a far distant goal ahead and his mind immersed in erroneous 'lessons' from one brief and inappropriate period of Britain's naval past, he swathed his straight path with

343

guile, lies and a stupendous disregard for a gale of diplomatic and technological change blowing outside the walls of his office.

His goal was unattainable. Had the politicians he despised granted him the six years he wanted he would not have caught up with the British let alone the *Entente* and Japanese alliance navies; had they granted him twenty, twenty-five years his battleships would have been obsolescent before the challenge from aircraft and more effective submarines. His 'Plan' provides an object lesson in the perils of a doctrinaire approach. Churchill thought him a stubborn, purblind old Prussian; there is no more to be said.

But he cannot bear the blame for the German disaster; that must lie with Wilhelm who appointed him and, guided by his own adolescent vanity, supported him and the battle fleet against all political, economic and military arguments. Wilhelm *was* the German disaster. That is not to say there were no other powerful ingredients, nor to deny that he was a product of his time and station. He was also himself—inadequate, incapable and so devoid of analytical or critical reasoning power that he was never more than a sounding board for received ideas and impressions. So he could never outgrow his time or his station—only bring them down to his own puerile, incompetent level. And he did.

Invested with supreme power, yet lacking the most elementary judgement of men, he appointed second-rate officials to head his government and Service departments. Exceptions like Bülow he retained so long as their flattery pleased him; those, like Count Metternich or Prince Lichnowsky who told him unpleasant things he disregarded and finally sacked. His judgement of events was as childish; he saw Germany's future not in terms of the choices open to her, but as *he* wanted it to be. And if this were not sufficient burden for his Ministers and Service chiefs, what he wanted changed according to his most recent impressions. The only thing to which he remained constant was his fleet.

Knowing only what *he* wanted, and reaching out for it greedily like a child without thought to others' reactions, then blaming them for the consequences of his thoughtlessness, he tried to lead Germany towards the world power and equal recognition with England's world Empire which he craved above all else, along several diverging paths at once. His Chancellors took one road, his Foreign Office others, his Army another, and his Navy the most dangerous of all while he strutted and postured, now before this column, now before that, proclaiming peaceable intentions one moment, showing his 'mailed fist' the next, writing fulsomely to 'Dear Nicky' while telling the English that the Russian Tsar was only fit to grow turnips, making up to the English while writing to 'Nicky' of their perfidy and giving the Russian Ambassador to believe that Germany would support Russian anti-British policy in India and the East—a pathological intriguer without purpose or consistency weaving an idiot web over Europe.

In the absence of rational leadership, the Army took over the leading role—which it had always assumed in any case. Some time at the end of 1912 or beginning of 1913 the Chancellor and the Foreign Office fell into step behind the Army and Wilhelm fell in behind them all, still making encouraging noises to Tirpitz and the *Admiralstab* as their separate paths took them further and further from the main body, vaguely disappointed that no one else bothered to notice them at all.

In the summer of 1914 the Army reached the position from which it intended to launch the assault to gain the Continent for themselves—and Germanism. But Tirpitz, way out on the wing, had found other enemies, and although he couldn't help the Army in its battles—indeed his large following had denied them the small extra margin of superiority which would have ensured easy victory —*they* had to face his enemy, then other powerful enemies which the naval enemy called in from time to time.

How easily—without Wilhelm—Germany could have achieved her destiny, either in peace with her irresistible economic development, or by the sword in easy stages.

As for England, she awoke in time. Despite those liberals and pacifists who insisted against all evidence that militaristic chauvinism could be *talked* away around a table by rational men of goodwill, and who accused those Englishmen who tried to rouse the country to its danger of the very war-mongering they were warning *against*—despite all this there were more than enough men of sound sense in positions of power.

And the Liberal government, despite being handicapped by its quota of Utopians, played a splendidly realistic hand. They first reduced naval construction when it was quite safe to do so, hoping that Wilhelm and Tirpitz might follow suit; but when this only spurred the Germans to greater efforts, the Liberals went ahead with naval programmes aimed to deter, and were so successful that, on the evidence from within Germany, they *should have deterred* if rational men had been assessing Germany's chances.

Unfortunately Wilhelm and his politicians deceived themselves about England's resolve, while the military, who had no judgement, gave the Liberal government just the excuse it needed to come in in time.

There was no British failure—save from those who encouraged German ambition by preaching peace as a higher value than integrity or self-preservation. Both in diplomacy and naval strategy the Liberals ran rings around Wilhelm's second eleven of *Real* politicians. One can only marvel at a golden age which could harness such diverse giants as Sir Edward Grey, Winston Churchill and Lloyd George, at a Navy which after a century of undisputed superiority could find such energy and such genius to adapt itself to new challenges, and at an Empire which could provide simultaneously the beginnings of a welfare state and the greatest Navy as an instrument for world peace.

Bibliography, References, Notes

Author, full title and publisher are given in small capitals the first time they appear, thereafter only author—or author and a shortened version of title if more than one work by the same author has been referenced—followed in brackets by the chapter in which the first reference appears. The references in small capitals, therefore, represent a *select* bibliography of the sources used; it is by no means a comprehensive bibliography of the vast and growing number of works on the naval rivalry, Anglo-German relations and the outbreak of World War; that would take a small book of its own. Where page numbers are missing it is usually because I have read the book or article in draft or proof prior to publication.

Abbreviations:

P.R.O.: Public Record Office, London

Nav. Lib.: Minister of Defence (Navy) Library, London

B.D.: Gooch and Temperley; *British Documents on the Origins of the War*; H.M.S.O. 1926-38

G.P.: Lepsius and others; *Die Grosse Politik der europäischen Kabinette*; Berlin 1922-7

Fear God: A. J. MARDER; *Fear God and Dread Nought: the correspondence of Admiral of the Fleet Lord Fisher of Kilverstone*; Cape 1952-9

Adty.; Admiralty, Whitehall

1st. Ld.; First Lord of the Admiralty

D.N.I.; Director of Naval Intelligence; Admiralty

N.I.D.; Naval Intelligence Division; Admiralty

D.N.O.; Director of Naval Ordnance; Admiralty

CHAPTER 1

1   B. v. BÜLOW; *Imperial Germany*; Cassell, 1914, 270
2   A. DORPALEN; *Heinrich von Treitschke*; Yale U.P. 1957, 232
3   P. ANDERSON; *Anti-English feeling in Germany, 1890-1902*; American U.P. 1939, 195
4   Dorpalen, 150; see also 234
5   ibid, 149
6   ibid, 145
7   H. SCHWARZ; *Russia and China*; Horizon, Vol. X, 1968, 1, 15
8   R. KIPLING; 'The White Man's Burden' from *The Five Nations*, London, 1903
9   A Biologist; *A Biological View of Foreign Policy*; *Saturday Review*; Feb. 1, 1896, 118-9
10 ibid
11 ibid
12 ibid
13 G. W. STEEVENS; *Under the Iron Heel*; Daily Mail, Sept. 24, 1897
14 T. R. PHILLIPS; *The Roots of Strategy*; Bodley Head, 1943 citing Frederick the Great's 'Military Instructions for Generals', 1741
15 V. R. BERGHAHN; *Germany and the Approach of War in 1914*; Macmillan, 1973
16 G. W. STEEVENS (1); Oct. 1, 1897
17 See G. MASUR; *Imperial Berlin*: Routledge & Kegan Paul, 1971
18 G. W. STEEVENS (1); Oct. 5, 1897
19 L. CECIL; ALBERT BALLIN: Princeton U.P., 1967, 110
20 B. v. BÜLOW; *Imperial* (1), 180. For detailed analysis and confirmation by a *Socialist*, see Angst to Tyrrell, March 14, 1915; P.R.O. FO 8000 104, pp 278-86
21 H. U. WEHLER; *Bismarck's Imperialism, 1862-1890*; *Past & Present*, 48, Aug. 1970, 152
22 B. v. BÜLOW; *Imperial* (1), 198
23 G. W. Steevens (1); Sept. 27, 1897
24 R. FULFORD (ed); *Your Dear Letter*; Evans 1971, p. 112 citing Crown Princess to Queen Victoria, Dec. 10, 1866
25 ibid, Jan. 30, 1871

26 ibid. Queen Victoria to Crown Princess, Jan. 27, 1865
27 R. FULFORD; *Dearest Mama*; Evans 1968; Crown Princess to Queen Victoria Apr. 28, 1863, describing the apparatus of torture for 'Willy'
28 Fulford; *Letter* (1) Crown Princess to Queen Victoria; Dec. 10, 1866
29 T. ARONSON; *The Kaisers*; Bobbs-Merrill, N.Y., 1971, 176-7
30 B. v. BÜLOW; *Memoirs 1897-1903*; Putnam 1931, 231-2, citing Wilhelm II to Crown Princess
31 See A. HURD; *The German Fleet*: Hodder, 1915 and A. Hurd; *The Kaiser's Dream of Sea Power*; Nineteenth Century & After, Aug. 1906, pp 215*ff*
32 G. W. Steevens (1) Oct. 11, 1897

CHAPTER 2

Tirpitz's character, appearance and career chiefly from:
J. STEINBERG; *Yesterday's Deterrent*; Macdonald 1965
A. VON TIRPITZ; *My memoirs*; Hurst & Blackett, 1919
B. VON BÜLOW; *Memoirs 1897-03* (1)
British naval attaché report 'Grand Admiral v. Tirpitz,' July 16, 1912; Nav. Lib. Ca 2053
A. V. TROTHA; *Gross Admiral von Tirpitz*; Breslau (hagiography!)
EX-KAISER Wilhelm II; *My Memoirs 1878-1918*; Cassell 1922
A. Hurd; *The German Fleet* (1)
J. MIDDLETON; *Tirpitz the Eternal*; The World's Work (U.S.) 1915 pp 642*ff*
D. WOODWARD; *Admiral Tirpitz*; History Today, Aug. 1963 pp 548*ff*
V. R. BERGHAHN: *Der Tirpitz Plan*; Droste, Düsseldorf 1971 (in conversation with author)
Paul M. Kennedy (in conversation with author and numerous articles listed below)

1 B. v. BÜLOW; *Memoirs 1897-1903* (1)
2 ibid, 65
3 See Steinberg; *Deterrent* (2)
4 Adml. Knorr minute on Tirpitz, cited W. Hubatsch; *Die Kulminationspunkt der deutsche Marinepolitik* ...; Historische

Zeitschrift CCXXVII (1953) 293, transl. M. BALFOUR; *The Kaiser and his Times*; Cresset, 1964, 203

5   See Steinberg; *Deterrent* (2), 79ff
6   ibid, 69
7   ibid, 67, citing v. Stosch memo. 1883
8   ibid, 66
9   Tirpitz: *Memoirs* (2), Vol. 1, 111
10 ibid, 60-1, dated Dec. 21, 1895
11 ibid, 62, dated Feb. 2, 1896
12 ibid, 63-4, dated Feb. 13, 1896
13 SEE PAUL KENNEDY; *Tirpitz, England and the Second Navy Law of 1900; Militärgeschichtliche Mitteilungen* 2, 1970 for fascinating evidence of Wilhelm's and Tirpitz's grand design from the very beginning.
14 Br. Naval Attaché (2)
15 See J. STEINBERG; *The Copenhagen Complex; Journal of Contemporary History*; Vol. 1, 3, 1966, 23ff.
    P. KENNEDY; *German World Policy and the Alliance Negotiations with England 1897-1900; The Journal of Modern History*, Dec., 1973
    P. KENNEDY; *Maritime Strategieprobleme der deutsche-englischen Flottenrivalität; Marine und Marinepolitik im kaiserlichen Deutschland, 1871-1914*: Droste, Düsseldorf 1972 pp 178ff
    P. J. KELLY; *The Naval Policy of Imperial Germany*; Ph.D. diss: (unpublished) Georgetown University 1970 (Thesis 3704)
    B. v. Bülow; *Memoirs* (1)
16 See Kennedy; *2nd Navy Law* (2)
17 Steinberg; *Deterrent*, 90-1, citing Senden's diary Feb. 13, 1896
18 ibid, 117 citing Holstein to Germ. Amb., London, Apr. 14, 1897
19 ibid, 116, citing Holstein to Bülow, Apr. 3, 1897
20 ibid, Appendix
21 A. v. TIRPITZ; *Politische Dokumente der Aufbau der deutschen Weltmacht*: Berlin 1924, 1, 136, cited Kennedy; *Strategieprobleme* (2)
22 A. v. Tirpitz; *Memoirs* (2), 1, 96
23 SIR CHARLES WALKER; *Thirty-six Years at the Admiralty*; London 1933, 12

24 J. A. Fisher, quoted A. J. MARDER; *British Naval Policy*, 1880-1905; Putnam, 1941, 176
25 Memo; Adml. F. Richards, 1893; P.R.O. ADM 116 878
26 Memo; Adml. F. Richards Nov. 1895 *idem*. See also Marder; *Naval Policy* (2), 176
27 Marder; *Naval Policy* (2), 263
28 *The Times* naval correspondent, June 28, 1897
29 another correspondent *idem*
30 naval correspondent *idem*
31 ibid

CHAPTER 3

1 Bülow; *Memoirs* (1), 3
2 Wilhelm II to Pr. Eulenburg, Aug. 20, 1897, *idem* 135
3 Tirpitz: *Memoirs* (2) 1, 96
4 Steinberg; *Deterrent* (2), 145 citing Begründung (or reasoned explanation) of Navy Bill.
5 P. Anderson (1) 204
6 Bülow; *Memoirs* (1) 133-5, citing Wilhelm II to Pr. Eulenburg Aug. 20, 1897
7 Kelly (2) 102, citing Capelle to Lieber, Oct. 24 1897
8 Bülow; *Memoirs* (1), 7
9 Kelly (2) 103
10 Bülow; *Memoirs* (1) 135-6
11 ibid, 109; see also 53ff
12 ibid, 113
13 See Steinberg; *Deterrent*, 164
14 For analysis of debate, see ibid 162ff
15 ibid 171 quoting Lucanus to Wilhelm II Dec. 7, 1897
16 ibid 184
17 ibid 185
18 ibid 194, quoting Richter
19 ibid 195, quoting Bebel
20 ibid 196, quoting Tirpitz to Wilhelm II March 26, 1898
21 See Marder; *Naval Policy*, (2) 291
22 ibid, 299

CHAPTER 4

1   See Kennedy; 2nd Navy Law (2) 36
2   See Kelly (2) 123-6 and Berghahn: Approach of War (1)
3   The Navy League Journal, No. 1. July 1895
4   Saturday Review, London, Sept. 11, 1897
5   See O. J. HALE; Publicity and Diplomacy: Appleton-Century
    1940 163ff: 'there is something almost pathological in the
    manner in which (German) journalists portrayed Germany
    as the single honest nation surrounded by thieves ...'
6   See Kelly (2) 127
7   Kennedy; German World Policy (2)
8   ibid
9   Kelly (2) 139ff
10 Kennedy; Strategieprobleme (2)
11 Kelly (2) 142
12 Bülow; Memoirs (1), 280
13 Kennedy; German World Policy (2)
14 The Peace Conference 1898-1900 (Adty. papers) P.R.O. ADM
    116/98
15 Bülow; Memoirs, (1) 223
16 ibid 233
17 As reference 14 above
18 ibid
19 Marder; Naval Policy (2), 346
20 Balfour (2) 215, citing GP XIV 4351
21 Fisher to ? Feb. 22, 1905; Fear God, 2, 51
22 R. H. BACON; The Life of Lord Fisher of Kilverstone; Hodder
    1929, 1, 115
23 ibid, 121-2
24 Marder; Naval Policy (2) 347-8, citing Col à Court
25 Fisher to Ld. Selbourne Dec. 1, 1900; Fear God 1, 168
26 Kennedy; Strategieprobleme, citing Tirpitz to Büchsel, July
    29, 1899
27 ibid, citing Tirpitz, Denkschrift zum Immediatvortrag, Sept.
    28, 1899
28 Bacon; Fisher (4) 1, 170
29 Tirpitz; Memoirs (2) 1, 157
30 For detailed analysis of this internal goal see V. R. Berghahn;
    Der Tirpitz Plan (2), and in summary see J. Steinberg's review

article on this in *Historical Journal* XVI 1 (1973) pp 196 *ff*; see also Berghahn: *Approach of War* (1)

31 Tirpitz; *Memoirs* (2) 1, 117
32 Kennedy; *Strategieprobleme* (2) citing Tirpitz *Denkschrift zum Immediatvortrag*, Sept. 28, 1899
33 Berghahn; *Der Tirpitz Plan* (2) 191
34 Kennedy; *Strategieprobleme*, citing Tirpitz as for ref. 32 above
35 Kelly (2) 163
36 Bülow to F.O. Oct. 31, 1899 cited Hale (4) 208
37 See Hale (4) 201 *ff*
38 Delbrück, Nov. 26, 1899 cited Steinberg; *Copenhagen Complex* (2) 27
39 Tirpitz; *Memoirs* (2) 1, 122
40 Kelly (2) 161
41 Kennedy; *German World Policy* (2), citing Bülow to Richthofen, July 26, 1899
42 Bülow; *Memoirs* (1) 306
43 Kennedy; *German World Policy* (2), citing GP XV 4396
44 Bülow; *Memoirs* (1) 306
45 ibid, 305
46 idem
47 ibid, 332
48 ibid, 353
49 Hale (4) 225
50 Kennedy; *German World Policy*, (2), citing Bülow to Hammann Dec. 31, 1899
51 Cecil (1) 153, citing *Nachrichten* Feb. 27, 1900
52 ibid
53 WILLY BECKER; *Fürst Bülow und England*: Griefswald 1929, 304, cited Kelly (2) 166
54 V. BERGHAHN; *Zu den Zielen des deutschen Flottenbaus ...*; *Historische Zeitschrift*, 1970, 63-4
55 Kennedy; *2nd Navy Law* (2) 36, citing Bülow papers, Vol. 24, draft of speech to Budget Comm. March 27 1900. Paul Kennedy notes that this passage was not reproduced in Bülow's *Denkwürdigkeiten*
56 Metternich, Summer 1900, cited Bülow; *Memoirs* (1) 422
57 Hurd; *German Fleet* (1), Appendix

CHAPTER 5

1   1st. Ld.'s minute Sept. 29, 1901 on D.N.I. memo. Sept. 14,
    1901, cited Marder; *Naval Policy* (2) 463-4
2   Bacon; *Fisher* (4) 1, 133
3   Fisher to Selborne Dec. 19, 1900; *Fear God* 1, 171
4   Bacon; *Fisher* (4) 1, 170
5   ibid, 166
6   ibid, 165
7   ibid, 240, citing J. L. Garvin
8   ibid, 241, citing J. L. Garvin
9   Fisher to Ld. Selborne Dec. 19, 1900; *Fear God* 1, 171
10 Fisher to Beresford Feb. 27, 1902; *Fear God* 1, 231-2
11 Fisher to Roseberry May 10, 1901; *Fear God* 1, 190
12 Kennedy; *Strategieprobleme* (2), citing Souchon Sept. 20, 1902
13 1902 Br. Naval Manoeuvres; Nav. Lib. Eb 06
14 P. Fontin in *Revue Maritime*, Oct. 1902; Nav. Lib. N.I.D.
    Reports 58
15 ibid
16 Tirpitz; *Memoirs* (2) 1, 138
17 Bacon report, May 13, 1903, cited Marder; *Naval Policy* (2),
    363-4
18 GP XVII 4983, cited L. ALBERTINI; (transl. Massey); *The
    Origins of the War of 1914*; O.U.P. 1952, 114
19 A. J. Marder's emphasis; see *Naval Policy* (2) 430
20 Paul Kennedy to author
21 June 1901; see E. L. WOODWARD; *Great Britain and the
    German Navy*; O.U.P. 1935, 49ff
22 June 27, 1900; see Bülow; *Memoirs* (1), 357-8
23 R. KIPLING; *The Rowers*, 1902
24 See Bülow; *Memoirs* (1) 572
25 'Notes on a visit to Kiel and Wilhelmshaven', Aug. 1902;
    P.R.O. ADM 116 940B
26 GP XVII 234
27 Bülow; *Memoirs* (1) 428
28 Fisher to Arnold White Aug. 6 1902; *Fear God*, 1, 259-61
29 See C. ANDREW; *German World Policy* ...; *Journal of Con-
    temporary History*, Vol. 1, 3, (1966) 137ff
30 SYDNEY LEE; *King Edward VII*; Macmillan 1925, 2, 217-8,
    citing Eckardstein; *Ten Years at the Court of St. James*, 230

31 Lee (5) 2 218
32 ibid, 237-8
33 F. PONSONBY; *Recollections of Three Reigns*; Eyre & Spottiswoode 1951, 170
34 Letter to *The Times*, May 10, 1922, cited Lee (5) 2, 238
35 Metternich to Bülow, June 2, 1903; GP XVII, 590, cited Lee (5), 241
36 Mallet to Bertie June 2, 1904 and Bertie to Mallet, June 11, 1904, from Bertie MSS, cited G. MONGER; *The End of Isolation*; Nelson 1963, 100-01
37 Spring-Rice to Roosevelt, 1904, cited Marder; *Naval Policy*, 476
38 B. v. BÜLOW; *Memoirs 1903-1909*; Putnam 1931, 22
39 ibid, 29
40 ibid, 30
41 Berghahn to author
42 Tirpitz; *Memoirs* (2) 1, 129
43 Tirpitz to Pr. Henry May 6, 1904, cited Kelly (2), 232
44 Note by R. Arbuthnot of an interview with Fisher, Jan. 6, 1904, cited Bacon; *Fisher* (4) 1, 249
45 P. KEMP; *The Fisher Papers*; Navy Records Society, 25, citing Fisher's Oct. 20, 1904 memo. for Ld. Selborne
46 ibid. For genesis of this idea and 'The Scheme' generally see Fisher memo. 'High Speed for Battleships' May 1904; P.R.O. ADM 116/942

CHAPTER 6

1 Bacon; *Fisher* (4) 2, 2
2 ibid 1, 240
3 Kemp (5) 17*ff*
4 Steinberg; *Copenhagen* (2), 31
5 ibid
6 Oct. 28, 30? 1904; A. J. MARDER; *From the Dreadnought to Scapa Flow*; O.U.P. 1961, Vol. 1, 111
7 J. STEINBERG; *Germany and the Russo-Japanese War*; American Historical Review, Dec. 1970, p 1978 citing Wilhelm II to Bülow Nov. 1, 1904 GP XIX, i, 6110
8 Tirpitz to Richthofen, Nov. 1, 1904, cited Steinberg; *Copenhagen* (2), 34

9 Nov. 1, 1904; *Fear God* 2, 47
10 Metternich to Bülow, Nov. 1, 1904; GP XIX 6111, cited Steinberg; *Russo-Japanese War* (6) p. 1978
11 Selborne to Balfour Nov. 26, 1904, cited G. Monger (5) 176
12 *Vanity Fair*, London Nov. 10, 1904
13 *Army & Navy Gazette*, London Nov. 12, 1904
14 *Vanity Fair*, London, Nov. 17, 1904
15 Wilhelm II marginalia on Naval Attaché report Nov. 17, 1904, cited Steinberg; *Copenhagen* (2) 34
16 See PAUL KENNEDY; *The Development of German Naval Operations Plans against England, 1896-1914*; English Historical Review, Oct. 1973
17 ibid
18 Berghahn; *Approach of War* (1)
19 Tirpitz's note Dec. 20, 1904 on Heeringen's memo. Dec. 14, 1904, cited Steinberg; *Russo-Japanese War* (6), p. 1980
20 Arthur Lee's speech Feb. 3, 1905, cited Woodward (5) 94-5
21 Wilhelm 2 to Tirpitz, Feb. 1905; cited Steinberg; *Copenhagen* (2), 39
22 See Kelly (2) 244ff
23 See ibid, 248ff
24 Müller to Tirpitz, Feb. 8, 1905; Tirpitz; *Aufbau* (2) 1, 15, cited Woodward (5) 112-3
25 Edward VII to Lansdowne Apr. 15, 1905, cited Lee (5) 340
26 Fisher to Lansdowne Apr. 22, 1905; *Fear God* 2, 55
27 Mallet to Bertie Apr. 24, 1905; Monger (5) 189
28 Lansdowne to Balfour Apr. 23, 1905; cited ibid, 190
29 ibid
30 Balfour to Edward VII June 8, 1905, cited Lee (5) 344
31 GP XXI 7082, cited Balfour (2) 246
32 D.N.I. memo on combined naval and military operations, July 1905; P.R.O. ADM 116/866B
33 Berghahn; *Der Tirpitz Plan* (2) 494
34 P-C. WITT; *Die Finanzpolitik des deutschen Reiches ...*; Mathieson (Lübeck) 1972, 141
35 Berghahn; *Approach of War* (1)
36 See Tirpitz; *Aufbau* (2) 20ff
37 To J. Corbett, July 28, 1905; *Fear God*, 2, 63
38 E. H. Moorhouse, quoted Bacon; *Fisher* (4) 1, 241
39 See A. HURD; *Who Goes There?*; Hutchinson 1941, 74-5

40 Tirpitz; *Aufbau* (2), cited Kelly 273
41 *British Naval Policy and Aspirations; Fortnightly Review,* London, Sept. 1905
42 War Office Intelligence Division memo March 20, 1906, cited Monger (6) 282
43 Grey to Spring-Rice, Feb. 19, 1906; BD 111, 299, cited Monger (6) 281
44 *The Times*, Apr. 23, 1906, cited Woodward (5) 106
45 To Capt. Fortescue, Apr. 14, 1906; *Fear God* 2, 71
46 Witt (6) 143

CHAPTER 7

1 Campbell-Bannerman speech, Glasgow, Jan. 1907, quoted J. A. SPENDER; *The Life of the Rt. Hon. Henry Campbell-Bannerman*; Hodder, 321
2 Marder; *Dreadnought* (6) 1, 127
3 *The Times*, May 10, 1906
4 R. CUSTANCE; *The Ship of the Line in Battle*; Blackwoods, 1912
5 A. T. MAHAN analysing Tsushima; *U.S.N. Inst. Proceedings,* June 1906
6 Naval Attachés Reports on Russo-Japanese War, Vol. 1, 167; Nav. Lib.
7 See P. PADFIELD; *The Battleship Era*; Hart-Davis 1972
8 To Ld. Spencer March 28, 1902; *Fear God* 1, 237-8
9 ibid
10 Bacon to Fisher Apr. 12, 1906; *Fear God* 2, 72
11 Fisher to Tweedmouth Apr. 24, 1906; *Fear God* 2, 79
12 Esher to Fisher Oct. 21, 1906, cited M. V. BRETT (ed); *Journals & Letters of Reginald Viscount Esher*; Nicholson & Watson 1934, 2, 198
13 Dec. 21, 1906, cited ibid 2, 209
14 Garvin to Bacon, cited Marder; *Dreadnought* (6) 1, 86
15 Fisher to G. Lambert Jan. 21, 1907; *Fear God* 2, 116
16 To Arnold White, Jan. 19, 1907; *Fear God* 2, 115
17 Remarks on War Plans by Adml. of Fleet Sir A. Wilson, cited Kemp (5) 454
18 Fisher's marginal comments on above

19 Kemp (5) 337ff
20 Oct. 23, 1906; *Fear God* 2, 102-3
21 To Knollys May 21, 1907, cited GEOFFREY BENNETT; *Charlie B*; Dawnay 1968 286-7
22 Fisher memo; 'War Arrangements' cited Kemp (5) 465
23 Transcript meeting between Tweedmouth, Fisher, Beresford; Adty; July 5, 1907; P.R.O. ADM 116 3108
24 cited PETER PADFIELD; *Aim Straight*; Hodder 1966, 161
25 *The Times* May 10, 1907
26 *Nation*, March 2, 1907, cited Spender; *Campbell-Bannerman* (7) 328
27 Dumas to Lascelles Jan. 9, 1907; Nav. Lib. Ca 2053
28 Memo; 'Limitation of Naval Armaments and size of battleships', Adty. Jan. 29, 1907; P.R.O. ADM 116 866B
29 ibid
30 As reference 27 above
31 Bülow in *Reichstag* Nov. 14, 1906, cited Hale (4) 290
32 Bülow; *Memoirs* (5) 254
33 cited Lee (5) 2, 540
34 E. GREY; *Twenty Five Years*; Hodders 1925, 203
35 See Grey's instructions to Br. delegates to Hague; BD VIII, 228
36 Grey's speech Aug. 1, 1907, cited Woodward (5) 133-4
37 reported *The Times* May 1, 1907
38 T. WOLFF; *Das Vorspeil*; Munich 1924, 233 cited Albertini (5) 1, 187
39 Marschall to Bülow Oct. 28, 1907; GP XXIII, i, 282ff
40 Sir Edw. Fry at Hague Conf; *The Times* Aug. 19, 1907
41 As ref. 39, cited Kelly (2) 309
42 Lord Reay; BD VIII 299-300, cited Woodward (5) 139
43 See Anderson (1) 165
44 P-C Witt (6) 140, 143
45 Därnhardt to Capelle, Feb. 4, 1907, cited BERGHAHN; *Der Tirpitz Plan und die Krisis des preussisch-deutschen Herrschaftssystems; Marine und Marinepolitik*; Droste, 1972, 102
46 See Kelly (2) 319ff
47 Tirpitz marginalia on Hollmann's *Denkschrift* June 1897, cited Steinberg; *Deterrent* (2) 132
48 Berghahn; *Tirpitz Plan und Krisis* (7) 102, also Kelly (2) 102-3
49 See Kelly (2) 332

CHAPTER 8

1   Wilhelm II to Edward VII June 20, 1907, cited Lee (5) 2, 536
2   Beresford to Adty. Nov. 12, 1907; P.R.O. ADM 116 3108
3   *Daily Express* Nov. 11, 1907
4   *Good Hope's* signal log as detailed in Beresford to Adty. Nov. 8, 1907; Carson Papers, Belfast
5   See Bennett; *Charlie B* (7) 290ff and Padfield; *Aim Straight* (7) 163ff
6   *Standard*, Nov. 11, 1907
7   Adty. to Beresford Nov. 13, 1907; Carson Papers, Belfast
8   Wilhelm II speech Nov. 12, 1907, cited Lee (5) 2, 558
9   Wilhelm II speech Nov. 13, 1907, *The Times*
10 ibid
11 cited *The Times* Nov. 14, 1907
12 ibid Nov. 15, 1907
13 ibid, citing *Journal*
14 ibid
15 *Daily Mail* Nov. 25, 1907
16 cited *The Times* Nov. 22, 1907
17 Wilhelm's 'Interview' with Col. Stuart-Wortley, *Daily Telegraph* Oct. 28, 1908
18 Sea Ld.s report to 1st Ld., Dec. 3, 1907, cited Marder; *Dreadnought* (6), 1, 137
19 Fisher to Cawdor, Nov. 25, 1907; *Fear God*, 2, 151
20 To Sir Edward Carson Jan. 21, 1908; Carson Papers, Belfast
21 To Sir Arthur Balfour March 7, 1908. Balfour Papers, Brit. Museum
22 Fisher to Grey Jan. 23, 1908; *Fear God*, 2, 155
23 Beresford to Balfour, March 7, 1908; Balfour Papers, Brit. Museum
24 Fisher to Tweedmouth Jan. 23, 1908; *Fear God*, 2, 158
25 Fisher to Esher Jan. 19, 1908; *Fear God*, 2, 155
26 Fisher to Spender Feb. 10, 1908; Spender Papers, Brit. Museum
27 *The Times* reports of debate, Jan. 14, 1908
28 cited in J. E. SUTTON; *The Imperial Navy*, 1910-1914; Doctoral diss:, Indiana University, 1953 (unpublished), p. 308
29 ibid, 301
30 *The Times* Jan. 14, 1908
31 ibid

32 Dumas report on Tirpitz Feb. 3, 1908; Nav. Lib. Ca 2053
33 Wilhelm II to Tweedmouth Feb. 14, 1908; Asquith Papers, Box 19, Oxford
34 Feb. 14, 1908, cited Lee (5) 2, 606
35 Esher Journal Feb. 19, 1908; Brett (7) 2, 285
36 cited Marder; *Dreadnought* (6) 1, 141
37 *The People* Jan. 12, 1908
38 M. Macdonald reported *The Times* March 3, 1908
39 ibid
40 Adty. memo on limitation of armaments Jan. 29, 1907; P.R.O. ADM 116 866B
41 *The Times* March 11, 1908
42 Esher Journal March 14, 1908; Brett (7) 2, 295
43 ibid, 2, 294; March 7, 1908
44 Metternich to Bülow March 8, 1908; GP XXIV 44-6, cited Woodward 168*ff*
45 ibid
46 March 28, 1908; *Fear God* 2, 170
47 Bacon; *Fisher* (4) 2, 75
48 Hardinge to Grey June 1908, cited Grey (7) 210*ff*
49 ibid
50 ibid
51 ibid
52 To McKenna June 12, 1908; *Fear God* 2, 182
53 ibid
54 Duchess Olga to Fisher June 17, 1908; *Fear God* 2, 183
55 June 14, 1908, cited Hale (4) 310
56 Metternich to Bülow, June 25, 1908; GP XXV ii, 479
57 Metternich to Bülow, July 16, 1908; GP XXIV, 99
58 ibid
59 ibid, 103
60 See Kelly (2) 349-50
61 Grey memo for Edward VII Aug. 6, 1908, cited Lee (5) 2, 616-7
62 Esher Journal Sept. 27, 1908; Brett (7) 2, 344
63 Bülow; *Memoirs* (5) 312-3
64 ibid
65 See Ponsonby (5) 245
66 Col. Trench despatch enclosed in Lascelles to Grey Aug. 21, 1908; P.R.O. ADM 116 940B

67 Dumas to Lascelles Aug. 6, 1908; P.R.O. ADM 116 940B

CHAPTER 9

1   Jan. 27, 1908; Carson Papers, Belfast
2   Feb. 2, 1908; idem
3   Memo by McKenna on Beresford affair, May 18 1909 P.R.O.
    ADM 116 3108
4   See Bennett; *Charlie B* (7) and Padfield; *Aim Straight* (7)
    182*ff*
5   *The Times* July 8, 1908
6   ibid, July 9, 1908
7   ibid
8   ibid
9   July 28, 1908; *Fear God* 2, 184
10 Padfield; *Aim Straight* (7) 188
11 Fisher to Esher Sept. 8, 1908; last two sentences Fisher to
    Arnold White, same date; both *Fear God* 2, 193-4
12 Fisher to W. May Sept. 28, 1908; *Fear God* 2, 196
13 See R. Bacon (D.N.O.) evidence before Royal Armaments
    Commn. 1935, cited P. NOEL-BAKER; *The Private Manu-
    facture of Armaments*; Gollancz 1937, 467*ff* and R. BACON;
    From 1900 Onwards; Hutchinson 1940 179*ff*
14 See Bacon; *Fisher* (4) 87
15 Naval Attaché's (Berlin) reports through Nov. 1908; Nav.
    Lib. Ca 2053
16 idem Nov. 16, 1908
17 Bacon's evidence; see note 13 above
18 Dec. 28, 1908; Asquith Papers, Box 21, Oxford
19 Bacon's evidence; see note 13 above
20 *Fear God*, 2, 220
21 Asquith Papers, Box 21, Oxford
22 Nav. Lib. Ca 2053
23 McKenna to Germ. Naval Attaché GP XXVIII 425-6
24 Sea Lds. memo for 1st Ld. Jan. 15? 1909; Marder; *Dread-
    nought* (6) 1, 155
25 R. S. CHURCHILL; *Winston Churchill* 1901-1914; Heinemann
    1967, 516-7
26 Jellicoe memo to McKenna Feb. 24, 1909, A. T. PATTERSON

(ed); *The Jellicoe Papers*; Navy Records Society, 17
27 V. BONHAM-CARTER; *Winston Churchill as I knew him*; Eyre & Spottiswoode 1965, 17
28 1909 speech, cited R. HYAM; *Winston Churchill before 1914*; *Historical Journal* XII (1969) 170
29 See Bonham-Carter (9) 169
30 speech Aug. 17, 1908, cited R. Churchill (9) 511-2
31 Feb. 1909 for Cabinet; Asquith Papers, Box 21, Oxford
32 Fisher to J. L. Garvin Feb. 17, 1909; A. M. GOLLIN; *The Observer and J. L. Garvin*; O.U.P. 1960, 70-2
33 Feb. 10, 1909; *Fear God* 2, 221
34 To Garvin; Gollin (9) 70-1
35 idem
36 Esher Journal Feb. 12, 1909; Brett (7) 2, 370
37 Bonham-Carter (9) 170
38 R. Churchill (9) 517
39 See Bülow *Memoirs* (5) 405
40 See Kelly (2) 356ff
41 See Woodward (5) 200
42 Tirpitz to Bülow Jan. 4, 1909 GP XXVIII, 51
43 ibid, 53
44 See Esher Journal Aug. 21, 1908; Brett (7) 2, 332
45 See Kennedy; *Strategieprobleme* (2)
46 See P-C Witt (6), Table XIV
47 See Kennedy; *2nd Navy Law* (2)
48 P. Anderson (1) 13 footnote
49 Ballin to Harden July 1909, cited Cecil (1) 160
50 Cecil (1) 168
51 Bülow; *Memoirs* (5) 398
52 ibid, 400
53 Esher Journal Nov. 12, 1908; Brett (7) 2, 359
54 Hurd; *German Fleet* (1) 141
55 See Kelly (2) 357ff
56 Bülow; *Memoirs* (5) 407-8
57 Ponsonby (5) 258
58 Feb. 21, 1909, *Fear God* 2, 222-3
59 See Marder; *Dreadnought* (6) 1, 163
60 E. Grey memo on conv. with Fisher March 4, 1909; *Fear God* 2, 227-8
61 Fisher to McKenna March 5, 1909; *Fear God* 2, 229

62 *Hansard* March 16, 1909
63 See Fisher to Garvin March 11, 1909; Gollin (9) 73
64 See Jellicoe's autobiographical notes cited Patterson (9) 12;
    'I had ascertained that the productive capacity of Krupp's
    works considerably exceeded that of our own gun-mounting
    firms.'
65 Esher to MVB March 18, 1909; Brett (7) 2, 377
66 See Gollin (9) 74
67 ibid, 75
68 *The Observer* March 21, 1909
69 5 am March 21, 1909; *Fear God* 2, 233-4
70 Fisher to Arnold White c. March 24, 1909; *Fear God* 2, 235-6
71 Speech March 29, 1909, cited Woodward (5) 230-1
72 Fisher to Davidson March 27, 1909; *Fear God* 2, 236-7
73 March 30, 1909; *Fear God* 2, 238
74 cited Woodward, 235
75 March 10, 1909; *Fear God* 2, 232
76 See Esher Journals March 20, 1909; Brett (7) 2, 378
77 Brit. Naval Attaché report March 30, 1909; Nav. Lib. Ca
    2053
78 idem May 24, 1909
79 See Bülow; *Memoirs* (5) 417-8
80 See Berghahn; *Approach of War* (1); Kelly (2) 357ff; Bülow;
    Memoirs (5) 421ff
81 *Daily Telegraph* Oct. 28, 1908
82 *The Memoirs of the* CROWN PRINCE *of Germany*; Butterworth
    1922, 87
83 See Bülow; *Memoirs* (5) 501ff
84 See Beresford-Balfour correspondence March-July 1909; Bal-
    four Papers, Brit. Museum
85 *The Times* March 25, 1909
86 See Fisher to Ponsonby May 4, 1909; *Fear God* 2, 248
87 Evidence succinctly compressed by Marder; *Dreadnought* (6)
    1, 194ff, but for Beresford's case see Bennett; *Charlie B* (7)
    300ff
88 'Conclusions' of Sub-Ctee Report, Cd. 256
89 to McKenna Aug. 19, 1909; *Fear God* 2, 260
90 Aug. 19, 1909; Gollin (9) 90
91 Aug. 15, 1909; Bacon; *Fisher* (4) 2, 100
92 to Dolphin Society; *The Times* Nov. 15, 1909

93 See Gollin (9) 86
94 Fisher to Arnold White Oct. 12, 1909; *Fear God* 2, 276
95 See Bacon; *Fisher* (4) 2, 106
96 To Arnold White Nov. 13, 1909; *Fear God* 2, 277
97 ibid
98 See Fisher to Garvin May 24, 1909; Gollin (9) 86
99 Brit. Naval Attaché report March 30, 1909; Nav. Lib. Ca 2053
100 See Kelly (2) 381
101 *Crown Prince Memoirs* (9) 68-9

CHAPTER 10

1   See K. H. JARAUSCH; *The Enigmatic Chancellor*; Yale U.P. 1972
2   See P-C Witt (6) Table XIV
3   Ballin's estimate; see Cecil (1) 121
4   *Crown Prince Memoirs* (9) 97
5   Cecil (1) 121
6   Brit. Naval Attaché Report Oct. 11, 1909; Nav. Lib. Ca 2053
7   Nov. 3, 1909, cited W. CHURCHILL; *The World Crisis* 1911-1914: Butterworth 1923, 39
8   American *Review of Reviews* Nov. 1909 607ff
9   Dr Rohrbach cited in 'A Letter from Berlin'; *Fortnightly Review*, London, Jan. 1910
10 ibid
11 *Daily Mail* Dec. 13, 1909
12 Sir Henry Angst to Tyrrell, Oct. 4, 1910; P.R.O. (Grey Papers) FO 800 104, pp 113-7; I am indebted to R. J. Crampton for bringing this fascinating correspondence between Sir Henry Angst, British Consul General in Zurich, and the British Foreign Office to attention; Angst was August Bebel's intermediary during a long clandestine correspondence with the Foreign Office; see R. J. Crampton; *August Bebel and the British Foreign Office*; History, June 1973, pp 218ff
13 *Daily Mail* Dec. 15, 1909
14 *Daily Mail* Dec. 18, 1909
15 Cabinet memo by Grey Nov. 10, 1910; P.R.O. ADM 116 3486

16 ibid
17 Tirpitz; *Aufbau* (2) 184*ff*, cited Kelly 399
18 Minute of Apr. 28, 1911; Marder; *Dreadnought* (6) 1, 227
19 Brit. Naval Attaché Report May 24, 1911; Nav. Lib. Ca 2053
20 Angst to Tyrrell, May 1, 1911; P.R.O. FO 800 104, p. 128
21 idem p. 171 Jan. 2, 1912
22 Esher to Sanders Feb. 7, 1911; Brett (7) 2, 444
23 speech March 13, 1911, cited Woodward (5) 303
24 GP XXVIII 396*ff*, cited Woodward (5) 303
25 May 4, 1911, cited Kelly (2) 402
26 Angst to Tyrrell May 1, 1911; P.R.O. FO 800 104 p. 127
27 idem p. 132 July 15, 1911
28 ibid
29 See Cecil (1) 178 See Berghahn; *Approach of War* (1)
31 July 4, 1911; Grey (7) 222
32 from Riezler diary, cited Jarausch (10)
33 cited W. Churchill; *World Crisis* (10) 47
34 V. Berghahn to author
35 See W. Churchill; *World Crisis* (10) 47
36 See J. RÖHL; *Adml. v. Müller and the approach of War 1911-1914*; *Historical Journal* XII 4 (1969) 653
37 W. LE QUEUX; *The Invasion of 1910*; London, 1906
38 *Fear God* 2, 376
39 Tyrrell to Spring-Rice Aug. 1, 1911; cited R. COSGROVE; *A Note on Lloyd George's speech at the Mansion House ...*; *Historical Journal* XII (1969) 699
40 See LORD RIDDELL; *More Pages from My Diary*: Country Life, 1934, 22
41 W. Churchill; *World Crisis* (10) 52
42 Grey (7) 238
43 Nicolson to Hardinge Aug. 17, 1911, cited Cosgrove (10) 700
44 Bonham-Carter (9) 236
45 Tirpitz to Capelle Aug. 3, 1911; Tirpitz; *Aufbau* (2) 1, 200*ff*, cited Kelly (2) 418
46 Capelle to Tirpitz Aug. 12, 1911; Tirpitz *Aufbau* (2) 1, 203, cited Kelly (2) 419
47 Jarausch (10)
48 BRANDENBURG; *From Bismarck to the World War*, 396, cited Sutton (8) 115
49 *The Times* Aug. 29, 1911

50 Oppenheimer to F.O. Oct. 21, 1911; P.R.O. ADM 116 940B
51 Müller diary Sept. 6, 1911, cited J. Röhl; *Müller* (10) 655
52 idem Sept. 12, 1911
53 ibid
54 Tirpitz to Wilhelm II Sept. 26, 1911; Tirpitz; *Aufbau*, (2) 1, 207, cited Berghahn; *Approach of War*
55 Wilhelm II to Bethmann Sept. 30, 1911; Tirpitz; *Aufbau* (2) 1, 216-8, cited Marder; *Dreadnought* (6) 1, 273
56 Röhl; *Müller* (10) 656
57 Sept. 20, 1911; *Fear God* 2, 286
58 Angst to Tyrrell Dec. 20, 1911; P.R.O. FO 800 104 p. 163
59 idem Jan. 2, 1912, p. 171
60 *Münchener Neueste Nachrichten*, Sept. 28, 1911, cited in Corbett to Grey Sept. 29, 1911; P.R.O. ADM 116 3474
61 ibid
62 ibid
63 See Albertini (5) 334
64 Jarausch (10)

CHAPTER 11

1   Fisher to Leyland Nov. 7, 1911; *Fear God* 2, 411
2   Fisher to Mrs C. Fisher Oct. 31, 1911; *Fear God* 2, 408
3   As for reference 1 above
4   ibid
5   To Arnold White Nov. 1911; *Fear God* 2, 416
6   Dec. 5, 1911; *Fear God* 2, 419
7   To G. Fiennes Dec. 26, 1911; *Fear God* 424
8   To G. Fiennes Feb. 8, 1912; *Fear God* 2, 429
9   Jan. 16, 1912; *Fear God* 2, 425
10 OSCAR PARKES; *British Battleships*: Seeley Service 1966
11 Fisher to Spender Oct. 31, 1911 and Fisher to G. Fiennes Feb. 8, 1912; *Fear God* 2, 409 and 429
12 Patterson (9) 26
13 J. A. SPENDER; *Life, Journalism and Politics*; Cassell 1927, 162
14 ibid 163
15 W. Churchill; *World Crisis* (10) 72
16 Spender; *Journalism/Politics* (11) 163
17 Esher to LB Nov. 23, 1911; Brett (7) 2, 63

18 See Riddell diary Dec. 9, 1911; Riddell (10) 32
19 Oct. 28, 1911 GP XXXI 11, cited Sutton (8) 116
20 W. Churchill; *World Crisis* (10) 53
21 ibid, 95
22 Adty. memo Feb. 3, 1912, cited W. Churchill; *World Crisis* (10) 96
23 Churchill to Grey Jan. 31, 1912; Marder; *Dreadnought* (6) 1, 276
24 Cassel to Ballin Feb. 3, 1912, cited W. Churchill; *World Crisis* (10) 98
25 Müller diary Feb. 7, 1912, cited Röhl; *Müller* (10) 658
26 Haldane to his mother, cited Cecil (1) 187
27 *The Times* Feb. 8, 1912
28 ibid Feb. 9, 1912
29 VISCOUNT HALDANE; *Before the War*; Cassell 1920 59
30 GP XXXI 336
31 *The Times* Feb. 13, 1912
32 ibid
33 *The Times* Feb. 11, 1912
34 *Die Flotte* XV Feb. 2, 1912, cited Sutton (8) 181
35 March 5, 1912; *Fear God* 2, 435-6
36 March 18, 1912
37 March 26, 1912, cited R. Churchill (9) 556
38 Marder; *Dreadnought* (6) 1, 284
39 Wilhelm II to Bethmann Feb. 27, 1912; Tirpitz; *Aufbau* (2) 1, 306-8
40 Bethmann to Wilhelm II March 6, 1912; Tirpitz; *Aufbau* (2) 1, 318
41 Jan. 10, 1912, cited Spender; *Journalism/Politics* 178ff
42 Haussmann writing in *März*, Apr. 1912, cited *The Times* Apr. 8, 1912; his attack in the *Reichstag* was on these lines
43 For the *Flottenverein* propaganda especially see Sutton (8) 181ff; see *The Times* spring and early summer 1912
44 See Sutton (8) 507ff, and Kennedy; *Naval Operations Plans* (6) re. Tirpitz's battle strategy for the fleet
45 ibid
46 *Die Flotte* XV May 5, 1912, cited Sutton (8) 194
47 Brit. Naval Attaché's report Apr. 30, 1912; Nav. Lib. Ca 2053
48 idem July 16, 1912
49 idem July 2, 1912

50 Adty. memo on general naval situation Aug. 26, 1912; Asquith Papers, Box 24, Oxford; this must have been worked up from a July paper as Churchill used similar phrases in a C.I.D. meeting July 11, see Marder; *Dreadnought* (6) 1, 296

51 Haldane; *Before War* (11) 67

52 See Balfour in *Nord und Süd* July 1912, cited Woodward (5) 375*ff*

53 March 22, 1912; R. Churchill (9) 1530

54 ibid

55 July 22, 1912, *The Times*

56 Feb. 19, 1912, cited W. Churchill; *World Crisis* (10) 105

57 Memo to Asquith, Grey July 17, 1912, BD X ii 601

58 Angst to Tyrrell Nov. 23, 1912; P.R.O. FO 800 104 p. 221

59 Dec. 3, 1912; Tirpitz; *Aufbau* (2) 1, 361*ff*, cited Röhl; *Müller* (10) 664

60 Dec. 8, 1912, GP XXXIX 119 note, cited Röhl; *Müller* (10) 664

61 Three separate accounts of this meeting given in full in Röhl; *Müller* (10) 661*ff*; they are from Müller's diary Dec. 8, 1912, Saxon Military Attachés report Dec. 12, 1912, and Bavarian Military Attaché's report Dec. 15, 1912

62 ibid

63 Bonham Carter (9) 262

64 Riddell diary March 31, 1912; Riddell (10) 51

65 W. Churchill; *World Crisis* (10) 120

66 Goschen to Grey Feb. 10, 1913; P.R.O. FO 800 23, cited R. LANGHORNE; *The Naval Question in Anglo-German relations 1912-1914*; *Historical Journal* XIV 2 (1971) 362

67 Grey to Goschen Feb. 15, 1913; idem

68 Angst to Tyrrell Feb. 14, 1913; P.R.O. FO 800 104 p. 230

69 March 26, 1913, cited Woodward (5) 409

70 Brit. Naval Attaché's report June 30, 1913; Nav. Lib. Ca 2053

71 ibid

72 idem Oct. 4, 1913

73 cited Woodward (5) 419

74 See GP XXXIX 51*ff*

75 See Jarausch (10)

76 Angst to Tyrrell Feb. 14, 1913; P.R.O. FO 800 104 p. 232

77 As for note 74

78 See *The Times* Feb. 5, 1914

79 Grey to Goschen Feb. 5, 1914, BD X ii 498, cited Langhorne (11) 367
80 GP XXXIX 77ff
81 Churchill memo 'Navy Estimates', printed for use of Cabinet Dec. 1913 P.R.O. ADM 116 3486
82 See Riddell diary Dec. 13, 1913; Riddell (10) 189-90
83 idem Dec. 18, 1913
84 Dec. 25, 1913, cited R. Churchill (9) 663
85 Churchill memo for Cabinet Jan. 10, 1914; Asquith Papers, cited Marder; *Dreadnought* (6) 1, 322-3; this differs interestingly from W. Churchill's version of the same memo in *World Crisis* (10) 175-7
86 W. Churchill; *World Crisis* (10) 176
87 Riddell diary Jan. 7, 1914; Riddell (10) 196
88 idem Jan. 18, 1914 197
89 idem Jan. 25, 1914 199
90 idem Feb. 1, 1914 201
91 idem Feb. 26, 1914 201
92 *The Times* Feb. 4, 1914
93 Adty. memo 'Requirements of Officers, 1920', Apr. 14, 1914; P.R.O. ADM 116 3486

CHAPTER 12

1 G. VON HASE; *Kiel and Jutland*; Skeffington, 7
2 Brit. Naval Attaché report Jan. 27, 1914; Nav. Lib. Ca 2053
3 v. Hase (12) 20
4 See Sutton (8) 550
5 See Sutton (8) 549
6 Diary Lt. R. Schwerdt, HMS *Lion*, cited W. S. CHALMERS; *The Life and Letters of David Beatty*; Hodder 1951, 128
7 v. Hase (12) 39
8 See FRITZ FISCHER; *Germany's Aims in the First World War*; Chatto & Windus 1967, 37
9 See Pr. Eulenburg to Prof. K. Breysig Sept. 22, 1919, cited in J. RÖHL (ed); *1914: Delusion or Design?*; Elek 1973
10 Jarausch (10)
11 See Pr. Lichnowsky memo Jan. 1915, cited Röhl; *Delusion?* (12) 82-3

12 For all these furious preparations, see V. R. BERGHAHN & W. DEIST; *Kaiserlichen Marine und Kriegsausbruch 1914; Neue Dokumente; Militärgeschichtliche Mitteilungen 1970,* particularly Hopman to Tirpitz July 7, 1914, p. 47

13 Hopman to Tirpitz July 6, 1914 idem 45

14 Tirpitz to Hopman 'beginning' July 1914 idem 46

15 ibid

16 See Sutton (8) 559-60

17 Hopman to Tirpitz July 20, 1914; Berghahn/Deist; *Kaiserlichen Marine* (12) 52

18 idem 53-4

19 Behnke to Jagow July 22, 1914, cited Sutton (8) 561

20 Röhl; *Müller* (10) 669

21 *Hansard* 5th Series IXV 726-9, cited Woodward (5) 478

22 W. Churchill; *World Crisis* (10) 193

23 See Cecil (1) 207

24 See W. Churchill; *World Crisis* (10) 194

25 Goschen to Grey July 29, 1914, cited Grey (7) 325

26 ibid

27 SCHMITT; *The Coming of the War, 1914;* Vol. 1 538, cited D. F. FLEMING; *The Origins and Legacies of World War 1;* Allen & Unwin 1969, 165

28 Lichnowsky to Jagow July 29, 1914, cited MONTGELAS & SCHÜCKING (eds); *Outbreak of World War;* N.Y. 1924, 391-2, cited Sutton (8) 569

29 July 31, 1914, cited Balfour (2) 350-1

30 Müller diary Aug. 1, 1914; Röhl; *Müller* (10) 669

31 See on this *volte face* the analysis of a Swiss Socialist in Angst to Tyrrell March 14, 1915; P.R.O. FO 800 104 pp. 278-86

32 Tirpitz; *Memoirs* (2) 1, 277

33 C. V. USBORNE; *Blast and Counterblast:* Murray 1935, 25

34 to his wife, July 28, 1914, cited R. Churchill (9) 710

35 Grey (7) 2, 14-15

36 Speech in Appendix to Grey (7) 2

37 W. Churchill; *World Crisis* (10) 228

EPILOGUE

1 Tirpitz; *Memoirs* (2) 1, 280
2 Bülow; *Memoirs* 1909-13; Putnam 1931, 143
3 ibid
4 Cecil (1) 94
5 ibid, 213
6 Hurd; *German Fleet* (2) Appendix
7 Tirpitz; *Memoirs* (2) 1, 283
8 Kennedy; *Strategieprobleme* (2)
9 See von Trotha (2) 104*ff*
10 Tirpitz; *Memoirs* (2) 2, 312
11 Tirpitz to Ch. of *Admiralstab* Oct. 1, 1914; Tirpitz; *Memoirs* (2) 2, 361
12 See DANIEL HORN (ed); *The Private War of Seaman Stumpf*; Frewin 1969, 74
13 Usborne (12) 46-7
14 ibid, 61
15 v. Hase (12) 97-8
16 See Horn (Epilogue) 295 note
17 Röhl; *Delusion?* (12) 100
18 See P. PADFIELD; *Guns at Sea*; Evelyn 1973, 273; also P. PAD-FIELD; *The Battleship Era*; Hart-Davis 1972, 221*ff*

Index

Index